At Lincoln's Side

At Lincoln's Side

John Hay's Civil War Correspondence and Selected Writings

Edited by Michael Burlingame

Southern Illinois University Press

Carbondale and Edwardsville

Frontispiece: Photograph of John Hay, dated 1861.
From the John Hay Papers, Library of Congress.

Library of Congress Cataloging-in-Publication Data

Hay, John, 1838–1905.
   At Lincoln's side : John Hay's Civil War correspondence and
selected writings / edited by Michael Burlingame.
      p.   cm.
   Includes bibliographical references (p.   ) and index.
   1. Hay, John, 1838–1905 Correspondence. 2. Statesmen — United
States Correspondence. 3. United States — History — Civil War,
1861–1865 Personal narratives. 4. Lincoln, Abraham, 1809–1865 —
Friends and associates. 5. United States — Politics and govern-
ment — 1861–1865. 6. Hay, John, 1838–1905. 7. Statesmen — United
States Biography.   I. Burlingame, Michael, 1941–   . II. Title.
E664.H41A4   2000   99-31085
973.7'092 — dc21   CIP
ISBN 0-8093-2293-5 (cloth: alk. paper)

The paper used in this publication meets the minimum requirements
of American National Standard for Information Sciences — Permanence of
Paper for Printed Library Materials, ANSI Z39.48-1992. ⊗

For Sue Burlingame Coover and Edwin R. Coover

Contents

Acknowledgments   *ix*

Introduction   *xi*

Part One. Civil War Correspondence

1. 1860–1862   *3*
2. 1863   *29*
3. 1864–1865   *72*

Part Two. Selected Writings

4. Hay's Reminiscences of the Civil War   *109*

    Letter to William H. Herndon (1866)   *109*

    Obituary of Tad Lincoln (1871)   *111*

    The Heroic Age in Washington (1872)   *113*

    Life in the White House in the Time of
    Lincoln (1890)   *131*

5. Biographical Sketches   *141*

    Elmer E. Ellsworth (1861)   *141*

    Edward D. Baker (1861)   *151*

Appendix 1: The Authorship of the Bixby Letter   *169*

Appendix 2: Mary Todd Lincoln's Unethical
Conduct as First Lady   *185*

Notes   *205*

Index   *281*

Acknowledgments

To John Y. Simon, dean of documentary editing in the field of American history, I am grateful for his encouragement as this volume and its companions have slowly gestated over the past several years.

At Brown University's John Hay Library, I have been the fortunate beneficiary of many kindnesses from Jennifer Lee, Samuel Streit, Jean Rainwater, Mary Jo Kline, Andrew Moel, Pat Soris, and their colleagues. To all I extend heartfelt thanks.

To their counterparts at Connecticut College, Yale University, the University of Chicago, the Illinois State Historical Library, Allegheny College, the Library of Congress, the Chicago Historical Society, the Lincoln Museum of Fort Wayne, the J. Pierpont Morgan Library, the Henry E. Huntington Library, the Lincoln Museum at Lincoln Memorial University, and the New York Public Library, I am indebted for their generous assistance.

The R. Francis Johnson Faculty Development Fund at Connecticut College helped defray the costs of research and travel involved in editing this volume.

In identifying Lincoln's word usage, I was assisted both by David Herbert Donald, my mentor at Princeton University and Johns Hopkins University, and by Dr. C. A. Tripp of Nyack, New York.

Appendix 1, "The Authorship of the Bixby Letter," is a much-expanded and revised version of my article "New Light on the Bixby Letter," *Journal of the Abraham Lincoln Association* 16 (winter 1995): 59–71. I am grateful to Thomas F. Schwartz, Illinois State historian and editor of the *Journal of the Abraham Lincoln Association,* for granting permission to use that article in this volume.

Appendix 2, "Mary Todd Lincoln's Unethical Conduct as First Lady," is a revised version of a talk given in 1994 to the Lincoln Fellowship of Wisconsin, which published it in pamphlet form as "Honest Abe, Dishonest Mary." Daniel Pearson kindly gave permission to reproduce that essay.

Douglas L. Wilson and Rodney O. Davis, codirectors of the Lincoln Studies Center at Knox College, have generously shared with me their vast knowledge of the Lincoln sources.

Wayne C. Temple, deputy chief director of the Illinois State Archives, has also given me the benefit of his legendary expertise on matters relating to Lincoln and his times.

My sister and brother-in-law, to whom this book is dedicated, have been hospitable far above and beyond the call of family duty in hosting me for long stretches while I conduct research in Washington, D.C. Others, including Thomas and Cathy Schwartz, Sarah Thomas, James and Mary Patton, and Robert Bray, have been generous in putting me up when I indulge in research binges in Illinois.

The lovely and long-suffering Lois McDonald has for many years uncomplainingly provided indispensable support and encouragement as I have pursued the historical Lincoln.

Introduction

Real history," John Hay declared, "is told in private letters. No man should ever destroy one that contains light on public men or public affairs."[1] The 227 surviving letters and telegrams that Hay wrote during the Civil War are a case in point. Like his Civil War diary,[2] they shed an unusually bright light on Abraham Lincoln. Through Hay's eyes, we see the president as a statesman in this 1863 letter: "The Tycoon is in fine whack. I have rarely seen him more serene & busy. He is managing this war, the draft, foreign relations, and planning a reconstruction of the Union, all at once. I never knew with what tyrannous authority he rules the Cabinet, till now. The most important things he decides & there is no cavil."[3] We also catch glimpses of Lincoln in more informal circumstances. At Ford's Theater, the president and Hay "occupied [a] private box & . . . carried on a hefty flirtation with the Monk Girls in the flies."[4] Hay described Lincoln's off-color humor to a journalist who had asked for an authentic Lincoln story: "I have been skulking in the shadow of the Tycoon, setting all sorts of dexterous traps for a joke. . . . Once or twice a gleam of hope has lit up my soul as he would begin 'That puts me in mind of Tom Skeeters out in Bourbon County' but the story of Skeeters would come out unfit for family reading."[5]

Some of the letters gathered here, along with excerpts from Hay's diary, appeared in 1908 in a three-volume private edition compiled by Henry Adams and Hay's widow, Clara Stone Hay.[6] Though their methods were eccentric (they provided only the initials of people and places mentioned by Hay), those editors deserve the gratitude of historians, for they persuaded many people to supply them with copies of Hay's letters, now available at Brown University.[7] Thirty-one years later, Tyler Dennett published a more scholarly version of the diary and letters, covering the years 1861–1870.[8] A great improvement over the Henry Adams–Clara Hay edition, Dennett's volume was nevertheless "rather casually edited," as the dean of Civil War historians, Allan Nevins, observed.[9] Dennett omitted much, annotated skimpily (and often inaccurately), and transcribed some passages erroneously. This volume contains many letters not included in the Adams–Hay and Dennett editions.

Hay's private correspondence, in the words of Horace White, is "breezy and sparkling as champagne, [*and*] most attractive as literature."[10] Theodore Roosevelt called Hay "without exception, the best letter-writer of his age."[11] Joseph Bucklin Bishop believed that there "have been few better letter-writers than John Hay." Bishop recalled that Hay "wrote more nearly as he talked than any man I have ever known, and, as he could not talk in a dull or uninteresting way, so he could not write a dull letter. Some day, when time shall have made it not indiscreet to publish a compilation of his letters, they should be given to the world. They will prove to be not only an intellectual delight, but an inestimable contribution to the history of the time in which he lived and in which he bore so honorable and useful a part." Bishop observed, "Unlike many brilliant letter-writers," Hay "did not write with the obvious expectation that his letters would be published. He let himself go freely, as was his wont in conversation."[12] In editing Hay's letters, Henry Adams hoped to provide "a unique example of table-talk . . . grave and gay, frivolous and solemn, quick and unaffected, unconscious, witty, and altogether unlike the commonplace."[13] He explained to Whitelaw Reid that "a few volumes of Table Talk of one of our best talkers would fill a yawning gap in our somewhat meagre library. Therefore I tried to select everything that resembled conversation;—everything that he said to you and me, without literary purpose."[14] Concurring with Adams's estimate, Theodore Roosevelt called Hay "the most delightful man to talk to I ever met, for in his conversation he continually made out of hand those delightful epigrammatic remarks which we would all like to make, and which in books many people appear as making, but which in actual life hardly anyone ever does any more than think about when it is too late to say them."[15]

The number of personal letters in this volume is relatively small, for not many have survived. According to his widow, Hay did not obey his own injunction about preserving historically important letters: "[*T*]here are very few letters written by Mr Hay from the White House in existence—he destroyed all that he wrote to his family."[16] (He even destroyed many of his photographs dating from the war years.) Fortunately, some family correspondence managed to escape its author's destructive urge. In addition, his letters to fellow White House secretary John G. Nicolay and to the journalist-soldier Charles G. Halpine are extant, despite Hay's repeated injunctions to those gentlemen that they burn his missives.

Hay's surviving official letters are also included here. Though lacking the literary brilliance of his personal letters, they help flesh out the historical record, supplementing Roy P. Basler's edition of Lincoln's collected works.[17]

Some letters that Hay composed for Lincoln's signature are reproduced in this volume. In 1866, Hay recalled that while in the White House, Lincoln "wrote few letters. He did not read one in fifty that he received. At first we tried to bring them to his notice, but at last he gave the whole thing over to me, and signed without reading them the letters I wrote in his name."[18] Hay made a similar statement to Lincoln's eldest son, who informed Nicholas Murray Butler that "it was the custom of John Hay to write in the name of Lincoln all letters of a non-political kind."[19] This assertion is supported by evidence in Hay's diary, which indicates that he composed a letter for Lincoln to George H. Boker in October 1863.[20] That same month, he recorded in his diary: "I induced the President to sign a letter I wrote to Col. Rowland approving his proposed National Rifle Corps."[21] The following year, Hay told Charles S. Spencer, who had requested a presidential letter that could be read to banqueters: "I regret that the President was literally crowded out of the opportunity of writing you a note for yr. banquet. He fully intended to do so *himself* & for that reason I did not prepare a letter for him."[22]

It is impossible to identify precisely other correspondence that Hay wrote for the president, but informed guesses can be made. In scrapbooks of his own writings, Hay pasted newspaper clippings of three letters bearing Lincoln's signature: to F. B. Loomis, 12 May 1864; to John Phillips, 21 November 1864; and to Lydia Bixby, also 21 November 1864. It seems likely that Hay wrote these letters for Lincoln to sign, or else he would not have preserved them in scrapbooks of his own compositions. The most noteworthy example of Hay's ghostwriting is the celebrated Bixby letter, whose authorship is examined in appendix 1. Stylistic considerations, along with Hay's statements to friends and the evidence of his scrapbooks, suggest that Hay is the author of that prose poem that is widely regarded as Lincoln's epistolary masterpiece, often ranked with the Gettysburg address and the second inaugural address.

(Hay also served as a ghostwriter for Mary Todd Lincoln on at least one occasion. In the James Wadsworth Papers at the Library of Congress is a letter in Hay's handwriting signed by Mrs. Lincoln. The editors of *Mary Todd Lincoln: Her Life and Letters* acknowledge that they "have been unable to locate the original of this letter, but the smoothness of its style indicates that it was either written out for Mrs. Lincoln's signature or edited for publication."[23] Robert Todd Lincoln said, "I do not believe it to be genuine; it is not at all like her style."[24] Bearing the date "June 1861," it was doubtless composed for her by Hay; not only is the manuscript in Hay's hand and style, but a newspaper clipping of it is pasted into one of Hay's scrapbooks.[25] Hay also wrote at least one reply to a correspondent of Mary Lincoln.)[26]

In light of Hay's statements to Herndon and Robert Todd Lincoln, it does not strain credulity to deduce that these letters were written by Hay. After all, he was Lincoln's secretary and a sophisticated prose stylist, and it is common practice for secretaries to write letters for their employers. Hay may have been a ghostwriter for political leaders even before he reached the White House; in 1860, he evidently composed a Thanksgiving proclamation for the signature of the governor of Illinois.[27]

In 1863, Hay took notes of a meeting Lincoln held with a delegation of Radicals from Missouri and Kansas. In that colloquy, Lincoln touched on such controversial matters as emancipation, the suspension of the privilege of the writ of habeas corpus, and accusations that he had behaved tyrannically. ("I do not intend to be a tyrant. At all events I shall take care that in my own eyes I do not become one. I shall always try and preserve one friend within me, whoever else fails me, to tell me that I have not been a tyrant, and that I have acted right. I have no right to act the tyrant to mere political opponents.")[28]

Hay never wrote an autobiography. "I am inclined to think that my life is an oughtnottobiography," he quipped three years before his death. "I have already most thoughtlessly said to half a dozen publishers that if I ever wrote it, I would give it to them, and I suppose that estops me from ever writing it."[29] He contemptuously dismissed as "rubbish" the reminiscences of Lincoln by the journalist Noah Brooks, who had known the president well and was to be his personal secretary during the second administration.[30] Despite his aversion to such memoirs, Hay wrote four pieces recalling his days at Lincoln's side; they comprise chapter 4 of this volume.

The first is Hay's 1866 letter answering William H. Herndon's questions about Lincoln. The second is an obituary of Tad Lincoln, the president's youngest son, who died in 1871. Of this document, Robert Todd Lincoln said: "John Hay's screed is like a picture."[31]

The third is a previously unpublished lecture, "The Heroic Age in Washington," which Hay delivered in the early 1870s. Hay rebuffed Richard Watson Gilder, who wanted it for *Scribner's Magazine:* "Are you still using that old lecture of yours on Washington during the War? If not wouldn't it make a capital magazine paper?"[32] Gilder was right, for "The Heroic Age" contains some vivid recollections of Lincoln, including his first day as president, when he conversed with the outgoing chief executive, James Buchanan: "The courteous old gentleman took the new President aside for some parting words into the corner where I was standing. I waited with boyish wonder and credulity to hear what momentous counsels were to come from that gray and weather-beaten head. Every word must have its value at such an instant. The ex-President said: 'I think you will find the water of the right-hand well at the White-House better than that at the left,' and went on with many intimate details of the kitchen and pantry. Lincoln listened with that weary, introverted look of his, not answering, and the next day, when I recalled the conversation, admitted he had not heard a word of it." In the summer of 1863, Hay observed the president respond to a telegram announcing that artillery fire could be heard near Knoxville, where General Ambrose E. Burnside was menaced by Confederate troops: "I took it to the President. He read it, and said, 'That is good.' I expressed my surprise at his taking so cheerful a view of Burnside's deadly danger. He said, 'I had a neighbor out West, a Sally Taggart, who had a great many unruly children, whom she did not take very good care of. Whenever she heard one squall in some out-of-the-way place, she would say, "Well, thank Goodness, there's one of my young ones not dead yet!" As long as we hear guns, Burnside is not captured.'"

Hay remembered that on the gloomy morning following the first battle of Bull Run, "when many thought seriously of the end," Lincoln "said, with some impatience, 'There is nothing in this except the lives lost and the lives which must be lost to make it good.' There was probably no one who regretted bloodshed and disaster more than he, and no one who estimated the consequences of defeat more lightly." This reminiscence lends credibility to a statement made by one of Hay's assistants in the White House,

William O. Stoddard, who claimed that Lincoln said after the Union defeat at Fredericksburg: "[*I*]f the same battle were to be fought over again, every day, through a week of days, with the same relative results, the army under Lee would be wiped out to its last man, the Army of the Potomac would still be a mighty host, the war would be over, the Confederacy gone, and peace would be won at a smaller cost of life than it will be if the week of lost battles must be dragged out through yet another year of camps and marches, and of deaths in hospitals rather than upon the field. No general yet found can face the arithmetic, but the end of the war will be at hand when he shall be discovered."[33] (Some historians regard Stoddard's account skeptically.)[34]

Hay also recounted Lincoln's reaction in 1859 to a pronouncement by Stephen A. Douglas on slavery expansion: "He came into the law office where I was reading, which adjoined his own, with a copy of *Harper's Magazine* in his hand, containing Senator Douglas's famous article on Popular Sovereignty. Lincoln seemed greatly aroused by what he had read. Entering the office without a salutation, he said: 'This will never do. He puts the moral element out of this [*slavery*] question. It won't stay out.'"

While besieged by applicants for government jobs, Lincoln "once estimated with some disgust the number of office-seekers who visited Washington at 30,000; but, he quickly added, 'There are some 30,000,000 who ask for no offices.'" In "The Heroic Age in Washington," Hay described an amusing encounter of the president and a favor seeker:

At a dark period of the war, a gentleman of some local prominence came to Washington for some purpose, and so as to obtain the assistance of Lincoln, he brought a good deal of evidence to prove that he was the man who originated his nomination. He attacked the great chief in the vestibule of the Executive Mansion, and walked with him to the War Department, impressing this view upon him. When the President went in his Warwick "waited patiently about till Lincoln did appear." He walked back to the White-House with him, clinching his argument with new and cogent facts. At the door the President turned, and, with that smile which was half sadness and half fun, he said: "So you think you made me President?" "Yes, Mr. President, under Providence, I think I did." "Well," said Lincoln, opening the door and going in, "it's a pretty mess you've got me into. But I forgive you."

To a friend, Hay described how Lincoln treated another office seeker more abruptly:

> I was sitting with him on one occasion when a man who had been calling on him almost daily for weeks in pursuit of an office was shown in. He made his usual request, when Lincoln said: "It is of no use, my friend. You had better go home. I am not going to give you that place." At this the man became enraged, and in a very insolent tone exclaimed, "Then, as I understand it, Mr. President, you refuse to do me justice." At this, Lincoln's patience, which was as near the infinite as anything that I have ever known, gave way. He looked at the man steadily for a half-minute or more, then slowly began to lift his long figure from its slouching position in the chair. He rose without haste, went over to where the man was sitting, took him by the coat-collar, carried him bodily to the door, threw him in a heap outside, closed the door, and returned to his chair. The man picked himself up, opened the door, and cried, "I want my papers!" Lincoln took a package of papers from the table, went to the door and threw them out, again closed it, and returned to his chair. He said not a word, then or afterward, about the incident.[35]

The fourth of Hay's Civil War reminiscences included here is "Life in the White House in the Time of Lincoln," which appeared in 1890 in *Century Magazine*, whose editor deemed it "pure gold — though all too short."[36]

In 1861, Hay wrote long obituaries of Elmer E. Ellsworth and Edward D. Baker, two men close to both him and Lincoln. Those obituaries are reproduced in chapter 5.

Living in the White House, Hay enjoyed easy access to Lincoln, who "loved him as a son," Charles G. Halpine believed.[37] Galusha Grow, Speaker of the U.S. House from 1861 to 1863, remembered that "Lincoln was very much attached" to Hay "and often spoke to me in high terms of his ability and trustworthiness." Grow was aware "of no person in whom the great President reposed more confidence and to whom he confided secrets of State as well as his own personal affairs with such great freedom."[38] In 1871, the editor of the *Sedalia* (Missouri) *Times*, who had known Hay well in Washington between 1862 and 1865, claimed that the assistant presidential secretary was a "trusted and intimate friend of Lincoln's" who "probably lived nearer to that good man's heart during the years of the civil war, than any other man."[39] Hay and the chief presidential secretary, John G. Nicolay, were (in their own words) "daily and nightly witnesses of the incidents, the anxieties, the fears, and the hopes, which pervaded the Executive Mansion and the National Capital."[40] Lincoln, they asserted, "gave them his unlimited confidence."[41]

Born in Salem, Indiana, in 1838, Hay grew up in Warsaw, Illinois, where his father was a physician. A gifted student, Hay at the age of twelve went to live with his uncle, Milton Hay, in Pittsfield, Illinois, a town settled by New Englanders; there he received more advanced schooling than he could find in Warsaw and also became friends with John G. Nicolay, a lad six years his senior. In 1855, Hay entered Brown University, the alma mater of his maternal grandfather. After graduating three years later, he returned to Illinois, again staying with his uncle, who was then practicing law in Springfield ("a city combining the meanness of the North with the barbarism of the South," Hay declared. Shakespeare's Dogberry "ought to have been an Illinoisan.")[42]

Once nominated as the Republican standard bearer in 1860, Lincoln, in need of help to answer his mail, turned to John G. Nicolay, an assistant to the Illinois secretary of state, Ozias M. Hatch. Lincoln often visited Hatch's office, which was "practically the Republican campaign headquarters for both city and State," and had thus became well acquainted with the industrious, efficient, German-born Nicolay.[43] At the suggestion of Milton Hay, his nephew John, who was desultorily studying law with him in Springfield, was chosen to aid Nicolay. The young Brown alumnus had little appetite for a political life. In early May 1860, he told a friend: "I am as yet innocent of politics. I occupy myself very pleasantly in thoroughly hating both sides, and abusing the peculiar tenets of the company I happen to be in, and when the company is divided, in saying, with Mercutio, 'A plague on both your Houses.' This position of dignified neutrality I expect to hold for a very long time unless Lincoln is nominated at Chicago."[44] Following the November election, Lincoln wanted both Nicolay and Hay to remain in his employ, but Congress had appropriated funds for only one presidential secretary. Milton Hay, who remarked that his nephew "had much enjoyed working with Mr. Lincoln," offered to pay John's expenses in Washington for six months. The president-elect demurred, insisting that he compensate Hay out of his presidential salary, but that proved unnecessary when the young man became a clerk in the Interior Department, assigned to duty in the White House. (In 1864, he was appointed a major in the army while continuing his work as an assistant presidential secretary.)[45]

The relations between Hay and Lincoln were like those between Alexander Hamilton and George Washington when the former served as the latter's principal aide. The journalist John Russell Young recalled that Hay "knew the social graces and amenities, and did much to make the atmosphere of the war environed White House grateful, tempering unreasonable aspirations, giving to disappointed ambitions the soft answer which turneth away wrath, showing, as Hamilton did in similar offices, the tact and common sense which were to serve him as they served Hamilton in wider spheres of public duty." (Hay's tactfulness was put to the test one day by a gentleman who insisted that he must see Lincoln immediately. "The President is engaged now," replied Hay. "What is your mission?" "Do you know who I am?" asked the caller. "No, I must confess I do not," said Hay. "I am the son of God," came the answer. "The President will be delighted to see you when you come again. And perhaps you will bring along a letter of introduction from your father," retorted the quick-witted secretary.)[46]

Young, who often visited the White House during the Civil War, called Hay "brilliant" and "chivalrous," quite "independent, with opinions on most questions," which he expressed freely. At times sociable, Hay could also be "reserved" and aloof, "with just a shade of pride that did not make acquaintanceship spontaneous." Hay, Young said, combined "the genius for romance and politics as no one . . . since Disraeli" and judged that he was well "suited for his place in the President's family." Young depicted Hay as "a comely young man with [a] peach-blossom face," "exceedingly handsome — a slight, graceful, boyish figure — 'girl in boy's clothes,' as I heard in a sniff from some angry politician." This "young, almost beardless, and almost boyish countenance did not seem to match with official responsibilities and the tumult of action in time of pressure, but he did what he had to do, was always graceful, composed, polite, and equal to the complexities of any situation which might arise." Hay's "old-fashioned speech" was "smooth, low-toned, quick in comprehension, sententious, reserved." People were "not quite sure whether it was the reserve of diffidence or aristocracy," Young remembered. The "high-bred, courteous" Hay was "not one with whom the breezy overflowing politician would be apt to take liberties." Young noticed "a touch of sadness in his temperament" and concluded that Hay "had the personal attractiveness as well as the youth of Byron" and "was what Byron might have been if grounded on good principles and with the wholesome discipline of home."[47]

Others added touches to Young's portrait. One of his professors at Brown recalled that Hay "was modest even to diffidence, often blushing to the roots of his hair when he rose to recite."[48] A college friend reported that Hay's "quick perception, ready grasp of an idea and wonderfully retentive memory, made a mere pastime of study. His enthusiasm was boundless, and his love for and appreciation of the beautiful in nature and in art was acutely developed. If he was smitten with the charms of a pretty girl, he raved and walked the room pouring out his sentiment in a flood of furious eloquence. He would apostrophize a beautiful sunset till the last glow had expired."[49] Hay's roommate at Brown, William Leete Stone, said he was "of a singularly modest and retiring disposition" yet with "so winning a manner that no one could be in his presence, even for a few moments, without falling under the spell which his conversation and companionship invariably cast upon all who came within his influence."[50]

Of that conversation, Joseph Bucklin Bishop observed:

> He loved to talk, and his keen joy in it was so genuine and so obvious that it infected his listeners. He was as good a listener as he was a talker, never monopolizing the conversation. . . . He talked without the slightest sign of effort or premeditation, said his good things as if he owed their inspiration to the listener, and never exhibited a shadow of consciousness of his own brilliancy. His manner toward the conversation of others was the most winning form of compliment conceivable. Every person who spent a half-hour or more with him was sure to go away, not only charmed with Hay, but uncommonly well pleased with himself.[51]

Clark E. Carr described Hay as a "bright, rosy-faced, boyish-looking young man." Carr had never met "a young man or boy who charmed me as he did when he looked at me with his mischievous hazel eyes from under a wealth of dark brown hair. He was, for those days, elegantly dressed,— better than any of us; so neatly, indeed, that he would . . . have been set down as a 'dude' at sight."[52] Logan Hay remarked that his cousin John was "a different type from the rest of the Hay family. He had a magnetic personality— more culture."[53] A newspaperman who saw Hay in 1861 recalled that he was "a young, good-looking fellow, well, almost foppishly dressed, with by no means a low down opinion of himself, either physically or mentally, with plenty of self-confidence for anybody's use, a brain active and intellectual, with a full budget of small talk for the ladies or anybody else, and both eyes keeping a steady lookout for the interests of 'number one.'"[54] In early 1861, Frederick Augustus Mitchel, who attended Brown when Hay was a student there, encountered Hay at Willard's Hotel, casually leaning against a cigar stand; in response to Mitchel's congratulations on being named assistant presidential secretary, Hay replied: "Yes. I'm Keeper of the President's Conscience."[55]

William Leete Stone remembered that Hay "was always a great favorite with the ladies."[56] Caroline Owsley Brown of Springfield depicted him as "a handsome young fellow, rather short, but slender and well formed, with bright, dark eyes that wrought havoc in the hearts of susceptible maidens, and a tongue that could have talked the traditional bird off of the bush." Drawn to many young women, he "flitted from flower to flower, with a sonnet to this one's sweet eyes, and to that damsel's rosy lips, with no worse result than a fleeting pang."[57] In 1860, another Springfield maiden deemed him "a very pleasant young fellow & very intelligent."[58] Later she recalled that at twenty-one, Hay was "a bright, handsome fellow of medium height and slight build, with good features, especially the eyes, which were dark, lustrous brown; red cheeks and clear dark complexion; small, well-shaped hands which he had a habit of locking together interlacing the fingers, and carrying at arm's length, which the girls thought particularly fetching." His style of dress also pleased girls. According to Anna Ridgely, he "wore a long, loose overcoat, flying open, his hands thrust into the pockets, which was also thought very graceful and attractive as he swung himself along the street, for he had a rocking walk in those days."[59]

In 1862, a young woman visiting Washington reported that the "nicest looking man I have seen since I have been here is Mr Hay the President's Secretary. I do not know him personally but he came into the Senate the other day to deliver a message from the President. He is very nice looking with the loveliest voice."[60] Other women found his eyes as well as his voice appealing. "Hay's marked feature was his eyes," said Helen Nicolay; they were "always kindly" and "sometimes depressed."[61] Hay's college sweetheart, Hannah Angell, praised his "wonderful hazel eyes" into which "you could look . . . a mile, & he looked a mile into yours." She also regarded him as "very attractive as a talker"; in conversation he was "given to abrupt, swift phrases."[62] (In 1864 a young Springfield woman felt differently: she "was disgusted with him" in part because "he talked in a most affected manner.")[63]

T. C. Evans, a reporter for the *New York World* who encountered Hay often during the Civil War, thought that he "was born to moderation and calmness in mien as in action, and they walked with him on either hand throughout his length of days, tokens of the equity of a balanced character, working with Nature as one who had discovered that her central note is calm and that she is commanded only by those who obey her." He appeared "to possess in a high degree a silent power of work, doing a great deal and saying little about it," while "his spirit was ever of unruffled serenity, his manner of invariable sweetness and charm, and his talk was apt, varied, refined, and of a markedly literary quality."[64]

A gentleman who boarded at the same club and dined with Hay frequently during Lincoln's presidency depicted him as "smooth-faced, ruddy-cheeked, vivacious, witty, polished, urbane and withal as full of intellectual activity as an egg of meat." Although "he constantly pursued his *belles lettres* studies and went much into society," Hay was "a hard practical worker," spending "twelve or fourteen hours a day of hard work at the White House." Hay "was always the same witty, genial, agreeable, effervescent and fascinating fellow" who obviously "had decided genius and unusual literary culture."[65]

A clerk who assisted Nicolay and Hay from 1861 to 1864, William O. Stoddard, said Hay was "quite young, and looks younger than he is; of a fresh and almost boyish complexion; quite a favorite among the ladies, and with a gift for epigram and repartee."[66] He enjoyed a reputation as "the best story-teller in Washington," with the exception of Lincoln.[67] Stoddard recalled that one Sunday when the White House was "silent as the graveyard," Hay burst in, "all one bubble." Hay, Stoddard reported, "is sober enough most of the time, but he had heard something funny, and he was good-natured about dividing it. Generally he can tell a story better than most boys of his age, but he broke down on that one before he got well into it." Hearing the laughter, Nicolay came over and asked Hay to repeat the story. Suddenly, Lincoln appeared, saying: "Now John, just tell that thing again." As Stoddard recalled, "His feet had made no sound in coming over from his room, or our own racket had drowned any footfall, but here was the President, and he sank into Andrew Jackson's chair, facing the table, with Nicolay seated by him, and Hay still standing by the mantel. The story was as fresh, and was even better told that third time up to its first explosive place, but right there a quartette explosion went off. Down came the President's foot from across his knee, with a heavy stamp on the floor, and out through the hall went an uproarious peal of laughter."[68]

Stoddard thought that Hay was less well qualified to be a presidential secretary than Nicolay, though he acknowledged that Hay "was more diplomatic" than the brusque young German. Stoddard recalled that "now and then Hay could express his inner opinions very well. He did so, sometimes when I read to him sundry poems, in return for a number of pretty good ones of his own that he came and read to me. It is on my mind that I admired his productions a number of sizes more than he did mine. We were the best of friends, nevertheless, and I recall his daily association with great pleasure."[69]

Hay could be critical of Stoddard, despite their friendship. Stoddard recalled Hay "almost angrily telling me that he considered me a kind of miracle of hard work and that I could do more without showing it than any other man he had ever seen. He abused me also for being what he called 'statuesque' and always inclined to strike attitudes and take positions.,— but I replied that the latter was just what we were wishing the army would succeed in doing."[70] When writing to Nicolay, Hay was even more critical of Stoddard. In 1863, he complained that "Stod[dard] is more & more worthless. I can scarcely rely upon him for anything."[71] That same year, Hay said that another assistant secretary, Nathaniel S. Howe, "is better than Stod[dard] as he is never stuffy and always on hand."[72] Hay thought Stoddard asinine as well as stuffy. "Stod[dard] has been extensively advertising himself in the Western Press," he told Nicolay in August 1864. "His asininity which is kept a little dark under your shadow at Washington blooms & burgeons in the free air of the West."[73] The following month, Hay sarcastically observed that Stoddard "has been giving the Northern watering places for the last two months a model of high breeding and unquestionable deportment."[74]

Another clerk who assisted Nicolay and Hay, Charles H. Philbrick, alleged in 1864 that "Hay does the ornamental . . . and the main labor is divided between three others of us who manage to get along tolerably well with it."[75] In 1866, Hay described the division of labor differently: "Nicolay received members of Congress, & other visitors who had business with the Executive Office, communicated to the Senate and House the messages of the President, & exercised a general supervision over the business. I opened and read the letters, answered them, looked over the newspapers, supervised the clerks who kept the records and in Nicolay's absence did his work also."[76] Hay's manner of handling the mail and callers can be inferred from instructions he gave to an assistant taking over his duties briefly: "Refer as little to the President as possible. Keep visitors out of the house when you can. Inhospitable, but prudent."[77] Hay took his responsibilities seriously; in 1862, his aunt reported that he "thinks there is a good deal resting on his shoulders."[78] William O. Stoddard recalled that after the Union defeat at the Second Battle of Bull Run, Hay "was mourning around somewhere as he always did after bad news, for his patriotism was fairly a burden to him."[79]

The following year, Thomas Wentworth Higginson called Hay "a nice young fellow, who unfortunately looks about seventeen and is oppressed with the necessity of behaving like seventy."[80] The journalist Henry King believed that Hay "most resembles Edgar A. Poe" in appearance; King added that Hay was "a thorough gentlemen, and one of the best fellows in the world."[81] Another journalist, William Howard Russell of the *London Times*, thought Hay a "nice smart odd witted" fellow who was "very agreeable and lively" though "rather young."[82] In 1865, William Henry Seward praised Hay as "a noble as well as a gifted young man, perfectly true and manly."[83] Seward's alter ego, Thurlow Weed, considered Hay "a bright, gifted young man, with agreeable manners and refined tastes."[84]

Some observers were less complimentary. In 1861, Henry Martin Smith, city editor of the *Chicago Tribune*, patronizingly disparaged Hay as "a nice beardless boy" and lamented that "Mr. Lincoln has no private secretary that fills the bill and the loss is a national one."[85] Similarly, Noah Brooks in 1863 told readers of the *Sacramento Union* that Lincoln "is affable and kind, but his immediate subordinates are snobby and unpopular."[86] Another wartime critic declared that Hay's "vanity" was "inordinate almost to the point of being disgusting."[87] The historian Henry Steele Commager called Hay "in many ways a very irritating young man, bumptious, clever, supercilious, yearning for culture and for the approval of the East."[88] More bluntly, the journalist-historian David Rankin Barbee said that "Hay was such a damned intellectual snob, . . . so superior to everybody, including Jehovah, that you want to puke as you read him."[89] In fact, Hay did not rank immodesty among the cardinal or even venial sins; rather, as he told a close friend, "Modesty is the most fatal and most unsympathetic of vices."[90] He prayed that his newborn nephew would "shun Modesty! It is the bane of genius, the chain-and-ball of enterprise."[91]

Early in 1865, Hay accepted a diplomatic post in Paris, for he had come to loathe some of the duties of a presidential secretary. In 1881, he declined James A. Garfield's invitation to resume his old post in the White House, explaining that the "contact with the greed and selfishness of office-seekers and the bull-dozing Congressmen is unspeakably repulsive. The constant contact with envy, meanness, ignorance and the swinish selfishness which ignorance breeds needs a stronger heart and a more obedient nervous system than I can boast."[92]

In addition, Hay may have been eager to avoid Mary Todd Lincoln, who disliked him because he thwarted some of her schemes to loot the public treasury. In the spring of 1862, he confided to Nicolay that Mrs. Lincoln "has mounted me to pay her the Stewards salary. I told her to kiss mine."[93] This response evidently did not please, for the following day Hay wrote, "The devil is abroad, having great wrath. His daughter, the Hell-Cat [*Mary Lincoln*], sent Stackpole in to blackguard me about the feed of her horses. . . . She is in 'a state of mind' about the Steward's salary. There is no steward. Mrs Watt has gone off and there is no *locum tenens*. She thinks she will blackguard your angelic representative into giving it to her 'which I dont think she'll do it, Hallelujah!'"[94] When William O. Stoddard left the White House in 1864, Nicolay exclaimed to Hay, "John! What'll we do with the Madam after Stod goes? You and I can't manage her."[95] Hay incurred the wrath of Mary Lincoln's partner in crime, White House gardener John Watt, because "I wont let Madame have our stationery fund."[96] The White House physician, Dr. Robert K. Stone, also believed that "Mrs. Lincoln was a perfect devil," and Stone's wife thought that "Mrs. Lincoln was insane on the subject of money."[97] (See appendix 2, infra, for further evidence of Mary Lincoln's unethical conduct as first lady.)

Unlike many of his contemporaries, Hay appreciated Lincoln's greatness well before the assassination. In 1863, the young secretary described his boss thus: "I am growing more and more firmly convinced that the good of the country absolutely demands that he should be kept where he is till this thing is over. There is no man in the country, so wise so gentle and so firm. I believe the hand of God placed him where he is."[98] That same year, Hay speculated that Lincoln "will fill a bigger place in history than he even dreams of himself."[99] Only one other historical figure loomed so large, Hay told William Herndon in 1866: "Lincoln with all his foibles, is the greatest character since Christ."[100] A quarter-century later, Hay summed up the essence of Lincoln's statesmanship:

> He never asked perfection of any one; he did not even insist, for others, upon the high standards he set up for himself. At a time before the word was invented he was the first of opportunists. With the fire of a reformer and a martyr in his heart he yet proceeded by the ways of cautious and practical statecraft. He always worked with things as they were, while never relinquishing the desire and effort to make them better. To a hope which saw the Delectable Mountains of absolute justice and peace in the future, to a faith that God in his own time would give to all men the things convenient to them, he added a charity which embraced in its deep bosom all the good and the bad, all the virtues and infirmities of men, and a patience like that of nature, which in its vast and fruitful activity knows neither haste nor rest.[101]

EDITORIAL METHOD

The following editorial conventions are used in this book. When Hay uses shorthand for *of the* (an inverted caret), *that* or *which* (a slash), and *the* (a dot), those words are silently supplied without brackets. Words that cannot be deciphered with certainty have been included within brackets followed by a question mark [*like this?*]. When Hay adds words above the line, with or without a caret, they have simply been inserted into the text. Contractions are retained. Raised letters have been reproduced as if they were not raised. All decipherable words of any significance that were crossed out have been reproduced as canceled text ~~like this~~. When words are illegible, square brackets are supplied, enclosing a blank space like this [   ]. When the editor inserts words into the text for clarification, they are italicized and placed within square brackets [*like this*]. When Hay inadvertently repeats a word, the second occurrence of the word is silently omitted. When Hay uses a period when a comma is called for, a comma has silently replaced the period. Otherwise, Hay's somewhat eccentric punctuation is unchanged. His misspellings are retained without the cumbersome use of [*sic*]. Familiar foreign terms are untranslated; less well known expressions in foreign languages are translated in the endnotes.

Persons mentioned by Hay are identified in endnotes when their name first appears, if information on them has been found. No annotation is made for those about whom nothing could be discovered. Sources for annotations derived from manuscript collections, newspapers, and specialized monographs and biographies are identified, but not those taken from easily available published sources.

Part One
Civil War Correspondence

1

1860–1862

I seize a moment of this quiet midnight to write to you before the days of the coming week bring their congressional nuisances and their swarms of visitors. I shall be so cross and surly by the middle of next week that I should be very unfit company for any one.

Warsaw dull? It shines before my eyes like a social paradise compared with this miserable sprawling village which imagines itself a city because it is wicked, as a boy thinks he is a man when he smokes and swears. I wish I could by wishing find myself in Warsaw.

I am cross because I am away from Warsaw. I believe honestly (if it is possible for me to believe anything honestly) that I shall never enjoy myself more thoroughly than I did that short little winter I spent at home.[2] It was so quiet and still, so free from everything that could disturb or bore me, that it seems in the busy days I am wearing out now like a queer little dream of contentment and peace, when I so obstinately and persistently left the dear old town that rainy, tearful, doleful Monday afternoon. I never before was so anxious to see Warsaw, or so reluctant to leave it. It is a good thing to go home. I seem to take a new lease on life; to renew a fast-fleeting youth on the breezy hills of my home. I feel like doing a marvelous amount of work when I return, and the dull routine of every-day labor is charmingly relieved by vanishing visions of green hills, grand rivers, and willowy islands that float in between me and my paper. And sometimes the pen will drop from tired hands and the desk will disappear and the annoyances of the chancery court will be forgotten in dreams of happy days in the old home, lit with eyes and melodious with the voices of those who are and ever have been

A' the world to me —

You know the rest.

By the way, have you seen the last — that is the October — number of the "Atlantic Monthly"? I have a terrible time denying the authorship of an article therein entitled "The New Cinderella."[3]

How pleasant those evenings in the dear old town that I remember with a heart full of joy. Write soon, sooner, soonest.

TO HANNAH ANGELL, SPRINGFIELD, 6 JANUARY 1861[4]

I felt so much better than usual this morning, that I walked quietly up to the State-House through the still winter sunshine. While I was there taking a unocular view of men and things (especially things — office-seekers) I was encountered by my physician who forthwith remanded me to my solitary confinement, comforting me with the assurance that if I would be a good boy today and use my Calendula regularly, I might uncover my eyes tomorrow and stay in the Hall of the Representatives all day;[5] buoyant with this cheering presage I returned home. But everything is fearfully quiet. My little sister (who is here at school) has fallen asleep. I cannot read. What must I do until tomorrow?

In such circumstances one grows retrospective. Many times in the dreary month which, bless God, is ended, have I lain quiet with darkened eyes dreaming of the beautiful city crowning the beautiful Bay [*Providence, Rhode Island*]. And sometimes I have thought of the green hills of Scituate, splendid in their summer bravery, and its shadowy intervales tender with deep glooms, flecked by the sifted sunshine. So what could I do better, than employ the free half of my left eye, in writing a few lines to postpone for a few more days the time when you will forget me! If I am fortunate enough to recover my health by the coming week, this winter will be very laborious to me. (If not, "gods wil bee dun" as Joe Lane feelingly observed when he heard the news from Oregon).[6] I shall be so busy with the business of the mythical being called "the public" that I shall have little time for private cares. So I write today to tell you that I am toujours le meme and to protest against your concluding that living here two years has "subdued my nature to the thing it works in." By the way let me say in explanation of the foregoing that in a North-west-windy ride of Eighty miles a month ago, I took a little cold, which pursued the same fighting tactics with me, that the ex-champion did with Benicia's child, in "shutting up my eyes."[7] I am recovering fastly. I rather wish some of the friends of my "flush days" knew that I was helpless and half-blind, so that their flinty hearts might be touched with compassion and they be led to spoil a sheet of paper in my behalf. Just think of it! Walter, Peckham, et id, omne genus have stopped communications with the West.[8] I am inclined to secede.

I showed part of your last letter (how long ago!) to Mr. Lincoln, at a little musical soiree, whereat he grinned his majestic delight. I am beginning to respect him more than formerly. He maintains a very dignified attitude before all strangers. Weed, Cameron, Bates & others have all been here and acknowledge their superior in the Cincinnatus of the prairie.[9]

Give my regards to your friends, who were mine & believe me yet yours.

To William Leete Stone, Washington, 15 March 1861[10]

If there is anything which more than all else causes me to regret the intolerable press of business about the President's office, it is the impossibility of answering the letters of my best friends. I have positively not had a moment's leisure since we arrived in this city. The throng of office-seekers is something absolutely fearful. They come at daybreak and still are coming at midnight.

You *know* that in any thing I can do, you can command me, but you over-rate my influence. Mr. Lincoln positively refuses to make any recommendations for positions in the departments; he rejects the entreaties even of his most intimate friends and relatives. I have a pile of unanswered letters from more than a dozen of my old friends, and it grieves me exceedingly to be unable to afford the assistance they ask.

To Jane Huntington Ridgely, Washington, 19 March 1861[11]

An enterprising genius has just opened a little collection of Japanese curiosities under Willard's, and everybody goes there and gets unmercifully cheated. I was beguiled into the shop to-day and my eyes fell upon these little mother-of-pearl trinkets. I inquired their possible use and was told they were used in Japanese gambling, but were sold here for counters. I remembered the pleasant whist-parties at your house, and take the liberty of sending them. There is nothing domestic about them. The box, the wood and the paper are all *d'outre mer*.

Mr. Baker and his *cara sposa* left us to-day.[12] It made me positively homesick. I would give everything for a day or two in Springfield. Not that I love Washington less, but that I love Springfield more. This town will be very pleasant after a while when we have leisure to enjoy it.

To HANNAH ANGELL, WASHINGTON, 29 MARCH 1861[13]

I met in the streets of this wilderness of a town an old friend of ours, the other day, who told me something that may account for your long silence. He said that you were to be married before long. I do not understand why you should cease writing to me on that account. You were very indulgent and long suffering through the dead months, when I was so hideously negligent and indolent. When, after long weeks of silence I would scribble a few disjointed lines, you would answer with the quick sympathy that taught you that the only object for which I wrote was to hear from you.

Every letter of yours was a bright shaft of sudden light, glancing into the murk of a colorless Western life. They were very pleasant to receive. I was vaguely dissatisfied to miss them. The effort of the lines that waked them was greater than you knew.

And now that the great joy has come to you once in a lifetime of loving happily, is there any good reason why you should hesitate to speak of it to me? The tenderness and dearness of new knowledge, should not prevent you from imparting it to me. The dearer and the tenderer, the sooner, as it seems to me, should you hasten to share it with one whose heart and mind has been in such utter sympathy with yours. It will not make your future less happy, to have its tangled web tinged by threads straying into it out of the past. You will not be sadder, while I will be happier, in the quiet continuation of a friendship that is connected with all of my life which is worth remembering. I should be very sorry to think that I must banish you, or that you would banish me, from all the associations of the time that glided so pleasantly on through a four years dream, by the still flow of the Narragansett's waves.

Believe me now and tomorrow and always, as years ago

Your friend

To Miss H. Louise Hickox, Washington, 10 May 1861[14]

Mrs. Lincoln desires me to say, that receiving your very kind letter on the point of her departure for New York she is unable at present to answer it, but begs me to assure you of her grateful appreciation of your good wishes & true sympathy.

To Hiram Barney, Washington, 17 May 1861[15]

The President directs me to acknowledge the receipt of your favour of the 11th inst and to state in reply that he does not know the present address of Mr. Barrell, if he is not in New York.

I will write to Mr. Barrell's friends in Illinois to send you his address. The President is much interested in him, as a worthy and very needy man.[16]

[*P.S.*] By the way, I had the pleasure last night of seeing a photograph of Miss Marcy.

To Charles L. Huntington, Washington, 18 May 1861[17]

Will you have the kindness to send me immediately the present address of Mr. Barrell, if you know it? The President wishes to recommend him to the consideration of Mr. Barney the Collector at New York, and knowing no one else who would be likely to know his present residence, I take the liberty of referring to you.

We had a very pleasant visit a few weeks ago from Charlie.[18] He was very well.

To William Dean Howells, Washington, 18 June 1861[19]

I was very glad to receive your letter, which I shall preserve as the autograph of a man who has proved that a good poetical thing may occasionally come out of the Nazareth of a great bacon state.[20] Some of your shorter pieces have taken a strangle hold of my fancy—particularly some graphic lines which you entitled "Dead."[21]

I have examined the situation of the Munich consulate and find that though the applications are somewhat numerous, none seem so well supported as yours. Besides, you have in Gov. Chase a sincere and earnest advocate. Still, though I think your chances hopeful, you know that it is easier to predict the destination of a thunderbolt than of an office.

I hope you may go and that the air of the Bavarian Capital may fill your brain anew with art and poetry and that your first song may be something about Ludwig and Lola.[22]

[*P.S.*] If you see Miss Denison soon I wish you would make her remember me.[23]

"MARY LINCOLN" TO CAPTAIN JOHN FRY, WASHINGTON, 20 JUNE 1861 (IN THE HAND OF JOHN HAY)[24]

It gives me very great pleasure to be the medium of transmission of these weapons, to be used in the defense of national sovereignty upon the soil of Kentucky.

Though long removed from my honored mother-state, I have never ceased to contemplate her progress in happiness and prosperity, with sentiments of fond and filial pride. In every effort of industrial energy, in every enterprise of honor and valor, my heart has been with her. And I rejoice in the consciousness that at this time when the institutions to whose fostering care we owe all that we have of happiness and glory, are rudely assailed by ungrateful and parricidal hands, the State of Kentucky, ever true and loyal, furnishes to the insulted flag of the Union, a guard of her best and bravest. On every field the prowess of Kentuckians has been manifested. In the holy cause of National Defense, they must be invincible.

Please accept, Sir, these weapons, as a token of the love I shall never cease to cherish for the State of my birth; of the pride with which I have always regarded the exploits of her sons; and of the confidence which I feel in the ultimate loyalty of her people, who, while never forgetting the homage which their beloved State may justly claim, still remember the higher and grander allegiance due to our Common Country.

"LINCOLN" TO CHARLES KING, WASHINGTON, 26 JUNE 1861[25]

It is with feelings of deep gratitude not unmingled with diffidence, that I accept the honor which the Trustees of Columbia College have through you, conferred upon me.

It gives me the greatest pleasure to receive from a source so universally respected, such a manifestation of confidence and good will. I accept it, less as a personal courtesy than as a grateful indication of the spirit which animates all classes of our people, to preserve inviolate the institutions to whose fostering protection we owe all the progress we have made, as well in material and political advancement as in the higher fields of literature and science.

To Frederick William Seward, Washington, 12 July 1861[26]

Let me introduce Mr. Felix van Reuth of Maryland, of whom I spoke to you some time ago.[27] You will oblige me by giving him the information he desired in regard to his application for a consular appointment.

To Francis P. Blair Jr., Washington, 7 August 1861[28]

The President begs you will pardon him for having broken his engagement yesterday, and says he will make an effort to go with you at 5 o'clock tomorrow afternoon.

To Hannah Angell, Washington, 12 August 1861[29]

I am frequently made to think of Providence. I never thought to have that dear old city enter into my mechanical routine as it has since I have been here. I think business impertinent when it concerns Providence. I have always kept Rhode Island as girls keep wedding cake — to dream on. Today I wrote two letters to Providence, both on business. To take the taste out of my mouth, I write to you, "in the dead unhappy night and while the rain is on the roof." That is all of Locksley Hall, that I intend to quote.[30]

How is it with you and how have you been? I was sorry not to come up to Scituate and help marry you.[31] I delayed answering your kind invitation, in the vague Micawberish hope that something would turn up to permit me to go, until it was too late.

Was it a pleasant time and did the laurels bloom kindly? I have almost forgotten the Ponongansett except when I dream of it.[32]

I am dreadfully lonesome here. When Ellsworth was murdered all my sunshine perished.[33] I hope you may never know the dry, barren, agony of soul that comes with the utter and hopeless loss of a great love. I think often of him whenever I ought to be jolly, with a tearless abandon which good people who hope for heaven can never conceive. You remember that impious rhyme of mine which I gave you once. It seems to me now like a wicked prophecy.

Why dont the changing years which improve all things change me? My good is slipping from me, and evil is developing simply. I would give all things to be Walter Noyes.[34] I saw Tom Caswell the other day & was glad to serve him.[35] That was not creditable to me. Tom has been growing steadily upward.

As for me I am not improving company for a good Christian lady, on a rainy night. Take a bad subject's blessing and Good Night.

To James A. Hamilton, Washington, 19 August 1861[36]

I am the unluckiest wretch that lives. I did not receive the kind note you sent me, until Friday night at Long Branch.[37] As it was horribly dull there, I concluded, instantly upon reading your kind invitation, to return to New York and go to you Saturday afternoon.[38] But then I found there was no telegraphic station at Irvington or Dobb's Ferry and that I could not apprize you of my coming. I went down town and lunched with Mr. Roosevelt at Exchange Place.[39] Coming back I was thunderstruck to find you had been at my hotel and were gone.

There were only three recourses left me. Suicide, intoxication, or profanity. As I never drink and am still living, you can imagine which I chose. I thought my stupidity could only be expiated by a rigorous penance. So I resolved not to return to Long Branch, not to enjoy myself in New York, but to go sulkily back to Washington, and stay at my desk until my luck changed.

Some day, before long, I will take my fate by the throat and conquer it. It has become a monomania with me to "eat salt" with you at Nevis and it shall be done.[40]

To Montgomery C. Meigs, Washington, 19 August 1861[41]

I am directed by the President to send you the enclosed telegram from the

Quartermaster of the Fire Zouaves [*Alexander M. C. Stetson*], who are endeavoring to resume their former position in the army.[42]

To John G. Nicolay, Washington, 21 August 1861[43]

Nothing new. An immense crowd that boreth ever. Painters, who make God's air foul to the nostril. Rain, which makes a man moist and adhesive. Dust, which unwholesomely penetrates one's lungs. Washington, which makes one swear.

There is not an item. We are waiting for your arrival to make one.

To Mrs. Fanny Campbell Eames, Washington, 21 August 1861[44]

If the events of the last few days were to be taken as an earnest of the future, I would invest my surplus shekles in a cheap tombstone, write "Miserrimus" on it, and betake myself to Prussic acid glacé. I have been like Poe's raven's "unhappy master whom unmerciful disaster followed fast and followed faster till he thought all life a bore." It is not a particularly hilarious chronicle, but here it is.

Finding it hideously dull at Long Branch (the gay & festive Jenkins of the [*New York*] Herald is paid by the line for making the world believe that the place is not ghastly and funereal) the crowd a sort of queer half-baked New Jersey confectionery, with a tendency to stammer when spoken to, and to flatten its nose against our windows while we ate.[45] I determined to go up to New York and accept a most kind invitation from Col. Hamilton to come to him Saturday. Arriving there, I found there was no telegraph to Irvington or Dobb's Ferry. I could not apprize him of my coming or arrange for him to meet me. I blasphemed at this a little, and went quietly down town and was busy for an hour or two. Coming back I found Mr. Hamilton's card at the Hotel. He had been and gone.

My rage transcended grief. I was so mad at myself that I was uncivil to everyone else. Mr. Dennison came in with brilliant plans for the next day.[46] I mildly but firmly requested him to mobilize himself for an instant trip to the Court of His most Sulphurous majesty. I concluded to take a royal revenge on myself by ordering myself back to Washington.

I came and found the air like a damp oven. They are painting the White

House and the painters from their horrid hair (I mean their brushes) shake pestilence & things. The people in the streets are stupid or scared. It is a bad neighborhood.

I can do nothing but wish it were "not me, but another man."

Let me tell you a fact which proves me insane or Washington preternaturally dull. Yesterday I went to dinner at Willards late & after taking my seat, I saw a solitary diner at a distance. I took up my soup and walked. I sat down & ate dinner with BING.[47] I was so dull he was almost endurable.

If you see Mrs. Lincoln dont hint to her that anything but inexorable necessity called me from Long Branch. I impressed her with the belief that the delay of another day, would break the blockade, recognize Davisdom, impeach the Cabinet and lose the Capital. Like a Roman matron she sacrificed her feelings to save the Republic.

I have not seen Mr. Eames since I returned.[48] I have not felt like proper company for a gentleman and a Christian. I have felt as outlawed as a Hasheesh eater.

There is another offshoot of English nobility coming over in a day or two, a son of the Earl of Mayo, Hon. Robert Bourke.[49] I hope [*Nathaniel P.*] Willis will find it out & by way of showing him a delicate attention, take him to the observation settee whence on clear afternoons is to be seen, windows favoring, the Presidential ensarking and bifurcate dischrysalizing. In view of his late letter I would mildly inquire "What next?"[50]

To John G. Nicolay, Washington, 24 August 1861[51]

Yours of the 22 received this morning.[52] I dont wish to hurry you, but write simply to say that Dr. Pope's prediction has been realized.[53] I am flat of my back with bilious fever. I had a gay old delerium yesterday, but am some better today. Dr. thinks I will be around in a day or two. Bob Lincoln came this morning bringing positive orders from his mother for me to join her at New York for an extension of her trip. I dont know where. Of course I cant go — as things look. There is no necessity whatever for you to return just now.[54] There is no business in the office and Stoddard is here all the time.[55] He can do as well as either of us. As soon as I get able, I shall leave. The air here is stifling. You had better stay as long as you like for there is nothing but idleness here. As soon as I get on my pins I shall shab.[56] It will be a sort of breach of etiquette but as Joe Gargery feelingly observes "Manners is manners, but your 'elth's your 'elth."[57]

Dont come till you get ready.

To Mr. Swain, Washington, 25 August 1861[58]

I did not receive your note until I had returned from Long Branch. I would like to see you today or very early tomorrow (Monday) morning.

To William Henry Seward, Washington, 27 August [1861][59]

Mr. Bleeker writes that Mr. Charles H. Todd a gentleman of character and fortune residing in Paris, is now in New York, and intends returning to France in a few days.[60] He suggests that if you would request an interview with Mr. Todd, valuable information as to the operations of the Rebel Com[*missione*]rs in Europe, &c might be obtained. He writes much more at length, but to save yr. time I have synopsized the matter.

To [Mrs. A. E. Edwards], Washington, 12 October 1861[61]

I send you a carte-de-visite, which I think is very good, all but the face, which don't look like anything in particular. The pantaloons, however, are in the highest style of the tailor life and photographic art.

I think the mug is absurd. The expression of the features reminds me of the desperate attempts of a tipsy man to look sober. But coat, trousers, and gloves are irreproachable.

To Albert Marshman Palmer, Washington, 24 October 1861[62]

The President, and myself, in a smaller way, are very much annoyed by applications from Strangers desiring letters of introduction to Mr. Barney and recommendations to places in the Customs. These are invariably refused.

But I write now, at the suggestion of the President, to say that if there is any vacancy in the Custom House which can be without detriment bestowed upon a citizen of Illinois it would give the President and Mrs. Lincoln great pleasure to have it bestowed upon Mr. George Barrell of Springfield, whose application endorsed by Mr. Lincoln has been for some time on file, and in relation to whom Mr. Barney himself addressed a letter of inquiry to the President. If Mr. Barney thinks of giving an appointment to any body in Springfield, they would prefer that it be Mr. Barrell, *rather than any one else.*

Please make this representation to Mr. Barney and oblige the President and yours truly

[*P.S.*] Be kind enough to answer this at your leisure. I suppose you have received my former note in regard to one Scott who has seemed to have somehow gotten a letter from Bob Lincoln.

To John G. Nicolay, Washington, ca. 10 November 1861[63]

Hell is to pay about Watt's affairs.[64] I think the Tycoon begins to suspect him. I wish he could be struck with lightning. He has got William & Carroll turned off, and has his eye peeled for a pop at me, because I wont let Madame have our stationery fund.[65] They have gone to New York together.

The "near horse" John says has seen his best days. He is getting stiff. When you get back, you can trade him.

To L. B. Wyman, Washington, 11 November 1861[66]

I am directed by the President to acknowledge the receipt this morning of your kind invitation for the 22nd of December next, and to state that nothing but the exigencies of public affairs could prevent him from availing himself of the privilege you have been so thoughtful as to tender.

The President regrets the more deeply the necessity that deprives him of the pleasure of meeting you, since at no former time have the memory and the example of our forefathers furnished a more instructive subject for our contemplation, than now, when the institutions they founded are threatened by armed insurrection, and all the powers of the Government are pledged to the support of the principles for which they toiled and suffered.

To [John Dean Caton], Washington, 12 November 1861[67]

Your letters and your telegram to Mr. Nicolay have been received. I am directed by the President to inform you that the entire subject of the Military Telegraph has been referred to the Department of War to be organized into a regular system, and Mr. Anson Stager has been appointed the Government Agent for that purpose.[68] He told me today that he would soon go West and while in Illinois will see you and endeavor to make an arrangement which will be entirely satisfactory to you.

To [William Henry Seward], Washington, [7 December] 1861[69]

The President directs me to say, in answer to the inquiry of the Secretary of State, that he is only waiting for his carriage to start immediately.

To A. C. Voris, Washington, 21 December 1861[70]

I am directed by the President to express to you his grateful acknowledgements for your kind favor of the 16th of this month.

To Albert Bierstadt, Washington, 21 December 1861[71]

I have been so very busy since I received your kind note containing the photographs that I have not had time to thank you. They are very fine. That one of me with the hat on is the best I have ever had.[72] I should be very much obliged if you would send me a few more of them. My friends stole all I had the first day.

Leutze is still very busy upon his cartoons for his great picture in the Capitol.[73] It will be a wonderful work when he completes it.

To Mary Ridgely, Washington, 1861[74]

I send you this book [*Silas Marner* by George Eliot] because it is new — that is its only recommendation. It sketches with the most miraculous fidelity characters that are not worth sketching. It reminds me of a satiric cartoon of a Dutch painter, representing Art knocking in vain at his door, and the artist within industriously engaged in drawing an old shoe. This woman has wonderful power but is wasting it on unworthy subjects.

There is something strange, almost startling in this story. There is not one single character in it who is not below mediocrity in mind, morals and manners. Yet these people, so drearily commonplace, in actual life, move us strongly in the book. It is not sympathy with the people; it is sympathy with the success of the portraits.

When women write books they make young people fall in love very foolishly. I want to write a novel on common-sense principles and change all that, some day, when I have grown rich and idle, and have forgotten to-day and yesterday.

We are very jolly here now, on a warfooting. We are hoping for a little brush with the traitors, but are very much afraid they will deprive us of that pleasure.

. . . I wish I were in Springfield for a little while. I am afraid to leave here just now, lest I should lose some fun in my absence.

To "My Dear Sir," Washington, 9 January 1862[75]

Please admit to the Ladies' Gallery Mrs. Bliss,[76] who goes to join some ladies already there.

To Andrew Johnson, Washington, 20 January 1862[77]

The President directs me to send you copy of dispatch just received from Baltimore:

"We have dispatch from Cincinnati announcing that Schoeff killed Zollicofer and routed his army at Somerset on Saturday.[78] Twelve hours fight. Heavy loss both"

To Josiah D. Canning, Washington, 3 February 1862[79]

The President directs me to acknowledge the receipt of your favour of the 18th January containing your patriotic and spirited song.

He wishes to express to you his hearty thanks for your kindness in remembering him.

To "My dear doctor," Washington, 2 March 1862[80]

Robert Lincoln has just sent me this letter to mail for him. I hope you continue well and enjoy the reports of the victories we have been sending you over the water.

To Anson G. Henry, Washington, 7 March 1862[81]

The President directs me to acknowledge the receipt of your favor of the 30th of December and to say that he fully appreciates the importance of your suggestions, and the sincerity of your efforts for the best interests of your state and the Nation.

At the same time he feels that he cannot without manifest impropriety, offer any advice as to the details of political action in the several states. Especially in cases where the avowed and earnest friends of the Government differ as to the best means of accomplishing the end which all equally desire, it would be an ungracious office for him, by adopting the suggestions and forwarding the views of certain of his friends, to seem to cast a censure upon those holding different opinions of right and expediency.

For this reason, while he earnestly hopes that the coming elections in Oregon may result in such a manner as to show the clearest possible evidence of the attachment of the people to the principles of constitutional liberty, he does not deem it proper at this distance, to make any suggestions in relation to the manner in which this most desirable result is to be accomplished.

The President directs me to convey to you the assurance of his unchanged personal regard.

To Edward A. Bedell, Washington, 24 March 1862[82]

As soon as I received your letter I went to see Gen: Richardson about it.[83] He said that after he had made one nomination, the Department informed him that a mistake had been made in notifying him, and that he had no further appointment at his disposal. He seemed to be very sorry about it and regretted particularly to disappoint you. If I were you I would not yet give up all hopes; for if during his term a vacancy occurs at the academy, for his district, he says you shall have it.

Study when you can so as to be sure of entering if you have the good luck to be appointed. You have written a very nice letter to me, which shows you have hitherto made good use of your time. Continue to study and you will not regret it, even if you fail to gain the position in the Navy you desire.

To John G. Nicolay, Washington, 31 March 1862[84]

Still nothing new in politics or war.

Madames Lisboa & Asta Buraga have had an awful quarrel originating in the Brazilienne uttering disrespectful opinions of the Chilienne's nose.[85] The Diplomatic Body in a ferment — met and agreed to keep it still — so of course everybody knows it.

Mrs Eames gives a little party next Wednesday night.[86] Dont you wish you were here.

Thats all.

The "enemy" [*Mary Lincoln*] is still planning Campaign in quiet. She is rapidly being reinforced from Springfield. A dozen Todds of the Edwards Breed in the house.[87]

Make Charlie write. I opened Cole's [*Austin Coleman Woolfolk*] letter as you told me but found nothing of what you said.[88]

I send Magazines by today's mail.

[*on verso of envelope*] Little Mac.[*General George B. McClellan*] sails today for down river. He was in late last night to see Tycoon. He was much more pleasant and social in manner than formerly. He seems to be anxious for the good opinion of everyone.

Nothing new as yet in any direction. Miss Mary Hamilton is at Eames. A first class woman every way.

What did you do with the safe key. I cannot find it anywhere.

The Logans are here all safe and sound.[89]

Call Charlie a cuss for not writing to me.

To John G. Nicolay, [Washington, 3 April] 1862[90]

I am engaged in a horse-trade. John lately discovered what he considered a splendid match for our off-horse, in the possession of Major Beckwith.[91] I have got him now trying him, a splendid fellow really, and I think I can bamboozle our friend Beckwith into a trade somehow.

I wish you would write me immediately to tell me what you have done & what remains to be done in the case of Reinmüller, the deserter. Carl Schurz has become much interested in him and bothers me horribly to do something. I want to know what you have done.

Mrs Eames had a nice party last night.

W. H. Russell is hideously outraged because Stanton had him ordered off the Ship on which he was going to Ft. Monroe.[92] No news from Mc. yet.

[*on verso of envelope*] Gen. McC is in danger. Not in front but in rear. The President is making up his mind to give him a peremptory order to march. It is disgraceful to think how the little squad at Yorktown keeps him at bay.[93]

To John G. Nicolay, Washington, 4 April 1862[94]

McClellan is at last in motion.[95] He is now moving on Richmond. The secret is very well kept. Nobody out of the Cabinet knows it in town. Dug Wallack is in a great fidget about it.[96] He knows something is in the wind but cant guess what.

Madame has mounted me to pay her the Stewards salary. I told her to kiss mine. Was I right?[97]

To [William Howard Russell], Washington, 4 April 1862[98]

I have referred your communication to the President who has given it due consideration. The President directs me to say that, with every disposition to oblige you, he is disinclined to overrule a decision of the Secretary of War founded on what appears to the Secretary, considerations of high public importance. To do so in your case alone would seem to all others an invidious distinction.

The President regrets that he cannot gratify you in the matter.

To John G. Nicolay, Washington, 5 April 1862[99]

The devil is abroad, having great wrath. His daughter, the Hell-Cat [*Mary Lincoln*], sent Stackpole in to blackguard me about the feed of her horses.[100] She thinks there is cheating round the board and with that candor so charming in the young does not hesitate to say so. I declined opening communications on the subject.

She is in "a state of mind" about the Steward's salary. There is no steward. Mrs Watt has gone off and there is no *locum tenens*.[101] She thinks she will blackguard your angelic representative into giving it to her "which I dont think she'll do it, Hallelujah!"

My horse trade has fallen through: the new horse though fine looking was vicious. So I took back the "near horse."

To [John G. Nicolay], Washington, 9 April 1862[102]

Glorious news come borne on every wind but the South Wind. While Pope is crossing the turbid and broad torrent of the Mississippi in the blaze of the enemy's fire and Grant is fighting the overwhelming legions of Beauregard at Pittsburgh [*Landing*], the little Napoleon sits trembling before the handful of men at Yorktown afraid either to fight or run.[103] Stanton feels devilish about it. He would like to remove him if he thought it would do.

Things go on here about as usual. There is no fun at all. The Hellcat is getting more Hellcattical day by day.[104]

Lamon has indicted Horace Greeley criminally for libel and thinks of going to New York to bring him down to the jail here. He would not be persuaded by his best friends.[105]

We have made Van Alen a Brig Gen.[106] The Senate however have not yet confirmed him. I am getting along pretty well. I only work about 20 hours a day. I do all of your work & half of my own now you are away.

Dont hurry yourself. We are getting on very well. I talk a little French, too, now. I have taken a devil of a notion to the Gerolts.[107] I went to see them the other day. The children were less scared than usual and they and Madame la Baronne talked long and earnestly of the state of your hygiene and said "it was good intentions you for to go to the West for small time."

The latest rumour in "our set" is that Mr. Hay and Miss Hooper are *engaged* as Count Gurowski calls it.[108] I wish I had that d'd old nuisance's neck in a slip noose. I am afraid the Hoopers will hear it and then my good times there will be up.

To Samuel C. Brown, Washington, 16 April 1862[109]

I am directed by the President to acknowledge the receipt of your esteemed favor of the 10th of April, accompanying the Resolutions of the Providence Conference of the Methodist Episcopal Church recently in session.[110]

He directs me to convey to you his thanks for your courtesy, and to express to you the gratification with which he received assurances of devotion to the government, so steadfast and so loyal, and a confidence in himself so generous and flattering, as were embodied in the Resolutions of the Conference.

To John G. Nicolay, Washington, 16 April 1862[111]

There is nothing new. Yes there is. A Pretty Girl at Willard's. Haight is going to introduce me tonight. Haight is a good egg. He votes straight Republican every time. He and Odell both went for Abolition in the Deestreck.[112]

The President has appointed Berrett one of the Com[*missio*]n[*ers*] under the Abolition Act.[113] I am glad. It is a graceful compliment & a proper *amende* for the former injury.

McDougall got skinned alive by Wade yesterday.[114] Mc. didnt mind it. He was pretty drunk.

Forrest is playing at the New Theater.[115] Thats all.

To Mrs. Carl Schurz, Washington, 20 April 1862[116]

The President returned home this evening. I represented your request to him. He replied that he would be pleased to see you tomorrow, Monday, morning early. If you would come as early as from 8 1/2 to 9 oclock in the morning you would be most likely to find him disengaged.

To Hiram Ketchum, Washington, 16 May 1862[117]

The President directs me to acknowledge the receipt of your favor under date of yesterday.

TO CALEB LYON, WASHINGTON, 21 MAY 1862[118]

Herewith I send you the Autograph of which you spoke some days ago. It is a longer letter than the President has before written in a month.

TO MRS. LINCOLN, WASHINGTON, 23 MAY 1862[119]

The Secretary of the Navy has called to ask whether you have any objection to the Marine Band beginning to play upon the lawn. If you have not, they will begin tomorrow. He waits for your answer.[120]

TO MRS. LINCOLN, WASHINGTON, [CA. 25 MAY 1862][121]

I communicated your answer to the Secretary of the Navy. He says he will be governed in the matter by your wishes. He requests me to ascertain whether you have any objection to the Band playing in Lafayette Square.[122]

TO MARY JAY, WASHINGTON, 20 JULY 1862[123]

Will you pardon me for an offense which seems to me unpardonable — omitting so long to thank you for your great kindness in sending me the photographs of your father and brother?

There have been very few hours that I could call my own from the time that you thus honored me until now. At last we have lost our chronic infliction of a Congress and are beginning to think of finishing the accumulated arrears of duties and pleasures.

What a wretched conclusion of all our little Generals [*George B. McClellan's*] boasting addresses and orders have we seen on the bloody banks of the Chickahominy! Sad as is the result to himself and the country I think you have reason to congratulate yourself upon the sagacity which so long ago foresaw the coming failure. You will perhaps remember that you then thought less of him than I did.[124]

How gloriously General Hunter has justified my statement that the future would prove his soundness in hatred of slavery. He has done the greatest thing of the war even though unfruitful of results.

Although the President repudiated his order he regards him none the less kindly, and so told the Border State Slaveholders the other day.[125]

The President himself has been, out of pure devotion to what he considers the best interests of humanity, the bulwark of the institution he abhors, for a year. But he will not conserve slavery much longer. When next he speaks in relation to this defiant and ungrateful villainy it will be with no uncertain sound. Even now he speaks more boldly and sternly to slaveholders than to the world.

If I have sometimes been impatient of his delay I am so no longer.

Please present my regards to those of your family whom I have the honor to know.

To Edward McPherson, Washington, 28 July 1862[126]

The time at which appointments will begin to be made under the Revenue law depends somewhat upon the Treasury Department. As soon as the matters connected with the new issue of currency are settled the appointments will begin to be made. Govr. Boutwell cannot say just when that will be, probably this week, beginning with California Oregon &c. extreme points.[127]

To William A. Wheeler, Washington, 29 July 1862[128]

The President directs me to acknowledge the receipt of your communication of the 24th asking the appointment of John A. Sabin as a Paymaster in the U.S. Army.

If it is an appointment in the regular service you desire the President directs me to say that there are no vacancies, and none to be at present created. Such an appointment therefore is an impossibility.

If however you desire an appointment in the volunteer force for Mr Sabin the President directs me to say that it will give him pleasure to recommend him for the earliest vacancy in that Department.[129]

To John G. Nicolay, Washington, 1 August 1862[130]

There is positively nothing of the slightest interest since you left. The abomination of desolation has fallen upon this town. I find that I can put in twenty four hours out of every day very easily, in the present state of affairs, at the Executive Mansion. The crowd continually increases instead of diminishing. The Tax business has begun to grind. Chase is having things very much his own way. He makes out a batch of twenty or thirty commissions at a time filling in the names & presenting them to the President to sign.[131]

To John G. Nicolay, Washington, 6 August 1862[132]

I send herewith several cards of introduction which General Todd has written for you to friends of his in the Pembina.[133] They are men of wealth and influence in the Territory of Dakotah, and may be of advantage to you to know.

I wrote the letter that accompanies this before I had heard that Bill Jayne was Todds opponent.[134] This of course alters the question so far as doing anything about the election is concerned.

Burn these letters as soon as you read them.

To John G. Nicolay, Washington, 11 August 1862[135]

You will have seen by the papers that Pope has been running his head into a hornets nest. He fought a desperate battle the other day—or rather Banks did—Pope coming up at the end of it.[136]

He stands now in good position eager for another fight and confident of licking the enemy.

The Tycoon has given orders that he shant fight unless there is a first rate chance of cleaning them out. The Tycoon thinks a defeat there would be a greater nuisance than several victories would abate.

There is no further news. It is horribly hot[—]all but me have gone to shaking again. Your infernal South windows always give me the chills. Stone has broken them up however and doses me remorselessly to keep them away.[137]

If in the wild woods you scrouge an Indian damsel steal her moccasins while she sleeps and bring them to me. The Tycoon has just received a pair gorgeously quilled, from an Indian Agent who is accused of stealing. He put them on & grinned. Will he remember them on the day when Caleb [B. Smith] proposes another to fill the peculating donor's office. I fear not, my boy, I fear not.

Your ducks are all as usual. Nobody in town but Mrs Seward and La Baronne de Gerolt. I sit on doorsteps sometimes with these and talk of many things, principally the knaveries of [*Schweinitz Krain?*].

To JOHN G. NICOLAY, WASHINGTON, 27 AUGUST 1862[138]

Where is your scalp? If anybody believes you dont wish you were at home, he can get a pretty lively bet out of me. I write this letter firing into the air. If it hits you, well. It will not hurt so much as a Yancton's rifle. If in Gods good Providence your long locks adorn the lodge of an aboriginal warrior and the festive tomtom is made of your stretched hide, I will not grudge the time thus spent, for auld lang syne. In fancys eye I often behold you the centre and ornament of a wildwood circle delighting the untutored children of the forest with Tuscan melodies, while from enraptured maidens comes the seductive invitation "Mush way—heap—boneby—bush—two bet." But by the rivers of Babylon you refuse to yield to dalliance, yea, you weep when you remember Washington whose magnificent distances are nevermore for you.

Washington is not at the present speaking an alluring village. Everybody is out of town and nobody cares for nobody that is here. One exception tres charmante, which is French for devilish tidy. Miss Census Kennedy is here with a pretty cousin from Baltimore which Ellicott [*light?*].[139] Stoddard is quite spoony about her while I am languidly appreciative.

Grover's Theater reopens next Saturday and Dahlgren breathes again.[140] Some pretty women are engaged to whom I am promised introductions. There is also a new Club House established in the city to which I have sometime gone to satisfy the ragings of famine.[141] I think you will patronize it extensively when you come back. I ride on Horseback mornings. I ride the Off Horse. He has grown so rampagious by being never driven (I have no time to drive) that no one else whom I can find can ride him. Stoddard, Boutwell & Leutze ride sometimes the near horse.

To MRS. D. K. CARTTER, WASHINGTON, 3 SEPTEMBER 1862[142]

The President directs me to state that he has sent your letter to your husband, as you desired, and has referred your request for a leave of absence for him to the consideration of the Secretary of State.

To [Montgomery C. Meigs], Washington, 12 September 1862[143]

The President directs me to refer the enclosed account to the attention of the Quartermaster General with the hope that it may be found proper to pay the claim of Mr. Heslop.[144]

Hay's endorsement of a bill submitted to the White House by Joseph Gawler, 17 September 1862[145]

I believe these items to be correctly stated.[146]

To Edwin M. Stanton, Washington, 26 September 1862[147]

The President directs me to refer the enclosed papers to your notice. Mr. Nay, who makes some grave charges against officers at New Orleans, is declared by the best man in Quincy, Ill, where he formerly lived to be a man of intelligence and good character.[148]

To Major J. C. Williams, Washington, 1 October 1862[149]

In reply to yours of this date to Mr. Nicolay, — The matter of Mr. Carlin was referred to the Secretary of War, by the President, and Mr. Carlin's letter was sent to his Brother, Col. Carlin 38th Ill. Vols.[150]

To Captain Joseph H. Bradley, Washington, 10 October 1862[151]

You will see by the enclosed letter that your discharge is considered by the Adjutant General's Office an honorable one.[152]

I think you are especially fortunate in extricating yourself so easily from the difficulty into which you entered by a reappointment into your old Regiment. Everything has been done in the case which could be done, and the rules of the Department have even been violated to oblige you.

To John G. Nicolay, Warsaw, Illinois, 28 October 1862[153]

McGregor's on his native heath, and having quietly a good time. I sit by the woodfire all day and talk with my mother and at night I do a little unobtrusive sparking. I am perfectly idle, and you, who always insist on being busy even when you ought to be pleasuring, can have no adequate conception of the enjoyment of the genuine *dolce far niente*. Just keep the army still for a week or so and I will bless you with my latest breath.

I shall stay here a few days and try to put beef on my bones and then return by way of Springfield and Cincinnati.

I spent only one day in Springfield. But it paid. I saw much of Alice Huntington and something of the Ridgleys. Alice is very delicate and sensitive. Her soul seems to be wearing out her body. Her devotion to music is absolutely pathetic.[154] Mary R is growing into a damned splendid woman. She has gone to Indianapolis to stay for some months.

Charlie Philbrick is going to Hell by a large majority.[155] He was hideously drunk all day and all night while I was there. Something must be done to reform him or he is gone up.

Please send me as soon as you receive this, five or ten dollars worth of postal currency. There is none at all here and it is almost impossible to get a dollar changed. Send it care of Milton Hay Springfield.

[*P.S.*] You cannot imagine the earnestness of denunciation which fills the West in regard to McClellan. *I have not heard one single man defend him.* If he should be sent West to command our troops his presence would demoralize the army. His continuance in command in the East begins to shake the confidence of some of our best friends in the Government.

Things look badly around here politically. The inaction of the Army & the ill success of our arms have a bad effect and worse than that, all our energetic and working Republicans are in the Army. The Captains of tens & Captains of Hundreds who, you know, do our best work, are all in the field, and we have gained no strength from Democratic accessions, as, in almost every case, as soon as a Democrat has his eyes opened, he enlists. This State is in great danger.

I have been astonished to hear so little objection to the [*emancipation*] proclamation. Republicans all like it and every Democrat who does not swear by Vallandigham comes up to it.[156]

But everything depends on the Army of the Potomac.

Thank God that Buell is finished finally![157]

Neither Latham Irwin or Stack were in Springfield.[158] So I have naught to say unto thee.

To EDWIN M. STANTON, WASHINGTON, 10 DECEMBER 1862[159]

The President directs me respectfully to commend to the consideration of the Secretary of War, the enclosed letter of Governor Salomon.[160]

To JEAN DAVENPORT LANDER, WASHINGTON, 12 DECEMBER 1862[161]

I send you with this the picture I promised.

Whenever you see it, pray do not fail to remember that it is the counterfeit presentment of your most obedient servant.

2

1863

To William Leete Stone, Washington, 8 January 1863[1]

Pray do not think me ungrateful for your kindness in sending me the advance chapters of your history, because I have not promptly acknowledged the receipt of them.[2]

I have read them with great interest and profit, and — what to my mind affords the best proof of the ease and purity of your style, — I have been so interested in the subject matter that I paid little attention to the dress in which your ideas were presented. It surpassed even my expectations of you, formed in college, to find you throwing aside the little arts of ornament and passionate expression which used to give such life to your youthful essays, and assuming so easily and naturally the calm and quiet style of the historian. I have no doubt that your book will form a most valuable addition to that department of history in which the name of your father has so long stood without a rival.

To Adam Badeau, Washington, 9 January 1863[3]

I am sure I shall never be able to convince you how glad I was to hear from you and with what pleasure and profit I read your exceedingly interesting letter. It is positively the only letter I have read from any man in the army who seemed to have any sort of inclination for accurate observation and philosophical deduction. You have given me a better idea of matters in your Department from your point of view than I had previously gained from all sources. I am very grateful to you.

It seems really odd to me that you can where you are, write so long and well considered a letter. This war seems to have paralyzed all pens except professional ones. Of all the bright fellows whom I knew at the beginning, there is scarcely one who retains any inclination or aptitude for writing. As for me, although I am far from ranking myself among men of letters, yet when I remember that I used to scribble to my own intense delight and by the kind sufferance of friends who read, I can hardly admit that the used up machine who sits at my desk is the same person still. I cant write any longer. I need a plunge into respectable society and an exile from Washington to save me from absolute inanity.

To [George Plumer Smith], Washington, 10 January 1863[4]

I received your favor of yesterday this morning and at once laid the matter before the President.

He directs me to state in reply that your statement is substantially correct, but that, for the present, he prefers that you would still withhold it from the public.[5]

To Mary Ridgely, Washington, 22 January 1863[6]

I suppose you have long before this decided that I was never again to be believed or trusted, it has been so long since you kindly gave me permission to send you these books. But I am not so much to blame as you would think. I have made myself a nuisance at the book-stores asking for them ever since I returned. The demand for them, Mr. Philp informs me, has been so great that the supply was temporarily exhausted and I have been compelled to wait until now for a complete set.[7]

I have just finished reading the entire work [*the French edition of* Les Miserables]. I think nothing approaching it in sustained excellence has been written in our day. It is a great novel, a splendid historical monograph, a brilliant theological disquisition, and a profound treatise of political philosophy. No man in our day has thought it worth while to use the vehicle of fiction for the transmission of such weighty and portentous truths. No philosopher or statesman has had sufficient grace and vigor of imagination to envelope his ideas in a garb so attractive, and no novelist has been gifted with that strength and scope of intellect which would enable him to grasp with so firm a hand the gravest problems of society and progress. In delicacy and fervor of fancy and depth of pathos, in sustained and unflagging power, and in absolute mastery of the machinery of artistic construction, I have read nothing that can even be brought into comparison with it.

Of course there will be many things in it which you will not approve, and many which you will not understand fully until you have finished the book; and even then if you are dissatisfied, it is not with the author but with society and the great social wrongs against which he is a crusader.

I envy you heartily, Miss Mary, the leisure which you are to devote to this wonderful book. I deeply regretted the quiet and "the tranquil mind," with which I should have read it in Springfield a year or two ago.

To William Dean Howells, Washington, 31 January 1863[8]

Allow me to introduce my friend and Kinsman Mr. John J. Thomasson son of the Honorable Wm P Thomasson of Kentucky one of the most prominent of the uncompromising loyalists of the Border States.[9] I commend him to your acquaintance.

To Ethan Allen Hitchcock, Washington, 1 February 1863[10]

The President directs me to say that he has no objection to your taking a copy of the letter you referred to yesterday, under the conditions which you proposed.[11]

To Benjamin F. Butler, Washington, 13 February 1863[12]

I have the honor to enclose to you, in accordance with the request of the writer, a letter sent for that purpose to the President.[13]

To Mrs. Charles Hay, Washington, 19 March 1863[14]

I started for Port Royal a week ago, but finding myself a little sick when I arrived at New York I thought it would be more prudent to return to Washington and make repairs before setting out.[15]

I am now getting quite well again and will soon make a fresh start to visit Charlie. I have a great deal to talk to him about and cannot of course write many things that I want to say. We hear rumours here of disaster to the colored troops. I am in hopes they may turn out to be untrue. I shall take a careful and deliberate survey of matters in the Department and can then understandingly advise Charlie for his own good.[16]

I saw a good deal of Augustus[17] in N.Y. and became acquainted with our cousin C. G. Thompson. He is a very agreeable old gentleman and a fine artist.

To George H. Stuart, Washington, 21 March 1863[18]

In accordance with the desire of the writer I have the honor, by direction of the President to send you the enclosed remittance, to be devoted to the purpose indicated in the letter accompanying.

To John G. Nicolay, [Washington, March 1863][19]

For two weeks send my letters to Hilton Head. After that, keep them for me here.

If I should get knocked over Gus will come down and take care of matters.

To John G. Nicolay, Stono River, S.C., 8 April 1863[20]

I arrived here tonight at the General's [*Hunter's*] Headquarters & was very pleasantly received by both him and Halpine.[21] They are both in fine health and spirits. Halpine is looking better than I ever saw him before. They asked after you. On the way down I had for compagnons du voyage Generals Vogdes and Gordon; Gordon on sick leave and Vogdes to report for duty.[22]

I hear nothing but encouraging accounts of the fight of yesterday in Charleston Harbor. Gen. Seymour Chief of Staff says we are sure to whip them, much surer than we were before the attack.[23] The monitors behaved splendidly.[24] The Keokuk was sunk and the Patapsco somewhat damaged but as a whole they encountered the furious and concentrated fire of the enemy in a style for which even our own officers had scarcely dared to hope.[25] The attack will soon be resumed with greater confidence and greater certainty of what they are able to do than before. An expedition is on foot for the Army from which they hope important results. The force of the enemy is much larger than ours, but not so well posted, and as they are entirely ignorant of our plans they are forced to scatter and distribute their strength so as greatly to diminish its efficiency. Our troops are in good order and fine spirits apparently. I think highly of Seymour, from the way he talks — like a firm, quick, and cool headed man. On the whole, things look well, if not very brilliant.

The General says he is going to announce me tomorrow as a Volunteer Aide, without rank. I am glad of it, as the thing stands. If I had not been published as having accepted, hesitated, and rejected such an appointment I would not now have it. But I want my abolition record clearly defined and that will do it better than anything else, in my own mind and the minds of the few dozen people who know me.

Vogdes & I came up here alone as the rest could not get transportation. Littlefield is still at Hilton Head but the General is glad to receive him & will put him in position immediately.[26] He directs me to say to you this, and to convey his kindest remembrances. I wish you could be down here. You would enjoy it beyond measure. The air is like June at noon & like May at morning and evening. The scenery is tropical. The sunsets unlike anything I ever saw before. They are not gorgeous like ours but singularly quiet and solemn. The sun goes down over the pines through a sky like ashes-of-roses and hangs for an instant on the horizon like a bubble of blood. Then there is twilight, such as you dream about.

I have as yet seen neither Charlie nor [*Volmy?*] They are on the De Ford where my quarters will be when I get there.[27] They are hanging around the outskirts of Charleston Harbor, sloshing about, "lo[o]se in the Deestreck," waiting for a plant.

April 9. Alas for the pleasant prognostications of the military men! The Genl. this morning recd the despatches which you will see before this, confessing that the attack has been a failure! I do not as yet know all the results of this bitter disappointment. Charleston is not to be ours as yet, and another instance is added to the many, of the President having clearer perceptions of military possibilities than any man in the Cabinet or the field. He thought it would fail.

[*P.S.*] Write to me care of Gen. Hunter. I have seen Admiral Dupont.[28] Rodgers, Fleet Captain, & Preston, Flag Lieutenant, desired to be remembered to you.[29]

To John G. Nicolay, [Stono River, S.C., 10 April 1863][30]

I have written some particulars of my interview with Admiral Dupont which I thought the President should know. Please give it to him, reading it yourself if you care to. I went up into the Harbor yesterday. Everything was quiet. The Grey-coated rascals were on both sides, waiting for another attack. A crowd of them were crawling cautiously over the bluff to look at the wreck of the Keokuk which has sunk near the shore. They are very busy throwing up new batteries on Morris Island, and did not fire on us though we were in easy range.

While I was gone, they published the order making me A[ide] D[e] C[amp]. [several words crossed out] They have made a d'd burlesque of the thing by giving me so much rank. I objected to being called Priv. Sec. & the Adj. said it should not be printed so. You can of course see *why* it happened so.

To Lincoln, Stono River, S.C., 10 April 1863[31]

I went yesterday morning to Charleston Harbor to deliver to Admiral Dupont the despatches with which the Navy Department had charged me. I found the Admiral on board the "Ironsides" which with the rest of the Monitor fleet was lying inside the Bar at the point where they had anchored after the engagement of Tuesday.[32] I delivered my despatches and while he was reading them, I had some conversation with Capt. Rodgers, Fleet Captain of the S[outh] A[tlantic] B[lockade] Squadron. He said that ["]although the attack had been unsuccessful & the failure would of course produce a most unhappy effect upon the country, which had so far trusted implicitly in the invincibility of the Monitors, all the officers of the Navy, without exception, united in the belief that what they had attempted was impossible, and that we had reason for congratulation that what is merely a failure had not been converted into a terrible disaster. The matter has now been fairly tried. With favoring circumstances, with good officers, with good management, the experiment has completely failed. We sailed into the Harbor not sanguine of victory. We fought only about 40 minutes, and the unanimous conclusion of the officers of the Navy is that an hour of that fire would have destroyed us. We had reached and touched the obstructions. To have remained there long enough to remove them would have ensured the destruction of some of the vessels. If the others had gone by the Fort, they would still have been the target of the encircling batteries. There was no sufficient land force to have taken possession of the city. There was no means of supplying them with ammunition and provision, for no wooden ship could live ten minutes in that fire. The only issue would have been the capture of the surviving & the raising of the sunken vessels. This would have lost us the command of the coast, an irremediable disaster. So the Admiral took the responsibility of avoiding the greater evil, by saving the fleet and abandoning an enterprise which we think has been fairly proved impossible."

The Admiral, who had been listening and assenting to the latter portion of what Rodgers had been saying, added, "And as if we were to have a visible sign that an Almighty hand was over us for our good, the orders you have given me[33] show how vast was the importance of my preserving this fleet, whose power and prestige are still great and valuable, for the work which I agree with the President in thinking most momentous, the opening & the control of the Mississippi River. After a fight of 40 minutes we had lost the use of 7 guns. I might have pushed some of the vessels past Fort Sumter, but in that case we ran the enormous risk of giving them to the enemy & thus losing the control of the coast. I could not answer for that to my conscience."

The perfect approval of their own consciences, which these officers evidently felt, did not prevent their feeling the deepest grief and sorrow for the unhappy result of the enterprise. Their whole conversation was as solemn as a scene of death. At one time I spoke of the estimation in which they were held by the Government and the country, which in my opinion rendered it impossible that blame should be attached to them, and their eyes suddenly filled with tears. A first repulse is a terrible thing to brave and conscientious men, accustomed only to victory.

I was several times struck by the identity of opinion and sentiment between Admiral Dupont and yourself. You had repeatedly uttered, during my last week in Washington, predictions which have become history.

When I left the Harbor, they were preparing the Torpedo raft for the destruction of the sunken Keokuk.

I have taken the liberty of writing thus at length, as I thought you should know the sentiments of these experienced officers in regard to this unfortunate matter. I hope, however the news may be received, that due honor may be given to those who fought with such bravery and discretion, the losing fight.

To John G. Nicolay, n.p., 14 April 1863[34]

Here is one of the cleverest things I have seen since the war began. It is an impromptu order of Halpine's on Miss Mary Brooks, a New York lady, who was down here on a visit with Mrs. Raymond.[35] The "Hay" is, of course, Charlie, not *the Colonel.*

We are living very pleasantly here since the return from Charleston of the K——'s.[36] The General has some fine horses and the rides are pleasant.

To John G. Nicolay, Hilton Head, S.C., 16 April 1863[37]

The General and the Admiral this morning received the orders from Washington, directing the continuance of operations against Charleston. The contrast was very great in the manner in which they received them. The General was absolutely delighted. He said he felt more encouraged, and was in better heart and hope than before, at this indication of the earnestness of the Government to finish this business here. He said however that the Admiral seemed in very low spirits about it. He talked despondingly about it, adhering to the same impression of the desperate character of the enterprise as I reported to the President after my first interview with him. Perhaps, having so strongly expressed his belief that the enterprise was impracticable, he feels that he is rebuked by an opposite opinion from Washington.

General Hunter however, is in the best feather about the matter. He believed before we came back, that with the help of the gunboats we could take Morris Island and from that point reduce Fort Sumter, and he is well-pleased to have another chance at it. Whether the intention of the Government be to reduce Charleston now, with adequate men and means, or by powerful demonstrations to retain a large force of the enemy here, he is equally anxious to go to work again.

I write this entirely confidentially for you and for the President to know the ideas prevalent here.

Gen. Seymour has been with you before this & has given to the Government the fullest information relative to military matters here. His arrival, I suppose, will only confirm the resolution already taken. Admiral Dupont's despatches by the Flambeau, of course put a darker shade on the matter than anything Seymour will say, as he was strongly in favor of staying there & fighting it out.

Charlie has been quite sick since I got here with Pneumonia. I am occupied nearly all the time taking care of him. I hope he will be well in a day or two that I may move with the new expedition. I am getting browned by equitation, and can digest an enormous quantity of beef and sleep.

Write to me when you have nothing else to do & be good enough to remember that I have a pretty extensive handle to my name.

I intended before I left to have written to Cole Woolfolk about the subject of our conversation but forgot it. Wont you?

To John G. Nicolay, Hilton Head, S.C., 23 April 1863[38]

In yours of the 15th received last night you say "there was verbal indication of much wrath at the report that Dupont intended to withdraw his fleet and abandon his [*position*]." I was surprised at this. If you have received my different letters you will see why. He would have obeyed orders, had he done so. You say we have gained *points d'appui* for future work. The Navy say not. They say they cannot lie off Morris Island to cover the landing of our troops (or rather the crossing from Folly Island, the only practicable route) without imminent danger of being driven ashore & wrecked by the first northeasterly breeze that comes. It is not for me to say what is or what is not possible. My old ideas have been horribly shattered when I have seen two men, each of whom I had formerly considered an oracle on every subject connected with ships, accusing each other of ignorance and charlatan[*erie*].

I do not think Dupont is either a fool or a coward. I think there is a great deal of truth in his statement that while the fight in Charleston Harbor demonstrated the great defensive properties of the Monitors, it also proved that they could not be relied upon for aggressive operations.

With an adequate force I think Hunter could dislodge the enemy from Morris Island & from that point make a hole in Fort Sumter, but even then, little has been done. The General is sanguine. He wants a fight. I hope he may have one before I return.

Today I start to Florida. Charlie has been very sick since I arrived & I have been with him most of the time. We will be gone only a few days and will see Fernandina, St. Augustine. I take the liberty of making a note or two on several letters you sent me and respectfully referring them to you.

To Mrs. Charles Hay, Hilton Head, S.C., 23 April 1863[39]

It seems to me absolutely providential that I came down here as I did. The day we returned from Charleston Charlie was taken sick and for two or three days got steadily worse. His physician said he had a slight bilious attack & treated him on that supposition. I was not satisfied and mentioned my ideas to the General who took the responsibility of dismissing the physician and calling in another a Dr. Craven who seems a very accomplished man.[40] He at once confirmed my suspicions & said it was a decided case of Pneumonia. This had been treated for several days as a mere bilious attack! As soon as Craven took hold of him he commenced getting better and is now entirely convalescent. I wont let him go to work again until he entirely recovers his strength. In the meantime the Doctor advises a short sea-voyage. We will start for Florida this afternoon and remain there a few days. The climate is cool and pleasant like the Northern June. I never felt better in my life than I do now. I ride a good deal, eat in proportion, and sleep enormously. I hope to weigh about a ton when I return.

I shall never cease to be thankful that I came as I did, for it would have been an even chance, that in another week he would have had his lungs damaged for life, by ignorance and incompetence.

As to our future military operations I know nothing. I do not believe the General does. We have not force enough to take Charleston & we hear no talk of reinforcements. The Admiral thinks it madness to attack again with the Ironclads. The Government at Washington think differently. They think he is to blame for giving up so soon. I do not know how it is to end.

I am not at all despondent however. If we rest on our arms without firing another gun the rebellion will fall to pieces before long. They are in a state of starvation from Virginia to Texas. All we have to do, is to stand firm and have faith in the Republic, and no temporary repulses, no blunders even can prevent our having the victory. The Elections in Connecticut have frightened the rebels & disheartened them more than the Charleston failure his [has] discouraged us.[41]

We received Mary's letter last night for which thanks.

To John G. Nicolay, Hilton Head, S.C., 1 May 1863[42]

I arrived here this morning from Florida where I have been spending a week on a tour of inspection & muster with Charlie & Major Smith.[43] I received yr. letter for which thanks. I am a Colonel s'il vous plait. Col John Hay Vol. A. D. C. &c.

I send you a recent number of the New South.[44] You see you are floating around anonymously. I wrote the leader "Last legs." Read the fate of treason there. Charlie is pretty well again.

Halpine says he has written you recently wishing Grand Headquarters to be posted.[45] When you write again tell me how badly I am needed. It goes agin the grain to come back without nary a fight.

The news generally from the North look cheering. We will lick the rebels yet. From Davis to Vallandigham they all shall rue their treason yet. I am getting fat and tanned.

I have had a great time in Florida. It is the only thing that smells of the Original Eden on the Continent. I wish I could buy the State for taxes & keep it for a Castle of Indolence.[46] As we sat in the shade at St. Augustine & watched the picaninnies catching crabs in the lazy sunshine on the seawall, the quaint old town lying sleepy and still before us & the orange groves filling the background with the vivid green of the tropics, while a sky without blemish of cloud hung like a visible benediction over all, I felt as useless and irresponsible as the lizards in the grass or the porpoises that leaped in the liquid basin of the bay. The memory of a land where people worked, was as dim and distant as the dream of home to the enchanted mariners sleeping beneath the whispering pines of the Lotos Islands. But when we weighed anchor and sailed all that changed & now we are back in actual life among the fleas & the work and the annoy of Hilton Head.

Fleas are a subject of refined gossip. A lady at the General's quarters the other day speaking on the all-engaging topic says, "I am comparatively free but Carrie there is absolutely alive with them." The horror of the unmarried sister, newly imported from the decorous North, may be imagined.

Give my love to all who ever speak of me. As for Mrs. Johnny Clark, how [two or three words crossed out] can I like the South & she in Washington?

I wish you would write to me & give me some idea of things in general from a central standpoint. I can gain nothing from newspapers. What is in the immediate future? And what is going to be done with *us*?

Remember me to Stod[*dard*].

To his grandfather, John Hay, Hilton Head, S.C., 2 May 1863[47]

Thinking that you might wish to know how your family are getting along in the land of the rebels, I take a few minutes this afternoon to inform you of our recent doings.

I have been here about a month. The climate is very pleasant and mild. When I left Washington there was quite a heavy snow-storm and when I got here it seemed like summer. The corn is in places nearly waist-high and the air is full of the fragrance of flowers, in the towns and in the woods.

Charlie I found quite sick with Pneumonia. It seemed quite providential that I got here as I did, as his physician was not a man of skill and had, as I suspected, entirely mistaken the nature of the disease. I had him dismissed and called in another, who confirmed my suspicions, and by changing the treatment relieved him very much, so that in a few days he was able to go on board a ship, and go with me and some other officers of the General's staff to Florida. We visited all the posts of this Department in that State & were gone more than a week and have just returned. Charlie has come back quite well and strong again. He had been too much overworked, and the rest and change of air improved his health very fast.

I never saw a more beautiful country than Florida. The soil is almost as rich as our prairie land. All sorts of fruit and grain grow with very little cultivation, and fish and game of every kind abound. I found there a good many sound Union people, though the majority are of course bitter rebels.

I send you a number of a newspaper published here in camp. It may be amusing to you.

Charlie joins me in sending love to you and all the friends.

To John G. Nicolay, Hilton Head, S.C., 12 May 1863[48]

I had intended to leave for the North today, but the uncertain state of Charlie's health prevents me. He is very unwilling to leave his work here, while he appears to be getting on comfortably, but the Surgeon tells me that his left lung is completely hepatized, or solidified, & that I had better remain with him a week or so longer, and if he is not then entirely recovered, to take him North & send him home. I send this letter by the Arago, which sails today, and will come myself by her next trip.[49] You need not answer this letter, therefore, as I will leave here as soon as an answer would be received.

I cannot, with all my ancient admiration for Admiral Dupont and the brave officers who command the iron-clad Navy, understand the lethargic apathy which has fallen on them since the battle in Charleston Harbor. General Hunter, fully appreciating the importance of making a diversion in these critical times in favor of Hooker and Rosecrans,[50] has repeatedly proposed to the Admiral expeditions against Savannah, against the S.C. batteries, against the rebel ironclads, &c, but all to no purpose. The Admiral objects to attempting "any thing in which success is not certain, for *fear of further damage to the prestige of the iron-clads!*"

Had the Navy, instead of rushing so blindly, and withal so gallantly against Fort Sumter and the encircling batteries, adopted Gen Hunter's plan and cooperated with him in the reduction of Morris Island & the Cumming's Point battery, the issue of that unfortunate fight might have been different. And even the day after, the Army here, thought that success was only to be obtained in that way. Seymour, sent to the Admiral by the General to urge that plan, did it in face of the Admirals opposition with such warmth that the conference ended in ill feeling between them. ~~I am expecting~~ I wonder every day how the kind relations between the General and the Admiral endure the strain of their great difference, the General ~~being~~ forever proposing fight and the Admiral continually declining.

The General, not having army enough to do anything alone, as he must keep garrisons at each of eight points in the Department & all with only about 20,000 men, is as busy as possible "stealing niggers" as Father Wickliffe used to say & making soldiers of them.[51] He has sent off one party to the interior swamps of Florida where there are said to be a large number of negroes banded together, under a cool and determined man. He is preparing another party to go to the mainland on a proselyting expedition among "our men and brethren." I wish he had more troops, but of course he can't ask for them at such a time. The draft I suppose will reenforce him up to the effective point. He has written to the President asking power to officer his negro regiments, like what was given to Genl. Thomas.[52] Without this he can do nothing you see. He has two hundred men and officers who are able and anxious to go into that service from whom to choose. I wish you would speak to the Prest. & Sec. Stanton about it.

I see by the papers that Lawrence, the Englishman who wrote Guy Livingston has been caught near Washington going over to the enemy & jugged.[53] I hope you will use all your influence to prevent his getting loose, until I get home & then I will relieve you. It was bad enough for him to write the most immoral novels of the age, but to fall in love with that "flamboyant [*deminess?*]" Secessia, is worse. Dont let up on him. Go to Judge [*Advocate Levi C.*] Turner & tell him to keep him a while longer. When I get home your mind may be easy.

General Hunter has this moment come in and ordered me to get ready to go to Stono with him. "How long will we be gone Sir?" "Perhaps a week." That means, take a shirt and toothbrush. Whether anything is going to happen or not I cant guess & I have been long enough in harness to ask no questions. We start in an hour. The General, Halpine and I.

If you should see "My mistress Dear"

"Tell her that next to Liberty
Her name was the last word my lips pronounced."

Intimate to the President what I have said about things of importance & consider it all entirely confidential otherwise, as there is no one even on the staff who knows all these things.

To John G. Nicolay, Hilton Head, S.C., 24 May 1863[54]

I take advantage of a transient boat to send a line.

On my return from a week at Beaufort & the Sea Islands, I learned that the General had sent Arthur Kinzie to Washington to bear a letter begging that the Govt. would release him from the orders which bind him to the dead body of the Navy here & would permit him to organize an expedition of his own into the Interior. I was very sorry that the letter had been dispatched in my absence as I should have preferred to use what influence my position would give me to bring the matter at once before the President and Secretary of War. There is positively nothing to hope for from the Navy at present. The Admiral so dreads failure that he cannot think of success. If anything is to be done here, General Hunter must, in the present aspect of affairs do it himself. The enemy are hurrying every available man away from the coast, to reenforce their great armies in the interior. Now is our time to strike them while & where they are weak. If the matter is not already settled, I hope you will exert yourself, for the good of the country to have it done.

Another thing about which I wrote before. Why is not authority given to Genl. Hunter to organize Negro Regiments? He very much needs it. He has written twice for it, and has gotten no answer. I wish you would, simply *pro bono publico*, have some resurrection made of the matter. Negroes are coming in, slowly as yet. But when our expeditions get on the Main he will be very much embarrassed for authority to do this.

I will start in a day or two. I write today because of the importance of the subject involved. The Arago is now lying at the wharf. I leave in her. But I thought a day or so might be gained by posting this today.

I am very sorry that I have to leave just as a prospect for some work opens. But I have been away as long as my conscience will permit to tax yr. forbearance.

Poor Charlie is in bad health. His lungs are affected. His physician thinks he must go North, which he flatly refuses to do as he thinks nothing ails him, and is only useful here now. I think I will bring him with me and send him home for a while.[55]

To General David Hunter, Washington, 9 June 1863[56]

Captain Kinzie is at last preparing to return and I take this opportunity of writing you. When I arrived here I found him still waiting an answer to your communication. The delay was caused by the following circumstances.

Some days before his arrival, Gen. Gillmore being in New York had become acquainted with some of our influential friends there, who, struck by his apparent energy and vigor of thought wrote to the President recommending him as the most suitable man in the Army to conduct the siege of Charleston.[57] His intimate knowledge of the country, his former services in that Department, and his enthusiastic desire to perform that piece of work, seemed to them to indicate him as a proper person for that duty. He came to Washington and on full and frequent conversations with officers of the Navy, they coincided in that opinion. General Halleck ~~alone objected~~ was slow to give his assent to the movement as he thought the troops might be needed to reinforce General Grant on the Mississippi. At this time Captain Kinzie came and the consideration of your communication was necessarily postponed until this matter was decided.

Immediately on my arrival, I saw Captain Fox, who told me that the Navy Dept. had decided to relieve Admiral Dupont & send to S.C. Admirals Foote & Dahlgren, at the same time speaking of General Gilmore's connection with the enterprise.[58] I found that his views harmonized entirely with your own as to the feasibility of the reduction of Fort Sumter from Morris Island. I said the same thing to the President, and he then gave it as his opinion that the troops might as well be employed in that enterprise as ~~in doing nothing~~ not, and that if they were needed elsewhere they could then be withdrawn. Orders were then drawn up, which while leaving the Department in your hands & the General command of all the troops, assigned to General Gilmore the conducting of the siege operations. These did not seem satisfactory, and after another days deliberation, it was decided that the number of troops in the Department was too small to require your services and those of General Gilmore together, so that an order was framed giving to Genl. G. the command of the Department during the proposed operations.

It may be superfluous for me to add any assurance that in this arrangement there has never been cast from any quarter a reflection upon you. On the contrary I have heard nothing but approval of your course from the President Mr Stanton & General Halleck. It was simply determined, first: that General Gilmore could be employed to great advantage at this time in operations against Charleston: and second: that it could far more conveniently be done by him singly than by a divided command.

It was impossible for the President to answer your letter pending these deliberations and even now he is too much occupied to write at length.[59]

I have taken the liberty of correcting some erroneous statements that I have seen in the newspapers relative to matters in the Department.

To Julian R. Campbell, Washington, 15 June 1863[60]

I am directed by the President to acknowledge the receipt of your favor of the 10th June, and to express his gratification to the gentlemen composing the Association you represent for the liberal and patriotic tone of the Resolutions which you enclosed.[61]

To Frederick William Seward, Washington, 2 July 1863[62]

W[illiam] Marsh, Consul at Altona insists upon it that he is starving & writes me numerous letters to prove that the process is unwholesome—

that he can get out of the habit by getting a better consulship, Elsinore for instance, which is vacant, and whose Vice-Consul, — says Marsh (& proves it by the enclosed) — would jump out of his Vice Consular skin with delight if Marsh were made Consul.[63]

Marsh is an honest, sincere fellow with wives and children & very little other household riches, writes bad verses and adores the starspangled bunting. I leave him in your merciful and over burdened hands.

I am yours to annoy.[64]

To John G. Nicolay, Washington, 18 July 1863[65]

I have received your first bulletin from Baltimore. Your style-t is improving. It is getting a fine old crusty military flavor. It has a smell of cartridges and ambulance about it. Macte virtute puer, which is old Italian for "go in my hearty."

Bob [Lincoln] & I had a fearful orgie here last night on whiskey and cheese. The house is gradually going to the bad since you left.

I saw Nettie Chase yesterday,[66] she says she is going to have a cage fitted up in the parlor for the buffalo you promised her.

The "great big beast of a Henglishman" who is going to take from us our joy and pride the dear little [Carlota] Gerolt, is here.[67] I find the cook unapproachable in the way of pizen.

Mrs Lincoln goes North early next week. She will remain in New York some days & then she & le dauphin Bobbe will away to the Montagnes Blanches.

Do what you can for me. I think there is no show for you here. They talk of making Merritt a General. If so you can never save your Bacon.

[P.S.] Here is a paper which Low sent you.

To John G. Nicolay, Washington, [19 July 1863][68]

I am in a state of entire collapse after yesterday's work. I ran the Tycoon through One hundred Court martials! a steady sitting of six hours!

Think of that in your dolce far &c & weep for the true & brave who stay behind.

Carlota de G. is married on Tuesday night. I go to see the last of it.

45

To an unidentified correspondent, Washington, 21 July 1863[69]

The President directs me to acknowledge the receipt of Field Marshall Bosco's communication of the 20th May, and to state that while he gratefully appreciates the feeling which induced the tender of service, he regrets that it will be impossible to give to that distinguished officer such a position in our Army as would alone be suitable to his rank.[70]

To [John G. Nicolay, Washington, 21 July 1863][71]

There is nothing new. Will not probably be any thing for a month or so.

Possess your soul in Patience. La Gerolt goes off today. The mari is a good sort of fellow—for an Englishman.

Be virtuous & you will be miserable.

To Charles Hay, Washington, 24 July 1863[72]

All right. Charlie is here.[73]

To John G. Nicolay, Washington, 28 July 1863[74]

Yours of the 19th is just received. I return you the envelope as a dreadful warning. You remember by the new law letters to the President must be prepaid. Tremble, & provide yourself with gum-backs!

I immediately asked Fry about the draft.[75] He says none is yet or soon will be ordered in Illinois. The old state is so thundering far ahead of her quota that they will perhaps let her run. Please have me enrolled at Springfield & various other towns. In these times no man should shirk his duty. I will have my name taken off the list here.

There is no news & I see no present prospect of any.

It would do you good to see how I daily hold the Tycoon's nose to the Court Martial grindstone.

I am getting as thin as a shad—yes, worse—as thin as a shadder.

Yet I forgive you.

To Captain Edward G. Bush, Washington, 31 July 1863[76]

The President has sent a request to General Meade to have you transferred to Col. Alexander.[77] Col. Fry wishes it done but cannot do anything till Gen. Meade's consent is gained. I doubted for a while whether it were best to send the paper to you or the General but concluded to send it directly to him.

Jack has been here. He is very well.

Nicolay is in Pike [*County, Illinois*], on his way to the Rocky Mountains. Write to me when you think of anything more I can do.

To Mrs. Ames, Washington, 5 August 1863[78]

Here is what I promised you.

It [*an enclosed photo*] represents the distinguished subject in his milder moods, when newsboys fear not to approach him, and schoolchildren ask him the time of day.

He would have surrounded himself with the terrors of war but his contraband, on whom he had relied to polish his sword, has been drafted, "and this infernal blazon must not be."

To Captain Edward G. Bush, Washington, 5 August 1863[79]

I opened this morning a letter from you to Nicolay from which I judge you have not received mine.[80] I have been doing all I could to have you transferred to Missouri for the last month. Nicolay went west about a month ago.[81]

I got the President to ask Meade to let you go. Meade assented. Col. Fry formally applied for you. Col. Townsend, after saying that regular officers were too valuable to waste in such a way at last sent the matter to the General in chief.[82] It was then approved and Genl. Cullum today tells me [*it*] has gone back [*to*] the A. G. Office for the necessary order.[83] I have asked Col. Williams' office to hurry it up as fast as possible. I suppose you will get it in a few days.

I am very sorry to hear of Theodore's dangerous condition & hope you may find him better.[84]

I suppose as I will see you as you pass through Washington on the way home.

To John G. Nicolay, Washington, 7 August 1863[85]

I have just received your letter from St. Louis & was glad to hear that you had not been drowned in the [*Sug Carty?*] or chawed up by the copperheads of [*Five-Five?*]. Your advice relative to John H. [*concerning?*] the fine old previous enrollment dodge was very good but it came too late. He had drawn a prize in the great lottery here and the P[*ost*] M[*aster*] Genl. had decided that this was his domicile & that he must do or die or substitute or pay. He intends to pass his physical examination — has a vague hope that he may be found saddled with consumption, gout, tic-dolorem, aneurism of several aortas, and hereditary insanity. He is [*page torn off at this point*] He thinks even if he passes the surgeons he can get a substitute for less than $300. They are selling rather cheap here now. I have taken considerable time to the matter & made careful inquiries, but I cant see how he can get out of paying, if the surgeons pass him. Fry says there is no way.

The draft fell pretty heavily in our end of town.[86] William Johnson (cullud) was taken while polishing the Executive boots and rasping the Imperial Abolition whisker.[87] Henry Stoddard is a conscript bold.[88] You remember that goodnatured shiny faced darkey who used to be my special favorite a year ago at Willards. He is gone, en haut de la spout. And the Gorgeous headwaiter, G. Washington. A clerk in the War Department named Ramsey committed suicide on hearing he was drafted.[89] Our friend Henry A. Blood was snatched from his jealous desk.[90] And Bob Lamon is on the [*torn off*] Bob [*Lincoln*] and his mother have gone to the white mountains. (I dont take any special stock in the matter & write the locality in small letters.) Bob was so shattered by the wedding of the idol of all of us, the bright particular Teutonne [*Carlota Wilhelmina Mariana von Gerolt*] that he rushed madly off to sympathize with nature in her sternest aspects. They will be gone some time. The newspapers say the Tycoon will join them after a while. If so, he does not know it. He may possibly go for a few days to Cape May where Hill Lamon is now staying, though that is not certain.

This town is as dismal now as a defaced tombstone. Everybody has gone. I am getting apathetic & write blackgua[r]dly articles for the Chronicle from which West extracts the dirt & fun & publishes the dreary remains.[91] The Tycoon is in fine whack. I have rarely seen him more serene & busy. He is managing this war, the draft, foreign relations, and planning a reconstruction of the Union, all at once. I never knew with what tyrannous authority he rules the Cabinet, till now. The most important things he decides & there is no cavil. I am growing more and more firmly convinced that the good of the country absolutely demands that he should be kept where he is till this thing is over. There is no man in the country, so wise so gentle and so firm. I believe the hand of God placed him where he is.

They are working against him like beavers though; Hale & that crowd but dont seem to make anything by it.[92] I believe the people know what they want and unless politics have gained in power & lost in principle they will have it.

I am getting on very comfortably. Howe is a very good fellow.[93] I hate to give orders to a man who was a Senator in Massachusetts while I was in jackets & button cinctured trowsers. Still he is better than Stod[*dard*] as he is never stuffy and always on hand.

I will wind up with a little gossip. Mrs. Davenport told it to [*Henry A.*] Wise & Wise told me. Mrs Davenport *loquitur.* "Have you heard the dreadful story about Miss Carroll of Baltimore?[94] Raped by a negro! What are we coming to?

Wise. How did she appear to like it?

Mrs D. You have heard about Mrs. Emory's maid? Gone to Philadelphia to be *confined!*

Wise. Who has gotten her that way; not Mr Emory, I hope.

Mrs D. No! you naughty fellow. Lord Lyons' valet.

Thats all I know of high life that would interest you. Take care of yourself & write when you have nothing better to do.

To John G. Nicolay, Washington, 13 August 1863[95]

Blair says Armstrong shall eat dirt or "off goes his head, so much for Buckingham."

"John A. Nicholay" I see by the papers was grafted for a soldier.[96] He was in great pucker for a while, profoundly interested in the substitute market and negotiating extensively with the Iraelitish gentry who do that some. But I got him at last started on the right track with Scheetz, for physical examination & in the course of an hour he came in perfectful radiant with the joyful intelligence that he was so thoroughly diseased that he would not live a week if he went into the army, flourishing his certificate to that effect like a medal of honor. The evening papers publish him in the list of exempts as Major General Debility. This will be of course attributed to you & not a woman in Washington will look at you, until you get yourself indicted for rape.[97]

There is not a bit of news or scandal. The heat has been something terrible for ten days. Men and horses dropping dead in the streets every day. Last night it rained & today it is very cool and breezy. Thank God you are not where other men are, or even where this Re Publican is.

To Charles G. Halpine, Washington, 14 August 1863[98]

How could you ever have called Waterbury a fair and honest man?[99] The outrageously unfair and prejudiced report recently published under his name would bring a blush to the cheek of a stage-horse. Who would get up, as he and Seymour claim, a partizan enrollment? Neither the President nor Stanton interfere with the details of that business. Fry is as sound a Democrat, I am sorry to say, as Waterbury himself, & certainly would favor no frauds against his own side. He is a splendid fellow, full of energy and will, but no Republican by any possibility. Did Robert Nugent do the dirt there?[100] Who is the outside cabal!

There was a very able and well-considered article in the Times yesterday, the 13th, on "terms of reconstruction."[101] Read it and ponder it. It is about right. The trash you read every day about wrangles in the Cabinet about measures of state policy looks very silly from an inside view, where Abraham Rex is the central figure continually. I wish you could see as I do, that he is devilish near an autocrat in this Administration.

I read with great interest your Washington letter in the Herald. It has an unwonted snap and vigor. I believe that people in general dont write as energetically as they used to. Energy in times like these spreads off into other channels. You have brought back from the war the old fire and verve. I think the article sometimes unjust, of course. We never shall agree on some points. You must pardon me for saying that if the Tycoon had kept his fingers from meddling with the war, we should now have had neither war nor government I think. I have to a great extent stopped questioning where I dont agree with him, content with trusting to his instinct of the necessities of the time and the wants of the people. I hardly ever speak of him to others than you, because people generally would say "Yes! of course: that's how he gets his little daily bread!" I believe he will fill a bigger place in history than he even dreams of himself.

Write to me occasionally will you!

[*P.S.*] I know of no man upon whose statements I can so entirely rely as upon yours about New York matters. I wish you would write me as fully as you can about the real feeling and sentiment there [*New York*] about the conscription: What sort of a party the News represents, if any at all and what is the real strength of factions there. Your communications shall be held strictly confidential as to yourself and only used for the information of the President in any case. Where you prefer I shall not even mention them to him. You know that New York is more the centre of public interest today than is Charleston. I hope you will write me as soon and as fully as you can. How is your own health and what are your plans. I am fearfully busy and overworked just now.

[*P.P.S.*] I heard Gen Hooker speak with great admiration of your Herald article.

To John A. Dahlgren, Washington, 16 August 1863[102]

It is only because I have always cherished for your name and fame so deep a regard, and because I think that any imputation cast upon you by the people at large would be a positive injury to the Navy, that I venture to write a word to bring to your notice the despatches of Mr. Fulton.[103] By every mail from the South come voluminous letters from that gentleman giving ~~the most~~ minute details of all army and naval operations, present and to come, ~~the most~~ accurate lists of forces, armaments & positions, ~~&c~~ and in fact all possible information which could injure us and benefit the enemy. Added to this he indulges in confident, and to us who know anything about the vast difficulties with which you contend, absurd predictions as to the ease and celerity with which you are to do your work, in effect representing the siege of Charleston as a matter ~~after-breakfast performance~~ only affording exercise enough for a morning's constitutional. He assigns, for instance, "two to six hours" as the limits between which

Fort Sumter is to be not only reduced but occupied. His letters are full of this injurious bombast. He has the trick also of closing his letters by predicting that the flag will wave &c before this letter is read.

Now we who know very well that you can and will do all that man can, and yet know that Mr. Fulton promises for you what cannot be done by human power, regret very deeply the effect of these absurdities upon the public mind. Mr. F. dates his letters on board your flagship and uses your name in his letters with reprehensible familiarity. People reading them say this man reflects the sentiments of the Admiral. It is only your friends who know that these utterances are entirely unauthorized. His last letters created such excitement as ~~temporarily to materially lower~~ to cause a material depression in the price of Gold on Wall Street.

A word to him from your Chief of Staff would no doubt enforce discretion.

I know you will pardon the freedom with which I have written. Those who know you and recognize your past as full of honor and your future as full of hope and glory for the American navy ~~do not wish~~ can not bear to see ~~any cloud cast upon your merited fame by the blunder of indiscreet friends, more than by the malice of envious enemies~~ that future discounted by blundering friends or envious enemies.

In that sense I have written freely & do not fear that you will misunderstand me.

To Schuyler Colfax, Washington, 20 August 1863[104]

I send you a word that I put into this morning's Chronicle.[105] I did not make it so strong as the truth or my own feelings would prompt because I wished it to seem impartial & judicial. *We* will say more from time to time.

To Colonel James B. Fry, Washington, 24 August 1863[106]

The inevitable Waterbury is again upon us. He has changed his base. He don't like the way the thing is done.

His experience as a political ballot stuffer for twenty years comes up and troubles his dreams. He is afraid you are stuffing the draft on him.

Read his wail[107] if you don't think life is too short and Lee too near. If you do, file it.

With a firm reliance on Providence and your waste-paper basket, you cannot fail.

I am going to the sea-shore; burst not with envy.[108]

To Charles Sumner, Washington, 24 August 1863[109]

The President directs me to thank you for your kindness in sending him the letters of Mr. Bright and Mr. Cobden, which I now return, and to express the gratification with which he has read them.[110]

To an unidentified correspondent, Washington, 9 September 186[3][111]

The subscriber, who never yet took a
Dinner with Fighting Joe Hooker,
This engagement will keep,
(If he dont fall asleep)
As punctual as General Blucher.

To Edwin M. Stanton, Washington, 10 September 1863[112]

The President directs me to request that you will give Mr. G. Rush Smith of Philadelphia an audience as soon as may be convenient.[113] Mr. Smith desires to see you on a matter of business.

To John G. Nicolay, Washington, 11 September 1863[114]

A week or so ago I got frightened at

"The brow so haggard the chin so peaked
Fronting me silent in the glass"

and sending for Stoddard (who had been giving the Northern watering places for the last two months a model of high breeding and unquestionable deportment) I left for a few days at Long Branch and two or three more at Providence. I was at the commencement at Brown University and made a small chunk of a talk.[115] I only staid a little over a week and came back feeling heartier.

I *must* be in Warsaw early in October on account of family affairs. As I infer from your letter that you cannot return before November, or as Judge Otto says before December I will have to give the reins up for a few days to Stoddard and Howe again.[116] I hope the daring youth will not reduplicate the fate of Phaeton.

Washington is as dull here as an obsolete almanac. The weather is not so bad as it was. The nights are growing cool. But there is nobody here except us old stagers who cant get away. We have some comfortable dinners and some quiet little orgies on whiskey & cheese in my room. And the time slides away.

We are [*quietly?*] jolly over the magnificent news from all round the board. Rosecrans won a great and bloodless victory at Chattanooga which he had no business to win.[117] The day that the enemy ran he sent a mutinous message to Halleck complaining of the very things that have secured us the victories, and foreshadowing only danger and defeat. You may talk as you please of the Abolition Cabal directing affairs from Washington: some well meaning newspapers advise the President to keep his fingers out of the military pie: and all that sort of thing. The truth is, if he did, the pie would be a sorry mess. The old man sits here and wields like a backwoods Jupiter the bolts of war and the machinery of government with a hand equally steady & equally firm.

His last letter is a great thing.[118] Some hideously bad rhetoric—some indecorums that are infamous—yet the whole letter takes its solid place in history, as a great utterance of a great man. The whole Cabinet could not have tinkered up a letter which could have been compared with it. He can snake a sophism out of its hole, better than all the trained logicians of all schools.

I do not know whether the nation is worthy of him for another term. I know the people want him. There is no mistaking that fact. But politicians are strong yet & he is not their "kind of a cat." I hope God wont see fit to scourge us for our sins by any one of the two or three most prominent candidates on the ground.

I hope you are getting well and hearty. Next winter will be the most exciting and laborious of all our lives. It will be worth any other ten.

To John Murray Forbes, Washington, 12 September 1863[119]

The President directs me to acknowledge the receipt of your letter transmitted by Mr. Sumner, and to express to you his sincere thanks for the suggestions it contains, as well as for the kind terms in which you have spoken of himself.

To an unidentified correspondent, Washington, 15 September 1863[120]

Your note is so very suggestive,
That I'll come, led by motives digestive —
  For Willards I ban
  Whenever I can —
I close for your henchman grows restive.

To Jean Davenport Lander, Washington, 19 September 1863[121]

Here is that wonderful lyric of Boker's.[122] Some of these times I want to hear you read it.

To Hiram Barney, Washington, 23 September 1863[123]

The President directs me to thank you for your kind favor of the 21st of September and to say in reply that it will give him pleasure to sit to Mr. Elliott at any time which may be convenient to him. He is unable to name any period which will be more convenient than another.[124]

To Cephas Brainerd, Washington, 24 September 1863[125]

The President directs me to acknowledge the receipt of the Pamphlet Edition of Mr. Sumner's Oration, and to thank you for your prompt courtesy in sending it.

To an unidentified correspondent, Washington, 24 September 1863[126]

Mon cher I cannot dine with thee,
For a beautiful dame hath invited me
   With her to dine,
   So your talk and wine
I resist, and like the Devil, they flee.

I go in beauty's smile to bask
And hang on her lips, (a Ravel task)
   While her sweet eyes shine
   O'er the sparkling wine
And flavor it so I could drink a cask.

But still when roystering far away,
I shall dream of thee, my seadog gay —
   And the tender dream
   Shall over me beam
From the soup till I swallow my pousse-café.

To John G. Nicolay, Washington, 25 September 1863[127]

I have nothing in the world to tell you. The town is miserably dry.

Maggie Mitchell is here drawing Ford's New Theater suffocatingly full.[128]

Miss Younger is prettier each day that she lives — which is unnecessary.

I hope you are getting fat. *Quant a moi* — I am as thin as a rail.

I shall have to go home the first week of October. I will only be gone, however, ~~about~~ a week or so.

[*P.S.*] Becky Stewart was married the other day to a very goodlooking & fine fellow named Grant.

That's all I know.

I am awfully busy. Stod[*dard*] is more & more worthless. I can scarcely rely upon him for anything.

None of yr. ducks are here. I have no where to go except Canterbury which is fine.[129]

Memorandum, 30 September 1863[130]

The Delegation from Missouri and Kansas arrived here last week and have been preparing their address for some days with care and labor.[131] This morning, Wednesday the 30th of September at 10:30 A.M., Jim Lane & C. D. Drake came up stairs and announced that the Delegation was waiting below.[132] They were ushered into the East Room by my order and the reporters for the Press excluded. The President delaying for a few moments Jim took me down to see the little army as he styled it, and we found them ranged along three sides of the East Room, the North End being open. He introduced me to several of the sovereigns and we waited for the President. The men were simply representative men from Missouri not better than the average. The frowziness of the ungodly Pike was there though it was a decenter and quieter crowd than would have come in the old days of the border murders.[133] An ill combed, black broadcloth, dusty, longhaired and generally vulgar assemblage of earnest men who came to get their right as they viewed it. They say things are in a bad way out there and they came here, a little vaguely, for redress.

The President came in and walked up the hollow square to the South end: there he faced and stood, straighter than usual. Mr Drake of St. Louis said, "Gentlemen! I have the profound honor of presenting you the President of the United States." The President bowed and the earnest Pikes bowed, stiffly, but with unmistakable respectfulness: legs that thrust out backward, some scraping some awkward spreading of the hands: & the Pikes stood erect again, stern and ruminant. An abortive attempt at clapping which expired in its youth. Drake said Mr Prest. we came for purpose of presenting a statement of fact and making certain requests, embodied in an address I hold in my hand. Will it please to hear it now? "It will!" said Pres. and Mr Drake read the address. After Mr. Drake had finished the reading of his address the President said:

I suppose the committee now before me is the culmination of a movement inaugurated by a Convention held in Missouri last month, and is intended to give utterance to their well-considered views on public affairs in that state.[134] The purpose of this delegation has been widely published and their progress to this city everywhere noticed. It is not therefore to be expected that I shall reply hurriedly to your address. It would not be consistent, either with a proper respect for you or a fair consideration of the subject involved to give you a hasty answer. I will take your address, carefully consider it and respond at my earliest convenience. I shall consider it, without partiality for or prejudice against any man or party: no painful memories of the past and no hopes for the future, personal to myself, shall hamper my judgment.

There are some matters which you have discussed upon which my impressions are somewhat decided, in regard to which I will say a few words, reserving the privilege of changing my opinion even upon these, upon sufficient evidence.

You have alluded to an expression I used in a letter to General Schofield, characterizing your troubles in Missouri as a "pestilential factional quarrel".[135] You do not relish the expression but let me tell you that Govr. Gamble likes it still less.[136] He has written me a letter complaining of it so bitterly that on the representation of my private Secretary I declined reading it & sent a note to him informing him that I would not.[137]

You have much to say in regard to Govr. Gamble's position. You will remember that at the very beginning of the War, your own Governor being disloyal, you elected a Convention, a large majority of whom were Union members, for whom I suppose you yourselves voted.[138] There were at that time no dissentions among Union men in your state. Your convention elected Mr Gamble Governor in place of the disloyal incumbent, seemingly with the universal assent of the Union people of the State. At that time Governor Gamble was considered, and naturally so, the Representative of the loyalty of Missouri. As such he came to Washington, to request the Assistance and support of the general government in the organization of a state militia force. It was considered here a matter of importance: it was discussed in a meeting of the Cabinet, and an arrangement which seemed satisfactory was finally made.[139] No one doubted the proper intentions of those who planned it. The only doubt was whether the arrangement could be properly carried out—whether this Imperium in Imperio would not breed confusion. Several times since that [time] Governor Gamble has endeavored to have the troops raised on this basis transferred to the exclusive control of the state. This I have invariably refused. If any new arrangement has been made of enrolling State troops independently of the general government I am not yet aware of it. Such organizations exist in some of the states. I have no more right to interfere with them in Missouri than elsewhere. If they are consistent with your state laws I cannot prevent them. If not, you should redress your proper wrong. I will however give this subject as presented by you, careful consideration.

I am sorry you have not been more specific in the statements you have seen fit to make about Gen. Schofield.[140] I had heard in advance of your coming that a part of your mission was to protest against his administration & I thought I should hear some definite statements of grievances instead of the vague denunciations which are so easy to make and yet so unsatisfactory. But I have been disappointed. If you could tell me what Gen Schofield has done that he should not have done, or what omitted that he should have done, your case would be plain. You have on the contrary only accused him vaguely of sympathy with your enemies. I cannot act on vague impressions. Show me that he has disobeyed orders: show me that he has done something wrong & I will take your request for his removal into serious consideration. He has never protested against an order — never neglected a duty with which he has been entrusted so far as I know. When Gen. Grant was struggling in Mississippi and needed reinforcement no man was so active and efficient in sending him troops as Gen. Schofield. I know nothing to his disadvantage. I am not personally acquainted with him. I have with him no personal relations. If you will allege a definite wrongdoing & having clearly made your point, prove it, I shall remove him.

You object to his order on my recent proclamation suspending the privilege of the writ of Habeas Corpus. I am at a loss to see why an order executing my own official decree should be made a ground of accusation to me against the officer issuing it. You object to its being used in Missouri. In other words that which is right when employed against yr. opponents is wrong when employed against yourselves. Still I will consider that.

You object to his muzzling the press. As to that, I think when an officer in any department finds that a newspaper is pursuing a course calculated to embarrass his operations and stir up sedition and tumult, he has the right to lay hands upon it and suppress it, but in no other case. I approved the order in question after the Missouri Democrat had also approved it.

(Mem[ber of the] Del[egation]) "We thought it was then to be used against the other side."

[President] Certainly you did. Your ideas of justice seem to depend upon the application of it.

You have spoken of the consideration which you think I should pay to my friends as contradistinguished from my enemies. I suppose of course that you mean by that those who agree or disagree with me in my views of public policy. I recognize no such thing as a political friendship personal to myself. You insist upon adherence to the policy of the proclamation of Emancipation as a test of such political friendship. You will remember that your State was one excluded from the operation of that decree by its express terms. The Proclamation can therefore have no direct bearing upon your state politics. Yet you seem to insist that it shall be made as vital a question as if it had. You seem to be determined to have it executed there.

[*Delegate*] "No sir, but we think it a national test question."

[*President*] You are then determined to make an issue with men who may not agree with you upon the abstract question of the propriety of that act of mine. Now let me say that I, who issued that proclamation after more thought on the subject than probably any one of you have been able to give it, believe it to be right and expedient. I am better satisfied with those who believe with me in this than with those who hold differently. But I am free to say that many good men, some earnest Republicans, and some from very far North, were opposed to the issuing of that Proclamation holding it unwise and of doubtful legality. Now when you see a man loyally in favor of the Union — willing to vote men and money — spending his time and money and throwing his influence into the recruitment of our armies — I think it ungenerous unjust and impolitic to make his views on abstract political questions a test of his loyalty. I will not be a party to this application of a pocket Inquisition.

You are aware of movements in the North of a different character — interfering with the draft — discouraging recruiting — weakening the war spirit — striving in all possible ways to weaken the Government merely to secure a partizan triumph. I do not take the party of your opponents in Missouri to be engaged in this line of conduct.

Del "They are."

[*President*] In a civil war one of the saddest evils is suspicion. It poisons the springs of social life. It is the fruitful parent of injustice and strife. Were I to make a rule that in Missouri disloyal men were outlawed and the rightful prey of good citizens as soon as the rule should begin to be carried into effect I would be overwhelmed with affidavits to prove that the first man killed under it was more loyal than the one who killed him. It is impossible to determine the question of the motives that govern men, or to gain absolute knowledge of their sympathies.

Del "Let the loyal people judge[.]"

Prest. And who shall say who the loyal people are? You ask the disfranchisement of all disloyal people: but difficulties will environ you at every step in determining the questions which will arise in that matter. A vast number of Missourians who have at some time aided the rebellion will wish to return to their homes and resume their peaceful avocations. Even if you would, you cannot keep them all away. You have your state laws regulating the qualifications of voters. You must stand by those till you yourselves alter them.

Del "Are we to be protected at the polls in carrying out these laws?"

Prest. I will order Gen. Schofield to protect you at the polls and save them from illegal interference. He will do it you may be assured. If he does not I will relieve him.

—Jim Lane at this point burst in boisterously, "Do you think it sufficient cause for the removal of a General, that he has lost the entire confidence of the people."

Presdt "I think I should not consider it a sufficient cause if he had lost that confidence unjustly, it would [not] be a very strong reason for his removal."

Lane "General Schofield has lost that confidence."

Presdt. "You being judge!"

—A confused murmur of delegates all crying in chorus, confirmation of Lane's statements.

The President very quickly said "I am in possession of facts that convince me that Gen Schofield has not lost the confidence of the entire people of Missouri.

Delegates: "All loyal people."

Prest "You being the standard of loyalty.

Lane "There are no parties and no factions in Kansas—All[141] our people demand his removal. The massacre of Lawrence,[142] is in the opinion of the people of Kansas, solely due to the embicility of Gen. Schofield."

Prest. "As to that, it seems to me that is a thing which could be done by any one making up his mind to the consequences, and could no more be guarded against than assassination. If I make up my mind to kill you for instance, I can do it and these hundred gentleman could not prevent it. They could avenge but could not save you."

—A member from the interior then felt called on to say something and said it. He began in a quiet hesitating way but gradually warmed up with his subject and bellowed like a mad bull, about "the sufferings me and the rest of the board suffers, with the guerillas achasing of us, and we a writing to Mr. Scovil for help & he not giving it to us, so we couldnt collect the broken bonds."

Prest. "Who's *us*? (very quietly but evidently desiring information.)

Del. "The *Board*." (As if that word would strike all questioning dumb.)

Presdt. "What board" (not struck dumb apparently[)]

Del. "The Board for collecting the broken bonds." getting a little nervous again.

Presdt. "Who appointed you & by what law, & how were you acting & by what right did you ask a military force from Gen. Schofield?"

These questions completed the ruin of the unhappy commissioner & he floundered in a maze of hopeless explanation, which represented him as a sportive and happy free plunderer on the estates of misguided traitors passing his time in rapid alternation from stealing secesh cattle to running from guerillas.

Another plethoric gentleman wailed gloomily for a quarter of an hour over scenes of cruelty he and a number of his friends had witnessed in their town and had not the manhood to prevent.

In every instance, a question or two from the President pricked the balloon of loud talk and collapsed it around the ears of the delegate to his no small disgust and surprise. The baffled patriot would retreat to a sofa & think the matter over again or would stand in his place and quietly listen in a bewildered manner to the talk and discomfiture of another.

I was compelled to leave for a little while. When I returned the delegation had departed. I instructed Mr. S[*toddard*] to take notes in my absence. He immediately developed them and they are as follows: They contain, he says only the language of the President.

In reply to an assertion that "We are your friends and the Conservatives are not the Presdt. said: These so called Conservatives will avoid, as a general thing, votes, or any action, which will in any way interfere with or imperil, the success of their *party*. For instance they will vote for supplies, and such other measures as are absolutely necessary to sustain the Government. They will do this selfishly. They do not wish that the Government should fall, for they expect to obtain possession of it. At the same time their support will not be hearty: their votes are not equal to those of the real friends of the Administration. They do not give so much strength. They are not worth so much. My Radical friends will therefore see that I understand and appreciate their position.[143] Still you appear to come before me as my friends *if I agree with you, but not otherwise.* I do not here speak of mere personal friendship, as between man and man, — when I speak of my friends I mean those who are friendly to my measures, to the policy of the government.[144]

I am well aware that by many, by some even among this delegation, — I shall not name them, — I have been in public speeches and in printed documents charged with `tyranny' and willfulness, with a disposition to make my own personal will supreme. I do not intend to be a tyrant. At all events I shall take care that in my own eyes I do not become one. I shall always try and preserve one friend within me, whoever else fails me, to tell me that I have not been a tyrant, and that I have acted right. I have no right to act the tyrant to mere political opponents. If a man votes for supplies of men and money; encourages enlistments; discourages desertions; does all in his power to carry the war on to a successful issue, — I have no right to question him for his abstract political opinions. I must make a dividing line, some where, between those who are the opponents of the Government and those who only oppose peculiar features of my administration while they sustain the Government.

In the Vallandigham case a commander in the field decided that a certain political enemy of the government had become dangerous in a military point of view, and that he must be removed. I believe that he was justifiable in coming to such a decision. In cases where political opponents do not in any way interfere with or hinder military operations, I have judged it best to let them alone.

My friends in Missouri last winter did me a great unkindness. I had relied upon my Radical friends as my mainstay in the management of affairs in that state and they disappointed me. I had recommended Gradual Emancipation, and Congress had endorsed that course. The Radicals in Congress voted for it. The Missouri delegation in Congress went for it, — went, as I thought, right. I had the highest hope that at last Missouri was on the right track. But I was disappointed by the immediate emancipation movement. It endangers the success of the whole advance towards freedom. But you say that the gradual emancipation men were insincere; —

that they intended soon to repeal their action; that their course and their professions are purely fraudulent. Now I do not think that a majority of the gradual Emancipationists are insincere. Large bodies of men cannot play the hypocrite.

I announced my own opinion freely at the time. I was in favor of gradual emancipation. I still am so. You must not call yourselves my friends, if you are only so while I agree with you. According to that, if you differ with me you are not my friends.

But the mode of emancipation in Missouri is not my business. That is a matter which belongs exclusively to the citizens of that state: I do not wish to interfere. I desire, if it pleases the people of Missouri, that they should adopt gradual emancipation. I think that your division upon this subject jeopardizes the grand result. I think that a union of all anti-slavery men upon this point would have made emancipation a final fact forever. Still, I do not assume any control. I am sorry to see anti-slavery men opposing such a movement, but I will take up the subjects you have laid before me, without prejudice, without pique, without resentment, and will try and do what is best for all, as affecting the grand result to which we all are looking.

The Delegation on the whole disappointed me badly. I expected more cohesion more discretion from what Cartter had told me & from what Hawkins Taylor retailed.[145] Their cause, incoherent, vague, abusive, prejudiced, and did no good that I can yet see. They claimed to advocate no man—but asked for Butler—to speak without prejudice—yet abused Schofield like drabs;[146] to ask for ascertained rights and they rambled through a maze of ridiculous grievances and absurd suggestions. In the main ignorant and well meaning, they chose for their spokesman Drake who is neither ignorant nor well-meaning, who covered the marrow of what they wanted to say in a purposeless mass of unprofitable verbiage which they accepted because it sounded well, and the President will reject because it is nothing but sound. He is a man whom only facts of the toughest kind can move and Drake attacked him with tropes & periods which might have had weight in a Sophomore Debating Club. And so the great Western Delegation from which good people hoped so much for freedom, discharged their little rocket, and went home with no good thing to show for coming—a little angry and a good deal bewildered—not clearly seeing why they have failed—as the President seemed so fair and their cause so good.[147]

To Ethan Allen Hitchcock, Washington, 1 October 1863[148]

The President directs me to say that he will not at present trouble you to return the manuscript. He has been much interested in what he has read, but is not able to give it at this time the attention it merits.

To Lincoln, Columbus, Ohio, 4 October 1863[149]

An accident detained me in Columbus to-day and gave me an opportunity of seeing Brough.[150]

He requests me to apologize for his seeming rudeness in not answering your letter, and hopes that the verbal reply sent by Govr Dennison was entirely satisfactory.[151]

He says they will carry Ohio by at least 25,000 votes, independent of the soldiers who will indefinitely increase it. The Vallandigham men have given up the fight here.

Brough is much more anxious about Curtin than about himself.[152]

Brough thinks that as yet in the Keystone State
The prospect is rather uncertain—
The fifth act is near, and we only can wait
Impatient, the rise of the *Curtain*.

A hazy joke, with which I close.

To Caroline Angell, Washington, 19 October 1863[153]

I have been wandering all over the world while your letter was waiting for me here.

The "one dollar" in regard to which you so kindly ask my inclinations, in the not improbable event of my being kept away from the Festival, has been due so long that the interest is, as nearly as I can compute, equal to what I send.

To Montgomery Blair, Washington, 20 October 1863[154]

The President directs me to send you the enclosed to do as you please with.[155]

"LINCOLN" TO GEORGE H. BOKER, WASHINGTON, 24 OCTOBER 1863[156]

It is with heartfelt gratification that I acknowledge the receipt of your communication of the 30th of September, and the accompanying medal, by which I am made an honorary member of the Union League of Philadelphia.

I shall always bear with me the consciousness of having endeavored to do my duty in the trying times through which we are passing, and the generous approval of a portion of my fellow-citizens so intelligent and so patriotic as those composing your Association, assures me that I have not wholly failed. I could not ask, and no one could merit, a better reward.

Be kind enough, sir, to convey to the gentlemen whom you represent, the assurance of the grateful appreciation with which I accept the honor you have conferred upon me.

TO CHARLES G. HALPINE, WASHINGTON, 24 OCTOBER 1863[157]

Its the Devil ye'll be catching when Edwin [*Stanton*] gets back from the West. I dined with Fox last night. After Dinner he tried to go to sleep but I kept one of the party sticking pins in him to keep his eyes open while I kept his ears open with the account of the O'Reilly banquet.[158] The laugh was forminst him but he stood it like a brick and grinned ghastly. He knows the authorship of the letters. Wise found it out a few weeks ago in New York and the whole Navy Department has been reading Miles' lucubrations with delight ever since. If you knew Fox you wouldn't blackguard him, and Wise I have often told you is the best man in this wicked world.[159]

I think Smith's Speech and Gurowski's letter will become classics.[160] The count cant make up his mind to deny the authorship of the letter. He was very drunk the night it was written & the style is so entirely legitimate that he cant bear to bastardize the letter.

Mrs. Hunter was immensely delighted and so was the General whom I saw late in the evening. We would be glad to see you (anywhere out of the limits of the District, as the Bladensburgian invitations used to read: you wouldnt live five minutes in the streets of Washington. The Tycoon of the War Department [*Edwin M. Stanton*] is on the war path: his hands are red and smoking with the scalping of Rosey [*Rosecrans*];[161] he would think nothing of flaying the Bard of Paris Island. Prenez Garde Monsigneur O'Reilly.

Write a letter to me when you have nothing else to do. I am as miserable as a rat. The town is dull. Miss Chase is so busy making her father next President that she is only a little lovelier than all other women. She is to be married on November 12th which disgusts me with life.[162] She is a great woman & with a great future.

I wish I were in N[ew] York and away from here. Nicolay is having a superb time among the mountains. I dont think the scoundrel will be back before Congress comes together.

I suppose you burn my letters. If you have not, do.

To Charles Sumner, Washington, 26 October 1863[163]

Your note of the 13th addressed to Mr. Howe has just been shown to me.[164]

The letter from Mr Bates and that from Mr Bright which you sent to the President, were returned by me as soon as the President had read them, within one or two days from the date of their receipt.[165] I hope they have not been lost in the mail.[166]

To "Mariner Brave," Washington, 26 October 1863[167]

I have so much work to do that I cannot come. I must "scorn delights & live a laborious day."

I expect to go to the Devil for it but I must toil this sabbaday.

Yours, feeling the cuss of Adam in its fulness.

To Benson J. Lossing, Washington, 29 October 1863[168]

Begging pardon for a long delay which has arisen from a series of mistakes, I send by mail today the photographic copy of the Proclamation of Freedom.

The blots on the edges of the paper are incidental to the copying, and are not in the original.

To Charles G. Halpine, [Washington], 22 November [1863][169]

Ever since I got your letter I have been skulking in the shadow of the Tycoon, setting all sorts of dextrous traps for a joke, telling good stories myself to draw him out and suborning Nicolay to aid in the foul conspiracy.[170] But not a joke has flashed from the Tycoonial thundercloud. He is as dumb as an oyster. Once or twice a gleam of hope has lit up my soul as he would begin "That puts me in mind of Tom Skeeters out in Bourbon County" but the story of Skeeters would come out unfit for family reading; and the dawning promise of a reminiscence of Menard County would turn to ashes as it developed a [*feeble?*] personality which would move rage & not laughter if repeated.

By the way, an infernal nuisance named [*George B.*] Lincoln Postmaster at Brooklyn fastened himself to the Tycoon the other day and tried to get into conversation on the subject of the succession.[171] The Honest Abraham quickly put him off with a story of his friend Jesse Dubois, who, being State Auditor, had control of the State House at Springfield, Ill.[172] An itinerant quack preacher wanted the use of the Representatives Hall to deliver a religious lecture. "What's it about" said Jesse. "The Second Coming of Christ" said the parson. "Nonsense" roared Uncle Jesse, "if Christ had been to Springfield once, and got away, he'd be damned clear of coming again." This wont do for you to repeat, being blasphemous & calculated to hurt the "Quaker vote." I charge you not to use it.

I give you my word of honor if he says a good thing within a week to faithfully report it to you.

Here is the *personnel* of the White House.

Edward McManus the chatty old greyhaired gentleman, from Italy, who has been through five administrations keeps the door below,[173] assisted by Thomas Burns also from Italy who has outlived the storms of two reigns.[174]

The President's Messenger who guards the door of the Abolition despot himself, is Louis Burgdorf a Teutonic worthy whose memory runs back to Franklin called Pierce [*President Franklin Pierce*], the recent architect of a Mausoleum of Hearts in the vicinity of Conquered, a city of New Hampshire.[175]

You might introduce with great effect a dig at Dick Busteed Genl. & Judge who has been daily visible here for some time.[176] I mention this on account of the unfounded and unjust prejudice you have against Richard. As for me I like him & think him a good egg.

After all, my dear Miles, you had better far get up your own jokes than ask anything authentic from me. They will fit in more neatly than the crude originals.

> God bless you Miles my darlint,
> May you die both late and aisy,
> And when you lie wid the top of aich toe
> Turned up to the roots of a daisy,
> May this be your epitaph nately writ
> Though the "World" abuse ye vilely,
> "A broth of a boy at a fight or a faist
> Was Private Miles OReilly."[177]

To John G. Nicolay, Washington, 24 November 1863[178]

Where is your umbrella? I cant find it. It is raining like the Devil, whose reign you know is infernal.

The enclosed note came for you this morning.

There is no news from the Army. When any comes I will shove it along.

To John G. Nicolay, Washington, 25 November 1863[179]

Grant's and Wilcox's despatches are so cheering this morning that I sent you a cautious despatch this morning.[180] Hooker (Fighting Joe) (Fightinger than ever) has done gloriously; carried the north slope of Lookout Mountain and gobbled a thousand prisoners. Thomas & Sherman have also done all they attempted & Grant is to advance today along his whole line.[181]

Burnside has sent a courier through to Wilcox and says he is all right as yet: is not hungry or thirsty & hasnt quite begun his share of the fighting.

Every thing looks well.

Dont, in a sudden spasm of good-nature, send any more people with letters to me requesting favors from S[tanton]. I would rather make the tour of a small-pox hospital.

To John G. Nicolay, Washington, 26 November 1863[182]

The newspapers of this morning have told you all you want to know & so I send no telegram. The news is glorious. Nature was against us, but we won in her spite. Had not the rapid current and drift swept away Hookers pontoons he would have utterly destroyed them.

Grant will immediately send a column to relieve Burnside & if possible destroy Longstreet.

The President is sick in bed. Bilious.

[*P.S*] I wish you would telegraph me when you think of returning.

To John A. Dix, Washington, 1 December 1863[183]

I have not been permitted until today to present to the President your communication of the 23d November. He directs me to express his deep regret that his illness will prevent him from giving, on this occasion, expression to the profound interest he feels in the success of a work so vast and so beneficent as that which you are about to inaugurate.[184]

To Charles G. Halpine, [Washington, ca. early December 1863][185]

I am really very sorry that the only thing you have ever asked for should not be one possible to be granted. There are no vacancies at West Point. And there are five mortgages already on those first occurring. The President has ordered Mr Collins' name to be filed for the earliest possible consideration but I really cannot encourage him to hope it will soon be reached.[186]

The President knew well and deeply respected the late Mr. Collins and would be glad to do anything practicable for his son but the pressure for these appointments is something fearful. The son of an officer killed in battle, especially if he be himself a soldier, always has the first claim. I will watch the matter & seize any opportunity to forward it.

The Prest was immensely amused with Miles' last.[187] He is too sick to read and not well enough to object to anything. So I had him at my mercy & read him into a fever.

The current here seems to be setting in the same direction as all over the country. That only one black coat can be elected & *that he will be.* I hear this from men whose sudden allegiance would surprise you. If I could come to New York or meet you anywhere I could tell you some odd things.

Gen. Etheridge is working to throw out enough Union members to carry the organization.[188] If he plays that game he will get his head broke.

H[*orace*] G[*reeley*] is here, busy and sanguine, as he always seems here.

George Wilkes comes down about once a week to get posted by Salmon P. [*Chase*] & goes back to blackguard Lincoln & Seward.[189]

I thank God I am not as other men are.

I send you the enclosed grave protest against the infamous belittling of the Executive Office of which you have been guilty. The white chokered stupidity of indefinite money bags is in it. Mark the feeble-minded condescension with which the writer ~~tells~~ informs the Prest "that there are certain forms & customs." Dont use this letter or Ill haunt you.

[*P.S.*] I think "Lord Palmerstin" is the best thing since Maguire died. That & the "Soldier Song" touch the extremes of fun and pathos.[190] You are a scoundrel to do so little of these things.

To Samuel C. Pomeroy, Washington, 29 December 1863[191]

The gentleman who bears this, Mr. [*Turck?*], brought from you a letter of introduction to the President. According to the invariable custom of this office, mere letters of introduction after being presented to the President are made the subject of a memorandum and destroyed. The gentleman is very anxious to regain a copy of your letter & it is impossible for him to do so unless you will write him another.

To Charlotte Brooks Everett Wise, Washington, 31 December 1863[192]

May all the days of the New Year be as happy to you, as you and yours have made to me many days of the Old.

3

1864–1865

To Captain Samuel Phillips Lee, Washington, 4 January 186[4][1]

On arriving at Point Lookout on Sunday morning,[2] I learned that Gen. Butler would not be there until evening. The captain of the Clyde told me his boat could not lie safely at the wharf. I therefore gave him permission to take her up to Smith's Creek for the night.[3] When Gen. Butler came, it was said by boats coming down that it would not be safe to encounter the ice in the river that night. I therefore went with the General to Baltimore & hither by rail, having sent orders to the Clyde to come home as soon as possible. I write this to explain the matter to you, knowing that a Commander who "loses his ship" has upon himself the burden of proof of innocence.

If you will cause my valise to be sent to me, you will very much oblige me.

To Joseph Holt, Washington, 7 January 1864[4]

I beg your pardon for the long delay in the matter of this note. I thought it might be possible to get something for the writer from the President but have not succeeded and do not know when I can.

To Charles G. Halpine, Washington, 9 January 1864[5]

Letters received.

To John G. Nicolay, Hilton Head, S.C., 21 January 1864[6]

I had a quiet passage down: sick nigh onto death with the sea-disorder: got here misanthropic and blasé Tuesday night. Will start in a day or two for Fernandina: as soon as Quarter-Master can send me.

Gen. Gillmore received me ~~very~~ cordially. He held the President's letter in a helpless sort of way, like a bachelor with a baby:[7] he didnt know what he was to do with it or me: had a vague idea that he was to split his army up into squads and watch the polls while I carried on the election: a confused notion that he was to drop everything for the next month or two and shoulder-strike through the Everglades, like Eph. Brewer in the 2nd Ward in Springfield on election day.[8] But was comforted when I told him I wanted no soldaten [*soldiers*] — only orders. These I will get when I want them. He is a noble fellow all over soldier and not a glimmer of politics about him. A goodlooking active man, and thoroughly wide awake. I think the double stars lit with discretion on his shoulders. His chief of Staff, Gen. Turner, is an Illinoisan of the best type.[9]

I dont anticipate any immediate military results in this department. Gillmore is getting his troops together and mounting some infantry for a raid. When it will come off, I do not exactly know. I dont think it is decided yet, the where or the when.

A. G. Brown of Salem Mass is here: one of Mr Chase's treasury agents.[10] I am sure I shall run counter to that influence wherever I go. Stickney is the head and representative of it in Florida.[11]

It is refreshing to see how in every company you fall among in the Army, the question of the Presidency is treated: as closed up, settled, signed sealed and delivered. Of course Mr Lincoln will stay where he is! Any other proposition is poohpooed.

If you can find *Gantt's address to the people of Arkansas* I would very much like to have it.[12] Also a copy of the last annual *Message of the President*.[13]

Give my love to all for whom in absence I sigh.

Last night was a glorious summer night. I got arrested and taken to the Guardhouse for being out in the moon in citizen's clothes. Why does my tailor so delay? "For tis their nature to."

[*P.S.*] My address for the Present had better be Hilton Head.

TO LINCOLN, HILTON HEAD, S.C., 21 JANUARY 1864[14]

I take advantage of a steamer sailing today to write you a word.

I have presented your letter and made known your wishes to General Gillmore.[15] He requests me to assure you that he will be glad to do all in his power to forward your wishes.

He is getting his command gradually in hand and concentrated, in view of some descent upon the main land when a good opportunity offers. I do not anticipate an immediate operation.

I will soon be supplied with transportation to proceed to Florida. From what I have been able to learn here, I hope we will be able to gain among the population already within our lines, the requisite nucleus for reorganization.

I will be in condition to report more definitely as soon as I go to Fernandina. I will inform you within a few days from there, of the immediate prospect.

P.S. Col. [*Edward W.*] Smith informs me that there having been frequent inquiries made by the enemy's pickets about your proclamation of December 8th he caused a thousand copies to be struck and surreptitiously sent among them.

I hope the leaven may work.

TO JOHN G. NICOLAY, AT SEA OFF THE COAST OF FLORIDA, 8 FEBRUARY 1864[16]

An A.D.C. of the General handed me this morning a bunch of letters from you for which thanks.

Our advance occupied Jacksonville Fla yesterday. I happened to be with the advance: having been sent forward several days ago to Fernandina and seeing an opportunity to do something, I pushed on with Major Brooks,[17] who staid at the mouth of the River, while I with some troops went on to Jacksonville with Seymour. We occupied the town without opposition except desultory firing. We lost but one man, severely wounded. He was the mate of the steamer "Genl Hunter," shot through the body, as he sprang ashore.

Jacksonville is the pleasantest looking Southern town I have yet seen.

I am now on my way to Fernandina to put into other hands the enrollment business on the coast. I will immediately return to Headquarters in the field to accompany Gen Gillmore in his advance. I do not anticipate any serious resistance. We have a large force and the enemy are unable to make a stand.

I think we will soon have the state back in the Union. If we get the "President's Tithe" it will be fully half the voters in the state, as the poor old carcass of a neighborhood has been plucked to the bone, by North & South.

The weather here is the finest I have ever stumbled on. I came down the St. John's River last night. There was no moon and the stars glistened in the warm wintry air with a steady softness. The harbor as I entered it lay in a charmed quiet. I saw for the first time in its glory the wonder of the southern seas—the phosphorescent light of the waves. As I rowed across every stroke of the oars splashed melted silver. This is absolutely true. I floated in a vast reservoir of molten metal, white and luminous.

Keep other fellows away from my Heart's idol & I will some of these days return & "do the like for thee, my lad."

I have written a chunk of a screed to the President which you can read & give him the substance if you can find any in it.

About a week ago I got my first taste of battle gunpowder & dodged my first shell.[18] I was in the artillery fight on Morris Island. It was very lively for an hour or two.

To Lincoln, mouth of the St. John's River, Florida, 8 February 1864[19]

The preparations which have been for some time making to fit out the expedition for the occupation of Florida, have hitherto prevented my paying as much attention as I would otherwise have done to the special purpose of my mission. The necessities of the military service have compelled me for part of the time to act as an Aide de Camp rather than as a Provost Marshal. But as the expedition seems now in a fair way to speedy and satisfactory accomplishment, I leave our advance (where I have been) to return to Fernandina, to get my books and papers, and then rejoin the Headquarters of General Gillmore on the mainland and do what I can in the special fulfillment of your wishes.

I have found among the few leading men I have met a most gratifying unanimity of sentiment. Those who have formerly been classed as Conservative are willing to accept readily the accomplished events of the war and to come back at once: while those of more radical views whom, we had reason to fear, would rather embarrass us, are heartily in favor of your plan as exhibited in the case of Louisiana and Arkansas. There is no opposition to be apprehended from either native Unionists or "Treasury agents."

The people are ignorant and apathetic. They seem to know nothing and care nothing about the matter. They have vague objections to being shot and having their houses burned, but dont know why it is done. They will be very glad to see a government strong enough to protect them against these everyday incidents of the last two years.

I have the best assurances that we will get the tenth required: although so large a portion of the rebel population is in the army & so many of the loyal people, refugees in the North, that the state is well-nigh depopulated. We will have almost a clean slate to begin with.

To John G. Nicolay, Hilton Head, S.C., 23 February 1864[20]

Our hitherto unopposed campaign in Florida has met with its first check. Gen. Seymour, thinking best under the circumstances to deviate from the instructions received from Gen. Gillmore, has advanced upon the enemy posted beyond Sanderson and has been pretty severely repulsed. I take the opportunity to give you a brief resumé of the situation to prevent exaggerated rumors from stampeding you in regard to us. This command has always been successful and consequently a check is an unheard-of thing to them and gives rise to a wild growth of canards.

Gen. Seymour, thinking it advisable to attack the enemy in his front, rather than to wait his attack in the positions indicated to him by Gen. Gillmore, on Saturday the 20th advanced 8 miles beyond Sanderson and attacked a large force which he found there. The enemy was strongly posted, and in overwhelming numbers, and our troops after fighting very well for about three hours were forced to leave the field, which they did in good order, bringing off their wounded and all their guns but five, which fell into the hands of the enemy. Our loss in killed wounded and missing, is 800. That of the enemy is probably less, as they fought more under cover.

Our force engaged was about 5000. The [strength] of the enemy is estimated variously, from ten to fifteen thousand. Hardee was there.[21] The principal part of the enemy came from Bragg's army.

The fighting on both sides was very fine. The conduct of our troops was superb. The negro Regiments, 54th 55th Mass. 8th U.S. and 3d S.C. under Montgomery behaved like veterans, standing like rocks in a fire that decimated their ranks.[22] The commanding officers of two regiments fell in the fight but they fought on without flinching. Montgomery himself in action always extorts the unbounded praise of the regular officers here.

Gen. Gillmore has sent down to the front Gen. Vogdes with two good brigades. We do not at present apprehend any further serious trouble. Seymour's command, though defeated, is not shattered or demoralized. They will now go at the work they should have done before, which is to strengthen and confirm their hold upon East Florida. Gen. Gillmore is much grieved at this unexpected occurrence. He is a man of great courage and fortitude, and wastes no time in complaining or bewailing. When I came up from Florida to announce this unpleasant news, his first thought was "I am sorry for the effect on *your* operations, Major." He is very heartily and earnestly enlisted in our work of giving a free government to Florida.

I am getting on pretty well in my work. I have been starting the enrollment in several places and most of the citizens seem glad of the opportunity to declare themselves and claim protection. The only question in my mind is whether there are actually now in the State 1435 legal voters according to Florida laws. There have been sent into the rebel army 16 regiments. There are many hundreds of loyal citizens now refugees in the North. The whole country seems pretty well depopulated. We shall get nearly all that remain. If these are not enough we must then as a last resort call a Mass Convention & adopt two amendments to the Constitution. One abolishing slavery & the other altering the election laws to admit actual *bona fide* residents of the State. Thus we can get our quota & I am inclined to think, only thus. However I will put the thing through as far as possible before resorting to this. In any case, I shall, of course, not commit the President or the administration to any policy we may think fit to adopt.[23]

This is rather a long letter to write to the Executive Mansion but I wish you would read it to the President. While I do not ask any suggestions from him, any that he would make would be very acceptable.

While this emergency lasts I have requested permission to act as A.D.C.

I cant think of leaving the field till it is ours. I dont believe I could take my daily tramp down the [*Pennsylvania*] Avenue, if I skedaddled just now. So for a few weeks longer possess your soul in patience. I expect to go down to the front again in a day or two. I have seen some rather rough incidents since I came here. But am pretty nearly emancipated from nerves. You know I had visions of an hour or two a day of irresponsible leisure, and consequent scribble. But I lack not only leisure, but inclination for anything but the matter in hand. A[*fter a*] few minutes hurried jotting of the day's memorand[*a*], the note book is remanded to the pocket.

[*P.S.*] If there are any wild reports from stampeded newspapermen will you be good enough to allow somebody to correct them from this abstract. Gillmore is so earnestly and heartily with us that I should be sorry to see him suffer in public estimation for what is no fault of his own. I do not wish to blame Seymour, as he may have had a good reason for what he did, but he is so impulsive and impetuous that I cannot consider him a safe leader. I have been so constantly *in* this Expedition that I may exaggerate in this quiet corner of the world, its effect on the public mind. But if people around you do talk about it, I pray you, "report us and our cause aright."

To Nathaniel P. Banks, Key West, Florida, 7 March 1864[24]

Permit me to thank you very cordially for the prompt and kind response to my letter from Hilton Head which I found on my arrival here this morning. I shall leave the matter with which I am charged in the hands of General Woodbury, and return tomorrow to the North.[25]

While I have been much gratified at the readiness displayed by the people of this State in availing themselves of the privileges of the Proclamation of December, I cannot but think that we must wait for further developments in military operations before we can hope for a reorganization of the state under a loyal government. I find nearly everybody willing to take the oath of allegiance prescribed by the President, but I find scarcely anyone left in the country. Whole counties seem almost thoroughly depopulated. The few that remain seem heartily tired of the war, and willing to swear allegiance in any terms to the power that will protect them, but there are really not enough, as it seems to me, to justify a movement just at present, for rehabilitation.

Northern emigration or a fuller occupation of the State, consequent upon the spring campaigns, will probably afford the requisite quota of voters. Until then, the Union people here may stand fast and wait.

Permit me, in leaving the South for a time, to express the feelings of respect and admiration with which I have watched your course in Louisiana. Beginning with a people sullenly acquiescent or openly hostile, your firmness tempered with justice and moderation, has accomplished the glorious result of the 22nd of February.[26] To no name in all her varied annals is the rescued state so indebted as to yours.

TO LT. COL. ELIAS M. GREENE, WASHINGTON, [2 APRIL] 1864[27]

Mr. Stanley, our young Briton, left his waterproof coat in the ambulance in charge of the driver on Monday.[28] If you can have it sent to me for him, you will add another to the many obligations for which I am
Yours very gratefully

TO JOHN G. NICOLAY, WASHINGTON, 3 APRIL 1864[29]

Obliged to send the flowers today. Webster is not in town. Better get manuscript & send something else when you return.

TO JOHN BROUGH, WASHINGTON, 5 APRIL 1864[30]

The President has ordered the pardon of the soldiers of the 12th Ohio, in accordance with your request.

TO BENJAMIN F. BUTLER, WASHINGTON, 6 APRIL 1864[31]

The President directs me to acknowledge receipt of your dispatch of this morning and to say that you will submit by letter or telegram, to the Secretary of War, the points in relation to the exchange of prisoners wherein you wish instructions; and that it is not necessary for you to visit Washington for the purpose indicated.[32]

To Charles G. Halpine, Washington, 13 April 1864[33]

I thank you for your kind and most unjust letter. I did call at your lair on Bleeker Street and you were not at home—nor was M. le General. I am *too old a soldier* to pass through your camp without reporting.

I thank you for offering to set me right with the pensive public, but the game is not worth so bright a candle. The original lie in the [*New York*] Herald was dirty enough & the subsequent commentaries were more than usually nasty.[34] But the Tycoon never minded it in the least and as for me, at my age, the more abuse I get in the newspapers, the better for me. I shall run for Constable some day on the strength of my gory exploits in Florida.

I am stationed here for the present. I fear I shall not get away soon again. I have a great deal to do. It is the best work that I can do if I must stay here.

To General Lorenzo Thomas, Washington, 13 April 1864[35]

The President directs me to acknowledge the receipt of your favor of the 30th March, and to state in reply that Mr Lewis has no authorization from him for any such purpose as you mention. He gave to Mr Lewis a letter introducing him to you, at the request of some very respectable gentlemen from Kentucky, and here his responsibility for Mr Lewis terminated.

The President does not wish you to be hampered in the execution of your duties by any consideration of the letter given by himself to Mr Lewis.[36]

To Amos Myers, Washington, 21 April 1864[37]

The President directs me to acknowledge the receipt of your favor of the 18th April & to state in reply, that if the Secretary of War presents to him the name of Mr. Hays as A.Q.M. upon your recommendation, he will nominate Mr Hays to the Senate for the Office.[38]

To Edward Lyulph Stanley, Washington, 25 April 1864[39]

I send you this morning the book of which I spoke last night. It affords ~~at once~~ a fair specimen of American ~~art~~ workmanship, and exhibits in a compact form the tribute which American literature is glad to pay to Loyalty.

I hope it may not be unacceptable, therefore to you whose interest in our affairs seems at once so friendly & so intelligent.

To Manning Leonard, Washington, 30 April 1864[40]

I have been much grieved to hear of the affliction that has fallen upon your family and am thus prevented from congratulating you upon your own convalescence as heartily as I would otherwise. I earnestly wish it were in my power to obtain for you from the President the letters you desire. But he has established a rule from which he never varies, of giving no letter of introduction abroad. Of course I would be glad to do anything for you that is possible but I cannot ever ask him to violate a rule which he has always observed in such cases. I have some acquaintance among our diplomatic & consular officers in Europe & will be glad to give you a note which you can use wherever it will be of service.

[*P.S.*] I know personally, our Ministers at Spain, Portugal, Russia, & a good many consuls all over Europe & the East.

Any letter which you could obtain from Mr. Hamlin would be valuable.

To William S. Rosecrans, Washington, 5 May 1864[41]

The President directs me to inquire whether a day has yet been fixed for the Execution of Citizen Robert Londen, & if so, what day?

To Charles Edward Hay, Washington, 8 May 1864[42]

I have received and read with great pleasure your long letter about the good fortune that has come to you. I congratulate you very heartily and say God bless you and her whom you have chosen [*Mary Ridgely, Charles's fiancée*].

I knew her very intimately when I was in Springfield, and have rarely met anyone so young who was so sensible, so good and true. I think I have never known a girl more sincere and conscientious. It is with none but the brightest anticipations and hopes for your future that I congratulate you and her.

I do not know whether you have yet made up your minds as to time and seasons. I want very much to see you and talk over a thousand things that it is inconvenient to write about. I hope that you will conclude to delay for a while the consummation of your intentions. You are both very young. You can of course trust each other fully. I doubt if you will ever meet a nicer girl anywhere and I think it will puzzle her to find a better fellow. So now in your jolly youth, you had better wait awhile, don't you think? You will be a Captain some of these fine mornings. You are now third on the list of Lieutenants. Why not wait that long at least?[43]

Although I know nobody whom I would sooner have chosen for a sister than her you have chosen for me, I cannot think of losing you, my dear boy, without a feeling of sadness. We have not been very much together, but we have been friends as well as brothers, and so the past is very much endeared to me. The woods and hills of dear old Warsaw, the rivers of Florida and the sands of South Carolina are all fastened on my heart by your companionship. Although I liked Col. W[oolfolk] very much, I was miserable at losing Mary Hay, and now you are about to obey the universal law and pass out of our exclusive possession. Of course I rejoice with you and applaud your choice. I am glad you have chosen so early and so wisely. But our home grows more desolate day by day as all of our dear ones leave it, not to return. I believe Gus and I, some of these days, will come back to Warsaw, jolly old cumberers of the ground, and pass with Father and Mother the last quiet days of their green old age. And you and yours will always be joyfully welcomed in my heart and my home.

"Lincoln" to Francis B. Loomis, Washington, 12 May 1864[44]

I have the honor to acknowledge the receipt of your communication of the 29th of April, in which you offer to replace the present garrison of Fort Trumbull with volunteers which you propose to raise at your own expense.[45]

While it seems inexpedient at this time to accept this proposition, on account of the special duties now devolving upon the garrison mentioned, I cannot pass unnoticed such a meritorious instance of individual patriotism. Permit me, for the Government, to express my cordial thanks to you for this generous & public spirited offer, which is worthy of note among the many called forth by these times of national trial.

To Charles D. Chase, Washington, 16 May 1864[46]

Sorry your father is not better. No necessity of being here.

To Richard McCormick, Washington, 16 May 1864[47]

I have been away from Washington for a great part of the time since I last saw you and so had nothing to write, for when one is in the army he cuts loose from his former life and begins to live idly and improvidently, doing his work and never looking beyond. But I have been recently remorselessly detached from my Corps, which is now under that splendid fellow Gillmore, thundering at the gates of Richmond, and ordered to special duty again at the Executive Mansion. I do not know when I can get away again.

I am not able to give you any definite information as to your affairs in the War Department. The representations and request of Govr. Goodwin have been under consideration, but the President referred them to the War Department, where I have no special entree and so know nothing of the prospects there.[48]

I see Raleston from time to time. He seems busy and prosperous. Washington is not a pleasant place just now. People live entirely upon political & military excitements. Congress plots and the army fights with more energy than in the days when you were with us.

Grant has fought one of the most wonderful series of battles on record during the past fortnight. No armies that the world has heretofore produced have stood pounding like that in Spottsylvania. He is waiting now for the mud to dry a little so that he can move upon Lee again.[49]

Before this reaches you, the campaign will have been definitely worked out and the nominations made at Baltimore—so I forebear prophecy.[50] I hope to see you here before long "bearing your sheaves with you."

However you come rely upon a hearty welcome from your friends— quorum est.

Remember me to the Govr. & Judge. Nicolay sends regards.

To "My dear Sir," Washington, 28 May 1864[51]

Gen. Smith certainly misapprehended me, if he has the impression that I said that the order of release of the persons mentioned by you was made at your special instance. I only told him that *his* name ~~was one~~ & yours were both attached to certain of the petitions ~~and that yours was another of the signatures~~ for release. I of course did not know and had no means of knowing at whose special request the releases were ordered.

To WILLIAM LEETE STONE, WASHINGTON, 3 JUNE 1864[52]

This morning I found yr. notes on my table, on returning from two months soldiering in the South. I immediately did as you wished with the letter to the Secretary of State. He has given me no answer.

To JOHN G. NICOLAY, WASHINGTON, 6 JUNE 1864[53]

Yours of yesterday just received & read to the President.[54] Swett is unquestionably all right in regard to the President, but his presentation of Col. [*Joseph*] Holt's name is entirely of his own suggestion.[55] He seemed not to have considered the bad effect of the contiguity of Illinois & Kentucky on his proposed ticket until I called his attention to it last night. He has never even mentioned Col. Holt's name to the Prest. for the place designated.

The President wishes not to interfere in the nomination even by a confidential suggestion. He also declines suggesting anything in regard to platform or the organization of the Convention. The Convention must be guided in these matters by their own views of justice & propriety.

Do not infer from what I have said above that the President objects to Swett presenting Col. Holt's name. He is, and intends to be absolutely impartial in the matter.

To JOHN G. NICOLAY, WASHINGTON, 6 JUNE 1864[56]

Your letter recd & answered, declines interfering

To MANNING LEONARD, WASHINGTON, 9 JUNE 1864[57]

I will not intrude upon your sorrow further than to express my deep sympathy for your great loss and my prayer that a merciful God may give you that consolation which mortal love is too weak to offer. I have sent your letter to my mother who will join me in my sympathy and prayers.

To [James B. Fry], Washington, 18 June 1864[58]

I beg to present the bearer John Cronan employed at the President's who desires a pass to Alexandria.

To John G. Nicolay, Washington, 20 June 1864[59]

I went plunging through the country after leaving you, missing my connections & buying tickets until I landed in Baltimore without a cent: had to borrow money of the Gustav to pay for my dinner & hack.[60] Got home tired dusty & disguss.

The Tycoon thinks small beer of Rosey's [*General Rosecrans's*] mare's nest.[61] *Too* small, I rather think. But let 'em work. Val[*landigham*]'s sudden Avatar rather startles the Cop[*perhead*]s here away.[62] Billy Morrison asks me how much we gave Fernandiwud [*Fernando Wood*] for importing him![63]

Society is *nil* here. The Lorings go tomorrow—lost lingerers.[64] We mingle our tears & exchange locks o' hair tonight in Corcoran's Row—some half-hundred of us.

I went last night to a Sacred Concert of profane music at Ford's. Young Kretchmar and old Kretchpar were running the machine.[65] Hermanns & Habelman both sung: & they kin ef anybody kin. The Tycoon & I occupied private box & (both of us) carried on a hefty flirtation with the Monk Girls in the flies.

Madame [*Mary Lincoln*] is in the North. The President has gone today to visit Grant. I am all alone in the White pest-house. The ghosts of twenty thousand drowned cats come in nights through the South Windows. I shall shake my buttons off with the ague before you get back.

Buy me some gold mines & a gas lead & give my love to Charlie Chase & drink my health in some of yr. chicory.

To George William Curtis, Washington, 20 June 1864[66]

Your letter to the President is not yet received.[67] Please cause a copy to be made.

To George William Curtis, Washington, 20 June 1864[68]

The official letter has come to hand.

To Charles Kappes, Washington, 24 June 1864[69]

The President has received your letter of the 21st June and directs me to reply that if you will come to Washington, he will give you a pardon which will exempt you from punishment for your desertion, on condition that you faithfully serve out yr. time.[70]

To George William Curtis, Washington, 27 June 1864[71]

Presidents response sent by mail today.[72]

To Quincy A. Gillmore, Washington, 2 July 1864[73]

I cannot refrain from tendering my hearty congratulations upon the forcible and authoritative endorsement that you today recd in the Senate. Nothing could afford better evidence of the futility of the worst efforts of yr detractors, than the overwhelming majority by which yr nomination was carried. You could not but have been gratified to see the warmth & energy with which some of the most distinguished [*Senators*] to whom you are personally unknown espoused yr cause, as the cause of honor & justice.

To Stephen A. Hurlbut, Washington, 8 July 1864[74]

I learn from some very good friends in New York that Mr. E. W. Vander-hoff of that city, is now under military arrest in New Orleans. I am not fully informed of the causes of this arrest and do not desire to interfere in your administration; but in consideration of Mr. Vanderhoff's feeble health and the earnest solicitations of his friends, I would be glad if he could be released on parole, or receive any other indulgence consistent with the public interest.

To Horace Greeley, Washington, 9 July 1864[75]

The President answers your letter by this day's mail.[76]

To Leonard Hay, Washington, 14 July 1864[77]

I start for New York tonight.

To Leonard Hay, Washington, 14 July 1864, 9 p.m.[78]

No train through tonight. Will start in the morning.

To Edward D. Neill, Washington, 14 July 1864[79]

I am going to New York tonight on business. Will be gone only a very few days.

I leave matters in your hands till my return. There will probably be little to do. Refer as little to the President as possible. Keep visitors out of the house when you can. Inhospitable, but prudent.

I have a few franked envelopes. Let matters of ordinary reference go without formality of signature. If you have any doubt about any matter, please reserve it till my return.

To Lincoln, New York, 16 July 1864[80]

Arrived this morning at 6 AM and delivered your letter [*to Horace Greeley a*] few minutes after.[81]

Although he thinks some one less known would create less excitement and be less embarrassed by public curiosity, still he will start immediately if he can have an absolute safe conduct for four persons to be named by him.[82]

Your letter he does not think will guard them from arrest and with only those letters he would have to explain the whole matter to any officer who might choose to hinder them. If this meets with your approbation I can write the order in your name as A A G, or you can send it by mail.

Please answer me at Astor House.[83]

To Lincoln, New York, 17 July 1864[84]

Gave the order yesterday. He promised to start at once and I suppose did so. I return this evening if connections can be made.

To William Cornell Jewett, Washington, 18 July 1864[85]

In the exercise of my duties [as] secretary in charge of the President's correspondence, it is necessary for me to use a certain discretion in the choice of letters to be submitted to the personal inspection of the President. In order to avoid a further waste of time on your part, I have to inform you that your letters are never so submitted. My proceeding in this matter has the sanction of the President.

To Alice W. Skinner, Washington, 23 July 1864[86]

I bow in abject penitence to yr. righteous indignation. I have no plea—no justification—but I *do* want yr. picture—the one with the hat.

Of course it is impertinent for me to ask for it. But I cant help it. It is yr. own fault, looking so charmingly when you had it taken. If you don't give it to me I shall go into a nunnery.

I might have known th. you wd have forgotten my name. After I had the honor of writing to you once or twice a long absence from Washington destroyed the continuity of all my correspondence, & when I returned to duty here I did not think I had the right of resuming my epistolary acquaintance with you. So though often [*hearing?*] about y[*ou*] fr[*om*] our friends & always very much interested in yr. welfare—no direct correspondence until the sight of the irresistible pho. determined me to take risk of the reply in asking for it. So I made the demonstration & am disastrously repulsed.

But not yet finally defeated. Suffering severely I admit with shattered ranks & torn banners, with purpose unfaltering I come back for my picture. You say yr. determination is fixed. [*Chg. mid July ladylike ergo Sabine.?*]

I am not making an argument M. E. No right to ask. no question of right. I beg entreat implore clamor for that sweet counterfeit. Give it to me not in justice but in grace.

Please Miss Eva let me sign myself this time in hope & the next time in mercy.

To [Samuel Cony], Washington, 29 July 1864[87]

The President directs me to acknowledge the receipt of your favor of the 22nd July inviting him to accompany the Committee of Congress in their tour of inspection upon the North Eastern Frontier, & to express his regret that public business will prevent his availing himself of the proffered courtesy.[88]

To Hannah Angell Coggeshall, Washington, 31 July 1864[89]

I have a young sister whom my mother desires to place at school somewhere in the East. She is, I think, about 17 years old.

I write to ask you what you know about Mrs. Buell's establishment. You know I have a weakness for Rhode Island & I should like to place her there, if it is as good as the best.

Pardon me for giving you this trouble but blame your unvarying kindness which emboldens me.

Present my regards to Mr. Coggeshall.

[P.S.] Please don't mention this to anybody else (but Mr. C. I mean)

To John G. Nicolay, New York, Sunday, August 1864[90]

[William H.] Marston is out of town so I am stranded here, badly bored with nothing to do but wait for tomorrow.[91]

I have lost my knife. I wish you would put one in an envelope & send it to me here.

Everybody is out of town. New York is duller than Washington. I saw Boutwell for a while today. He takes rather an encouraging view of the political situation. I wont go to see Greeley unless the Prest desires it.

I shall be here all day tomorrow.

To Morton McMichael, Washington, 2 August 1864[92]

The President directs me to request that you will visit him at Washington as soon as convenient.

To Carl Schurz, Washington, 9 August 1864[93]

Your letter of yesterday is in the hands of the President.[94]

I received your letter written from Philadelphia to me and immediately communicated its contents to the President. As you remember the answer it called for could not be furnished by me. I have on three or four occasions since endeavored to get an answer for you, but have written nothing simply because I had nothing to write. The letter which you addressed to Mr. Nicolay some time ago reached him in the West & was transmitted to me.[95] I immediately made inquiries in relation to its subject matter and on being informed that the Bill you referred to had not passed I communicated that fact to you addressing the point where your letter was dated.

I wish to assure you that your correspondence is always carefully placed before the President as soon as received, if marked *Private*, without inspection, & that it is always a pleasure for me to be honored by any request from you within my power to execute.

To Francis G. Young, Washington, 10 August 1864[96]

The President directs me to say that there are no appointments within his immediate gift of the nature you desire. But if any General in the field should apply for you to fill a position upon his staff to which he is entitled to nominate an officer, of if any Governor shall desire to issue to you a commission in the Volunteer service within his power to bestow, the President will readily remove any existing obstacle to your accepting such position or commission.

To Hannah Angell Coggeshall, Washington, 10 August 1864[97]

I thank you very cordially for your kind letter and your more kind offer of farther friendly service to my sister. But it does not seem to me possible for the child to live at a boarding house and attend a day school. I regret this on account of the high character I have heard given to Miss Shaw's establishment by yourself and Capt. Ives. But a boarding school seems to me indispensable unless I could be near.

This being head of the family is turning my hair grey in the flower of my youth.

To Carl Schurz, Washington, 11 August 1864[98]

The President directs me to request that you will proceed at once to Washington and report to him in person.

To John G. Nicolay, Warsaw, Illinois, 25 August 1864[99]

I arrived home yesterday, fagged. I have made an examination of something less than a hundred Boarding schools and convents and we have at last after a family council held last night, pretty well settled upon the Convent of Visitation at St. Louis.[100]

I shall stay here until the term begins & go with Ellie there, and then come at once back to Washington early in September.

We are waiting with the greatest interest for the hatching of the big peace Snakes at Chicago.[101] There is throughout the country, I mean the rural districts, a good healthy Union feeling & an intention to succeed, in the military & the political contests, but everywhere in the towns, the copperheads are exultant and our own people either growling & despondent or sneakingly apologetic. I found among my letters here, sent by you, one from Joe Medill inconceivably impudent, in which he informs me that on the Fourth of next March thanks to Mr. Lincoln's blunders & follies we will be kicked out of the White House.[102] The damned scoundrel needs a day's hanging. I wont answer his letter till I return & let you see it. Old Uncle Jesse [K. Dubois] is talking like an ass — says if the Chicago nominee is a good man, he dont know &c &c. He blackguards you & me — says we are too big for our breeches — a fault for which it seems to me either Nature or our tailors are to blame. After all your kindness to the old whelp & his cub of a son, he hates you because you have not done more. I believe he thinks the Ex[ecutive] Mansion is somehow to blame because Bill married a harlot & Dick Oglesby is popular.[103]

Land is getting up near the stars in price. It will take all I am worth to buy a tater-patch. I am after one or two small pieces in Hancock [*County*] for reasonable prices; 20 to 30 dollars an acre. Logan paid $70,000 for a farm a short while ago, & everybody who has greenbacks is forcing them off like waste paper for land. I find in talking with well informed people a sort of fear of Kansas property: as uncertain in future settlement & more than all, uncertain in weather. The ghost of famine haunts those speculations.

You were wrong in thinking either Milt or Charlie Hay at all copperish. They are as sound as they ever were. They of course are not quite clear about the currency, but who is?

Our people here want me to address the Union League. I believe I wont. The snakes [*Democrats*] would rattle about it a little & it wd. do no good. I lose my temper sometimes talking with growling Republicans. There is a diseased restlessness about men in these times that unfits them for the steady support of an administration. It seems as if there were appearing in the Republican party the elements of disorganization that destroyed the whigs.

If the dumb cattle are not worthy of another term of Lincoln then let the will of God be done & the murrain of McClellan fall on them.

[*P.S.*] My sister Mary is here & she & Charlie desire to be remembered.

To John G. Nicolay, Warsaw, Illinois, 26 August 1864[104]

I this morning received Derby's circular with my interpolated title.[105] Please send him the enclosed under your frank. He of course knows better.

It is reported here that Greeley Raymond & the Ex. Com. are trying to run Lincoln off, having given up beat.[106] Most of our people are talking like damned fools. My father on the contrary is the most sanguine man I have met. He says we will carry this State with a fair working majority. Some of the Dutch [*Germans*] are bit with the Fremont mania.[107] But the returned soldiers are all for Lincoln, if they can be kept right till November.

The worst thing I have noticed is that prominent & wealthy Republicans who still continue all right in politics & go their length on the President, are getting distrustful of the issue and forcing off their greenbacks into land at fancy prices. One firm here have $80,000 in Govt. Bonds which they intend to keep, but they say, "if a Copperhead is elected in November, which is not impossible, we will lose it all by repudiation."

John T. Stuart is legging a little for Fillmore as the fogy candidate in the Convention which meets tomorrow.[108] But I suppose they cant control the McClellan current. I wait the result with some interest—not very much, as I have scarcely a doubt as to what they will do. If the Cop[perhead]s do roll us over this fall, will it not make Kansas land a very unsafe speculation. I anticipate anarchy & disorganization of society if those devils get full control especially in the border States.

Has the appointment of Land Patent Secretary yet been made?[109] Charlie Philbrick is perfectly steady now I am told. I saw him when last in Springfield & he was straight as a string. If you could make it proper at yr. end of the line I am very sure you could not get a man more thoroughly discreet & competent. He made a most favorable impression on me when I saw him—all of one evening. The subject was not mentioned by either of us.[110] Stod[dard] has been extensively advertising himself in the Western Press. His asininity which is kept a little dark under your shadow at Washington blooms & burgeons in the free air of the West.

If there were any reason for hoping for our national future, Govt. securities wd be the best possible investment. But it is the growing despondency that has driven lands so high that a poor man cannot buy.

To John G. Nicolay, Warsaw, Illinois, 7 September 1864[111]

I had hoped to be in Washington before this but have been unlucky in many things. I have not yet spent one single day in recreation but have been busy ever since I left New York. Have placed Helen at school and gotten back here: attended to some business of my father's which could not be postponed: spent all my money in railroad tickets and drawn a hundred more to get back & find myself at the end of my trip worse tired out than if I had staid at Washington. I am today quite sick. I had made an engagement with Charlie Philbrick to leave Springfield tomorrow night for Washington but am unable to keep it.[112] Had a chill this morning. I have written to Charlie to go on without me.

If I am not in bed on Monday morning next I will start for Washington. If I am, I cannot say when "I will arise & go (from) my Father."

I have been struck more than ever this summer with the beauty of our river scenery. Charlie Hay & I had a plan for going to Nauvoo but failed for want of time.[113] You will enjoy all that when you come. I have told my mother of your intended pilgrimage to the old haunts of the Mormons & she directs me to assure you of the pleasure with which she will welcome you when you come. You can certainly find no quieter place to write your romance this side of the Great Desert. There is absolutely no society here. You can pass a couple of months here entirely undisturbed by visitors. If I could come with you I could introduce you to all the pretty views and attractive bridle paths but if you come alone you could soon find them for yourself. I would give a great deal to pass a month here. But all this after the War.

The Republicans here are talking better and *sassier* since the nomination of McClellan.[114]

To Miss "C.," Washington, 20 September 1864[115]

I have just returned fr. a visit to W[arsaw]. I find everything much changed since the time we remember. The memory of those times emboldens me to make the request which is the object of this note.

I wish you wd. send me yr. photograph. It will be one of the pleasantest illustrations of a period that I fear is finally past. I shall be very grateful if you will oblige me in this. At least whether you do or not, let me have the pleasure of calling myself once more very sincerely yr. friend.

To [Edward G. Bush], Washington, 21 September 1864[116]

Thinking you may have returned by this time to Saint Louis I send the pass you were so kind as to request.

I had a pleasant time among the hills at Warsaw. My sisters often spoke of you, & wished you could visit us.

Things are looking nicely in the whole field. Sheridan gave us a neat but not gaudy little victory the other day.[117]

To [George Wilkes], Washington, 21 September 1864[118]

I have read with great pleasure yours of yesterday. Of course I was not surprised at it. I do not see how any patriotic and candid man thinking as you do, could act otherwise. This nation may have sinned grievously, but neither you nor I believe ~~that~~ it deserves that the murrain of McClellan should fall upon it.

To John G. Nicolay, Washington, 24 September 1864[119]

Your despatch was just brought in.[120] I took it to the President & he told me to tell you you had better loaf around the city a while longer. You need some rest & recreation & may as well take it in N.Y. as anywhere else. Besides you cant imagine how nasty the house is at present. You would get the "painter's cholic" in 24 hours if you came home now.

Politicians still unhealthily haunt us. Loose women flavor the ante room. Much turmoil & trouble. But there are small compensations. The Youngs are here. They are pretty exceedingly. They have grown fat and fair.

The world is almost too many for me. I take a dreary pleasure in seeing Philbrick eat steamed oysters by the 1/2 bushel. He has gotten a haven of rest in the family of some decayed Virginia gentry. Really a very lucky chance. Good respectable & not dear.[121]

Schafer must be our resource this winter in clo[thes]![122] If you dont want to be surprised into idiocy dont ask Croney & Lent the price of goods. A faint rumour has reached me & paralyzed me. I am founding a "Shabby Club" to make rags the style this winter.

Write to me some morning while you are waiting for your cocktail & tell me how's things. Give my love to the fair who are so lucky to know

Yours truly

[P.S.] Isn't it bully about Sheridan!

Please let Billy have enclosed immediately.

To Francis Lieber, Washington, 29 September 1864[123]

The President has received the copies of your terse and vigorous article which you have had the goodness to send him, and he bids me return you his cordial thanks. Its clearness of statement and compactness of logic will doubtless be of great value in the coming canvass.[124]

To George Jacob Holyoake, Washington, 7 October 1864[125]

The President directs me to acknowledge the receipt of your kind letter of the 4th of September and to assure you of his grateful appreciation of the generous terms in which you have been pleased to speak of him.[126]

To John G. Nicolay, Washington, 8 October 1864[127]

Nothing as yet ripples the surface.

Every body is anxious about next Tuesday's work.

Raymond went home the other day rather discouraged about money matters.

If you should care to go out to the convent I send you the necessary introduction. Dont go, unless you want to.

The Surgeon General sends a very ready response to yr. note in behalf of Dr. Porter. I send it to you that you may be armed to meet him.

If you come across Grover you may trust every word he says as to facts.[128] As to sentiments, you can appreciate them yourself. He may be a little too hard on the Radicals & a little too conservative himself.

General Meigs has lost his only son—a very brilliant young engineer.[129]

Miss Bacon was duly married on the 6th. You & I were not there. Public business.

To Mrs. Henry P. Westerman, Washington, 10 October 1864[130]

In reply to your request for a donation to the Tazewell Co. Fair, the President desires me to transmit six photographs, with autographs.

To John G. Nicolay, Washington, 10 October 1864[131]

Here are yr. mails for this morning. We are very busy. Mr. Matile is sick.

Pennsylvania fellows are very confident. You will know the result before this gets there.

Kelly was here this morning.[132] He seemed to be in a great hurry, as he only staid 2 hours & a half, & didn't talk about himself more than 9/10ths of the time.

No fun—no Christmas.

Thank God you are not here. We are dreary enough. The weather is nasty.

[*P.S.*] Love to Ed. Bush.

To GEORGE G. MEADE, WASHINGTON, 12 OCTOBER 1864[133]

The President directs suspension of execution in case of Albert G. Lawrence 16th Mass. Vols. until his further order.

To ANDREW G. CURTIN, WASHINGTON, 13 OCTOBER 1864[134]

Since telegraphing you the President has recd. Your letter from Erie.

To THE UNION COMMANDANT AT NASHVILLE, WASHINGTON, 13 OCTOBER 1864[135]

The sentence of Jesse Broadway has been commuted by the President to imprisonment for three years.

To JOHN G. NICOLAY, WASHINGTON, 13 OCTOBER 1864[136]

I suppose you are happy enough over the elections to do without letters. Here are two. I hope they are duns to remind you that you are mortal.

Indiana is simply glorious.[137] The surprise of this good thing is its chief delight. Pennsylvania has done pretty well. We have a little majority on home vote as yet & will get a fair vote from the soldiers, and do better in November.[138] The wild estimates of Forney & Cameron founded on no count or thorough canvass are of course not fulfilled, but we did not expect them to be.[139]

Judge Taney died last night.[140] I have not heard anything this morning about the succession. It is a matter of the greatest personal importance that Mr Lincoln has ever decided.

Winter Davis' clique was badly scooped out in the Mayoralty election in Baltimore yesterday.[141] Chapman (regular Union) got nearly all the votes cast.[142] I have nothing from you as yet.

To Henry J. Raymond, Washington, 17 October 1864[143]

My friend Mr. Wm. N. Grover Esq. of St. Louis, U. S. District Attorney for Eastern Dist. of Missouri was recently taxed, among others, by Senator Lane's Western Committee, for $200.00.[144] Mr. Grover, not recognizing the right of this Committee to make such assessments, refused to honor the draft, but sent to me the sum asked for in two different checks of $100.00 each, the first of which I gave to Senator Harlan here, and the second I enclose to you.[145] He prefers to make his contributions thus voluntarily and to give them this destination, rather than the one demanded by the Western Branch Committee.

To Montgomery C. Meigs, Washington, 26 October 1864[146]

The President directs me to write this note to introduce Capt. Henry S. Fitch of Illinois, and to ask for him an interview upon matters of business.

To Gustavus Koerner, Washington, 26 October 1864[147]

The assignment of drafted men from St. Clair and Monroe counties to 43d Illinois vols has been made, as requested by you.

To Myer S. Isaacs, New York, 1 November 1864[148]

The President directs me to acknowledge the reception of your favor of the 26th October.[149]

You are in error in the assumptions you make in regard to the circumstances of the recent interview to which you refer, between certain gentlemen of the Hebrew faith, and the President. No pledge of the Jewish vote was made by these gentlemen and no inducements or promises were extended to them by the President. They claimed no such authority, and received no such response as you seem to suppose.

The President deems this statement due to you, and directs me to thank you for your letter.

To [Charles E. Allen], n.p., 1 November 1864[150]

The President directs me to acknowledge the reception of your letter of the 26th October, informing him that you hold subject to his order a Chair and Liquor Case voted to him at the recent Sanitary Fair, in your city.

He further desires me to say that while he cordially and gratefully appreciates the compliment thus conferred, ~~and~~ he begs the privilege of requesting that these articles be disposed of, in such a manner as may ~~be~~ contribute most effectually to the object which he, no less than you, has at heart, the relief of the suffering soldiers of the Union.

To H. Warren Stimson, Washington, 2 November 1864[151]

I have received your letter written October 25th.[152]

I read it to the President. He thought it, as I did, a manly and soldierly statement of the case, and ordered it to be filed in the Bureau of Engineers, to be considered as soon as any vacancies occur.

I cannot tell you whether you will be successful or not, but I can assure you that your application will be fairly and favorably considered.

I shall be glad to do anything I can to aid you.

To Francis B. Carpenter, Washington, 2 November 1864[153]

I presented to the President the case of Pratt.[154] He always requires in these matters the formality of an affidavit.

I send the paper back for the oath. Let Mrs. Pratt take a swear at it & return it to me.

I thank you for having made this matter the occasion of writing me a most acceptable letter.

To [John G. Nicolay], Washington, 7 November 1864[155]

I have nothing to say till the day after tomorrow. God save the Republic!

To Francis B. Carpenter, Washington, 19 November 1864[156]

The President made order for release of Pratt conditionally on paying back his last bounty, & sent it to the Navy Department for execution.

We are very busy.

"Lincoln" to Lydia Bixby, Washington, 21 November 1864[157]

I have been shown in the files of the War Department a statement of the Adjutant General of Massachusetts, that you are the mother of five sons who have died gloriously on the field of battle.

I feel how weak and fruitless must be any words of mine which should attempt to beguile you from the grief of a loss so overwhelming. But I cannot refrain from tendering to you the consolation that may be found in the thanks of the Republic they died to save.

I pray that our Heavenly Father may assuage the anguish of your bereavement, and leave you only the cherished memory of the loved and lost, and the solemn pride that must be yours, to have laid so costly a sacrifice upon the altar of Freedom.

"Lincoln" to John Phillips, Washington, 21 November 1864[158]

I have heard of the incident at the polls in your town, in which you bore so honored a part, and I take the liberty of writing to you to express my personal gratitude for the compliment paid me by the suffrage of a citizen so venerable.

The example of such devotion to civic duties in one whose days have already extended an average life time beyond the Psalmist's limit, cannot but be valuable and fruitful. It is not for myself only, but for the country which you have in your sphere served so long and so well, that I thank you.

To James S. Thomas, Washington, 22 November 1864[159]

The President directs me to say that he has received your telegram in reference to Genl. Pleasanton.[160]

To [ALICE W. SKINNER, WASHINGTON], 25 NOVEMBER [1864][161]

I am not ungrateful & I never will be for that friendship you offer me. It is worth more to me than you imagine. I cannot thank you enough for the letter you have written me. I do not know anyone else like you. You are so true & firm and brave. God forbid that I should not appreciate & treasure & cherish that honest frank friendship of which I scarcely feel myself worthy, though I am about as good as most men.

But you are better than most women. I cannot flatter you & would not if I could. I wish I knew some faults of yours that I might prove my sincerity by telling you of them, as you do.

Here is one of Edmond About's queer little stories.[162] I sent to New York for it for you. If I can get something here that is clever and not wicked (so hard in French you know) I will send it to you. There are no F. books in the W[ashington]n shops.

The reason why you had not heard from Ives is that I had not given him yr. carte.[163] I gave it to him when your question waked my remorse. I had not forgotten him but I [hid it like a?] miser in my own book for a month before I delivered it: which you will pardon. Write to me. You cannot do anything kinder & more generous.

To GEORGE B. SMITH, WASHINGTON, 25 NOVEMBER 1864[164]

The President directs me to acknowledge the receipt of a Choice piece of Roasting Beef and the very kind letter by which it was accompanied, and to tender you his thanks for both.[165]

To [CHARLES S.] SPENCER, WASHINGTON, 25 NOVEMBER [1864][166]

I regret that the President was literally crowded out of the opportunity of writing you a note for yr. banquet. He fully intended to do so *himself* & for that reason I did not prepare a letter for him. But the crush here just now is beyond endurance.

You had a glorious time as I see by the papers. The present universal acclamation must be very grateful to you whose sagacity saw earlier than most the way the hand of our good genius was pointing & who heard the name the voice of the people was beginning to syllable before the tones grew loud enough for the rest of the world to recognize in them the voice of God.

To Benjamin F. Butler, Washington, 26 November 1864[167]

The President directs me to return Mr. Clemens' letter, and to thank you for your kindness in submitting it to his perusal.[168]

To William Leete Stone, Washington, 28 November 1864[169]

I send a letter to Draper, which I fear will do you no good.[170] You are really better entitled to be heard in the matter than I am. He knows your name at least, which is more than he knows of me.

I am sorry you exaggerate my influence so. All I can do I would be glad to do for you, but I have no power over offices. I cant control a single appointment in the gift of the government. If I could, you know you would not have to ask twice for anything within my reach.

To an unidentified Major, n.p., 21 December 1864[171]

The President is well acquainted with the facts in the case of the Rebel Captain McHenry and made the order for his release understandingly. I had not seen this paper before. He made another order in the case, on the request of Hon. S. M. Cullom M. C. from Illinois, a few days since.[172]

To James Speed, Washington, 24 December 1864[173]

The President directs me to ask from you a suggestion as to the amount of Bond requisite in this case.

To Fay Worthen, [Washington], [1864?][174]

The boy Thomas is at Annapolis all right.

Recollection of a remark by Lincoln, ca. early 1865[175]

I . . . remember, too, that Lincoln, not many days before he went to join the august assembly of just men made perfect, said to me, "A man who denies to other men equality of rights is hardly worthy of freedom; but I would give *even to him* all the rights which I claim for myself."

To Ethan Allen Hitchcock, Washington, 16 February 1865[176]

The President desires that this may be done as soon as practicable.

To Edward McPherson, Washington, 23 March 1865[177]

The date of the President's letter to Mrs. Gurney is the 4th of September 1864. The interview referred to, took place long before.[178]

To Charles Edward Hay, Washington, 31 March 1865[179]

I have been a little neglectful of my duties to you lately. I have written almost no letters except on business for some time.

I am getting very hurried as the time approaches for me to give my place in the Executive Office to some new man. The arrears of so long a time cannot be settled in a day.

You have probably seen from the papers that I am to go to Paris as Secretary of Legation. It is a pleasant and honorable way of leaving my present post which I should have left in any event very soon. I am thoroughly sick of certain aspects of life here, which you will understand without my putting them on paper, and I was almost ready, after taking a few months' active service in the field, to go back to Warsaw and try to give the Vineyard experiment a fair trial, when the Secretary of State sent for me and offered me this position abroad. It was entirely unsolicited and unexpected. I had no more idea of it than you have. But I took a day or two to think it over, the matter being a little pressing, — as the Secretary wanted to let Mr. Bigelow know what he was to expect, — and at last concluded that I would accept.[180] The President requested me to stay with him a month or so longer to get him started with the reorganised office, which I shall do, and shall sail probably in June.

Meanwhile Nicolay, whose health is really in a very bad state, has gone off down the coast on a voyage to Havana, and will be gone the "heft" of the month of April, and I am fastened here, very busy. I don't like to admit and will not yet give up that I can't come on to your "happiest-day-of-your-life;" but I must tell you that it looks uncommonly like it just now. But whether I come or not, I will be with you that day in my love and my prayers that God will bless you and yours forever.

I very much fear that all my friends will disapprove this step of mine, but if they know all that induced me to it they would coincide.

To Charles H. Philbrick, Washington, 6 April 1865[181]

I must insist that you shall be more regular in your attendance at the office. The work is getting badly behind-hand and the current work even cannot be kept up. June will come before any progress is made in the work of preparing the office for the new Secretary.

You will please come here every morning and report for duty to Mr. Neill, who has been charged with the duty of arranging the office.[182]

To Benjamin F. Butler, Washington, 10 April 1865[183]

The President will be pleased to see you at Nine o'clock tomorrow (Tuesday) morning.

To Manning Leonard, Washington, 13 April 1865[184]

I have read with great pleasure your letter of the 31st March & am very glad to learn that your health has been so improved by your recent voyage.

I shall sail as soon as the President can spare me. I have intended to get away in June next, and think it not unlikely that I will succeed. Of course I will not go as long as my services here seem essential.

I am to be Secretary of the Legation of the United States at Paris. I think it will be a pleasant place for study and observation. I shall no doubt enjoy it for a year or so — not very long, as I do not wish to exile myself in these important and interesting times. Every young man has a work to do at home, in this age: I go away only to fit myself for more serious work when I return.

I have sent your letter to my mother who is always pleased to hear about you.

To Henry J. Raymond, Washington, 20 April 1865[185]

A day or two before the President's death, I handed him the enclosed copy of the safe conduct written for Mr. Greeley, to complete the record of the Niagara matter.[186] He then told me that you and Mr. Greeley were the only persons to whom he had ever given copies of the printed record. He also showed me a copy of the letter written to you in relation to the matter, in which he refers to the future publication of the correspondence. I send you this copy to complete the record in your hands. Mr. Greeley has the original.

Of course you understand that this was given Mr. Greeley to be used — provided the rebel Commissioners consented to come to Washington on the terms proposed by the President — simply to guard them against detention or annoyance on the way. No word of mine, nor of the President could have been taken to mean that this was an arrangement superseding the former one, or that the subsequent note "To whom it may concern" nullified this safe conduct.[187]

To Andrew Johnson, [Washington], 24 April 1865[188]

The bearer James Johnson, was the barber of the late President. Unless you have already selected some one to take charge of your shaving &c, I am sure you cannot find a better man.[189]

To Edwin M. Stanton, Paris, 26 July 1865[190]

I received your kind note from Mr. Moore just as I left the Hotel in New York for the Steamer.[191] I have so often thanked you for your consideration and kindness that I have no words left to renew the assurances of my grateful appreciation. It is not probable that the time will ever come that I can be of use to you. If it ever does, I shall free myself from the obligations that embarrass me, but never from those that bind me to you.

I know you generally care very little what people say or think about you, but it cannot but be gratifying even to you to know that confidence in you strengthens the confidence of good people in the government, and stiffens their hopes for the future. And I want you to let me say that in a very long journey this summer, embracing nearly every State in the North and the Border, I was surprised to see the near unanimity in this matter. You know that there were many meddlers whose knuckles you had rapped, many thieves whose hands you had tied, and many liars whose mouths you had shut for a time by your prompt punishments, who had occupied themselves in traducing you, so as to shake the faith of many decent people in you. That is all over now. Very frequently, when I had occasion to speak of you, I found you were understood and appreciated by strangers just as you are by your friends. It is already known, as well as the readers of history a hundred years hence will know, that no honest man has cause of quarrel with you, that your hands have been clean and your heart steady every hour of this fight, and that if any human names are to have the glory of this victory, it belongs to you among the very few who stood by the side of him who has gone to his better reward, and never faltered in your trust in God and the People.

Not everyone knows, as I do, how close you stood to our lost leader, how he loved you and trusted you, and how vain were all the efforts to shake that trust and confidence, not lightly given & never withdrawn. All this will be known some time of course, to his honor and yours.

It is not my habit to say this sort of thing, nor yours to listen to it. I wanted to tell you this when I saw you last, and now say it, and have done.

Part Two
Selected Writings

4

Hay's Reminiscences of the Civil War

Letter to William H. Herndon, Paris, 5 September 1866[1]

I am so constantly busy that I have had no quiet day in which I [could] write you what you desired in your letter several months ago. I have been Chargé d'Affaires nearly all summer, my day filled with official business and my night with social engagements equally imperative. Even now, I write because I am ashamed to wait any longer and have a few minutes disposable. I will answer your questions as you put them without any attempt at arrangement.

Lincoln used to go to bed ordinarily from ten to eleven o'clock unless he happened to be kept up by important news, in which case he would frequently remain at the War Department until 1 or 2. He rose early. When he lived in the country at Soldiers Home, he would be up and dressed, eat his breakfast (which was extremely frugal—an egg, a piece of toast coffee &c) and ride into Washington, all before 8 o'clock. In the winter at the White House he was not quite so early [to rise]. He did not sleep very well but spent a good while in bed. Tad usually slept with him. He would lie around the office until he fell asleep & Lincoln would shoulder him and take him off to bed.

He pretended to begin business at ten oclock in the morning, but in reality the anterooms and halls were full before that hour—people anxious to get the first axe ground. He was extremely unmethodical: it was a four-years struggle on Nicolay's part and mine to get him to adopt some systematic rules. He would break through every regulation as fast as it was made. Anything that kept the people themselves away from him he disapproved—although they nearly annoyed the life out of him by unreasonable complaints & requests.

He wrote very few letters. He did not read one in fifty that he received. At first we tried to bring them to his notice, but at last he gave the whole thing over to me, and signed without reading them the letters I wrote in his name. He wrote perhaps half-a-dozen a week himself—not more.

Nicolay received members of Congress, & other visitors who had business with the Executive Office, communicated to the Senate and House the messages of the President, & exercised a general supervision over the business.

I opened and read the letters, answered them, looked over the newspapers, supervised the clerks who kept the records and in Nicolay's absence did his work also.

When the President had any rather delicate matter to manage at a distance from Washington, he very rarely wrote, but sent Nicolay or me.

The House remained full of people nearly all day. At noon the President took a little lunch—a biscuit, a glass of milk in winter, some fruit or grapes in summer. He dined at fr. 5 to 6. & we went off to our dinner also.

Before dinner was over members [*of the U.S. House of Representatives*] & Senators would come back & take up the whole evening. Sometimes, though rarely he shut himself up & would see no one. Sometimes he would run away to a lecture or concert or theatre for the sake of a little rest.

He was very abstemious—ate less than any one I know. Drank nothing but water—not from principle, but because he did not like wine or spirits. Once, in rather dark days early in the war, a Temperance Committee came to him & said the reason we did not win was because our army drank so much whiskey as to bring down the curse of the Lord upon them. He said drily that it was rather unfair on the part of the aforesaid curse, as the other side drank more and worse whiskey than ours did.[2]

He read very little. Scarcely ever looked into a newspaper unless I called his attention to an article on some special subject. He frequently said "I know more about that than any of them." It is absurd to call him a modest man. No great man was ever modest. It was his intellectual arrogance and unconscious assumption of superiority that men like [*Secretary of the Treasury Salmon P.*] Chase and [*Massachusetts Senator Charles*] Sumner never could forgive.

I cant write any more today. I may see you before long—I dont know—& so I wont waste time by telling you what you must know as well as I do.

I believe Lincoln is well understood by the people. Miss Nancy Bancroft [*i.e., George Bancroft*] & the rest of that patent leather kid glove set know no more of him than an owl does of a comet, blazing into his blinking eyes.

Bancrofts address was a disgraceful exhibition of ignorance and prejudice.[3] His effeminate nature shrinks instinctively from the contact of a great reality like Lincoln's character.

I consider Lincoln Republicanism incarnate—with all its faults and all its virtues. As in spite of some weaknesses, Republicanism is the sole hope of a sick world, so Lincoln with all his foibles, is the greatest character since Christ.

OBITUARY OF TAD LINCOLN[4]

Most of those who read the dispatch announcing the death of Thomas Todd Lincoln will never think of the well-grown gentleman who died on Saturday at Chicago. The name of "Tad"—a pet name given by himself with this first stammering utterances and adopted by his fond parents and the world—recalls the tricksy little sprite who gave to that sad and solemn White House of the great war the only comic relief it knew. The years that have followed, spent in study and travel, produced an utterly different person. The Tad Lincoln of your history ceased to exist long ago. The modest and cordial young fellow who passed through New-York a few weeks ago with his mother will never be known outside of the circle of his mourning friends. But "little Tad" will be remembered as long as any live who bore a personal share in the great movements whose center for four years was at Washington.

He was so full of life and vigor—so bubbling over with health and high spirits, that he kept the house alive with his pranks and his fantastic enterprises. He was always a "chartered libertine," and after the death of his brother Willie, a prematurely serious and studious child, and the departure of Robert for college, he installed himself as the absolute tyrant of the Executive Mansion. He was idolized by both his father and mother, petted and indulged by his teachers, and fawned upon and caressed by that noisome horde of office-seekers which infested the ante-rooms of the White House. He had a very bad opinion of books and no opinion of discipline, and thought very little of any tutor who would not assist him in yoking his kids to a chair or in driving his dogs tandem over the South Lawn. He was as shrewd as he was lawless, and always knew whether he could make a tutor serviceable or not. If he found one with obstinate ideas of the superiority of grammar to kite-flying as an intellectual employment, he soon found means of getting rid of him. He had so much to do that he felt he could not waste time in learning to spell. Early in the morning you could hear his shrill pipe resounding through the dreary corridors of the Executive residence. The day passed in a rapid succession of plots and commotions, and when the President laid down his weary pen toward midnight, he generally found his infant goblin asleep under his table or roasting his curly head by the open fire-place; and the tall chief would pick up the child and trudge off to bed with the drowsy little burden on his shoulder, stooping under the doors and dodging the chandeliers. The President took infinite comfort in the child's rude health, fresh fun, and uncontrollable boisterousness. He was pleased to see him growing up in ignorance of books, but with singularly accurate ideas of practical matters. He was a fearless rider, while yet so small that his legs stuck out horizontally from the saddle. He had that power of taming and attaching animals to himself, which seems the especial gift of kindly and unlettered natures. "Let him run," the easy-going President would say; "he has time enough left to learn his letters and get pokey. Bob was just such a little rascal, and now he is a very decent boy."

It was evident that with all his insubordination and reckless mischief the spoiled child was at heart of a truthful and generous nature. He treated flatterers and office-seekers with a curious coolness and contempt, but he often espoused the cause of some poor widow or tattered soldier, whom he found waiting in the ante-rooms, and it was most amusing to see the hearty little fellow dragging his shabby protégés into the Executive presence, ordering the ushers out of the way, and demanding immediate action from headquarters. The President rarely refused a grace of this kind, and the demands were not so frequent as to lose the charm of novelty.

One of the tricks into which his idleness and his enterprise together drove him, was the occasion of much laughter to the judicious, and much horror to the respectable in Washington. He invested, one morning, all his pocket money in buying the stock in trade of an old woman who sold gingerbread near the Treasury. He made the Government carpenters give him a board and some trestles, which he set up in the imposing porte-cochere of the White House, and on this rude counter displayed his wares. Every office-seeker who entered the house that morning bought a toothsome luncheon of the keen little merchant, and when an hour after the opening of the booth a member of the household discovered the young pastryman the admired center of a group of grinning servants and toadies, he had filled his pockets and his hat with currency, the spoil of the American public. The juvenile operator made lively work of his ill-gotten gains, however, and before night was penniless again.

Although still a mere child at the death of his father, this terrible shock greatly sobered and steadied him. His brother Robert at once took charge of his education, and he made rapid progress up to the time of his sailing for Europe with his mother. He has ever since remained with her, displaying a thoughtful devotion and tenderness beyond his years, and strangely at variance with the mischievous thoughtlessness of his childhood. He came back a short while ago, greatly improved by his residence abroad, but always the same cordial, frank, warm-hearted boy. In his loss the already fearfully bereaved family will suffer a new and deep affliction, and the world, which never did and never will know him, will not withhold a tribute of regret for the child whose gayety and affection cheered more than anything else the worn and weary heart of the great President through the toilsome years of the war.

THE HEROIC AGE IN WASHINGTON[5]

No one has stood among the memorials of the Past without a feeling of intense curiosity as to the character and the life of the men who reared them. It is not the cyclopean granites of Stonehenge that fill the mind with wonder and awe as you stand in their mysterious circle on the stricken waste of Salisbury Plain. It is the vague and mystical fragments of the history of the Druids which give to that mighty ruin its tantalizing charm. And when we sail in to the Piraeus from the blue Egean, and see the Parthenon towering in its marred but immortal loveliness, like a battered coronet on the brow of the Acropolis, it is not alone its beauty and majesty that conquers and controls our hearts. It is the same tantalizing enigma as to the true character of that marvelous race which called into being this absolute perfection of form. We ask of the splintered columns and crumbling friezes the question which history but imperfectly answers. Could we but have been there! Could we but have seen the monoliths of Thebes go up into the sky of that elder Africa! Could we but have heard the first greeting which the Memnon, fresh and shining from the Theban chisels, shouted to the sun, over the Nile waters in the morning of time, how much of life and philosophy we imagine would have been plainer now. Half the joy and half the pain of travel is in this vain imagining. But these fancies all seemed to grow at once vain and delusive to me as I stood last ~~October~~ year among the brand-new ruins of Chicago. All the gray mystery of an antiquity without a beginning seemed to have fallen upon them in a night. Standing amid that vast and impressive desolation with the key in your hand, the riddle was not the less difficult to unlock. The builders are living and breathing as we are; we think the same thoughts which found expression in these broken walls and melted columns, eat and drink and love and grieve and hope and go on with work kindred to that which ~~now~~ has so suddenly taken its place in the Past. The decay which was then historical has become traditional. Even the remembrance of those ruins has been effaced in the wonder of that marble resurrection which has sprung from the incredible and dauntless energy of that vivid and virile life of the North West. ~~But can we so~~ In the space of a year you have given us three cycles of history to study, the glory the disaster and the renewal, such as would fill the annals of a thousand ordinary years. But can we say we wholly comprehend it? We are ourselves a part of the life those ruins and that Renaissance symbolize, of the civilization which they express. ~~You~~ We have heard the prayers and the oaths, the laughter and the cries, to the sound of which those walls went up. There is no unknown quantity in the problem they present. There it is—make of it what ~~you~~ we will. If ~~you~~ we come to nothing, ~~do~~ we may not blame time or history for the dust that is in ~~y~~our eyes.

It is not merely distance and the lapse of years which makes historical objects fabulous and wonderful. Moses descending from Mt. Sinai with the tables of the law was as reverend and worshipful to the children of Israel as he is to us. A child meets every day facts and fancies as strange and puzzling as the marvels of Mother Goose. It is that loyal element of belief and worship in men's hearts which makes mythologies and traditions. The time of great beliefs and passionate convictions is also the time of great deeds. The hour when a people forgets itself and struggles for a great lofty principle is its heroic age, and as time passes on the creations of poets and the adoration of believers will hang around all its events and garlands of fable. Already we begin to see the progress of their loyal religion. Only a decade has passed since the beginning of our Iliad, and yet how many names have passed into reverend tradition, have become spells to conjure with, have begun a new career as living principles and examples. The occasion was so momentous, the issues were so vast and weighty, the activities so vivid and exacting, that in those hours we had no time for weighing and sifting the significance of men and things. We have juster views of them now than we had then; perhaps those who never saw them will know them better than we. These deeds we took part in may mean something altogether different to the wider judgment of the future. History may place an entirely different value on those brothers of ours with whom we have touched elbows, whose lives lay open to us, and whose deaths were in our arms. But whether this be so or not, whether history is to rectify the errors and prepossessions of the present, or whether the wonder and reverence of posterity is to distort still further the facts of that extraordinary time, making the personages of that day loom like evening shadows vast and vague across the chronicles of the time, one thing is certain:—that those four years from 1861 to 1865 are our Heroic Age. The fables and traditions of the future springing from this date will divide the mythology of the Republic with the memories of 1776. Before the impressions of those hours pass away, it is not amiss for those who saw something of that wonderful history to compare their impressions and their reminiscences, to fix if possible some definite ideas of what they saw before it all glides away into myth and fairy fables. I hope the hour we are to pass in this way to-night will not be utterly wasted.

I do not come to rake up the ashes of old animosities. The strifes which preceded the colossal contest of 1860 are dead. They now seem as petty as our little quarrels of to-day will appear hereafter. But in that contest there was a quality which raised it above ordinary elections. There was a sudden pause for consideration—a casting up of the balance of the national life. Men asked themselves seriously whether there were anything worth fighting for in political principles. The answer was in that vast majority of Lincoln's. The first words I ever heard from him in that momentous Summer [*of 1859*] which preceded the struggle were singularly significant of this moral tendency our politics at that moment began irresistibly to take. He came into the law office where I was reading, which adjoined his own, with a copy of *Harper's Magazine* in his hand, containing Senator Douglas's famous article on Popular Sovereignty.[6] Lincoln seemed greatly roused by what he had read. Entering the office without a salutation, he said: "This will never do. He puts the moral element out of this question. It won't stay out." This was the gathering and growing conviction of the whole country. All measures had been adopted to evade the frightful responsibility of decision. But it was coming, and everybody knew it. Even those who obstinately looked and talked the other way, felt an uncomfortable assurance that they were drifting stern-foremost to the solution of the matter. There was no halting on either side. A few tranquil souls got into the muddy back-water, and looked with imbecile content on those who were plunging with the current. But they exercised no control—no influence even upon the course of events. ~~In the North and in the South alike there was a tremendous progress of opinion seen every day between the election and the inauguration of Lincoln. There was never a time, even in our history, where men always count for so little, which exhibits so plainly the tyrannous power of popular tendencies. The seeds of opinion long ago planted, which had lain apparently dead for years, suddenly germinated and burst into flower. Those Southern leaders who opposed Secession, and they were numerous and able, were heard with respectful contempt.~~ The ~~Northern~~ statesmen who met in Washington for that famous Peace Congress, which is now utterly forgotten—how many people here know anything about it?—wasted those February days in some of the cleverest and most useless talk ever uttered by man. Their words were as wise and as futile as the hootings of a congregation of politic owls that had come together in the gathering darkness, which seemed to them their congenial twilight. But it was not the gloom of night, sacred to the owls. It was the deathly obscurity of the eclipse and the hurricane. There was not a word of this weighty deliberation and discussion that reached the ears or the heart of the world. There was no hope of them as the Conference opened, there was no disappointment as it closed.[7] There was a little impatience as it went on for the time and the talk thus wasted. The country was looking toward sunset for the feet of one whose garments were rolled in blood. Contravening the natural movement of the race, the Pioneer came to the East, and the West paid with its heart and conscience the debt of its civilization. There was something singularly solemn and impressive in that progress of Lincoln to Washington [*in February 1861*]—scarcely less so than his journey home again. When in the gray of Winter twilight, from the platform of a car at the Springfield station, he bade farewell to his friends and neighbors, asking their prayers to the God "without Whose aid

I cannot succeed, and with which I cannot fail," the key-note of the journey was struck.[8] There was something of religious fervor in the welcome everywhere extended to him, and the thronging crowds that came out under the harsh skies to bid him God-speed. He took none of these honors to himself. He knew he was but the standard-bearer. The reverence and the cheers were for the flag. In this ~~very~~ city, as he looked out upon the vast assembly that had come to testify their faith to the principle he represented, he said, "These people ~~are worthy~~ know the worth of their Republic, and you can't take it away from them." He was but the symbol of the power the people honored because it was their own, and never for an hour did he forget this. So his reward was great. His love for the Republic was paid by love for him. He belonged to no Church. Yet he was the uncanonized saint of all the Churches. He never uttered a prayer in public. Yet prayers for him fastened our cause daily with golden chains around the feet of God. He was cold and ungrateful to his friends, as Republics are. And yet men who never saw him thronged at his bidding the road of death as to a festival. I do not wish to make a faultless monster of him. But he comes nearer than any man I ever knew or imagined to being a type of Democratic Republicanism incarnate.

~~Some of you may think that in going through Baltimore he did an act incompatible with heroism. But you should remember that therein he obeyed the peremptory injunctions of his civil and military advisers — of Mr. Seward, who does not lack sagacity; of Gen. Scott, who did not lack courage. There is no reason to doubt the conclusion arrived at then that a public reception would have occasioned bloodshed, and Lincoln's time was not yet come. Death in a brawl in those treason-haunted streets would have been an inglorious anticipation of that great danger.[9]~~

When he arrived in Washington, the picture was as confused and bewildering as a dissolving view. The old time was passing away, and all things had not become new. The old race of self-serving, swaggering politicians, whose ruling principle was selfishness tempered by whisky, was losing its absolute control. We had enough of them in the North. It is a product as difficult to exhaust as the Canada thistle. There are still conscript fathers among us to whom the same remark could be addressed as that which Wigfall,[10] in his last night in the Senate [*23 March 1861*], hurled at a distinguished fellow-member, who had exclaimed, in a moment of disgust, "If these things continue, I shall go and live among the Comanches." "Don't," roared Wigfall; "the Comanches are my constituents, and have already suffered sufficiently by contact with the vices of the whites." It is true that our Solons are not even yet all our fancy would paint them, but they are an improvement on the class represented by the Virginian statesman described so injuriously by Benton, who, as Benton said, when he had his hand full of trumps and his belly full of oysters would ask Heaven for nothing.[11] The flavor of whisky and tobacco has not yet departed from our politics, but it is less marked than in the good old times, when, as poor Harry Wise once said, "You had to wear your overshoes into the best society of Washington."[12] No! we are bad enough yet. There is work enough yet for the reformer in our politics. There are ~~thieves and Yahoos~~ men in Congress yet who would not adorn an evangelical tea-party, but it is not as bad a case as it was in that Winter before the war, when the North was dumb before the mighty catastrophe it foresaw, and the South was loud, and reckless, and arrogant, going forth to its secession as to a great pic-nic, with positively no thought of accountability. ~~But as it is now, there is nothing so bad in bulk as that swarm of slave-drivers who went away cursing their country and its liberties. Let us not be either uncharitable nor vainglorious. But we cannot help seeing how, when with the coming of the great Evangel of Freedom, the legion of devils that sprang from the worship of slavery was driven out of Northern hearts, they rushed into that unthinking herd which straightway plunged to the abyss of rebellion.~~ Not yet is our political body fully clothed and in its right mind, but still there was something that departed on that Fourth of March which we could well spare. The exodus has sometimes reminded me of Tennyson's lines:

> Arise and fly
> The reeling fawn, the sensual feast!
> Move onward working out the beast
> And let the ape and tiger die.

And besides the positively bad, there was much of vapid and frivolous that went at that time; of quirks and quibbles, of petty intrigue, of scouring of the outside of the cup and platter to the neglect of the weightier matters of the law. Let us eat and drink, for to-morrow we are not going to die by any means, was the unuttered motto of these sordid [*men*], and if any soul had been required of them they would have been in deadly trouble to meet the requisition. There seemed to me then, and now, a ~~profound~~ certain significance in the conversation which took place in the President's room at the Capitol, on Inauguration Day, between Buchanan and Lincoln, between the petty past and the great future.[13] The courteous old gentle-man took the new President aside for some parting words into the corner where I was standing. I waited with boyish wonder and credulity to see what momentous counsels were to come from that gray and weather-beaten head. Every word must have its value at such an instant. The ex-President said: "I think you will find the water of the right-hand well at the White-House better than that at the left," and went on with many intimate details of the kitchen and pantry. Lincoln listened with that weary, intro-verted look of his, not answering, and the next day, when I recalled the conversation, admitted he had not heard a word of it. Through every chamber of his heart and brain were resounding those solemn strains of long-suffering warning which he that day addressed to the South: "With you, not with me, rests the awful issue. Shall it be peace or the sword?"[14]

This shadow of resolute earnestness rested on every man in Washington who was worthy of the name of manhood during that month of prepara-tion. Everywhere you could see among the crowds on the avenue and in the Hotels that spirit of hushed expectancy with which we watch the piling of the clouds for a Summer storm. While there were many who hoped it might blow over or be conjured away, the most expected it, and were determined not to give way. The men in the Government meanwhile exhausted every expedient of persuasion and compromise which could be found in the arse-nal of politics, and though many of you doubtless blamed them for this, I believe the result gave them reason. The crisis was too tremendous to jus-tify them in affording to the South the slightest pretext for its ~~crime~~ action. ~~It was due to the North, it was due to the world, that they should push their patience even to the perilous verge of weakness.~~ They were right in assign-ing to the hands of the ~~criminal~~ foredoomed side the fearful task of fling-ing open the horribly-creaking gates of the temple of War.

Otherwise the result would have been less perfect and magnificent. ~~Had we not forgiven our brethren seventy times seven, it would never have been possible to have roused the North to such vast and unanimous resist-ance at last. If the current of Niagara could be dammed for ten years, the gathered torrent would wash Tammany Hall Congress clean. Everything is possible with this packed and accumulated force. A great mind forgives insults and wrongs; only a weak one forgets them. The North, for the sake of the Union, passed over a thousand affronts and injuries, but every one of them made up the sum of that mighty cry of indignation that burst all along the border at the echo of the first shot against Sumter.~~ All those blows which had seemed to break up and divide the North were but welding it together to that imposing unity with which it rose to the conflict. The day before, we had appeared hopelessly divided. But before the smell of powder disappeared from Charleston Harbor, the flag floated from every newspaper office in the country. From the opposite poles of opinion men thronged to the call of their country. Long-estranged enemies stood shoulder to shoulder; Gov. Andrew gave into the hands of Ben Butler the sword of the Puritans.[15] The coldest conservatives sprang forward to the front and the wildest radicals kept time with the new music. Douglas and Lincoln joined hands. Millard Fillmore put on the uniform of a militiaman, and Wendell Phillips stood for the first time in his life under the Star and Stripes, and "welcomed the tread of Massachusetts men marshaled for war."[16]

> Throughout the land there goes a cry:
> A sudden splendor fills the sky.
> From every hill the banners burst
> Like buds by April breezes nurst.
> In every hamlet, home, and mart
> The fine beat of a single heart
> Keeps time to strains whose pulses mix
> Our blood with that of Seventy-six!

In the awe of that sudden awakening, men saw clearly the hand of God, and even the shrill voice of the agitator was hushed. At the session of the Wyoming Conference [*of the Methodist Church*], in place of the usual resolution against Slavery, they said *Whereas*, Divine Providence has taken the work of emancipation into His own hands; therefore, *Resolved*, That we stand still, and see the salvation of God.

It is not often given to the life of a nation to see a moment of moral exaltation like this. The world may wait long before it will see again a gathering like that of the manhood of the nation which swept down almost with the swiftness of thought to Washington and the border. You know when the quota of the States were full, how those who were left out clamored to get in. How they overflowed the limits of their own States, and gave infinite trouble to the mustering officers by their change of venue. They committed perjuries and frauds to get a chance to be shot at. And among those who came in those first splendid days was to be found the finest flower of our great Western civilization. What recruits they were! One Rhode Island company had a half-dozen millionaires in the ranks.[17] And, what is far better than millionaires, there were parsons, and scholars, and poets, men of wit and men of genius, willing to waste the spoil of the ages they had accumulated in study, as a mere protest of civilization against barbarism. That was the army which England called a horde of hirelings enlisted to butcher the gentlemen of the South. England said that in English—and so we understood and remembered it. But let us not be unjust to the Motherland. The whole world repeated the taunt in its various dialects. Russia did not, nor did Patagonia, for the same reason. They did not know enough about us even to make a mistake. But the Diplomatic Body, posted in Washington for the express purpose of telling the truth about us, sent nothing over the ocean but calumnies and misrepresentations. What a farce it all was! These off-shoots of aristocracy or fungus-growths of despotism, the diplomats of Washington burrowing like moles away from the fierce light of a dawning epoch, stuffing their ears with cotton that they might deny the existence of the storm of lightning and thunder which was clearing the foul air of its long-gathered poisons. The ancient philosophers said that the music of the spheres was so loud we could not hear it. The blaze of that boreal light was so bright that not a man in the diplomatic service at Washington could see it. Yet every street and avenue swarmed with heroes. Men worthy of the myth of romance crowded the hills around Washington. Why should I enumerate names? Each heart here recalls a different one, and feels that no words could do justice to his memory. But I will mention two whom I knew most intimately, whose names have been consecrated by death as the first conspicuous victims of the solemn sacrifice—Baker and Ellsworth.[18]

Of Baker I do not speak as a politician, though he had attained the highest place open to a foreigner; nor as a lawyer, though distinguished at the bar of three States; nor as a soldier, although the magic and magnetism of his presence once brought victory to our flag on the rocky slope of Cerro Gordo. But there was something almost superhuman about Senator Baker as an orator. He was ~~almost utterly~~ unknown in the East, for his great successes were attained at an early day in the West, where there were few journals and no reporters. He could not write a speech. He was forced to depend upon the stimulus of the occasion for all he accomplished. But that was always sufficient. He never rose without making a better speech than he intended. No one who ever saw him in action, the grand and simple presence, the thin gray hair, the eye that flashed pale fire, the eagle face, and heard that silver snarling trumpet of his voice, could ever dismiss the vision from his mind. Two or three times he was supremely great. At the funeral of Broderick he mourned the death of that brave and generous rowdy in strains of lyric beauty as fine as any uttered over the urns of the dead victors of Marathon.[19] At the great meeting in the Union-square [*in New York*], in April [*1861*], he was the only orator up to the level of the august occasion. But his last speech was perhaps the most intensely dramatic. He was stationed at Ball's Bluff with his regiment, and riding into town one day, he dismounted at the Capitol, and walked, booted and spurred, with the dust of the road on his uniform, into the Senate Chamber. The Kentucky Lucifer, John C. Breckinridge, was making a brilliant and impassioned plea for the Rebellion.[20] As he concluded, Baker, moved by a sudden and irresistible impulse, threw down his hat and his gauntlets, and, striding to his seat, claimed the floor. It was granted him, and he delivered, without an instant's preparation, a full, complete, and rounded oration, not less distinguished by its law and its logic than by its beauty and energy of utterance. A few days later he was dead—pierced through and through by Rebel lead on that fatal bluff of the Potomac, a victim of the pitiable vacillation which then paralyzed the military arm. He was grandly buried, and nobly praised in the Senate House. [*Massachusetts Senator Charles*] Sumner called him the Prince Rupert of battle and debate. Yet, in spite of this preeminence of genius and place, though he was the first Senator who had ever died in fight, he had made such rare and swift apparitions in public that the fame he so eagerly hungered for has been denied him; and if you find anything of exaggeration in my words about him, it is only another proof of the insufficiency of co[n]temporary evidence in dealing with its phenomenal men.

But if Baker is ill-known, Ellsworth has fared still more hardly. This brilliant meteor, which shone with such ~~blinding~~ light for a moment in our sky and then went out forever, has left no trail of truthful history. Often I have heard the remarks, "He was lucky in his death. He was a short-boy, or a charlatan, or a fop." I will believe no one in the world knew him so well as I did, and I have no authority to force my knowledge of him upon the world. From the hour when I first met him, when he was a penniless law-student, eating dry bread to save his pennies for books, he shared my scanty purse and I shared his magnificent dreams. And I will say this of him, that I never yet saw so much of manhood embraced within five feet and a half from spur to plume. He was a soldier born to command men, and he was an artist also, a ready and persuasive stump speaker, a close, relentless student, but everything in him was subordinate to a feverish and passionate love of arms and lust of fame. He had that intense and romantic devotion to the flag which is only seen among young and imaginative men. I have seen him take the colors in his hands and caress them as a mother does her child. He was, perhaps, not a man of our time. He was too purely a soldier to be a perfect Republican. He was full of reveries of conquest. ~~Before the war began, in Springfield, one day, when the question of peaceable secession was under discussion, he swept his hand angrily over a map of Mexico which hung on the wall of his garret, and said: "There is an unanswerable argument against the recognition of the Southern Confederacy."~~ At 20 years of age he had matured a plan for the conquest of Mexico by armed emigration, and anything which trenched upon this fancy of his he considered a personal wrong to himself. In his poverty and hunger he never gave up his arrogant claims upon the future. People who saw these fantastic and grotesque pretensions in the shabby boy dismissed him without a further thought. They did not know the enormous strength and industry and capacity which made his conceit and arrogance reasonable. A good deal is pardonable in a youth who knows he can manage all the men of his age whom he meets, who can work twenty-four hours without rest or sleep. There are men who say he died in an act of reckless audacity. True; but a youth of 22 who never does anything rash will not be worth killing when he grows older. His death was not without result. It kept some young men out of the army; it drew many in. The Forty-Fourth New-York was his fittest monument.[21] He received the consecration of tears from men to whom they were unknown. As I stood by his corpse at the Navy-Yard, a Fire Zouave, whose ugly face had been washed almost clean with brine, said to me: "Did you know him?" "Yes." "Then," he replied, in a voice broken by sobs, "you knowed the bulliest little cuss that ever stood around in a pair of boots." I have never heard a more heartfelt eulogy. Sometimes we think he should have died hereafter. But who knows? It is by the bier of men like this that we are assailed by the burning questions of immortality. It is there we feel how impossible it is that such a wealth of life, of force, of intelligence should be annihilated. Somewhere that soul of fire pursues its ardent career. Somewhere that soul of fire pursues its ardent career. Somewhere that keen and imperious spirit is working and striving, casting new schemes and marshaling new clans along the lines of limitless development.

But the heroism of that time was not confined to the ranks of the fighting men — not to the men at all. The soldiers who poured out their blood upon the frozen fields performed no more precious service than the women who filled every camp and hospital with the light of their purity and their loving charity. Here all words become weak. It is to suit such occasions as those that all the songs and romances which have been written since the birth of literature in honor of women were made. ~~Every age in its own way has worshipped women. There was a true reverence in the chisel that carved the imposing beauty of Our Lady of Milo. A virile devotion to woman, which they imagined to be religion, gave that miraculous power to the matchless pencils of Raphael and Murillo. Dante and Shakespeare have given us in still more enduring verse the high ideals of feminine worth and loveliness. But it will require the united excellences of all these masters to fitly embody those impulses of unutterable devotion and gratitude excited by the conduct of American women in those days.~~ Your hearts go before me to recall all they did. Over the horror and the savagery of war the story of their labors and their love floats with a tenderness and beauty which is all divine. It gilds the darker pictures over which it hovers, like the halo woven of mist and rainbows which hangs forever in caressing loveliness over the rushing terror of Niagara. And not alone those who went out to the wars, but those silent saints and martyrs of the household displayed a glory of heroism and by whose light The Diadems of the Angels are made dim. For thousands of years the world has quoted and admired that saying of the Spartan mother to her son when she gave him his shield, "Come home with it, or on it." But that was the expression of a personal impulse of pride and courage. Beyond the pride of the American mother in her son, was her love of country, and high enthroned above her love of country was that devotion to ~~the principles of freedom~~ principle by which her soul was anchored fast to the immutable throne of Heaven. No higher point of heroism was ever reached by mortal than that of the Boston mother, who said to Gov. Andrew at the funeral of her only son slain in a disastrous battle: "I was proud and grateful when you gave William his commission. I am prouder and more grateful now." The stream can rise no higher than its source. Whenever we saw an exceptional jet of virtue or nobility darting up into the Southern sky, shaking its pure diamond lights and flashes in the air, we could be sure there was a higher and purer fountain of ~~purity~~ patriotism and virtue, far away in the Northern hills, in the heart of ~~his~~ a mother.

Of course there was much in those days which was mean and sordid. The comedy of selfishness is never lacking to any such scene.[22] But it really appears to me now that the proportion was about the same as that of farce to tragedy in the old-fashioned theaters—one act of farce to five of tragedy. I remember Mr. Lincoln once estimated with some disgust the number of office-seekers who visited Washington at 30,000; but, he quickly added, "There are some 30,000,000 who ask for no offices." But those who came were either of a singularly aggravated type, or the circumstances of the time made one impatient of their peculiarities. There is no one who can appreciate the tightness of a shoe except the man whose toe is pinched; and so the heart of the office-seeker knoweth its own bitterness. To him, the disposition of his post-office was a matter of more account than a battle or an earthquake. A dozen times the same dispatch was received in different names. "Unless Muggins gets the Podunk P.O. the Republican party is dead in this State." You rarely found an office-seeker who wanted a place for its own sake. He wanted to help the cause, and could do it better from that vantage ground than from any other. Their spirit of disinterested abnegation was crystallized in that classic joke of Artemus Ward, who said that he had already given one second cousin to the war, and rather than not have the war prosecuted he would sacrifice all his wife's relations.[23] It was not always avarice that drove men to office-seeking. They were often worthy people who had carried their precinct for the ticket and wanted recognition. I knew one high-toned gentleman who sold out a flourishing business and accepted an unpaid Consulate in Norway, where he shivered through an Arctic night of six months, simply to show his neighbors he possessed the confidence of the administration. There never was a President who so little as Lincoln admitted personal considerations in the distribution of places. He rarely gave a place to a friend—still more rarely because he *was* a friend. He had one characteristic which was often imputed him as a fault, but which I think a most creditable quality. He was entirely destitute of gratitude for political services rendered to himself. He filled his Cabinet with enemies and rivals, and refused any reward to those energetic politicians who did so much to nominate him in Chicago.[24] This, I cannot but think, is true Republicanism. The Republic is ungrateful. It ought to be. It is worthy of our best work without gratitude. It accepts our best service as Heaven accepts our prayers, not because either needs them, but because it is good for us to serve and to worship. There was a whimsical incident illustrating this ingratitude of Lincoln. At a dark period of the war, a gentleman of some local prominence came to Washington for some purpose, and so as to obtain the assistance of Lincoln, he brought a good deal of evidence to prove that he was the man who originated his nomination. He attacked the great chief in the vestibule of the Executive Mansion, and walked with him to the War Department, impressing this view upon him. When the President went in his Warwick "waited patiently about till Lincoln did appear." He walked back to the White-House with him, clinching his argument with new and cogent facts. At the door the President turned, and, with that smile which was half sadness and half fun, he said: "So you think you made me President?" "Yes, Mr. President, under Providence, I think I did." "Well," said Lincoln, opening the door and going in, "it's a pretty mess you've got me into. But I forgive you."

Nothing was more remarkable, during the whole progress of the war, than that gradual growth and consolidation of opinion which at last assured and accomplished the victory and prepared the reconstruction. The first rush to arms was rather at the bidding of an earnest patriotism to defend the flag and "redress wrongs long enough endured" than the result of any logical reasoning process. But as the fight went on, month by month and year by year, in spite of all temporary reverses and checks, it was to be seen that the circle of fire was continually narrowing around the Rebellion, and the issue ceased to be doubtful. The conviction of ultimate triumph never deserted the best men at headquarters. You remember how Gen. Sherman spoke of Grant's assurance of victory—which resembled, Sherman says, "a Christian's faith in his Savior." It was the same with Lincoln. Even the morning after Bull Run, when many thought seriously of the end, he said, with some impatience, "There is nothing in this except the lives lost and the lives which must be lost to make it good." There was probably no one who regretted bloodshed and disaster more than he, and no one who estimated the consequences of defeat more lightly. He was often for a moment impatient at loss of time, and yet he was not always sure that this was not a part of the necessary scheme. There are those who think his tranquillity in those terrible scenes was shallowness or unthinking levity. There could be no greater error. The solemnity which you see in the Gettysburg address and the Second Inaugural is but a shadow of the momentous spiritual contests which he fought out alone with his own questioning soul. I have here a paper written by him, in a time of profound national gloom, with religious soul-searching, never intended to be published nor to be seen by other eyes than his own. ~~To-night for the first time it is made known to others than myself.~~ You shall see how this patriarch and prophet wrestled in secret with his God:

"The will of God prevails. In great contests each party claims to act in accordance with the will of God. Both *may* be, and one *must* be wrong. God can not be *for* and *against* the same thing at the same time. In the present civil war it is quite possible that God's purpose is something different from the purpose of either party—and yet the human instrumentalities, working just as they do, are of the best adaptation to effect this purpose. I am almost ready to say this is probably true—that God wills this contest, and wills that it shall not end yet. By His mere great power on the minds of the now contestants, He could have either *saved* or *destroyed* the Union without a human contest. Yet the contest began. And having begun, He could give the final victory to either side any day. Yet the contest proceeds."[25]

I know of nothing in the whole range of history or of literature more remarkable than this paper—this unflinching facing of absolute truth—this cold cross-examination of omnipotence. Many men are honest with each other. This one was mercilessly honest with himself. In these deeply-solemn musings, which carried him down to the very bed-rock of things, he passed a large portion of his time during the Summer of 1862; and they produced the act which is more his own than any other of his life—the Proclamation of Emancipation. His singular justness of spirit was displayed in his treatment of this question before it was finally decided. If any one tried to dissuade him from it, he gave the argument in its favor. If others urged it upon him, he exhausted the reasoning against it. Even when it was resolved upon, written, copied, and lying in his desk only waiting promulgation, a delegation of clergymen waited on him to insist upon such a measure, and he confounded them all by his close and logical argument against it. They went away sorrowful, and a few days after, like lightning from a clear sky, came the long-pondered liberating word, melting with a flash four million shackles.[26]

In the later years of the war there was less of this doubt and reverie. A certain assurance of the result had come to be generally accepted, and Washington had like the Mithridates supped so long upon the poison of sensations that they had become her natural food and ceased to affect her. When Early came up the Valley in 1864 and thundered at the very gates of the Capitol, there was less excitement in Washington about it than there was in New-York.[27] In the morning of the battle fought in the Northern suburb, though every discharge of the guns shook all the windows in Washington on the way to the front, I saw no excitement among its tranquil citizens, except among those who had put on their best clothes and hired buggies to take their sweethearts out to see the fight, and were turned back by the hard-hearted guard. ~~And in the evening, after the repulse of the enemy, when a party went out to bury the dead, when the shallow graves were ready, the corporal sung out, "Mourners to the front. Draw pocket-handkerchers." Like Hamlet's grave-digger, the fellow had no feeling of his vocation.~~ An almost unnatural serenity took the place of the feverish interest with which the war had begun. One night, when Burnside was at Knoxville, and Longstreet had gone from Chattanooga to capture or destroy him, a dispatch came from [*Union General John Gray*] Foster, at Cumberland Gap, saying, "Scouts just in report hearing firing in the direction of Knoxville." I took it to the President. He read it, and said, "That is good." I expressed my surprise at his taking so cheerful a view of Burnside's deadly danger. He said, "I had a neighbor out West, a Sally Taggart, who had a great many unruly children whom she did not take very good care of. Whenever she heard one squall in some out-of-the-way place, she would say, 'Well, thank Goodness, there's one of my young ones not dead yet!' As long as we hear guns, Burnside is not captured."[28]

As the great struggle neared its close, the impatience of early days, the hot and righteous anger against the wrong, began to give way, and that commonest ~~fault~~ trait of noble minds, excessive magnanimity and generosity, was clearly indicated as the political danger that threatened the new Administration. Not only in the President was this conspicuous—this malice toward none, this charity for all—but in those most trusted members of his Cabinet, who had seen the war through from its beginning, there was the same tendency. There could have been no harshness of punishment or example with a government of which Lincoln was the head and Seward the Prime Minister. The history of governments affords few instances of an official connection hallowed by a friendship so absolute and sincere as that which existed between these two magnanimous spirits. Lincoln had snatched away from Seward at Chicago the prize of a laborious life-time, when it seemed within his grasp. Yet Seward was the first man named in his Cabinet and the first who acknowledged his personal preeminence. There were others who never could see or comprehend the greatness of the Western Statesman. Jung Stilling said of Goethe, ~~falsely,~~ that his heart, which few knew, was as great as his mind, which all knew. Seward had acumen and generosity enough to see and admit that this goodness of heart, which every one talked about, was the least of Lincoln's claims to respect. There were many distinguished people who would go to the White House with the intention of patting the President on the head, and who generally came away confused and dissatisfied at finding he stood six feet four in his slippers. Seward was the first man who recognized this, and from the beginning of the Administration to that dark and terrible hour when they were both struck down by the hand of murderous treason, there was no shadow of jealousy or doubt ever disturbed their mutual confidence and regard. The only word of regret at Lincoln's superior fortune I ever heard from the Secretary was a noble and touching one, at the hour when the fight of faction had grown fiercest. "Lincoln always got the advantage of me, but I never envied ~~so much as in~~ him anything but his death." On that Good Friday morning, when for the first time in four years the sound of hostile guns was silent, and the fighting men had already turned the toes of their army shoes homeward, the best and most powerful friends the South had in the world were the President and his Chief Secretary. Yet we may be sure that that most precious of sacrifices was in that great fated purpose which takes in the world in its scope. The nation was welded again into one mind by the death and burial of its prophet-leader, just as it was by the first shot against the flag. A Peter the Hermit preaching a Holy war with that fiery tongue of his was not more eloquent than the dumb corpse of Lincoln, moving home in triumph. In the princely palace of Liechtenstein, at Vienna, there is a great canvas of Rubens called the Triumph of Decius. The warrior lies dead in his car, his white face staring sternly at the sky, around him the golden spoils of sack and battle and the sacred laurels of victory; and bound to his chariot wheels throng princes and leaders, the clanking of whose fetters soothe the fierce soul of the hero on his way to the shades. It was superbly impressive.

The very spirit of the old glory of force and violence was there. But I could only think how vastly fuller of the better grandeur of a freer age was that funeral march of Lincoln to those sunset prairies of his love. Around his catafalk thronged the mourning people he had served so purely. The tearful benedictions of ransomed millions called forever down upon him the cherishing smile of God. In the ~~solemn~~ chiming of the silver-throated bells you might hear the echoing chorus, Well done! and almost fancy in the solemn hush of his midnight pauses the awful rushing of unseen wings as of the convoying legions of the just made perfect. That was the apotheosis of the hero. He had fought the good fight. He had kept the faith. He had become a spiritual force and essence. His great character and example went abroad on the wings of every wind that blew.

The mob of France by one cent subscriptions made a great gold medal of him. A friend of mine found a peasant family in the Hartz mountains crying like children over the news of his death. A member of the Austrian Reichsrath [*Parliament*] said to me, "Already he has become a Myth, a Demigod, a type of ideal Democracy."[29] It needed not even his death to give him this supernatural character among the humble people of his own land. In a prayer-meeting at Hilton Head one night a young negro said he would like to see Linkum. A gray-headed patriarch rebuked the rash wish, saying "No man see Linkum. Linkum walk as Jesus walk. No man see Linkum."[30]

This is the true touchstone of the heroic man and the heroic age, if living he is a toiler and dead he is a principle. Lincoln needed no lapse of years to become immortal. In one flash of blinding light he sprang fullpanoplied into the religion of the peoples.

As in the old tragedies, after the fall of the hero came the ~~fanfare~~ flourish of the trumpets and the entry of the forces, so after Lincoln had gone from Washington came in the victorious soldiers. It seems to me no such touching pageant was ever seen. There was not a regiment with half its complement of men. There was scarcely a soldier or an officer with a whole uniform. There was scarcely a banner but what was blackened with smoke and riddled with the fiery hail of fight. Yet as it marched past the reviewing generals, past Grant, and Sherman, and Stanton, and the representatives of the Old World all in gala dress, no one doubted any more that this was the greatest army that ever went to war. In that colossal and inspiring picture of Kaulbach, which shows the legendary fight of Attila, then on two fields and two contests, the one between the soldiers striving in deadly combat on the turf, and the other a shadowy battle set in the upper air, among the ghosts of the heroes slain below.[31] So all hearts that day were divided in reverence and gratitude between our two armies, the one on its way homeward crowned with love and laurels preparing its own unselfish disarmament and its return to the peaceful interests of the country it had saved; and the men of the other, invisible forevermore in those wasted columns, who had gained their promotion on the battle-field to a higher and wider sphere of duty, fulfilling now the scheme of the Lord of Hosts in some activity above the clouds. Thus they passed on, the victors and the martyrs. Out of the army into peace, out of our sorrow into holy memories. And with the sweet and thrilling sounds of the bugles and the rising dust of the columns smitten into golden glory by the sun setting over Georgetown Heights, passed away the Heroic Age from Washington.

Life in the White House in the Time of Lincoln[32]

The daily life of the White House during the momentous years of Lincoln's presidency had a character of its own, different from that of any previous or subsequent time. In the first days after the inauguration there was the unprecedented rush of office seekers, inspired by a strange mixture of enthusiasm and greed, pushed by motives which were perhaps at bottom selfish, but which had nevertheless a curious touch of that deep emotion which had stirred the heart of the nation in the late election. They were not all ignoble; among that dense crowd that swarmed in the staircases and the corridors, there were many well-to-do men who were seeking office to their own evident damage, simply because they wished to be a part, however humble, of a government which they had aided to put in power and to which they were sincerely devoted. Many of the suitors who presented so piteous a figure in those early days of 1861 afterwards marched, with the independent dignity of a private soldier, in the ranks of the Union Army, or rode at the head of their regiments like men born to command. There were few who had not a story worth listening to, if there were time and opportunity. But the numbers were so great, the competition so keen, that they ceased for the moment to be regarded as individuals, drowned as they were in the general sea of solicitation. Few of them received office; when, after weeks of waiting one of them got access to the President, he was received with kindness by a tall melancholy-looking man, sitting at a desk with his back to a window which opened upon a fair view of the Potomac, who heard his story with a gentle patience, took his papers and referred them to one of the Departments, and that was all; the fatal pigeonholes devoured them. As time wore on, the offices were filled, the throng of eager aspirants diminished and faded away. When the war burst out, an immediate transformation took place. The house was again invaded and overrun by a different class of visitors; youths who wanted commissions in the regulars; men who wished to raise irregular regiments or battalions without regard to their state authorities; men who wanted to furnish stores to the army; inventors full of great ideas and in despair at the apathy of the world; later, an endless stream of officers in search of promotion or desirable assignments. And from first to last, there were the politicians and statesmen in Congress and out, each of whom felt that they had the right by virtue of their representative capacity to as much of the President's time as they chose, and who never considered that they were many hundreds and that the President was but one.

It would be hard to imagine a state of things less conducive to serious and effective work, yet in one way or another, the work was done. In the midst of a crowd of visitors who began to arrive early in the morning and who were put out, grumbling, by the servants who closed the doors at midnight, the President pursued those labors which will carry his name to distant ages. There was little order or system about it; ~~his secretaries~~ those around him strove from beginning to end, to erect barriers to defend him against constant interruption, but the President himself was always the first to break them down. He disliked anything that kept people from him who wanted to see him, and although the continual contact with importunity which he could not satisfy, and distress which he could not always relieve, wore terribly upon him and made him an old man before his time, he would never take the necessary measures to defend himself. He continued, to the end, receiving these swarms of visitors, every one of whom, even the most welcome, took something from him, in the way of wasted nervous force. [*Massachusetts Senator*] Henry Wilson once remonstrated with him about it: "You will wear yourself out." He replied, with one of those smiles in which there was so much of sadness, "They don't want much; they get but little, and I must see them."[33] In most cases he could do them no good, and it afflicted him to see he could not make them understand the impossibility of granting their requests. One hot afternoon a private soldier who had somehow got access to him, persisted, after repeated explanations that his case was one to be settled by his immediate superiors, in begging that the President would give it his personal attention. Lincoln at last burst out, "Now, my man, go away! I cannot attend to all these details. I could as easily bail out the Potomac with a spoon."[34]

Of course it was not all pure waste; Mr. Lincoln gained much of information, something of cheer and encouragement from these visits. He particularly enjoyed conversing with officers of the army and navy, newly arrived from the field or from sea. He listened with the eagerness of a child over a fairy tale to [James A.] Garfield's graphic account of the battle of Chickamauga; he was always delighted with the wise and witty sailor-talk of [John A.] Dahlgren, [Gustavus V.] Fox and [Henry A.] Wise.[35] Sometimes a word fitly spoken had its results. When R. B. Ayres called on him, in company with Senator [Ira] Harris, and was introduced as a captain of artillery who had taken part in a recent unsuccessful engagement, he asked "How many guns did you take in?" "Six" Ayres answered. "How many did you bring out?" the President asked, maliciously. "Eight." This unexpected reply did much to gain Ayres his merited promotion.[36]

The President rose early, as his sleep was light and capricious. In the summer, when he lived at the Soldiers' Home,[37] he would take his frugal breakfast and ride into town in time to be at his desk at eight o'clock. He began to receive visits nominally at ten o'clock, but long before that hour struck the doors were besieged by anxious crowds, through whom the people of importance, Senators and members of Congress, elbowed their way after the fashion which still survives. On days when the Cabinet met, Tuesdays and Fridays, the hour of noon closed the interviews of the morning. On other days it was the President's custom, at about that hour, to order the doors to be opened and all who were waiting, to be admitted. The crowd would rush in, thronging the narrow room, and one by one, would make their wants known. Some came merely to shake hands, to wish him Godspeed; their errand was soon done. Others came asking help or mercy; they usually pressed forward, careless, in their pain, as to what ears should overhear their prayer. But there were many who lingered in the rear and leaned against the wall, hoping each to be the last, that they might in tete a tete unfold their schemes for their own advantage or their neighbor's hurt. These were often disconcerted by the President's loud and hearty,

"Well, friend, what can I do for you?" which compelled them to speak, or retire and wait [*for*] a more convenient season.

The inventors were more a source of amusement than of annoyance. They were usually men of some originality of character, not infrequently carried to eccentricity. Lincoln had a quick comprehension of mechanical principles, and often detected a flaw in an invention which the contriver had overlooked. He would sometimes go out into the waste fields that then lay south of the Executive Mansion to test an experimental gun or torpedo. He used to quote with much merriment the solemn dictum of one rural inventor that "a gun ought not to rekyle; if it rekyled at all, it ought to rekyle a little forrid."[38] He was particularly interested in the first rude attempts at the afterwards famous mitrailleuses [*machine guns*]; on one occasion he worked one with his own hands at the Arsenal, and sent forth peals of Homeric laughter as the balls, which had not power to penetrate the target set up at a little distance, came bounding back among the shins of the bye-standers. He accompanied Colonel Hiram Berdan one day to the camp of his sharp-shooters and there practiced in the trenches his long-disused skill with the rifle. A few fortunate shots from his own gun, and his pleasure at the still better marksmanship of Berdan led to the arming of that admirable regiment with breech loaders.[39]

At luncheon time he had literally to run the gauntlet through the crowds who filled the corridors between his office and the rooms at the west end of the house occupied by the family. The afternoon wore away in much the same manner as the morning; late in the day he usually drove out for an hour's airing; at six o'clock he dined. He was one of the most abstemious of men; the pleasures of the table had few attractions for him. His breakfast was an egg and a cup of coffee; at luncheon he rarely took more than a biscuit and a glass of milk, a plate of fruit in its season; at dinner he ate sparingly of one or two courses. He drank little or no wine; not that he remained always on principle a total abstainer, as he was during a part of his early life, in the favor of the "Washingtonian" reform;[40] but he never cared for wine or liquors of any sort, and never used tobacco.

There was little gaiety in the Executive house during his time. It was an epoch, if not of gloom, at least of a seriousness too intense to leave room for much mirth. There were the usual formal entertainments, the traditional state dinners and receptions, conducted very much as they have been ever since. The great public receptions, with their vast rushing multitudes pouring past him to shake hands, he rather enjoyed; they were not a disagreeable task to him, and he seemed surprised when people commiserated him upon them. He would shake hands with thousands of people, seemingly unconscious of what he was doing, murmuring some monotonous salutation as they went by, his eye dim, his thoughts far withdrawn; then suddenly he would see some familiar face,—his memory for faces was very good—and his eye would brighten and his whole form grow attentive; he would greet the visitor with a hearty grasp and a ringing word and dismiss him with a cheery laugh that filled the Red Room with infectious good nature. Many people armed themselves with an appropriate speech to be delivered on these occasions, but unless it was compressed into the smallest possible space, it never got utterance; the crowd would jostle the peroration out of shape. If it were brief enough and hit the President's fancy, it generally received a swift answer. One night an elderly gentleman from Buffalo said "Up our way, we believe in God and Abraham Lincoln," to which the President replied, shoving him along the line, "My friend, you are more than half right."

During the first year of the administration the house was made lively by the games and pranks of Mr. Lincoln's two younger children, William and Thomas—Robert, the elder was away at Harvard, only coming home for short vacations. The two little boys, aged eight and ten, with their western independence and enterprise, kept the house in an uproar. They drove their tutor wild with their good natured disobedience; they organized a minstrel show in the attic; they made acquaintance with the office seekers and became the hot champions of the distressed. William was, with all his boyish frolic, a child of great promise, capable of close application and study. He had a fancy for drawing up railway time tables, and would conduct an imaginary train from Chicago to New York with perfect precision. He wrote childish verses, which sometimes attained the unmerited honors of print. But this bright, gentle, studious child sickened and died in February 1862. His father was profoundly moved by his death, though he gave no outward sign of his trouble, but kept about his work the same as ever. His bereaved heart seemed afterwards to pour out its fulness on his youngest child. He was a merry, warm-blooded, kindly little boy, perfectly lawless and full of odd fancies and inventions, the chartered libertine of the Executive Mansion. He ran continually in and out of his father's cabinet, interrupting his gravest labors and conversations with his bright, rapid and very imperfect speech — for he had an impediment which made his articulation almost unintelligible, until he was nearly grown. He would perch upon his father's knee and sometimes even on his shoulder while the most weighty conferences were going on. Sometimes, escaping from the domestic authorities, he would take refuge in that sanctuary for the whole evening, dropping to sleep at last on the floor, when the President would pick him up and carry him tenderly to bed.[41]

Mr. Lincoln's life was almost devoid of recreation. He sometimes went to the theatre, and was particularly fond of a play of Shakespeare well acted. He was so delighted with Hackett in Falstaff that he wrote him a letter of warm congratulation which pleased the veteran actor so much that he gave it to the New York Herald, which printed it with abusive comments. Hackett was greatly mortified and made suitable apologies; upon which the President wrote to him again in the kindliest manner saying: "Give yourself no uneasiness on the subject. . . . I certainly did not expect to see my note in print; yet I have not been much shocked by the comments upon it. They are a fair specimen of what has occurred to me through life. I have endured a great deal of ridicule, without much malice; and have received a great deal of kindness, not quite free from ridicule. I am used to it." This incident had the usual sequel; the veteran comedian asked for an office, which the President was not able to give him and the pleasant acquaintance ceased.[42] A hundred times this experience was repeated; a man would be introduced to the President whose disposition and talk were agreeable; he took pleasure in his conversation for two or three interviews and then this congenial person would ask some favor impossible to grant, and go away in bitterness of spirit. It is a cross that every President must bear.

Mr. Lincoln spent most of his evenings in his office, though occasionally he remained in the drawing room after dinner, conversing with visitors or listening to music, for which he had an especial liking, though he was not versed in the science and preferred simple ballads to more elaborate compositions. In his office, he was not often suffered to be alone; he frequently passed the evening there with a few friends in frank and free conversation. If the company was all of one sort, he was at his best; his wit and rich humor had free play; he was once more the Lincoln of the Eighth Circuit, the cheeriest of talkers, the riskiest of story tellers; but if a stranger came in, he put on in an instant his whole armor of dignity and reserve.

He had a singular discernment of men; he would talk of the most important political and military concerns with a freedom which often amazed his intimates, but we do not recall an instance in which this confidence was misplaced.

Where only one or two were present, he was fond of reading aloud. He passed many of the summer evenings in this way when occupying his cottage at the Soldiers' Home. He would there read Shakespeare for hours with a single secretary for audience.[43] The plays he most affected were Hamlet, Macbeth, and the series of Histories; among the latter, he never tired of Richard the Second. The terrible outburst of grief and despair into which Richard falls in the Third Act, had a peculiar fascination for him; we have heard him read it at Springfield, at the White House and the Soldiers' Home.

> For heaven's sake, let us sit upon the ground,
> And tell sad stories of the death of kings: —
> How some have been deposed, some slain in war;
> Some haunted by the ghosts they have deposed;
> Some poisoned by their wives, some sleeping killed;
> All murdered: — For within the hollow crown
> That rounds the mortal temples of a king,
> Keeps death his court: and there the antick sits
> Scoffing his state and grinning at his pomp;
> Allowing him a breath, a little scene
> To monarchize, be feared, and kill with looks;
> Infusing him with self and vain conceit, —
> As if this flesh which walls about our life,
> Were brass impregnable; and humored thus,
> Comes at the last, and with a little pin
> Bores through his castle wall, and farewell, King![44]

He read Shakespeare more than all other writers together. He made no attempt to keep pace with the ordinary literature of the day. Sometimes he read a scientific work with keen appreciation but he pursued no systematic course. He owed less to reading than most men. He delighted in Burns; he said one day after reading those exquisite lines to Glencairn, beginning "The bridegroom may forget the bride," that "Burns never touched a sentiment without carrying it to its ultimate expression and leaving nothing further to be said." Of Thomas Hood he was also excessively fond. He often read aloud "The Haunted House." He would go to bed with a volume of Hood in his hands, and would sometimes rise at midnight and, traversing the long halls of the Executive Mansion in his night clothes, would come to his secretary's room and read something that especially pleased him. He wanted to share his enjoyment of the writer; it was dull pleasure to him to laugh alone.[45] He read Bryant and Whittier with appreciation; there were many poems of Holmes that he read with intense relish. "The Last Leaf" was one of his favorites; he knew it by heart, and used often to repeat with deep feeling,

> The mossy marbles rest
> On the lips that he has pressed
>   In their bloom;
> And the names he loved to hear,
> Have been carved for many a year,
>   On the tomb;

giving the marked Southwestern pronunciation of the words "hear" and "year." A poem by James Knox "Oh Why Should the Spirit of Mortal be Proud" he learned by heart in his youth, and used to repeat all his life.[46]

Upon all but two classes the President made the impression of unusual power as well as of unusual goodness. He failed only in the case of those who judged men by a purely conventional standard of breeding, and upon those so poisoned by political hostility that the testimony of their own eyes and ears became untrustworthy. He excited no emotion but one of contempt in the finely-tempered mind of Hawthorne; several English tourists have given the most distorted pictures of his speech and his manners.[47] Some Southern writers who met him in the first days of 1861, spoke of him as a drunken, brawling boor, whose mouth dripped with oaths and tobacco—when in truth, whiskey and tobacco were as alien to his lips as profanity. There is a story current in England, as on the authority of the late Lord Lyons, on the coarse jocularity with which he once received a formal diplomatic communication—but as Lord Lyons told the story [*marginal note:* to John Hay] there was nothing objectionable about it.[48] The British Minister called at the White House to announce the marriage of the Prince of Wales. He made the formal speech appropriate to the occasion; the President replied in the usual conventional manner. The requisite formalities having thus been executed, the President took the bachelor diplomatist by the hand, saying "And now, Lord Lyons, go thou and do likewise."

The evidence of all the men admitted to his intimacy is that he maintained, without the least effort or assumption, a singular dignity and reserve, in the midst of his easiest conversation. Charles A. Dana says "Even in his freest moments one always felt the presence of a will and an intellectual power which maintained the ascendancy of the President." In his relations to his Cabinet "it was always plain that he was the master and they were the subordinates. They constantly had to yield to his will, and if he ever yielded to theirs it was because they convinced him that the course they advised was judicious and appropriate."[49] While men of the highest culture and position thus recognized his intellectual primacy there was no man so humble as to feel abashed before him. Frederick Douglass beautifully expressed the sentiment of the plain people in his company: "I felt as though I was in the presence of a big brother and that there was safety in his atmosphere."[50]

As time wore on and the war held its terrible course, upon no one of all those who lived through it was its effect more apparent than upon the President. He bore the sorrows of the nation in his own heart; he suffered deeply, not only from disappointments, from treachery, from hope deferred, from the open assaults of enemies and from the sincere anger of discontented friends, but also from the world wide distress and affliction which flowed from the great conflict in which he was engaged and which he could not evade. One of the most tender and compassionate of men, he was forced to give orders which cost thousands of lives; by nature a man of order and thrift, he saw the daily spectacle of unutterable waste and destruction which he could not prevent. The cry of the widow and the orphan was always in his ears; the awful responsibility resting upon him as the protector of an imperilled republic kept him true to his duty, but could not make him unmindful of the intimate details of that vast sum of human misery involved in civil war.

Under this frightful ordeal his demeanor and disposition changed; so gradually that it would be impossible to say when the change began; but he was in mind, body and nerves a very different man at the second inauguration from the one who had taken the oath in 1861. He continued always the same kindly, genial and cordial spirit he had been at first; but the boisterous laughter became less frequent year by year; the eye grew veiled by constant meditation on momentous subjects; the air of reserve and detachment from his surroundings increased. He aged with great rapidity.

This change is shown with startling distinctness by two life-masks; the one made by Leonard W. Volk in Chicago, April 1860, the other by Clark Mills in Washington in the Spring of 1865.[51] The first is of a man of fifty-one and young for his years. The face has a clean, firm outline; it is free from fat but the muscles are hard and full; the large mobile mouth is ready to speak, to shout or laugh; the bold, curved nose is broad and substantial, with spreading nostrils; it is a face full of life, of energy, of vivid aspiration. The other is so sad and peaceful in its infinite repose that the famous sculptor Augustus St.-Gaudens insisted, when he first saw it, that it was a death-mask. The lines are set, as if the living face, like the copy, had been in bronze; the nose is thin and lengthened by the emaciation of the cheeks; the mouth is fixed like that of an archaic statue; a look as of one on whom sorrow and care had done their worst without victory is on all the features; the whole expression is of unspeakable sadness and all-sufficing strength. Yet the peace is not the dreadful peace of death; it is the peace that passeth understanding.

5

Biographical Sketches

ELMER E. ELLSWORTH[1]

The beginnings of great periods have often been marked and made memorable by striking events. Out of the cloud that hangs around the vague inceptions of revolutions, a startling incident will sometimes flash like lightning, to show that the warring elements have begun their work. The scenes that attended the birth of American nationality formed a not inaccurate type of those that have opened the crusade for its perpetuation. The consolidation of public sentiment which followed the magnificent defeat at Bunker's Hill, in which the spirit of indignant resistance was tempered by the pathetic interest surrounding the fate of [*Dr. Joseph*] Warren, was but a foreshadowing of the instant rally to arms which followed the fall of the beleaguered fort [*Sumter*] in Charleston harbor, and of the intensity of tragic pathos which has been added to the stern purpose of avenging justice by the murder of Colonel Ellsworth.

Ephraim Elmer Ellsworth was born in the little village of Mechanicsville, on the left bank of the Hudson, on the 23d day of April, 1837. When he was very young, his father, through no fault of his own, lost irretrievably his entire fortune, in the tornado of financial ruin that in those years swept from the sea to the mountains. From this disaster he never recovered. Misfortune seems to have followed him through life, with the insatiable pertinacity of the Nemesis of a Greek tragedy. And now in his old age, when for a moment there seemed to shine upon his path the sunshine that promised better days, he finds that suddenly withdrawn, and stands desolate, "stabbed through the heart's affections, to the heart." His younger son died some years ago, of small-pox, in Chicago, and the murder at

Alexandria leaves him with his sorrowing wife, lonely, amid the sympathy of the world.

The days of Elmer's childhood and early youth were passed at Troy and in the city of New York, in pursuits various, but energetic and laborious. There is little of interest in the story of these years. He was a proud, affectionate, sensitive, and generous boy, hampered by circumstance, but conscious of great capabilities, — not morbidly addicted to day-dreaming, but always working heartily for something beyond. He was still very young when he went to Chicago, and associated himself in business with Mr. Devereux of Massachusetts.[2] They managed for a little while, with much success, an agency for securing patents to inventors. Through the treachery of one in whom they had reposed great confidence they suffered severe losses which obliged them to close their business, and Devereux went back to the East. The next year of Ellsworth's life was a miracle of endurance and uncomplaining fortitude. He read law with great assiduity, and supported himself by copying, in the hours that should have been devoted to recreation. He had no pastimes and very few friends. Not a soul beside himself and the baker who gave him his daily loaf knew how he was living. During all that time, he never slept in a bed, never ate with friends at a social board. So acute was his sense of honor, so delicate his ideas of propriety, that, although himself the most generous of men, he never would accept from acquaintances the slightest favors or courtesies which he was unable to return. He told me once of a severe struggle between inclination and a sense of honor. At a period of extreme hunger, he met a friend in the street who was just starting from the city. He accompanied his friend into a restaurant, wishing to converse with him, but declined taking any refreshment. He represented the savory fragrance of his friend's dinner as almost maddening to his famished senses, while he sat there pleasantly chatting, and deprecating his friend's entreaties to join him in his repast, on the plea that he had just dined.

What would have killed an ordinary man did not injure Ellsworth. His iron frame seemed incapable of dissolution or waste. Circumstance had no power to conquer his spirit. His hearty good-humor never gave way. His sense of honor, which was sometimes even fantastic in its delicacy, freed him from the very temptation to wrong. He knew there was a better time coming for him. Conscious of great mental and bodily strength, with that bright outlook that industry and honor always give a man, he was perfectly secure of ultimate success. His plans mingled in a singular manner the bright enthusiasm of the youthful dreamer and the eminent practicality of the man of affairs. At one time, his mind was fixed on Mexico, — not with the licentious dreams that excited the ragged *Condottieri* who followed the fated footsteps of the "gray-eyed man of Destiny,"[3] in the wild hope of plunder and power, — nor with the vague reverie in which fanatical theorists construct impossible Utopias on the absurd framework of Icarias[4] or Phalansteries. His clear, bold, and thoroughly executive mind planned a magnificent scheme of commercial enterprise, which, having its centre of operations at Guaymas, should ramify through the golden wastes that stretch in silence and solitude along the tortuous banks of the Rio San José. This was to be the beginning and the ostensible end of the enterprise. Then he dreamed of the influence of American arts and American energy penetrating into the twilight of that decaying nationality, and saw the natural course of events leading on, first, Emigration, then Protection, and at last Annexation. Yet there was no thought of conquest or rapine. The idea was essentially American and Northern. He never wholly lost that dream. One day last winter, when some one was discussing the propriety of an amputation of the States that seemed thoroughly diseased, Ellsworth swept his hand energetically over the map of Mexico that hung upon the wall, and exclaimed, — "*There* is an unanswerable argument against the recognition of the Southern Confederacy."

But the central idea of Ellsworth's short life was the thorough reorganization of the militia of the United States. He had studied with great success the theory of national defence, and, from his observation of the condition of the militia of the several States, he was convinced that there was much of well-directed effort yet lacking to its entire efficiency. In fact, as he expressed it, a well-disciplined body of five thousand troops could land anywhere on our coast and ravage two or three States before an adequate force could get into the field to oppose them. To reform this defective organization, he resolved to devote whatever of talent or energy was his. This was a very large undertaking for a boy, whose majority and moustache were still of the substance of things hoped for. But nothing that he could propose to himself ever seemed absurd. He attacked his work with his usual promptness and decision.

The conception of a great idea is no proof of a great mind; a man's calibre is shown by the way in which he attempts to realize his idea. A great design planted in a little mind frequently bursts it, and nothing is more pitiable than the spectacle of a man staggering into insanity under a thought too large for him. Ellsworth chose to begin his work simply and practically. He did not write a memorial to the President, to be sent to the Secretary of War, to be referred to the Chief Clerk, to be handed over to File-Clerk No. 99, to be glanced at and quietly thrust into a pigeon-hole labelled "Crazy and trashy." He did not haunt the anteroom of Congressman Somebody, who would promise to bring his plan before the House, and then, bowing him out, give general orders to his footman, "Not at home, hereafter, to that man." He did not float, as some theorists do, ghastly and seedy, around the *Adyta* [*inner shrines*] of popular editors, begging for space and countenance. He wisely determined to keep his theories to himself until he could illustrate them by living examples. He first put himself in thorough training. He practised the manual of arms in his own room, until his dexterous precision was something akin to the sleight of a juggler. He investigated the theory of every movement in an anatomical view, and made several most valuable improvements on Hardee.[5] He rearranged the manual so that every movement formed the logical groundwork of the succeeding one. He studied the science of fence, so that he could hold a rapier with DeVilliers, the most dashing of the Algerine swordsmen.[6] He always had a hand as true as steel, and an eye like a gerfalcon. He used to amuse himself by shooting ventilation-holes through his window-panes. Standing ten paces from the window, he could fire the seven shots from his revolver and not shiver the glass beyond the circumference of a half-dollar. I have seen a photograph of his arm taken at this time. The knotted coil of thews and sinews looks like the magnificent exaggerations of antique sculpture.

His person was strikingly prepossessing. His form, though slight, — exactly the Napoleonic size, — was very compact and commanding; the head statuesquely poised, and crowned with a luxuriance of curling black hair; a hazel eye, bright, though serene, the eye of a gentleman as well as a soldier; a nose such as you see on Roman medals; a light moustache just shading the lips, that were continually curving into the sunniest smiles. His voice, deep and musical, instantly attracted attention; and his address, though not without soldierly brusqueness, was sincere and courteous. There was one thing his backwoods detractors could never forgive: he always dressed well; and sometimes wore the military insignia presented to him by different organizations. One of these, a gold circle, inscribed with the legend, NON NOBIS, SED PRO PATRIA [*not for us, but for our country*], was driven into his heart by the slug of the Virginian assassin.

He had great tact and executive talent, was a good mathematician, possessed a fine artistic eye, sketched well and rapidly, and in short bore a deft and skillful hand in all gentlemanly exercise.

No one ever possessed greater power of enforcing the respect and fastening the affections of men. Strangers soon recognized and acknowledged this power; while to his friends he always seemed like a Paladin or Cavalier of the dead days of romance and beauty. He was so generous and loyal, so stainless and brave, that Bayard himself would have been proud of him.[7] The grand bead-roll of the virtues of the Flower of Kings contains the principles that guided his life; he used to read with exquisite appreciation these lines: —

> "To reverence the King as if he were
> Their conscience, and their conscience as their King, —
> To break the heathen and uphold the Christ, —
> To ride abroad redressing human wrongs, —
> To speak no slander, no, nor listen to it, —
> To lead sweet lives in purest chastity, —
> To love one maiden only, cleave to her,
> And worship her by years of noble deeds,
> Until they won her";

and the rest, —

> "high thoughts, and amiable words,
> And courtliness, and the desire of fame,
> And love of truth, and all that makes a man."

Such, in person and character, was Ellsworth, when he organized, on the 4th day of May, 1859, the United States Zouave Cadets of Chicago.

This company was the machine upon which he was to experiment. Disregarding all extant works upon tactics, he drew up a simpler system for the use of his men. Throwing aside the old ideas of soldierly bearing, he taught them to use vigor, promptness, and ease. Discarding the stiff buckram strut of martial tradition, he educated them to move with the loafing *insouciance* of the Indian, or the graceful ease of the panther. He tore off their choking collars and binding coats, and invented a uniform which, though too flashy and conspicuous for actual service, was very bright and dashing for holiday occasions, and left the wearer perfectly free to fight, strike, kick, jump, or run.

He drilled these young men for about a year at short intervals. His discipline was very severe and rigid. Added to the punctilio of the martinet was the rigor of the moralist. The slightest exhibition of intemperance or licentiousness was punished by instant degradation and expulsion. He struck from the rolls at one time twelve of his best men for breaking the rule of total abstinence. His moral power over them was perfect and absolute. I believe any one of them would have died for him.

In two or three principal towns of Illinois and Wisconsin he drilled other companies: in Springfield, where he made friends who best appreciated what was best in him; and in Rockford, where he formed an attachment which imparted a coloring of tender romance to all the days of his busy life that remained.[8] This tragedy would not have been perfect without the plaintive minor strain of Love in Death.

His company took the Premium Colors at the United States Agricultural Fair, and Ellsworth thought it was time to show to the people some fruit of his drill. They issued their soldierly *défi* and started on their *Marche de Triomphe*. It is useless to recall to those who read newspapers the clustering glories of that bloodless campaign. Hardly had they left the suburbs of Chicago when the murmur of applause began. New York, secure in the championship of half a century, listened with quiet metropolitan scorn to the noise of the shouting provinces; but when the crimson phantasms marched out of the Park, on the evening of the 15th of July, New York, with metropolitan magnanimity, confessed herself utterly vanquished by the good thing that had come out of Nazareth. There was no resisting the Zouaves. As the erring Knight of the Round Table said,—

"men went down before his spear at a touch,
But knowing he was Lancelot; his great name conquered."

There were one or two Southern companies that issued insulting defiances, but, after a little expenditure of epistolary valor, prudently, though ingloriously, stayed afar,—as is usual in New Gascony. With these exceptions, the heart of the nation went warmly out to these young men. Their endurance, their discipline, their alertness, their *élan*, surprised the sleepy drill-masters out of their propriety, and waked up the people to intense and cordial admiration. Chicago welcomed them home proudly, covered with tan and dust and glory.

Ellsworth found himself for his brief hour the most talked-of man in the country. His pictures sold like wildfire in every city of the land. School-girls dreamed over the graceful wave of his curls, and shop-boys tried to reproduce the *Grand Seigneur* air of his attitude. Zouave corps, brilliant in crimson and gold, sprang up, phosphorescently, in his wake, making bright the track of his journey. The leading journals spoke editorially of him, and the comic papers caricatured his drill.

So one thing was accomplished. He had gained a name that would entitle him hereafter to respectful attention, and had demonstrated the efficiency of his system of drill. The public did not, of course, comprehend the resistless moral power which he exercised, — imperiously moulding every mind as he willed, — inspiring every soul with his own unresting energy. But the public recognized success, and that for the present was enough.

He quietly formed a regiment in the upper counties of Illinois, and made his best men the officers of it. He tendered its services to Governor [*Richard*] Yates immediately on his inauguration, "for any service consistent with honor." This was the first positive tender made of an organized force in defence of the Constitution. He seemed to recognize more clearly than others the certainty of the coming struggle. It was the soldierly instinct that heard "the battle afar off, the thunder of the captains, and the shouting."

Still intent upon the great plan of militia reform, he came to Springfield. He hoped, in case of the success of Mr. Lincoln in the canvass then pending, to be able to establish in the War Department a Bureau of Militia, which would prove a most valuable auxiliary to his work. His ideas were never vague or indefinite. Means always presented themselves to him, when he contemplated ends. The following were the duties of the proposed bureau, which may serve as a guide to some future reformer: I copy from his own exquisitely neat and clear memorandum, which lies before me: —

"First. The gradual concentration of all business pertaining to the militia now conducted by the several bureaus of this Department.

"Second. The collection and systematizing of accurate information of the number, arm[s], and condition of the militia of all classes of the several States, and the compilation of yearly reports of the same for the information of this Department.

"Third. The compilation of a report of the actual condition of the militia and the working of the present systems of the General Government and the various States.

"Fourth. The publication and distribution of such information as is important to the militia, and the conduct of all correspondence relating to militia affairs.

"Fifth. The compilation of a system of instruction for light troops for distribution to the several States, including everything pertaining to the instruction of the militia in the school of the soldier, — company and battalion, skirmishing, bayonet, and gymnastic drill, adapted for self-instruction.

"Sixth. The arrangement of a system of organization, with a view to the establishment of a uniform system of drill, discipline, equipment, and dress, throughout the United States."

His plan for this purpose was very complete and symmetrical. Though enthusiastic, he was never dreamy. His idea always went forth fully armed and equipped.

Nominally, he was a student of law in the office of Lincoln and [William H.] Herndon, but in effect he passed his time in completing his plans of militia reform. He made in October many stirring and earnest speeches for the Republican candidates. He was very popular among the country people. His voice was magnificent in melody and volume, his command of language wonderful in view of the deficiencies of his early education, his humor inexhaustible and hearty, and his manner deliberate and impressive, reminding his audiences in Central Illinois of the earliest and best days of Senator Douglas.

When the Legislature met, he prepared an elaborate military bill, the adoption of which would have placed the State in an enviable attitude of defence. The stupid jealousy of colonels and majors who had won bloodless glory, on both sides, in the Mormon War, and the malignant prejudice instigated by the covert treason that lurked in Southern Illinois, succeeded in staving off the passage of the bill, until it was lost by the expiration of the term. Many of these men are now in the ranks, shouting the name of Ellsworth as a battle-cry.

He came to Washington in the escort of the President elect. Hitherto he had been utterly independent of external aid. The time was come when he must wait for the cooperation of others, for the accomplishment of his life's great purpose. He wished a position in the War Department, which would give him an opportunity for the establishment of the Militia Bureau. He was a strange anomaly at the capital. He did not care for money or luxury. Though sensitive in regard to his reputation, for the honor of his work, his motto always was that of the sage Merlin,—"I follow use, not fame." An office-seeker of this kind was an eccentric and suspicious personage. The hungry thousands that crowded and pushed at Willard's thought him one of them, only deeper and slier. The simplicity and directness of his character, his quick sympathy and thoughtless generosity, and his delicate sense of honor unfitted him for such a scramble as that which degrades the quadrennial rotations of our Departments. He withdrew from the contest for the position he desired, and the President, who loved him like a younger brother, made him a lieutenant in the army, intending to detail him for special service.

The jealousy of the staff-officers of the regular army, who always discover in any effective scheme of militia reform the overthrow of their power, and who saw in the young Zouave the promise of brilliant and successful innovation, was productive of very serious annoyance and impediment to Ellsworth. In the midst of this, he fell sick at Willard's. While he lay there, the news from the South began to show that the rebels were determined upon war, and the rumors on the street said that a wholesome North-westerly breeze was blowing from the Executive Mansion. These indications were more salutary to Ellsworth than any medicine. We were talking one night of coming probabilities, and I spoke of the doubt so widely existing as to the loyalty of the people. He rejoined, earnestly,—"I can only speak for myself. You know I have a great work to do, to which my life is pledged; I am the only earthly stay of my parents; there is a young woman whose happiness I regard as dearer than my own: yet I could ask no better death than to fall next week before Sumter. I am not better than other men. You will find that patriotism is not dead, even if it sleeps."

Sumter fell, and the sleeping awoke. The spirit of Ellsworth, cramped by a few weeks' intercourse with politicians, sprang up full-statured in the Northern gale. He cut at once the meshes of red tape that had hampered and held him, threw up his commission, and started for New York without orders, without assistance, without authority, but with the consciousness that the President would sustain him. The rest the world knows. I will be brief in recalling it.

In an incredibly short space of time he enlisted and organized a regiment, eleven hundred strong, of the best fighting material that ever went to war. He divided it, according to an idea of his own, into groups of four comrades each, for the campaign. He exercised a personal supervision over the most important and the most trivial minutiae of the regimental business. The quick sympathy of the public still followed him. He became the idol of the Bowery and the pet of the Avenue. Yet not one instant did he waste in recreation or lionizing. Indulgent to all others, he was merciless to himself. He worked day and night, like an incarnation of Energy. When he arrived with his men in Washington, he was thin, hoarse, flushed, but entirely contented and happy, because busy and useful.

Of the bright enthusiasm and the quenchless industry of the next few weeks what need to speak? Every day, by his unceasing toil and care, by his vigor, alertness, activity, by his generosity, and by his relentless rigor when duty commanded, he grew into the hearts of his robust and manly followers, until every man in the regiment feared him as a Colonel should be feared, and loved him as a brother should be loved.

On the night of the twenty-third of May, he called his men together, and made a brief, stirring speech to them, announcing their orders to advance on Alexandria. "Now, boys, go to bed, and wake up at two o'clock for a sail and a skirmish." When the camp was silent, he began to work. He wrote many hours, arranging the business of the regiment. He finished his labor as the midnight stars were crossing the zenith. As he sat in his tent by the shore, it seems as if the mystical gales from the near eternity must have breathed for a moment over his soul, freighted with the odor of amaranths and asphodels. For he wrote two strange letters: one to her who mourns him faithful in death; one to his parents. There is nothing braver or more pathetic. With the prophetic instinct of love, he assumed the office of consoler for the stroke that impended.

In the dewy light of the early dawn he occupied the first rebel town. With his own hand he tore down the first rebel flag. He added to the glories of that morning the seal of his blood.

The poor wretch who stumbled upon an immortality of infamy by murdering him died at the same instant.[9] The two stand in the light of that event — clearly revealed — types of the two systems in conflict to-day: the one, brave, refined, courtly, generous, tender, and true; the other, not lacking in brute courage, reckless, besotted, ignorant, and cruel.

Let the two systems, Freedom and Slavery, stand thus typified forever, in the red light of that dawn, as on a Mount of Transfiguration. I believe that may solve the dark mystery why Ellsworth died.[10]

EDWARD D. BAKER[11]

Rivers form no less striking features in the pictures of history than in the face of nature. When dignified by the passage of armies, their course runs broadening through fame. The crossing of the Rubicon by the legions of the bankrupt Roman centuries ago, has given to the rhetoric of the world a metaphor crystallized into the ordinary speech of men who never heard of the Gallic war. We never realized that the shock of arms was coming between the Sardinian King and the Austrian Kaiser until the troops of Francis-Joseph stood on the Italian brink of the Ticino.[12] The Danube, the Elbe, and the Po run through their ancient dominions sad with the memories of slaughter and of battles.

Hitherto the western world has had no dower of associations to link with its streams. The peaceful charms of growing opulence and advancing arts were all that hallowed our rivers after we had forgotten our vague traditions of savage ambuscade and midnight massacre. But they can never again claim that happy immunity from the red suggestions of strife. The waters of the Missouri are darkening with a tint more deep than the amber of the mountains; the Mississippi will soon become the sepulchre of heroes; and the fair ripples of the Potomac, that have never blushed before except with the dalliance of the evening sunlight streaming rosily over the Virginian hills, will henceforth flow grimly into history stained with the costliest blood of the land. As if the significance of the forward movement of the armies of the republic were not enough to stamp the crossing of the river indelibly into the mind of the world, the noblest lives in the army were sacrificed at Alexandria and Ball's Bluff, whose fame will rescue the event from all the possibilities of oblivion. The boast of Virginians becomes justified, and the ground becomes "sacred soil," when hallowed by blood like that of Elmer Ellsworth and Edward Dickinson Baker. These heroic men, falling gloriously on the southern shore of the dividing river, call eloquently to their countrymen who, pressing on to avenge them, are too busy to weep for them. Now shall their history be written. When the storm is over-past, and peace brings leisure for eulogy, it will be time to tell the story and educe the lessons of their lives. To posterity, therefore, we will intrust the work of worthily honoring the dead Senator. At present we can only snatch from forgetfulness the simple facts of his life, and say what manner of man we have lost. The scattered garlands which affection to-day is casting upon his grave shall be hereafter gathered and woven into unfading chaplet of enduring fame. "Forget not the faithful dead" was the pathetic adjuration of the dying warrior-poet Koerner;[13] and it is ill for a republic when its martyrs begin to be forgotten.

Edward Dickinson Baker, United States Senator from Oregon, who died in battle near Conrad's Ferry on the 21st day of October, 1861, was born in the city of London on the 24th day of February, in the year 1811. His father, Edward Baker, was a man of education and refinement.[14] His mother was the sister of Captain Thomas Dickinson of the British navy, an officer of great ability and distinction, who fought under Collingwood at Trafalgar.[15] When Edward was four years of age his family came to America and lived for about ten years in the city of Philadelphia. He always fondly remembered his residence in Philadelphia, and his citizenship was through life, both to him and to Philadelphians, a source of mutual pride.

Early in the spring of the year 1825 the elder Baker, impelled by that spirit of restless adventure and enterprise that seems the heritage of all the race, gathered up his household gods and turned his face once more to the sunset. Over the trackless mountains, along the strange rivers, through the still wildernesses where life was bursting into beauty and bloom, he journeyed until, tired of wandering, he rested in the rich valley of the Wabash.[16] Only a little while though; for in a year or so we find him at the pleasant old town of Belleville, in the county of St. Clair, the earliest settled of all Central Illinois, filled with a population more wealthy and refined than that which settled in the Southern peninsula between the Mississippi and the Ohio, or that which fought and traded along the Illinois and Rock rivers. Most of the educational and social advantages of the State clustered at that early day around the villages facing the trading station that Laclede had built and called St. Louis,[17] and those that nestled cozily in the winding valley of Kaskaskia. In later years these towns have lost their ancient prosperity, and all that reminds the visitor of what has been is the dignified idleness of the men and the still, proud beauty of the women.

Finding in the good county of St. Clair a congenial social atmosphere, the elder Baker pitched there his tent, and opened an academy for boys, which he continued with great success for many years, conducting it upon a system of instruction then called the Lancasterian plan.[18] His son, Edward, then a handsome lad of fifteen, by the grace and dignity of his bearing, by his personal beauty, and by the astonishing charm of conversation which even at that early day distinguished him, became a general favorite in the best society there. He was always received with kindness in the family of Governor Edwards,[19] a magnificent old gentleman in fair top-boots and ruffled wristbands, who added to a character of great generosity and executive ability the *grand Seigneur* airs of the Old School. Young Baker availed himself with avidity of the treasures of the Governor's library, the best in the State. He was always a ravenous reader. He had one of those rare memories — wax to receive, and marble to retain. He was indebted to its trustiness and quickness for much of his success as a debater. He was rarely mistaken, and never at fault for a fact or an allusion. Thus reading and remembering, dreaming and growing, he passed the pleasant days in pleasant Belleville, in congenial study and edifying society. He took much interest in the political contests that convulsed the State upon the old and always mischievous question of Slavery — in which, singularly enough, Northern and Eastern men favored the introduction of Slavery, while the Governor and his Kentucky associates opposed it. By their untiring efforts Slavery was prohibited, and Illinois remained a free State.

From Belleville young Baker went to Carrollton, in Greene County, a town of less social culture, though filled with a wealthy and sterling population. Here he studied law in the office of Judge Caverly,[20] and practiced for some time with indifferent success. He married here a lady of high character and position,[21] who still survives him, in desolation and sorrow, on the far shore of the Pacific Ocean.

He removed to Springfield, afterward the capital city of the State, in 1835. In 1837, when Dan Stone[22] — the member who joined Abraham Lincoln in what his opponents styled the "Abolition protest"[23] — resigned his seat in the Legislature to assume a place on the Supreme Bench. Baker was elected to fill the vacancy thus created, and re-elected soon thereafter. He paid little attention to Legislative business; was often out of his seat, and more pleasantly employed. He was, however, always called on when an obnoxious measure was to be defeated or an opponent demolished. He mastered details with great ease when he cared, but he did not often care. He was State Senator from 1840 to 1844 defeating in the canvass John Calhoun, who afterward became memorable on account of an election manoeuvre in Kansas not wholly unconnected with candle-boxes.[24]

All this time he was applying himself assiduously to the practice of law. His infallible memory, his quickness of perception, and his ardent eloquence, were powerful agencies in the management of juries, and were usually successful against the most determined energy and labor. His bonhomie and impetuosity of delivery were irresistible to Western men; and his Kentucky admirers delighted to liken him to the great lights of the Southwestern bar, Barry[25] and Grundy.[26] He was fortunate in being associated with men of industry and learning, such as Judge Logan, the Nestor of the profession in Illinois;[27] M. Hay;[28] and, for a while, Albert T. Bledsoe, lately Assistant Secretary of War in the Southern Confederacy.[29]

It would be hard to find in any backwoods town, at the period of which I have been speaking, a coterie of equal ability and equal possibilities with those who plead, and wrangled, and electioneered together in Springfield. Logan, one of the finest examples of the purely legal mind that the West has ever produced; M'Dougal, who afterward sought El Dorado;[30] Bissell[31] and Shields,[32] and Baker, brothers in arms and in council, the flower of the Western chivalry and the brightest examples of Western oratory; Trumbull, then as now, with a mind pre-eminently cool, crystalline, sagacious;[33] Douglas, heart of oak and brain of fire, of energy and undaunted courage unparalleled, ambition insatiate and aspiration unsleeping;[34] Lincoln, then as afterward, thoughtful, and honest, and brave, conscious of great capabilities and quietly sure of the future, before all his peers in a broad humanity, and in that prophetic lift of spirit that saw the triumph of principles then dimly discovered in the contest that was to come.

Baker was elected to Congress in 1844, from the Sangamon District. He occupied his seat there, serving with distinction, when the Mexican war broke out. Though opposed to the war in its inception, the call of his country was imperative to him. There was something in his veins that would not let him be quiet when there was fighting going on. He had had some little experience of soldiering in the Black Hawk War—as who had not? Lincoln was a captain there, Robert Anderson and Jefferson Davis were together in an expedition up the Mississippi, and Abraham Lincoln and

Jefferson Davis probably bivouacked together in the Iowa forests and dreamed of battles by the dying fire.[35]

Baker left Washington and came to Springfield and called a thousand young men around him. They were immediately accepted by the Government as the "Fourth Illinois," and embarked for the war. Arriving at Matamoras, on the discovery of dangerous irregularities that absolutely demanded attention, Colonel Baker was sent to Washington as a bearer of dispatches. When he came there Congress was in session. He availed himself of his right of membership, and in a speech of great fire and force he plead the cause of the Volunteers, then resigned his seat, and went back to the war. He joined his regiment in time to share in the victorious termination of the siege of Vera Cruz. He advanced into the interior with the main body of Scott's army, and gained an opportunity for hot work at Cerro Gordo.[36] When Shields's Brigade had turned the Mexican position in the rear of the mountain, and the column emerged from the chaparral into the Jalapa road, a concealed battery suddenly opened with deadly effect upon the Illinoisans. Shields fell with a hurt in his breast large enough to let out the life of any man but him; and Baker, without an instant's confusion or hesitation, took command of the brigade, and charged magnificently upon the enemy's guns, taking the position which enabled him to cut off the retreat, and completing the utter rout of the Mexican army. It was in reference to this incident, and in remembrance of the conduct of Burnett's regiment,[37] that he said, last April, in Union Square, "I know what New York can do when her blood is up."

He was succeeded in his Congressional District by Abraham Lincoln, and shortly thereafter he removed to Galena, up in the lead-mines. The inevitable popularity that always attended his footsteps like a shadow followed him into the North, and placed him in Congress again within a very few months after his arrival in Galena. It is impossible for people living in cities, or in the heart of a dense population, to form any adequate conception of the intense affection and eager interest that a handsome, jolly, eloquent, and discreet partisan leader excites among his constituency of the backwoods. The rural school-houses and groves form the arena of his triumphs. His wit is rewarded by hearty laughter, and his eloquence by yells of approbation. Where excitements are few, a popular orator, who can make men laugh and cry, becomes entwined with their sluggish, emotional natures, and a speech is to them not an incident of an evening, but the event of a week. They show their appreciation of him by always designating him by some affectionate and slightly depreciatory epithet, which, though at first annoying, becomes in time a badge of honor and a cry of onset. They are hardly the most elegant names to go into the measures of history, but no titles have ever been more lovingly given than Honest Old Abe — the Little Giant — Old Tippecanoe[38] — Old Zack[39] — the Old Wheel-Horse. In this power of enchaining the love of a people, who though rude are always manly, and never grow maudlin in their devotion, but retain in their utterances of praise the privilege of judicious abuse, Baker was unparalleled. Though free from all degrading vices, the worst men loved him; and the rough dwellers in the mines and the timber came eagerly to hear him discourse of things above the reaches of their souls.

He served these last years in the House of Representatives with great industry and success. His principal oratorical effort of these days was the pathetic and musical eulogy he pronounced at the death of his old commander [*Zachary Taylor*], when the honest and sagacious old warrior went to heaven from the Executive mansion. Declining a re-election, his restless and original brain fastened upon a project as wild as it was engaging. Forming a business connection with the Panama Railroad Company, he sent a body of four hundred men under his brother, the genial and talented Dr. Alfred Baker, soon following them himself. Those who have read the narrative of Lieutenant Strain,[40] where the intensity of suffering charms while you shudder, may form an idea of the dispiriting experiences of this little band. In the depth of the matted rankness of the forests — on the humid banks of sluggish rivers — lying in the night amidst the tangled luxuriance of the wilderness — the moist splendors of tropical summer around them, and the wild voices of tropical and savage life in the pathless jungles filling the unquiet air — one by one they sunk beneath the insidious beguiling of the malarious atmosphere, and the Northern strength melted in the Southern fervors. At last their untiring leader fell sick, nearly unto death, and his brother brought him tenderly home, to see familiar skies and breathe the honest air of the prairies again.

He recovered slowly; but his heart leaned always westward. It is men like him that form the dazzling crest of the foremost wave of emigration, that never ceases to roll onward till caught and shattered into quiet by impassable boundaries. He went to California in 1852. The wild tumult of earlier years had begun to settle into the habitudes of civilized life, and the arts of peace had begun to supplant the savageries of nature. People were arriving at that point of social and moral development when they thought, on the whole, it was as well to litigate a claim as to fight about it. Retainers began to supplant revolvers, and briefs to supply the place of bowies; which was a bad thing for surgeons, and a very good one for lawyers.

Among the lawyers of California Baker was easily chief. The astonishing ease and felicity of his diction, his marvelous quickness of apprehension, bred a careless habit in him that often exposed him to the charge of indolence and superficiality.[41] There never was a greater mistake, though this delusion is one very frequently entertained in the case of men of great sprightliness of mind. Baker never neglected or slighted his business. His cases required little hard work, but they always received it. There was nothing slovenly or heedless about any of his habits of thought. His pleadings were always eminently safe, and his forensic harangues were models of perspicuity and force, without ornament or verbiage. His popularity increased with his success. He took his place at once, almost without effort, at the head of the profession in the State. A large proportion of all important civil causes were brought to him; and those social philosophers whose principles, embodied in practice, ran counter to the established prejudices of courts and statutes became imbued with a kind of superstitious confidence in his powers. There was certainly nothing lacking in Baker to the perfect advocate if he had cared to become so. His fascinating power with juries — his clear analytic processes of thought — his torrent of tempestuous eloquence, made him well-nigh irresistible. His success was commensurate with his powers.

He was popular in California, in spite of his politics. It was not possible for a man of such positive and aggressive character to seek power and position by subserviency to the prejudices of the people. By ancient affiliations, by accustomed habits of thought, by strong instincts of a liberal philanthropy, he was identified with the party opposed to the extension of slavery. In those early days the population of the Golden State had not yet perfectly polarized its constituent elements upon this subject of slavery. The free State colonists were largely, of course, in the ascendant; but a majority of them, led by the old traditions of organization, joined with the Southern residents on the question of propagandism. The majority was thus hopelessly against the Republicans when their party, struggling from the ashes of old defeats, unfurled the banner of Free Soil upon the Pacific shore. But there never was a fight more dauntless than that made by the forlorn hope of Republicans — Baker, Stanford,[42] Nunes,[43] Tracy,[44] and a handful of followers — in the diggings and ranches of California. There was none of that sleepy security that characterizes the wordy wars of Eastern tribunes. When a man went to talk for Fremont[45] among the squatters of Mariposa, or inveigh against slavery among the refuse ruffianism of the Gulf that haunted Yuba and Sonoma, or expound a hated doctrine to the desperadoes of Tuolumne, he took his life in his hand, and considered his pistols and knife as necessary companions as his pamphlets and papers. And who was so qualified as Baker for a strife like this? His geniality beguiled as much as his courage impressed. Because he was always known to be ready for a fight, it was never necessary. He won the hearts of the rough people who cursed his doctrine, and his name became coupled in the mouths of the mountaineers with every expletive of profane admiration. He was utterly at home on the hustings. Those who are acquainted only with his grave senatorial efforts can form no adequate idea of the ready, sparkling, ebullient wit — the glancing and playful satire, mirthful while merciless — the keen syllogisms — and the sharp sophisms, whose fallacies, though undiscoverable, were perplexing — and the sudden splendors of eloquence that formed the wonderful charm of his backwoods harangues. His fame became coextensive with the coast; and the people, in allusion to "the good gray head which all men knew," used to call him the "Gray Eagle."

Years passed on, and Baker made money and friends in California. At last the great party of the North became divided on the interminably vexing question of slavery in the Territories. Broderick — one of the truest diamonds that ever existed in the rough — after battling with unavailing pluck for what he deemed truth and justice in the Senate, came back to rally his clansmen for conflict with a haughty and implacable organization. Here was a conflict that at once enlisted all the soul of Baker. It was not so forlorn in prospect as his former one, and a glimmer of hope is very inspiriting in politics. A coalition was effected between the Republicans and the Douglas Democrats, by which Baker and M'Kibbin[46] became the candidates for Congress against the distinctive pro-slavery men. The story of that well-fought campaign was not a particularly pleasant one. It was like all sudden insurrections of free thought and manhood against powerful and disciplined tyranny. The Broderick ticket was defeated, and the baffled Senator was bullied into a criminal folly [*a duel*] that his better judgment condemned, and was slain. His last words were, "They have killed me because I was opposed to the extension of slavery and a corrupt Administration."

The words and the event fell heavily on the heart of the nation. Far more crushingly they rested on the saddened spirits of his friends. The dull heaviness of their grief forbade parade, and made ceremony mockery. The American mind runs naturally to committees when great men fall. But there was that within the hearts of Broderick's friends, like the anguish of the royal Dane, "passing show." By common consent Baker was the funeral orator. With none of the ordinary accessories of solemn burials, the dead Senator lay in the great square of the city, and the saddened people flocked silently to the scene. From all the streets of the crowded town they gathered in the hush of the autumnal noon, till the square was filled with the mourning multitudes, whispering with lowered voices of the virtues of the departed, and striving to come near enough to gaze upon the calm features of the murdered tribune, turned stonily to the brightness of the skies. Aloft the church bells were jangling mournfully, and their wild lament, floating down to earth, deepened the emotion of the hour. As their ringing vibrated into silence the voice of the orator stole out upon the air, tremulous with tender feeling and musical with the memories of dead friendship. The mind of the mighty multitude, softened by the excitement of their sorrow, lay plastic to his hand, and for an hour the homage of tears and sobs was paid to Baker's genius and Broderick's memory, until he ended in those grandly pathetic words, whose touching music breathes alike the abandon of sorrow and the joy of ultimate fame:

"The last word must be spoken, and the imperious mandate of death must be fulfilled. Thus, O brave heart! we bear thee to thy rest. Thus, surrounded by tens of thousands, we leave thee to the equal grave. As in life, no other voice among us so rang its trumpet blast upon the ear of freemen, so in death its echoes will reverberate amidst our mountains and our valleys until truth and valor cease to appeal to the human heart.

"Good friend! true hero! hail and farewell!"

It is worth while to die if one could be mourned so gloriously.

After the death of Broderick and the impunity of his murderer, Baker, as if to free himself from the haunting presence of the unatoned crime, went to Oregon. He entered with all his might into the election of 1859 in that State, working with his usual self-forgetting energy for David Logan, a young friend from Springfield.[47] Logan, though making a most brilliant canvass, was defeated for Congress; but the Legislature was carried, and Baker, who had by this time become the Republican party of Oregon, was proposed for the Senate. As soon as it became apparent that a Republican would be elected, the opposition, unused to any thing but victory, and unable in any other way to baffle defeat, "took to the bush," and actually spent several days in the tall timber to prevent an election being held. The sergeant-at-arms organized a hunting party, and going into the woods soon bagged enough for a quorum, and Baker was elected to the Senate of the United States. He had at last attained the summit of political ambition. As far as his nativity would permit him to be honored, he had been. He had arrived at the goal of a brilliant career before he had completed his half-century of years. And the end was not far.

Coming to California, on his way to the East, he scattered his perfect and jewel-like speeches all along his route. One evening, in San Francisco, after it had been surmised that his being elected by a coalition would induce lukewarmness of sentiment and expression, he took occasion to renew his fealty to the principles of his life. I do not think this wonderful speech was ever reported. Every word of it seemed to flame and sparkle with the miraculous fire of genius. It brought the audience to their feet. The very spirit of liberty seemed ennobled by his apostrophe.

He at once took his place among the foremost debaters of the Senate. For the first time in his life he was placed in a position which was entirely appropriate to him. The decorum and courtesy that usually marks the intercourse of Senators was most grateful to his habits of thought and feeling. The higher range of discussion, and the more cultivated tone of sentiment and discourse prevalent there gave him an opportunity, that all his life had lacked, of doing his best among his equals. Among these refined members of the most august of representative assemblies, there was none more courteous, more polished, than this Western lawyer, this rouser of the dwellers in the backwoods. He shed honor enough upon Oregon to atone even for General [Joseph] Lane.

Let it be remembered to his lasting praise, now that he is gone, in proof of the paternal and cherishing interest which he always exhibited in behalf of the common soldiers, that he exerted himself to the utmost in procuring the late increase in the rations of the rank and file. The heightened health and comfort of our brave soldiery will be the best monument to his wise forethought and liberal humanity.

In fervid, impressive oratory—in that peculiar ability which starts a man to his feet unprepared, and enables him to always do himself justice in the hurry and glow of debate, it would be hard to say what equal Baker has left in the Senate. His mind was always fully determined upon questions at issue. His convictions were firm and ardent. His opulence of expression and imagery was absolutely inexhaustible. Other men, upon the frame-work of a great idea, by labor and toil produce finished orations, and when they are done, however ornate, the fulfillment is found to lag behind the intention. But Baker never labored and never pondered; and so powerful and ready were the processes of his mind, so rich the resources of his imagination, and so warm and glowing the fervors of his spirit, that the creations of his genius came forth in the full perfection of their finished grace and beauty, with a light and a life and a color fairer than he had known.

He was especially great upon great occasions. He was a man whom the subtle magnetism of events always inspired. Those who heard will surely never forget the magnificent burst of red-hot rhetoric with which he electrified the crowding thousands that filled Union Square last April. It was a mighty assemblage—great in numbers—tremendous in earnestness—awful in aroused enthusiasm. We saw that day how hard it was for common men to address that crowd. Some simply raved, mastered by emotion. Some, wishing to be solemn, prosed. There were few who could ride on that whirlwind and direct that storm. Baker was one. From the instant when his graceful form was discovered on the stand—his handsome face, pale but quiet; his eye fierce in its brilliancy; his white hair crowning the splendid head like a halo; and the tones of his clear, firm voice rang out on the air in the words, "The majesty of the people is here to-day to sustain the majesty of the Constitution"—to the moment when he closed in a gust of passionate plaudits, he held the audience fettered and still. A visible thrill ran through the dense mass when, in closing, he consecrated himself anew to the service of his country in these words of exquisite melody:

"And if from the far Pacific a voice, feebler than the feeblest murmur upon its shore, may be heard to give you courage and hope in the contest, that voice is yours to-day; and if a man whose hair is gray, who is well-nigh worn out in the battle and toil of life, may pledge himself on such an occasion and in such an audience, let me say—as my last word—that, as when, amidst sheeted fire and flame, I saw and led the hosts of New York as they charged in contest upon a foreign soil, for the honor of your flag; so again, if Providence shall will it, this feeble hand shall draw a sword never yet dishonored, not to fight for distant honor in a foreign land, but to fight for country, for home, for law, for government, for constitution, for right, for freedom, for humanity, and in the hope that the banner of my country may advance, and wheresoever that banner waves there glory may pursue and freedom be established!"

This was no idle trick of rhetoric. Before the echoes of his words had died he was hard at work recruiting the California regiment. It filled rapidly. Men came from a distance to join in squads or singly. Many came from Philadelphia and its outlying country. He liked to receive these. "There must be a fighting streak somewhere about us Quakers," he used to say. There was an inspiration in this man's words and presence that made men love to fight under him. His regiment soon was over-full. The President appointed him a Brigadier-General. He declined it. The same friendly hand desired to place upon his shoulder-straps the double star of a Major-General. He quietly refused it, and kept the eagles to which his regiment entitled him. As for honors, he had enough of them in another field. He went into this war for use, not fame.

The time for use was coming and for fame as well, though hidden behind the forbidding mask of disaster and death. It seems as if Colonel Baker himself was not unmindful of his coming fate. It is so easy for people after a battle to remember that the dead were haunted by the coming probabilities, and for sentimental youths to say before a skirmish their farewell to the world, that newspaper reports of presentiments are usually not devoid of ludicrous associations. But sometimes you see, in a man whose character renders a suspicion of affectation impossible, an awful solemnity, born neither of fear nor of responsibility, but as if the black plumes of the wings of Azrael, the Death Angel, had touched him, or the ghostly gales out of the opened gates of eternity had blown for an instant over his brow. Else why that solemn farewell to his parents penned by the dauntless Ellsworth, as live a man as ever breathed, in the dead of the last midnight that he ever watched? Why the strange reckless bewilderment of the brave Lyon[48] on that disastrous day when his gallant heart was breaking under the double conviction that death had marked him, and the Government had forgotten him? Colonel Baker for several days was oppressed by this overhanging consciousness. He became as restless as an eagle in his camp. He came down to Washington and settled all his affairs. He went to say farewell to the family of the President. A lady—who in her high position is still gracefully mindful of early friendships—gave him a bouquet of late flowers. "Very beautiful," he said, quietly. "These flowers and my memory will wither together." At night he hastily reviewed his papers. He indicated upon each its proper disposition "in case I should not return." He pressed with quiet earnestness upon his friend Colonel Webb,[49] who deprecated such ghostly instructions, the measures which might become necessary in regard to the resting-place of his mortal remains. All this without any ostentation. He performed all these offices with the quiet coolness of a soldier and a man of affairs, then mounted his horse and rode gayly away to his death.

On the 20th day of October, the movement of General M'Call[50] upon Dranesville having excited the attention of the enemy at Leesburg, and a regiment of gray uniforms having been observed cautiously advancing from the west and taking position behind a hill near Edwards's Ferry, General Stone, commanding the army of observation on the Potomac,[51] resolved upon an armed reconnaissance to ascertain the position and feel the strength of the rebel force across the river. A scouting party sent out from Conrad's Ferry scoured the country rapidly in the direction of Leesburg, and when within about a mile of the town were suddenly confronted by what in the uncertain light appeared to be rows of tents, but which were afterward ascertained to be merely openings in the frondage of the woods. Upon this report, brought back by the mistaken scouts, Colonel Devens, of the Massachusetts Fifteenth,[52] was ordered to attack and destroy the supposed camp at daybreak, and return to Harrison's Island, between Conrad's and Edwards's Ferries, or, in case he found no enemy, to hold a secure position and await sufficient force to reconnoitre. Colonel Baker was ordered to have his Californians at Conrad's Ferry at sunrise, and the rest of his brigade ready to move early.

Colonel Devens crossed and proceeded to the point indicated, and General Stone ordered a party of Van Allen's cavalry under Major Mix,[53] accompanied by that most accomplished of English dragoons, who veils his titles under the sobriquet of Captain Stewart,[54] to advance along the Leesburg road and ascertain the condition of the heights in the vicinity of the enemy's battery near Goose Creek. This was performed in dashing style. They came upon a Mississippi regiment, received and returned its fire, and brought off a prisoner.

Meantime Colonel Devens had discovered the error in regard to the supposed encampment, and had been attacked by a superior force of the enemy and fallen back in good order upon the position of Colonel Lee,[55] who had been posted to support him on the bluff. Presently he again advanced, his men, as General Stone reports, behaving admirably, fighting, retiring, and advancing in perfect order, and exhibiting every proof of high courage and good discipline.

At this juncture Colonel Baker, who early in the morning had conferred with the commanding general at Edwards's Ferry and received his orders from him, began transporting his brigade across the narrow but deep channel that ran between Harrison's Island and the Virginia shore. The means of transportation were lamentably deficient — three small boats and a scow, which the soldiers say was miserably heavy and water-logged. With such means the crossing was slow and tedious. While they were toiling across, Devens and Lee, with their little commands, were in desperate peril in front, the wide battalions of the enemy closing exultingly around them, with savage prudence availing themselves of every advantage of ground, and flanking by the power of numbers the handful of heroes they dared not attack in front. Baker was not the man to deliberate long when the death-knell of his friends was ringing in his ears in the steady, continuous rattle of the rebel musketry. He advanced to the relief of Devens with a battalion of his Californians under Wistar,[56] the most gallant of the fighting Quakers, and a portion of the Twentieth Massachusetts. With this devoted band, 1720 men all told, for more than an hour he stood the fire of the surrounding and hidden foe, as from the concealing crescent of the trees they poured their murderous volleys. Bramhall[57] and French[58] struggled up the precipitous banks with a field-piece and two howitzers, which did good service till the gunners dropped dead, and the officers hauled them to the rear to prevent their falling into the enemy's hands. Every man there fought in that hopeless struggle as bravely as if victory were among possibilities. No thought was there of flight or surrender even when all but honor was lost. Their duty was to stand there till they were ordered away. Death was merely an incident of the performance of that duty; and the coolest man there was the Colonel commanding. He talked hopefully and cheerily to his men, even while his heart was sinking with the sun, and the grim presence of disaster and ruin was with him. He was ten paces in their front, where all might see him and take pattern by him. He carried his left hand nonchalantly in his breast, and criticised the firing as quietly as if on parade. "Lower, boys! Steady there! Keep cool now and fire low, and the day is ours!" All at once, as if moved by one impulse, a sudden sheet of fire burst from the curved covert of the enemy, and Edward Dickinson Baker was promoted, by one grand brevet of the God of Battles, above the acclaim of the field, above the applause of the world, to the heaven of the martyr and the hero.

When with dirges due I saw him borne to his grave, with the dull cadence of muffled drums, with draped banners, and slow-pacing soldiers, and all the solemn adjuncts with which affection seeks to alleviate and homage to ennoble death, I could not but think of what Douglas said last year. When the October elections had made a Republican success an event beyond contingency, Douglas, always a magnanimous man and a true friend, said in conversation, "We Springfield people will take the capital next year. Lincoln in the White House, Baker, and M'Dougal, and I in the Senate—we will make Washington jolly in spite of politics."

Alas, for the dead hours of honest friendship! the goodly fellowship of noble spirits! Where are the good fellows who were friends at Springfield in the happier days? [John J.] Hardin's[59] spirit went up through the murky canopy whose baleful shadow hung over the battling legions at Buena Vista—[William H.] Bissell passed from lingering pain to Paradise, honored in the highest by the State that he had honored—Douglas lies under the prairie sod in the dear old State, whose half-estranged heart burned with more than the old love for him before he died—Baker rests glorious in death, a precious offering to the Spirit of Freedom to which through life his worship was paid—and Lincoln stands, lonely in his power, a sadder, silenter, greater man than of old, time beginning to sift its early snows upon the blackness of his hair, his heart heavy with the sorrows of a nation, his mind and soul pledged to solemn and self-abnegating effort to keep from detriment in his hands the costly treasure of Constitutional Government.

For this Douglas toiled and Baker died. High examples are not without their uses; and, perchance, from the grave of the dead Senator may spring the living flowers of sacrifice and bright endeavor. Let no man now excuse himself from the service of his country by paltry suggestions of rank, of position, of diverse usefulness. Baker sacrificed more than others can. He was a Senator; he became a recruiting-officer. He was a man of extensive affairs; he neglected all for the camp. He was a man of delicate and scholarly tastes; he forsook books for bayonets, and slighted letters to study tactics. He had a family, which he tenderly loved; he bade farewell to his wife, and enlisted his son in his regiment. He enjoyed life with the intense vitality of a perfect manhood; he gave his life for his country.

And all with no bravado, no barbaric thirst for excitement. He obeyed an imperious mandate of duty; and warfare with him rose to the dignity of religion. Through the storm and gloom of the present his prophetic spirit caught the distant sunshine of a righteous peace, to which the war was a necessary and painful introduction. Let us all remember those eloquent words of lofty cheer with which, standing in his place, bronzed in the summer weather, his fatigue uniform travel-stained and dusty from camp and field, the warrior-statesman closed his reply to the sneering cavils of the fallen angel of Kentucky [*Senator John C. Breckinridge*]—and let them end this sketch of him whose memory may safely be confided to the jealous keeping of impartial fame: "There will be some graves reeking with blood, watered by the tears of affection; there will be some privation; there will be some loss of luxury; there will be somewhat more need for labor to procure the necessaries of life. When that is said, all is said. If we have the country, the whole country, the Union, the Constitution, free government—with these will return all the blessings of well-ordered civilization; the path of the country will be a career of greatness and glory such as, in the olden time, our fathers saw in the dim visions of years yet to come; and such as would have been ours to-day if it had not been for the treason for which the Senator too often seeks to apologize."

Appendixes
Notes
Index

Appendix 1

The Authorship of the Bixby Letter

One of the most extravagantly admired of all Lincoln documents is the letter of condolence to the Widow Bixby, dated 21 November 1864. James G. Randall declared that it "stands with the Gettysburg address as a masterpiece in the English language."[1] Carl Sandburg called it "a piece of the American Bible. 'The cherished memory of the loved and lost' — these were blood-color syllables of a sacred music."[2] Comparing the Bixby letter with the Gettysburg address, Sandburg added: "More darkly than the Gettysburg speech the letter wove its awful implication that human freedom so often was paid for with agony."[3] Another Lincoln biographer claimed that "Lincoln's three greatest writings" — the Gettysburg address, the letter to Mrs. Bixby, and the second inaugural address — are the compositions "upon which assessment of his literary achievement must ultimately be based."[4] In *Lincoln the Writer,* two literary scholars praised "the haunting strain of poetry" in the Bixby letter, the Gettysburg address, and the second inaugural address: "All three great prose-poems were the direct outgrowth of the circumstances of his last years working on the heart of Lincoln the poet. In a greater sense they were the outgrowth of his whole life, of all those mysterious qualities of heredity and environment that went into the making of his genius."[5] Even more rhapsodic was the appraisal of Daniel Kilham Dodge, who painted a picture of Lincoln as he wrote to the widow Bixby: "[W]e can imagine how that great heart throbbed and that strong, beautiful right hand rapidly traversed the paper while he was bringing comfort to a bereaved patriot mother. There was as true lyrical inspiration at work in the plain office of the White House that twenty-first day of November, 1864 as that which impelled Wordsworth to compose the 'Ode on Intimations of Immortality.'"[6] A New Yorker thought the Bixby letter superior to the Gettysburg address: "It is cleaner English, better constructed and shows a heartfull of emotion and sympathy."[7] Henry Watterson called it "the most sublime letter ever penned by the hand of man."[8] Here is the text of that much-lauded missive:

> I have been shown in the files of the War Department a statement of the Adjutant General of Massachusetts, that you are the mother of five sons who have died gloriously on the field of battle. I feel how weak and fruitless must be any words of mine which should attempt to beguile you from the grief of a loss so overwhelming. But I cannot refrain from tendering to you the consolation that may be found in the thanks of the Republic they died to save. I pray that our Heavenly Father may assuage the anguish of your bereavement, and leave you only the cherished memory of the loved and lost, and the solemn pride that must be yours, to have laid so costly a sacrifice upon the altar of Freedom.[9]

The manuscript of this document has not been seen since 24 November 1864, when it was delivered to Mrs. Bixby, who evidently did not preserve it. Her granddaughter believed that the widow "was secretly in sympathy with the Southern cause . . . and had 'little good to say of President Lincoln.'" She added, "I remember so clearly my surprise when my mother told me how Mrs. Bixby resented" the letter.[10] The widow's great-grandson similarly recalled, "In my boyhood days I was advised by my Father that my Great-Grandmother was an ardent Southern Sympathizer, and when she received the letter, she destroyed it in angry [sic]." On another occasion he asserted that Mrs. Bixby, "originally from Richmond, Virginia, destroyed it shortly after receipt without realizing its value."[11]

Some respectable Bostonians looked askance at Mrs. Bixby. Sarah Cabot Wheelwright, who at the age of twenty-six became acquainted with her, described the widow in unflattering terms: "Another woman to whom I gave work," she recalled forty years after the event, "was a Mrs. Bixby, who had been recommended to me by Mrs. Charles Paine as being very deserving." She was, as Mrs. Wheelwright remembered, "a stout woman, more or less motherly-looking, but with shifty eyes." Although she did not like the widow, Mrs. Wheelwright approached her in an attempt to help convey "small comforts" to Union prisoners of war. When the widow suggested that she could expedite such an errand of mercy through one of her sons, Mrs. Wheelwright visited her home. "I did not like the look of things at all," Mrs. Wheelwright remembered, and the woman was very evasive; would give me no definite information, said her son was not there, and asked if I would not meet him somewhere. I said I would and told her to send him to the ladies [*waiting*] room in the Albany Station at a certain time. I was there at the time appointed, and presently a very ill looking man, who had lost some of the fingers of his right hand, came towards me. He began with some familiarity, but I soon put a stop to him, finding I could get no information from him, and sent him off. Soon after this I received a very distressed letter from Mrs. Paine, saying that the police on finding that we were helping this woman had told her that she kept a house of ill-fame, was perfectly untrustworthy and as bad as she could be.[12]

The Boston constabulary would not have been surprised to learn that Mrs. Bixby lied about her sons. In fact, she had lost only two, not five, of them in the war. Of the three survivors, one had deserted to the enemy, another may have done so, and the third was honorably discharged. The famous letter of condolence was a response to an appeal from Massachusetts governor John A. Andrew. Mrs. Bixby had presented William Schouler, adjutant general of Massachusetts, documents indicating that five of her sons had died while serving in the Union army. Schouler then praised Mrs. Bixby to Governor Andrew as "the best specimen of a true-hearted Union woman I have yet seen." The governor, in turn, told the authorities in Washington that the case of the widow Bixby was "so remarkable that I really wish a letter might be written her by the President of the United States, taking notice of a noble mother of five dead heroes so well deserved." As all the world knows, the White House honored the request. Schouler delivered the letter, which has not been seen since.[13]

In the absence of a manuscript, doubts about its authorship arose. Some contend that John Hay actually wrote the letter, which Lincoln then signed. One participant in "the furious controversies that have raged" over this question noted that they threatened "to become as important in the annals of this country as *le affair Dreyfus* was in France, with this difference — no scandal, though a lot of dirt and deception, attaches to it; no duels, except verbal ones, have been fought over it; and no one . . . has been imprisoned because of it."[14]

One of the first to suggest that Hay might have written the Bixby letter was William E. Barton in his 1926 volume, *A Beautiful Blunder*. Cryptically

Barton said that "[f]rom a very high source comes a suggestion that there is an unpublished mystery with respect to this matter. It can mean, as I judge, nothing else than that John Hay wrote the letter." (The "high source" was Nicholas Murray Butler, as correspondence in the Barton Papers at the University of Chicago makes clear.) Barton, however, doubted Hay's authorship, in part because no one in the Hay family had ever heard such a claim and also because "versatile and gifted as John Hay was, he could not have written that letter. It is Lincoln's own, and there is no other letter just like it anywhere."[15]

Seven years later, Rollo Ogden of the *New York Times* asserted that the Bixby letter "was doubtless signed by Lincoln and is certainly characteristic of his language; but it was actually written by John Hay."[16] When queried about his source, Ogden replied: "I know of no scrap of documentary evidence, but Mr. Hay in his lifetime told more than one person that he really wrote the letter which Lincoln signed. Among others he confided this fact to . . . W[*illiam*] C[*rary*] Brownell, who told me of it at the time. Naturally, Mr. Hay took pains never publicly to claim the authorship, and, I presume, left nothing which set the matter straight."[17]

In addition to Brownell, Hay informed Walter Hines Page that he had composed the Bixby letter. A year after Ogden's editorial appeared, the Reverend Mr. G. A. Jackson published the following letter:

"When I lived at Knebworth, Cora, Lady Strafford . . . occupied for a time Knebworth House . . . and the late Mr. Page . . . used to spend weekends there. On one occasion, Lady Strafford told me, he noticed a copy . . . of Lincoln's letter [*to Mrs. Bixby*] and asked her if she knew the true history of it. He then related that John Hay had told him that when the news of the mother's bereavement was given to Lincoln he instructed Hay to write a suitable reply of condolence. This Hay did, and handed it to Lincoln," who "was so surprised that Hay had so perfectly captured his style of composition that he had the letter exactly as Hay wrote it sent to the mother as coming from himself."[18]

Six years later Nicholas Murray Butler, president of Columbia University, corroborated the story in his autobiography. According to Butler,

Theodore Roosevelt admired the Bixby letter greatly and had a framed photograph of it in one of the guest rooms at the White House. John Morley occupied this room while the guest of President

Roosevelt in 1904. His attention was attracted to the Bixby letter, of which he had never heard, and he too admired it greatly.

One morning during his visit to Washington, Morley called on John Hay, then Secretary of State, whose house was on the opposite side of Lafayette Square from the White House. Morley expressed to Hay his great admiration for the Bixby letter, to which Hay listened with a quizzical look upon his face. After a brief silence, John Hay told Morley that he had himself written the Bixby letter. . . . Hay asked Morley to treat this information as strictly confidential until after his [*Hay's*] death. Morley did so, and told me that he had never repeated it to any one until he told it to me during a quiet talk in London at the Athenaeum on July 9, 1912. He then asked me, in my turn, to preserve this confidence of his until he, Morley, should be no longer living.[19]

Morley apparently gave J. A. Spender a similar account. As Spender recalled: "The story about the Bixby letter and John Hay is familiar to me but I cannot remember from whom I first had it. Certainly not from John Hay himself but possibly from Lord Morley, who was an intimate friend of many years. Hay was a very punctilious man and it was unlike him to claim the authorship of anything that he wrote on behalf of his chief, but he may have let a word slip in private talk with an English friend. But the whole story may be founded on Hay's known accomplishment as a writer and somebody's suggestion that the Bixby letter is not in Lincoln's style."[20]

Louis A. Coolidge, a Washington correspondent for a Boston newspaper, also confirmed the story when he "emphatically" stated "that President Lincoln had nothing to do with the Bixby Letter." Coolidge covered Washington from 1891 to 1904 and in that latter year served as the literary director of the Republican National Committee. The identity of Coolidge's informant is unknown, but it may well have been Hay.[21]

Spencer Eddy, Hay's personal secretary, told his sister that Hay had actually written the Bixby letter. She assumed that Hay himself or his close friend Henry Adams was the source of her brother's information.[22]

Lending further credence to the story is Hay's 1866 statement to William Herndon that Lincoln "wrote very few letters. He did not read one in fifty that he received. At first we tried to bring them to his notice, but at last he gave the whole thing over to me, and signed without reading them the letters I wrote in his name."[23] Presumably, Lincoln would have asked Hay to write letters for him at especially hectic times, such as late November 1864. On the nineteenth of that month, Hay told Francis B. Carpenter, "We are very busy."[24] A week later, he wrote Charles S. Spencer: "I regret that the President was literally crowded out of the opportunity of writing you a note for yr. banquet. He fully intended to do so *himself* & for that reason I did not prepare a letter for him. But the crush here just now is beyond endurance."[25]

Most Lincoln specialists, following Barton's example, have resisted the notion that Hay wrote the Bixby letter. In 1943, Roy P. Basler, editor-to-be of *The Collected Works of Abraham Lincoln*, dismissed Walter Hines Page's recollection as a "matter of British tea-table gossip," and Hay's letter to Herndon as "inadequate, inaccurate, and incorrect." John Morley's statement to Nicholas Murray Butler, in Basler's view, was ambiguous: when Hay said he "wrote" the Bixby letter, he probably meant only that he had simply taken down the words dictated by Lincoln. Basler was evidently unaware of the testimony of W. C. Brownell and of Louis A. Coolidge.[26] Basler also cast doubt on Mrs. Wheelwright's unflattering account of the widow Bixby: "I simply cannot accept the Wheelwright story because it [*is*] too obviously damning. . . . Methinks the good Mrs. Wheelwright sounds a little bit like a psychopathic gossip who cannot refrain from spreading it on and from putting an uncouth and forward lower-class individual in his [*sic*] place. Of course, this is deducing too freely, but when I am suspicious I am hard to convince."[27]

To clinch his case, Basler argued that "the internal evidence of style seems to mark the letter as Lincoln's. . . . If the student will read aloud the best of Lincoln's lyrical passages in the 'Farewell Address,' 'Gettysburg Address,' or 'Second Inaugural Address' and then read aloud the 'Letter to Mrs. Bixby,' he will find it exceedingly difficult to believe that anyone other than Lincoln composed such sentences as 'I feel how weak and fruitless must be any word of mine which should attempt to beguile you from the grief of a loss so overwhelming. . . .'" Basler invited skeptics to "procure a copy of Thayer's *Life and Letters of John Hay* and read a few of Hay's compositions."[28]

Basler's view was widely accepted, as Don E. Fehrenbacher observed in 1987: "Since the original letter was lost, and its words survived as they were printed in a Boston newspaper, there is no way of verifying or disproving some dubious gossip that attributes the authorship to John Hay. Nevertheless, there seems to be general agreement among scholars in the field that the words of the Bixby letter are characteristically and peculiarly Lincoln's."[29]

Among the Lincoln specialists endorsing Basler's view was F. Lauriston Bullard, chief editorial writer of the *Boston Herald* and head of the Lincoln Group of Boston. Three years after Basler's article appeared, Bullard published *Abraham Lincoln and the Widow Bixby*, which emphatically denied that Hay had composed the letter. Bullard pointed to several considerations that made him doubt the claims of Hay's authorship: Hay was not exactly in his right mind on the day when he spoke with John Morley about the Bixby letter; Hay never informed Richard Watson Gilder that he wrote that document; and Hay in 1904 told William E. Chandler that the "letter of Mr. Lincoln to Mrs. Bixby is genuine." Bullard concluded (uncannily echoing the words of William E. Barton): "Gifted and versatile though John Hay was, . . . the young man . . . could not have written the letter to Mrs. Bixby." Walter Hines Page's testimony "is not of value," Bullard declared, and the *New York Times* editorial writer's account was "no more conclusive" than Page's. Bullard also cited a letter he had received from Tyler Dennett, Hay's biographer, stating that although "Hay is not remembered by members of his family ever to have denied the authorship, it seems not to have been remembered by anyone except John Morley that he ever claimed it." Dennett added that he did "not regard the Butler-Morley statement as conclusive."[30]

Bullard's argument from Tyler Dennett's authority is weak, for Dennett told Roy Basler that Hay may well have written the Bixby letter:

As for his style in that period and shortly thereafter, I think it is sometimes sufficiently in the vein of the Bixby letter to make plausible the assumption that he drafted the letter. There are many passages in Hay's letters from Paris and elsewhere immediately after the Civil War, and many passages in his letters and diaries when he was in Madrid [*1869–1870*] which have the rhythm and even the alliteration which appeared in Lincoln's style. In this period Hay had a tendency to overwrite his paragraphs and while it may seem lese majesty to say so it [*h*]as always seemed to me that the Bixby letter is a trifle overwritten. . . . I still incline to the opinion, which I cannot prove, that Hay not only disposed of a great many letters for the President but even wrote and signed some. Furthermore it seems to me not only plausible but reasonable that a young and impressionable man like Hay, under the influence of such a strong personality and in such intimate association would be likely to take on some of the characteristics of his senior. Hay was, particularly in that period, a very imitative person, as the Pike County ballads indicate. In fact Hay's imitative capacity is one of the important clues to understanding the man. He drew very heavily on his associations in a great variety of ways down to the latter years of his service as Secretary when the imitative quality seems to have faded out.[31]

Dennett also told Edward C. Stone that he was "of the opinion that John Hay could have drafted it [*the Bixby letter*]. In fact, it seems to me just a trifle over-written for Lincoln."[32]

In an extended review of Bullard's volume, William H. Townsend praised the author and belittled "the whisperings, insinuations and vague, indefinite recollections" of Page, Brownell, Coolidge, and Morley. Such "remote and nebulous hearsay evidence," Townsend declared, "could not even get in the back door of a courtroom or any other place where facts are analyzed and testimony weighed with care and impartiality."[33]

Other Lincoln specialists concurred, including Louis A. Warren. "Knowing Mr. Lincoln as I do," Warren asserted, "I do not think he would delegate it to some secretary. I cannot conceive how with the background built up as it has been built up the request made so explicit as it was upon Mr. Lincoln that he would delegate anybody to do the task but would most certainly do it himself in the finest way possible."[34] Logan Hay believed that at most John Hay wrote the original draft of the Bixby letter, which Lincoln then revised.[35] Paul Angle scoffed at Nicholas Murray Butler and others who contended that Hay wrote the Bixby letter: "As to the genuineness of the letter itself there has never been the slightest doubt in my mind. Nicholas Murray Butler's recent statement to the effect of John Hay once claiming authorship of the letter does not seem to me to be worthy of the slightest confidence."[36] Angle conceded that Hay and Nicolay may have written some letters that Lincoln signed, but added: "I have seen a very few letters which I thought were undoubtedly composed by either Hay or Nicolay and signed by Lincoln, but they were of no importance whatever. I am certain that Lincoln handled his own correspondence in the overwhelming majority of cases. Butler's assertions are, in my opinion, only the baseless imaginings of an old man. . . . I don't think that John Hay wrote

the original letter and my opinion will not be changed by the mere assertion of anyone, least of all Nicholas Murray Butler."[37] Harry E. Pratt shared
Angle's skepticism about Butler's memory: "Personally I don't believe Butler quoted Hay correctly. I have little use for Butler's historical scholarship
after he wrote a preface for the Hidden Lincoln [*by Emanuel Hertz*] without even reading it."[38]

Not everyone agreed with Basler. In the 1940s, both Sherman Day Wakefield, secretary of the Lincoln Group of New York and author of *How Lincoln Became President,* and David Rankin Barbee, a journalist and amateur
historian with a prodigious appetite for original research, filed dissenting
opinions.[39] Barbee accepted the Morley and Page stories at face value and
argued that Lincoln would never have used the term *our Heavenly Father.*
He dismissed William H. Townsend as Bullard's "feather-brained booster
from Lexington, Kentucky."[40] (Townsend reciprocated the contempt, calling Barbee "a professional Confederate," an "embittered professional
Southerner," and "a jackass." Bullard also condemned Barbee's "vitupera-
tive style," which he deemed "quite unworthy of any serious student.")[41]
Wakefield made several points, perhaps the most telling of which is his
analysis of Bullard's *coup de grace,* Hay's letter to William E. Chandler calling the Bixby letter "genuine." All Hay meant to imply, according to Wakefield (and Bullard seems to concede this vital point) is that the letter was
not a fake. A "genuine" Lincoln letter, in Hay's view, could be one that a
secretary wrote and the president then signed. That is all that Wakefield
and Barbee—as well as Morley, Page, Brownell, and Coolidge—meant to
suggest: that Hay composed the document to which Lincoln affixed his
signature. Wakefield also argued that Hay could well have written such a
profound letter.

In 1953 Basler seemingly ended the dispute by including the Bixby letter in *The Collected Works of Abraham Lincoln* with the following annotation: "Controversy over the claim that John Hay composed this letter has
somewhat abated, with the claim remaining unproved."[42] Two years later,
Lincoln the President: Last Full Measure, by James G. Randall and Richard
N. Current, appeared, endorsing Basler's conclusion. In the five pages Randall devoted to the Bixby letter (Randall wrote the chapter that discusses
the Bixby letter), Randall failed to mention the testimony of Walter Hines
Page, W. C. Brownell, or Louis A. Coolidge. He ignored Hay's 1866 letter to
Herndon, which asserted that Lincoln "signed without reading them the

letters I wrote in his name." Randall dismissed Nicholas Murray Butler's account of John Morley's recollection as "flimsy statements," arguing that "careful historians" agree that "reminiscence is not enough, and it must be repeated that the idea of Hay's authorship rests upon indirectly reported conversations." The Bixby letter, Randall concluded, "is sincere and heart-to-heart" and "a fine example of Lincoln's personal tact."[43]

Thus matters have stood for decades. In 1982, Mark E. Neely Jr. declared flatly, "There is not a scrap of reliable evidence to prove" that Hay wrote the Bixby letter.[44] But as William E. Barton had warned, "one never knows out of what dusty pigeonhole will emerge some letter or document that casts an entirely new light on such a problem."[45] Such a document was donated to Brown University in 1954 as part of John Hay's papers: a scrapbook of newspaper clippings, mostly from the late 1860s and early 1870s. Hay's handwriting identifies some of their sources. The overwhelming bulk of the items pasted into the 110 pages are Hay's own poems, along with reviews, notices, and commentary on his books, lectures, and poetry. Two pages contain clippings dating from the Civil War: "Ye Armie Gambolier," a poem written by Hay in South Carolina in April 1863; "A Paper of Pins of J[efferson] D[avis]," signed J. H.; an article announcing Hay's appointment as colonel in 1863; an 1865 notice of Hay's imminent departure for Paris to assume the duties of the secretary of the American legation; four more Hay poems—"A New Nursery Ballad," "Boudoir Prophecies," "The Advance Guard," and "God's Vengeance"—and the Bixby letter.[46]

In 1952, a similar scrapbook was donated to the Library of Congress.[47] Primarily filled with clippings of Hay's anonymous and pseudonymous journalism from 1860 to 1865, it too contains the letter to the widow Bixby as well as a few others signed by the president, including one to John Phillips, written the same day as the Bixby letter.[48] (Louis A. Warren plausibly concluded that "the person who composed the letter to Deacon Phillips wrote the note to the Widow Bixby.")[49] It is difficult to understand why Hay would have pasted the Bixby letter in these scrapbooks, full of his own literary creations, unless he had composed it himself.

Further support for the argument in favor of Hay's authorship can be found among the Hay Papers, which became available at Brown University a year after Basler had seemingly settled the question in his 1953 edition of Lincoln's collected works. Among Hay's manuscripts are many documents supporting William L. Werner's contention that the style of the Bixby letter resembles Hay's more than Lincoln's.[50] A professor of American and comparative literature at Pennsylvania State University, Werner found "three false notes" in the Bixby letter: the phrase *our Heavenly father*, the word *gloriously*, and the word *Republic*. A search of Lincoln's collected works and a reading of Hay's published and many of his unpublished works reveal that Werner had a point, but that he could have made it stronger if he had also called attention to the words *beguile* and *cherished*, as well as the phrases *I pray that our Heavenly father* and *I cannot refrain from tendering*.

In his brief article, Werner declared that *gloriously* was "just the word young Hay would use" and cites five examples of Hay's wartime use of *glorious* or *gloriously*. Lincoln, on the other hand, Werner observed, "was a man without glory in his dictionary or in his heart. I cannot find the word 'glorious' at all, apart from this letter [*to the Widow Bixby*]."[51]

The word *gloriously* appears four times in Lincoln's writings before his presidency, and only twice during it. In Hay's writings, *gloriously* appears at least ten times, seven of which were during the Civil War. The word *glorious* appears at least seventy-seven times in Hay's writings, but only thirty-one times in Lincoln's. Of those thirty-one instances, five are found in documents that may well have been written by William Henry Seward for Lincoln's signature.

In his collected works, Lincoln seldom used the word *glory*, especially during his presidency. There is but one instance in his writings between 1860 and his death, and that occurs in a letter that Hay may well have written for him. In his pre-1860 writings, *glory* can be found only eight times. Hay used the word *glory* far more frequently than did Lincoln. Hay's published works and his unpublished writings at Brown University contain seventy-nine instances compared to Lincoln's nine. Lincoln's collected works contain one example of *glorify*, while Hay used it at least six times. Lincoln's collected works do not contain a single example of *glories;* Hay used it at least ten times in his writings. Neither *inglorious* nor *ingloriously* appears in Lincoln's collected works. Hay used them at least six times.

In sum, Hay uses *glory* and its derivatives (*glorious, gloriously, glories, inglorious, ingloriously,* and *glorify*) at least 179 times, and Lincoln, only forty-eight (or forty-two if we exclude the six instances in documents that seem to have been composed by Hay or Seward for the president). Thus, Werner is justified in suspecting that Hay would have been more likely to employ *gloriously* than Lincoln would have.

Werner contended that Hay often used the word *republic* when referring to the United States, while Lincoln seldom did. The president's "favorite word (apart from formal documents) is 'Union'," he observed; "in the famous letter to Horace Greeley there are seven Unions and no synonyms. Sometimes, as in the Gettysburg address, he uses 'nation,' and at other times he used 'country.'" On the other hand, Werner maintained, "'Republic' is a favorite word of John Hay."[52]

Werner's hypothesis is not well supported by the writings of both men. In Lincoln's collected works, *republic* appears as a synonym for *nation* or *Union* thirteen times.[53] Hay used it in that context at least eighteen times.

Werner's argument that Lincoln was less inclined than Hay to use *our Heavenly father* is hard to confirm, for Hay seldom employed that locution, and in some of Lincoln's formal state papers (perhaps composed by Secretary of State William Henry Seward) it does appear. If Hay did not use the phrase *our Heavenly Father* often, he did in 1885 console a friend thus: "*I pray that our Heavenly Father may* comfort you in *your bereavement.*"[54] This language duplicates part of the Bixby letter: "*I pray that our Heavenly Father may* assuage the anguish of *your bereavement.*" Nowhere in Lincoln's published writings outside the Bixby letter can the construction *I pray that our Heavenly Father* be found.

Hay used a similar construction in an 1866 letter: "I cannot intrude upon your sacred grief, but I pray that God may sustain and comfort and uphold you."[55]

Curiously, Werner did not call attention to Hay's inordinate fondness for the word *beguile*, which occurs nowhere in Lincoln's collected works except for the Bixby letter. Hay used it at least thirty times, most often during the Civil War. In fact, in 1861 he used the word twice in his obituary of Edward D. Baker (see chapter 5 in this volume) and twice in an article for the *Missouri Republican* (25 June 1862).

Werner also failed to note that Hay, unlike Lincoln, frequently used the word *cherish*, an example of which can be found in a letter of condolence to Mrs. H. H. Richardson: "I lost in him one of the friends I most *cherished* and valued—and the loss to the country is irreparable."[56] In another letter of consolation, he said: "We had seen him so recently, and he was so firm and active in mind, so full of interest and hope for the future of the country, so unflinching in his support of the principles he had *cherished* so long and well, that we had hoped to see him, restored in health, long occupying his high position of citizen and patriot, where he was so needed."[57] He used the word at least forty-five other times. The word *cherish* appears only nine times in Lincoln's collected works, and two of the documents containing it were probably written by someone other than Lincoln.

Werner might have strengthened his case if he had noted that other constructions in the Bixby letter are Hay's rather than Lincoln's, such as "But *I cannot refrain from tendering* to you the consolation . . ." Five months before the Bixby letter was written, Hay told Quincy A. Gillmore, "*I cannot refrain from tendering* my hearty congratulations upon the forcible and authoritative endorsement [*that*] you today rec[*eive*]d in the Senate."[58] *I cannot refrain from tendering* does not appear in Lincoln's collected writings, though *I cannot refrain from* does on one occasion: "It is useless for me to say to you (and yet *I cannot refrain from* saying it) that you must not let your approaching election in Ohio so result as to give encouragement to Douglasism."[59] Hay used that expression several times. In 1858, he wrote to a friend, "*I cannot refrain from* availing myself of the opportunity presented by your letter of expressing to you my gratitude for your great kindness."[60] In 1866, he told Frederick W. Seward, "*I cannot refrain from* writing you my congratulations."[61] Four years later, he told a Spanish political leader, "*I cannot refrain from* expressing my admiration and delight at your magnificent discourse."[62] In 1874, he endorsed a friend's application for membership in a social club, saying, "*I cannot refrain from* saying a word in his favor."[63] In a letter of condolence to Henry James, Hay wrote in 1882: "*I cannot refrain from* sending you one line of sympathy and regard."[64] In another letter of condolence, he said "*I cannot refrain from* saying that Mrs. Hay and I have a share in your sorrow."[65]

Moreover, the tone of the Bixby letter resembles that in several of Hay's messages of condolence:

To Manning Leonard in 1864: "I will not intrude upon your sorrow further than to express my deep sympathy for your great loss and my prayer that a merciful God may give you that consolation which mortal love is too weak to offer."[66]

To William Henry Seward in 1865: "I do not dare to attempt the poor consolation that esteem and devotion can offer."[67]

To a Mr. Marshall in 1865: "I hope you will not think me intrusive in say-ing to you how much we were all grieved and shocked at hearing of the sudden death of your father."[68]

To "My dear Curtis" in 1867: "I hope you will not think me intrusive in offering you my heartfelt sympathy in your great affliction."[69]

To John G. Nicolay in 1885: "I do not dare to try to write any word of comfort to you. There is no comfort possible in such a disaster. I can only say I sympathize with you in this dark hour with all my heart. . . . Noth-ing is left but the memory of her sweet and loving character — her clear, strong intellect — her true and honest heart."[70]

These are far different from Lincoln's 1862 letter of condolence to Fanny McCullough:

> It is with deep grief that I learn of the death of your kind and brave Father; and, especially, that it is affecting your young heart beyond what is common in such cases. In this sad world of ours, sorrow comes to all; and, to the young, it comes with bitterest agony, because it takes them unawares. The older have learned to ever expect it. I am anxious to afford some alleviation of your present distress. Perfect relief is not possible, except with time. You can not now realize that you will ever feel better. Is not this so? And yet it is a mistake. You are sure to be happy again. To know this, which is certainly true, will make you some less miserable now. I have had experience enough to know what I say; and you need only to believe it, to feel better at once. The memory of your dear Father, instead of an agony, will yet be a sad sweet feeling in your heart, of a purer, and holier sort than you have known before.[71]

It might be objected that the tone of the Bixby letter does in fact resem-ble that of Lincoln's letter of condolence to the parents of Elmer E. Ellsworth:

> In the untimely loss of your noble son, our affliction here, is scarcely less than your own. So much of promised usefulness to one's coun-try, and of bright hopes for one's self and friends, have rarely been so suddenly dashed, as in his fall. In size, in years, and in youthful appearance, a boy only, his power to command men, was surpass-ingly great. This power, combined with a fine intellect, an indom-itable energy, and a taste altogether military, constituted in him, as

seemed to me, the best natural talent, in that department, I ever knew. And yet he was singularly modest and deferential in social intercourse. My acquaintance with him began less than two years ago; yet through the latter half of the intervening period, it was as intimate as the disparity of our ages, and my engrossing engagements, would permit. To me, he appeared to have no indulgences or pastimes; and I never heard him utter a profane, or an intemperate word. What was conclusive of his good heart, he never forgot his parents. The honors he labored for so laudably, and, in the sad end, so gallantly gave his life, he meant for them, no less than for himself.

In the hope that it may be no intrusion upon the sacredness of your sorrow, I have ventured to address you this tribute to the memory of my young friend, and your brave and early fallen child.

May God give you that consolation which is beyond all earthly power.[72]

David Rankin Barbee argued that Hay, not Lincoln, wrote the letter to the Ellsworths.[73] It is entirely possible that Hay at least helped draft it, for he was an extremely close friend of Ellsworth, and a passage from the letter to the Ellsworths ("*May God give you that consolation which is* beyond all earthly power") strongly resembles a passage in Hay's 1864 letter of condolence to Manning Leonard: "my prayer that a merciful *God may give you that consolation which* mortal love *is* too weak to offer." Also noteworthy is the parallel between these words to Leonard — "I will not intrude upon your sorrow" — and these to the Ellsworths — "In the hope that it may be no intrusion upon the sacredness of your sorrow."

Thus, on stylistic grounds, Werner has a far better case than Basler. In fairness to Basler, it should be noted that many of Hay's writings cited above were unavailable to scholars at the time he published his article on the Bixby letter or while he was editing Lincoln's collected works. Nor did Basler have the benefit of computers able to retrieve specific words of Lincoln from his collected works.[74]

The evidence adduced here may not ultimately clinch the case, but in combination with Hay's statement to Herndon in 1866; with the stylistic fingerprints of John Hay throughout the letter (*beguile, cherish, gloriously, I cannot refrain from tendering, I pray that our Heavenly Father*); and with the reminiscences of John Morley, Walter Hines Page, Louis Coolidge,

W. C. Brownell, and Spencer Eddy, Hay's scrapbooks suggest that it is highly probable that Hay, not Lincoln, is the true author of "the most beautiful letter ever written."

This conclusion, of course, does not injure Lincoln's literary reputation; the author of the Gettysburg address and the second inaugural address will long command the world's admiration.[75] As a journalist noted in 1925, "if under the merciless hand of investigation it should be shown that this remarkable document [*the Bixby letter*] was not only based upon misinformation but was not the composition of Lincoln himself, the letter to Mrs. Bixby would still remain ... 'One of the finest specimens of pure English extant.'"[76] Rather than diminishing Lincoln, the conclusion reached here should enhance the status of John Hay among literary critics and scholars.

Appendix 2

Mary Todd Lincoln's
Unethical Conduct as First Lady

The allusions in Hay's correspondence to the unethical conduct of Mary Todd Lincoln in the White House have been called "bitter phrases written in irritation by an immature secretary," which "have been among the loudest notes in posterity's chorus of denunciation of Mrs. Lincoln."[1] In fact, there is much additional evidence regarding the first lady's corruption. Lending credence to Hay's criticisms of Mary Lincoln are long-suppressed passages from the diary of Orville Hickman Browning which were not made public until 1994.

When serving as a member of the Illinois state senate (1836–1840), Browning (1806–1881) had befriended Lincoln, then a representative from Sangamon County. In the capital, they lodged at the same house and spent much time together.[2] Browning recalled that over the next three decades, "our relations were very intimate: I think more so than is usual. Our friendship was close, warm, and, I believe, sincere. I know mine for him was, and I never had reason to distrust his for me. Our relations, to my knowledge, were never interrupted for a moment."[3] One historian described Browning as "Lincoln's life-long associate in law and politics, his cherished adviser and his intimate friend" and concluded that "hardly anyone [was] closer to him."[4] From July 1861 to January 1863, Browning, as a U.S. senator, visited the White House almost every day while Congress was in session.[5]

Most of Browning's diary was published in the 1920s and 1930s; a few passages relating to Mary Todd Lincoln were omitted at the insistence of its owner, Eliza Miller. Upon selling it to the Illinois State Historical Library in 1921, she stipulated that the library not publish those entries because she did not want to dishonor the memory of Browning or embarrass Robert Todd Lincoln and his family. In compliance with her wishes, the library refused to let scholars examine these passages in the manuscript diary until March 1994, when the restrictions were lifted. Here are those censored passages:

29 July 1861: "Soon after I got back to the Senate a messenger arrived with a very beautiful bouquet from Mrs Lincoln, with a note to me, saying among other things that I would always find a very true friend in her if I would give my influence and support to Mr Woods [*William S. Wood*] when his name came up [*for Senate confirmation*] as Commissioner of public buildings—that he was very popular and very worthy[.]"

31 July 1861: "[*John P.*] Usher of Indiana [*assistant secretary of the interior*] told me a great deal of scandal about Mrs. Lincoln[.]"

3 March [*1862*]: "[*Thomas*] Stackpole one of the employee's at the Executive Mansion called at my room at the Capitol this morning, in company with [*John*] Watt, who came to ask me to get the President to give Watt the appointment of public gardener, or agent to buy seeds for [*the*] Patent Office.

"After they had left Stackpole returned to say that Watt ought to have some appointment which would take him away from Washington. He added that he [*Watt*] exercised a bad influence over Mrs Lincoln, and unless he was removed from here and a new leaf turned over at the White House, the family there would all be disgraced.

"That he [*Watt*] had in the beginning of the Administration suggested to Mrs Lincoln the making of false bills so as to get pay for private expenses out of the public treasury and had aided her in doing so, to such an extent that the President had to be informed of it, at which he was very indignant, and refunded what had been thus filched from the government out of his private purse.

"That Watt's wife was now nominally stewardess at a salary of $100 per month, all of which, by private arrangement, went into Mrs Lincoln's pocket.

"That she had purchased a service of silver plate, for her private use in New York, and had it charged in a bill for repairing the government plate, [*and did*] tell the President that the new set had been given to her.

"That the President's message [*to Congress last December*] had been furnished to [*Henry*] Wycoff by her, and not by Watt as is usually supposed—that she got it of [*John D.*] Defrees, Sup[*erintendent*] of government printing, and gave it to Wycoff in the Library, where he read it—gave it back to her, and she gave it back to Defrees. He also said the President had ordered that Wykoff should not be admitted to the White House, but that Mrs Lincoln was now in the habit of meeting him in the Green House, Watt arranging the interviews.

"He told me many other things which were painful to hear, and which will result in the disgrace of the family at the White House, unless they are corrected."[6]

12 April 1866: "Met Mrs Cuthbert, housekeeper at the White House in President Lincolns time. Met her on the steps of the Capitol. She stopped me to ask me to aid in getting her some employment. She said she was very destitute and in distress. That Congress allowed $600 per annum for the Stewardess at the White House, but that she never got it—it was all taken and appropriated by Mrs Lincoln, and she was left pennyless."

3 July 1873: "At breakfast I took a seat by [*U.S. Supreme Court*] Judge [*David*] Davis. . . . I referred to Mrs Lincoln; spoke of her unhappy and ungovernable temper, but added that great injustice had been done her; that her faults had been exaggerated, and that I believed that all the charges against her of having pilfered from the White House were false. The Judge replied that the proofs were too many and too strong against her to admit of doubt of her guilt; that she was a natural born thief; that stealing was a sort of insanity with her, and that she carried away, from the White House, many things that were of no value to her after she had taken them, and that she had carried them away only in obedience to her irresistable propensity to steal. He told me that after Mr Lincoln's death a bill was presented to him as adm[*inistrator of the president's estate*] by a merchant of New York, for $2,000, for a dress for the last inauguration; a very large bill for furs, the amount of which I do not remember, and a bill by Mr Perry, a merchant of Washington for 300 pairs of kid gloves, purchased by her between the first of January and the death of Mr Lincoln, all of which he refused to pay; and that the only bill which had been proven against the estate, and which he had paid, was one for $10 for a country newspaper, somewhere in Illinois. He also told me that Simeon Draper had paid her $20,000 for his appointment as cotton agent in the city of New York."

The rogues mentioned by Browning were close to Mary Lincoln. Simeon Draper, a "well-known real-estate developer" in New York,[7] was described by a contemporary as "an active politician, very popular with his fellow workers in the Republican organization, and prominent in the movements of the party."[8] Henry Villard recalled hearing him speak during the 1856 presidential campaign, during which Draper served as chairman of the Republican Central Committee: "I remember well the admiration I felt every time I saw his commanding figure and heard his stentorian voice."[9] On 7 September 1864, Lincoln named Draper to replace Hiram Barney as collector of customs in New York. The collectorship was a lucrative post, with an annual salary of $6,340 and supplemental "pickings and fees" amounting to about $20,000 a year; the collector also controlled 1,200 jobs.[10] Barney had been appointed in 1861 at the behest of the Horace Greeley-William Cullen Bryant faction in New York politics; Draper represented the other faction, headed by William Henry Seward and Thurlow Weed.[11] Shortly after becoming collector, Draper also won the valuable privilege of selling the cotton that General Sherman had captured in Savannah in December 1864. Earlier in the Civil War, Draper had intervened to keep John Watt from revealing what he knew about Mary Lincoln's unethical conduct. (This matter is treated more fully below.)

Draper may have been one of the targets of Mary Todd Lincoln's attempt at a "shakedown" that "smacked more than slightly of blackmail."[12] In 1867, assuming "an attitude of threat very strongly savoring of extortion," she demanded that men appointed to high office by her husband aid her financially by purchasing her old clothes, which she was selling in New York.[13] She agreed to write letters to be shown to political figures who had benefited from her husband's patronage. If those gentlemen did not then offer assistance, her brokers — S. C. Keyes and William Brady — would threaten to expose them by publishing the letters.

It is not known if Draper was one of the men she intended to shake down, but Abram Wakeman certainly was. Wakeman had been named surveyor of the port of New York at the time that Draper became collector. To her broker William Brady, Mary Todd Lincoln wrote: "Please call and see Hon. Abram Wakeman. He was largely indebted to me for obtaining the lucrative office which he has held for several years, and from which he has amassed a very large fortune. He will assist me in my painful and humiliating situation, scarcely removed from want. He would scarcely hesitate to return, in a small manner, the many favors my husband and myself always showered upon him. Mr. Wakeman many times excited my sympathies in his urgent appeals for office, as well for himself as others. Therefore he will be only too happy to relieve me by purchasing one or more of the articles you will please place before him."[14]

When the public learned of this scheme, a newspaper denounced Mary Todd Lincoln as "a termagant with arms akimbo, shaking her clenched fist at the country, and forgetful of her dead husband and all manner of propriety, demanding gold as the price of silence and pay that is her due because she was the wife of a President." The editor could not "imagine a more shocking exhibition, or one more calculated to put the country to the blush in her behalf."[15] Another paper found her acts consistent with earlier behavior: "Her conduct throughout the administration of her husband was mortifying to all who respected him. . . . She was always trying to meddle in public affairs, and now she will have it known to the whole world that she accepted costly presents from corrupt contractors."[16]

Draper and Wakeman were not the only men named to influential posts in the New York custom house at the urging of Mary Todd Lincoln. In February 1861, she threw a temper tantrum, insisting on the appointment of Isaac Henderson, publisher of the *New York Evening Post*, as naval agent in the New York custom house. Henderson's candidacy was backed by William Cullen Bryant and Parke Godwin.[17] An unsavory self-made man, Henderson evidently had sent Mary Lincoln diamonds as a bribe. She then tried to persuade her husband to appoint Henderson to a lucrative post. When he resisted, she threw a fit. In February 1861, her hysterics delayed Lincoln, who was late for a meeting with Herman Kreismann. Curious about the president-elect's tardiness, Kreismann called at the Springfield hotel where the Lincolns were staying on the eve of their departure for Washington. There he found Mrs. Lincoln in the throes of a tantrum. Lincoln said, "Kreismann, she will not let me go until I promise her an office for one of her friends." He yielded to her importuning and in April nominated Henderson as naval agent.[18] Henderson was dismissed when accused of misconduct three years later. (He allegedly demanded commissions from contractors doing business with the Brooklyn Navy Yard; by one estimate he extorted $70,000.) Although eventually acquitted by a court in 1865, Henderson was believed guilty by Parke Godwin and other observers.[19]

Thomas Stackpole was a watchman at the White House who in 1863 became the steward of the mansion. William P. Wood, superintendent of the Old Capitol prison, claimed that Stackpole, whom he deemed "a subtle partisan, Yankee Democrat" with "an eye to business and . . . anxious to make an extra dollar whenever occasion offered," had gained the confidence of Mary Lincoln and then used her influence to obtain trading permits, which he sold to his friend John Hammack, a Washington restaurateur and "a Virginia-bred Democrat and rabid secessionist." Hammack in turn peddled them to his customers.[20] (Mary Lincoln had direct contact with Hammack; in May 1865 she acknowledged receiving $84 from him.)[21]

Mrs. Lincoln admitted to Alexander Williamson, her sons' tutor in the White House, that she had helped Stackpole "as a friend": "through me he gained many favors, from my good husband"; "much, was done for S[tackpole] in my husband's administration & he realized much money, from my own good nature to S[tackpole] as well as my husband's."[22] Stackpole returned some favors; on her behalf in February 1865 he borrowed $2,000.[23]

William S. Wood, "a former hotel manager and organizer of pleasure excursions," came to Springfield in January 1861 at the suggestion of Thurlow Weed to "take charge of all the arrangements for the journey of the President-elect to Washington." Henry Villard, who saw him at that time, recalled that Wood "was a man of comely appearance, greatly impressed with the importance of his mission and inclined to assume airs of consequence and condescension."[24] According to David Rankin Barbee, Wood was a "scoundrel" who "was sent to Springfield by the Eastern Railroads to entice Lincoln to make that roundabout journey to Washington for the inauguration. By lies and other propaganda he worked on the imagination of Lincoln until Uncle Abe actually imagined that if he took the direct route to Washington, over the Baltimore & Ohio Railroad, he would be assassinated."[25] One observer noted that on the journey to the capital, Wood's "attentions were devoted exclusively to the whims and caprices of Mrs. Lincoln."[26] The following month, Wood presented the first lady with a gift of fine horses.[27]

As first lady, Mary Lincoln became an influence peddler, expediting the cases of clamorous office-seekers in return for such gifts.[28] Her closest friend in Washington, the black modiste Elizabeth Keckley, "said that politicians used to besiege Mrs. Lincoln, and that presents would be sent to her from people whom she had never seen." The donors would attend

White House receptions and declare, "*Mrs. President* Lincoln, I hope you admired that set of furs I sent you lately."

She would reply, "Oh, was it you sent them; really I am at a loss to thank you for your kindness."

"Not at all, madam, it was but a slight and worthless token of the deep esteem I have for the talents of one whose intrinsic merit would, irrespective of your present exalted station, would make you an ornament in the highest circles of the most civilized society."

Pleased with such "fulsome flattery," Mary Lincoln found it "difficult to refuse" when the gentleman than asked a favor. After a few months of this, the president "shut down on it" (to use his own words) and "many scenes" occurred "when his wife was goaded on to ask for places by office-seekers."[29]

Mary Lincoln scrutinized gifts closely. When John A. Logan presented her with a ring which he claimed "had cost him several hundred dollars," she sent it to a New York jeweler, who estimated its value at $18. The first lady returned the bauble.[30]

Wood was evidently one of those who employed flattery and gifts to win public office. Mary Lincoln urged Ward Hill Lamon to use his influence with the president to get Wood appointed despite Lincoln's misgivings.[31] David Davis, who found the appointment of Wood "incomprehensible," was told by the president that "it would be ruinous to appoint him — *ruinous to him.*"[32]

It is hard to know what to make of Lincoln's statement; perhaps it had something to do with the rumors that his wife was committing adultery with Wood. In June 1861, the president received a pseudonymous letter about "the scandal" involving Mary Lincoln and Wood, who went on shopping trips with the first lady to Manhattan.[33] The president spoke sharply to his wife about this matter; Schuyler Colfax later recalled "the war she had with Mr. Lincoln" about her relations with Wood. According to Colfax, the first couple "scarcely spoke together for several days."[34] An Iowan, referring to Wood, claimed that Mary Lincoln "used to often go from the White House to the Astor House in New York to pass the night with a man who held a high government office in Washington, given to him by her husband."[35] Senator Richard Yates hinted broadly that Mary Lincoln had not been "true to her husband,"[36] and John Watt told a journalist in 1867 that "Mrs. Lincoln's relations with certain men were indecently improper."[37]

After learning from a congressional delegation that Wood was corrupt, Lincoln obtained his resignation. While serving as commissioner-of-public-buildings-designate (the Senate had not yet acted on his nomination), Wood told one Samuel A. Hopkins: "I understand that you are here ... trying to get work from the government in the way of engraving. I want to tell you, as a friend, that there is no use at all of trying; that the work will be given to the American Bank Note Company and the National Bank Note Company." When Hopkins protested that his firm could do the work better and cheaper than those competitors, Wood explained that the contract would not go to him because Wood himself had an interest in the American Bank Note Company and that influential New York Republicans such as George Dennison had an interest in the National Bank Note Company. Hopkins then said he was trying to sell the government some cannons for $500 apiece. Wood replied, "Well, I can help you in that matter. Say nothing about the price; we can make something out of that. If the government wants them, they can as well afford to pay more as less. I will take you down and introduce you to Mr. Leslie, the chief clerk of the War Department." After Hopkins told this story on 30 August 1861 to a congressional committee investigating government contracts, members of the committee promptly informed Lincoln, and Wood was replaced on September 6.[38]

A week later, Mary Todd Lincoln denounced Wood "as a very bad man" who "does not know, what truth means." Everyone, she claimed, knew him "to be a most unprincipled man." Her wrath had been occasioned by Wood's charge that her friend, the White House gardener John Watt, was disloyal.[39]

A native of Scotland who had been living in Washington for over a decade by 1861, Watt had served as the presidential gardener since the early 1850s. In January 1861, the thirty-seven-year-old Watt became a major in the Washington, D.C., militia. On September 9, he was appointed first lieutenant in the Sixteenth U.S. Infantry, but the Senate revoked his commission on 3 February 1862. He later told authorities that he "was commissioned by President Lincoln and detailed for special duty at [the] White House and never served with his Regiment," and that he "also acted as recruiting officer at Washington D.C." A congressional report stated that he served as "one of the commanders of the bodyguard of President Lincoln" and "one of his personal aids and attendants." In March 1862, he was appointed to visit Europe on behalf of the Interior Department's Patent Division to inspect seeds. Returning the following year, he enlisted in the Thirteenth New York Artillery as a private on August 12, rose to the rank of corporal, and in 1865 accepted a commission as a second lieutenant in the Thirty-eighth U.S. Colored Troops, serving until 1867. He died in Washington in 1892, survived by his wife, Jane Masterson Watt. They had no children.[40]

Before the Lincolns entered the White House, Watt had acquired an unsavory reputation. As Executive Mansion gardener during the Buchanan administration, he had been chastised by the commissioner of public buildings, John B. Blake, for submitting unreasonable bills. Blake, "astonished" at a seed bill, told Watt in 1859, "You must raise your own seed hereafter." Blake also protested against an "enormous" bill "for making and sharpening tools." Sternly, the commissioner warned him not to "incur the smallest debt without first consulting the public gardener or myself."[41]

Early in Lincoln's first term, Watt continued to attract unfavorable attention. John F. Potter, chairman of the House Select Committee on the Loyalty of Government Employees, informed the president in September 1861 of damning testimony about Watt's pro-Confederate sympathies. Two independent witnesses confirmed that he had, shortly after the first battle of Bull Run, proclaimed that the South could not be defeated and that the Union army consisted of human trash.[42] (Mary Lincoln vehemently denied these allegations.)[43]

This is the gentleman who, according to the White House servant Thomas Stackpole (quoted in Browning's diary) "had in the beginning of the Administration suggested to Mrs. Lincoln the making of false bills so as to get pay for private expenses out of the public treasury and had aided her in doing so."[44] It is not clear just when Watt and the first lady began conspiring to defraud the government. John P. Usher, assistant secretary of the interior, informed Browning in late July of scandals involving Mrs. Lincoln. The first known example of her padding bills occurred the following month, when she tried to charge a state dinner for Prince Napoleon to the account of Watt. He had apparently billed the Interior Department $900 for the August 3 banquet, but Interior Secretary Caleb B. Smith rejected her claim. Secretary Smith told Thurlow Weed, the political partner of Secretary of State William Henry Seward, that because he thought the cost exorbitant, he consulted with Seward, who "had also dined the Prince, having the same number of guests, and giving them a duplicate of the dinner at the White House. In fact," Weed later recalled, "Mr. Seward ordered both dinners from the same restaurant, and, by his own bill, knew the cost of each. For what Mr. Seward paid $300, Mrs. Lincoln demanded $900." Thwarted by Smith's refusal, the first lady then "made her gardener make out a bill for plants, pots etc. of the required amount, certified it herself and drew the money." This "occasioned scandal."[45]

The gardener's account used to hide the cost overrun was described by a White House gatekeeper, James H. Upperman, who complained to Secretary Smith on 21 October 1861 about "sundry petit, but flagrant frauds on the public treasury," the products of "deliberate col[l]usion." According to Upperman, Watt had in mid-September authorized payments to Alexander McKerichar, a laborer on the White House grounds, for flowers ($700.75) and for 215 loads of manure ($107.50), as well as hire of a horse and cart for twenty-seven days in August to haul it to the Executive Mansion ($47.25). These bills were apparently for goods and services not provided. Another gentleman, Charles F. Cone, was paid $33.75 for working at the White House for twenty-seven days in August and $47.25 for the hire of horse cart and driver, even though, Upperman said, "this individual is no labourer and has rendered no such service as charged for as can be proved by sundry persons, that he does not work at any kind of labour and was at the time refer[r]ed to, and can yet be found in a certain locality on P[ennsylvani]a Avenue anytime during working hours." As for Cone's delivery charges, Upperman contended that "it can be proved that no such horse cart or driver rendered any such service in said grounds." Moreover, Upperman claimed, William Johnson was paid $155.00 for 310 loads of manure that were never delivered. Upperman said, "I imagine his whereabouts to be doubtful as nobody knows him." Augustus Jullien, a French cook employed in the White House kitchen, received $67.50 for work done on the grounds in July and August, although he "has at no time rendered any such service." Similarly, Francis P. Burke, a presidential coachman, was paid $33.75 for labor on the grounds for August, as was White House butler Peter Vermeren.[46]

In late October 1861, Mary Lincoln, through Watt, begged Secretary Smith to see the president, evidently about these embarrassing revelations made by the White House gatekeeper. In response to a query from the commissioner of public buildings, Lincoln on October 26 said he would "determine in a few days what he would do." Watt insisted that "the arrangement of the accounts was made by [William S.] Wood & that he assured Mrs L[incoln] that the transaction was right & legal and that she had no idea that anything was done which was not authorized by law." Secretary Smith told his cabinet colleague William Henry Seward that he "would be glad to have her relieved from the anxiety under which she is suffering."[47]

Smith provided such relief by covering up the scandal. After interviewing Watt, McKerichar, and Benjamin Brown French (who had replaced Wood as commissioner of public buildings) about the $700 flower bill, Smith concluded "that the voucher was correct, and that it had been rightfully paid by Mr. French," and therefore he "pursued the matter no further."[48] He did not consult Upperman, Burke, Jullien, Johnson, Vermeren, Cone, or others knowledgeable about the matter. Gatekeeper Upperman then protested to Solomon Foot, chairman of the Senate Committee on Public Buildings and Grounds, citing as his sources Burke, Jullien, and Vermeren, as well as the former public gardener, Thomas J. Sutter, and George W. Dant, a messenger and clerk to the commissioner of public buildings.[49] Nothing came of his complaint. According to Thurlow Weed, the Interior Department and Congress "measurably suppressed" this story out of "respect for Mr. Lincoln."[50] Congressman Benjamin M. Boyer confirmed this story, adding that the president paid the bill himself and withdrew the government check.[51] A congressional committee was made aware of this scandal, but Democratic Senator James A. Bayard of Delaware agreed to hush it up, saying, "The thing's a swindle, gentlemen, but this is the wife of our President, the first lady in this land and we only disgrace ourselves by this exposure."[52]

Commissioner French also knew more about Mary Lincoln's misconduct than he was willing to reveal. In 1865, he wrote about her in his journal: "She is a most singular woman, and it is well for the nation that she is no longer in the White House. It is not proper that I should write down, even here, all I know! May God have her in his keeping, and make her a better woman."[53]

On 11 March 1862, the president asked the "watchdog of the treasury department," first comptroller Elisha Whittlesey, to help him stop the padding of bills: "[O]nce or twice since I have been in this House, accounts have been presented at your bureau, which were incorrect—I shall be personally and greatly obliged to you if you will carefully scan every account which comes from here; and if in any there shall appear the least semblance wrong, make it known to me directly."[54]

Later, when Watt threatened to blackmail the first lady, he evidently received some form of hush money. According to Isaac Newton of the agriculture division of the Interior Department, the gardener "entered into a conspiracy to extort [$]20,000 from the President by using three letters of Mrs. Lincoln."[55] In those documents, the first lady apparently asked Watt "to commit forgery and perjury for purpose of defrauding the Government."[56] In 1867, Watt offered to sell a journalist an account of his relations with Mary Lincoln; it contained "a note to Watt signed by Mrs. L. (which is genuine) proposing to cover up their schemes etc."[57] Simeon Draper, who (according to David Davis's remarks as recorded in the Browning diary) had paid Mary Lincoln $20,000 to help him obtain his position as agent for selling the cotton seized in Savannah by General Sherman, called on Watt and "with much bluster & great oaths" threatened to have him imprisoned. Watt then "fell on his literal marrow bones & begged, & gave up the letters & the conspiracy got demoralized & came down, down, to 1500 dollars which was paid, and the whole thing [was] settled."[58] In March 1862, Watt was named special agent for Newton's agriculture division to purchase seeds in Europe, at an annual salary of $1,500 plus travel costs.[59] (This well-documented story lends credence to the Browning diary entry for 3 March 1862, which describes how Stackpole urged Browning "to get the President to give Watt the appointment of public gardener, or agent to buy seeds for [the] patent office.") After failing to be paid for his services in Europe, Watt in 1863 billed the president $736 to compensate him for Mary Lincoln's hotel bills, cash advances, and "Commissary stores." The vouchers for these payments and advances from Watt to the first lady were held by Simeon Draper.[60] Watt told Simon Cameron, "You know very well what difficulties I had to contend with in regard to Mrs. Lincoln. . . . I paid about $700.00 for Mrs. Lincoln on one trip to Cambridge, Mass."[61]

The Watt affair became the talk of the capital. David Davis told his wife in February 1862, "I got a letter from Washington & the gossip is still about Mrs. Lincoln and the gardener Watt."[62] The press reported that Watt, at Mary Lincoln's instigation, bought two cows "and charged them to the manure fund—that is, a fund voted in one of the general appropriation bills to provide manure for the public lands." This bill was rejected, probably by Secretary Smith. Watt facilitated the sale of a White House rug to a Washington photographer to pay an outstanding bill; the carpet was replaced at public expense.[63]

Secretary Smith also questioned other bills. According to the *New York World*, when Mary Lincoln ordered $800 worth of china from E. V. Haughwout & Co., she evidently tried to hide other purchases, amounting to $1,400, by having the total bill ($2,200) applied to the china alone. When the skeptical interior secretary raised questions, the merchant reportedly acknowledged that the overcharge was made to disguise the unspecified items. Haughwout & Co. denied the allegations in a letter to Manton Marble, editor of the *World*. In turn, Marble defended the story, and rather than retract it, he threatened to "expose what I know about Mrs. Lincoln's practices in her New York purchases—her silver service—the champagne[,] manure bills etc. etc. to say nothing of wallpaper seed commissions, shawls, contracts, etc. etc. etc."[64] John Watt claimed that "a bill of $6,000 contracted with Haughwout & Co. for silverware was paid for by a bill charged against gilding gas-fixtures."[65]

It was reported that Mary Lincoln also suggested to a New York merchant that he provide the White House with a $500 chandelier, charge $1,000 for it, and thus allow her to disguise $500 worth of jewelry purchases. The businessman refused to cooperate and apparently lost the sale of the chandelier.[66] It was widely rumored that Mary Lincoln "appropriated the manure piles which had always been the perquisites of the gardener" and used the funds from the sale of that commodity for her own purposes.[67]

In February 1862, Watt lost his White House position after agreeing to accept the blame for an indiscretion committed by the first lady, who had a reputation as "one of the *leaky vessels*—from whom contraband army news, gets afloat."[68] Two months earlier, the *New York Herald* had published excerpts of the president's annual message to Congress before its official release. When the House Judiciary Committee investigated the matter, Mary Lincoln's close friend and "social adviser," Henry Wikoff, admitted that he had telegraphed the president's message to the *Herald* but refused to tell where he had gotten it. Watt then "confessed" to the committee that he had been Wikoff's source. In fact, as Thomas Stackpole told

Browning, the first lady was the true culprit. During the investigation, Lincoln visited Capitol Hill and "urged the Republicans on the Committee to spare him disgrace."[69]

According to Alexander K. McClure, Mary Lincoln "was the easy prey of adventurers, of which the war developed an unusual crop, and many times they gained such influence over her as to compromise her very seriously."[70] Her friendship with Wikoff, which scandalized proper society, was a case in point. Born to wealthy Philadelphia parents in 1813, Henry Wikoff attended Yale, from which he was expelled, and ultimately graduated from Union College. He spent much time in Europe, where he pursued pleasure single-mindedly. Eventually, he became something of a journalist and an off-again, on-again friend of James Gordon Bennett, editor of the *New York Herald*. In 1851, he achieved notoriety by kidnapping a woman he loved. Convicted of abduction, Wikoff served fifteen months in jail; his account of this misadventure, *My Courtship and Its Consequences*, sold well. Later in the 1850s, he worked for Bennett in Washington, acting as a go-between for the publisher in his dealings with President James Buchanan.[71]

Wikoff had charm as well as notoriety. John W. Forney described him glowingly:

> You might travel a long way before meeting a more pleasant companion than the cosmopolitan Wikoff. He has seen more of the world than most men, has mingled with society of every shade and grade, has tasted of poverty and affluence, talks several languages fluently, is skilled in etiquette, art, and literature, and, without proclaimed convictions, is a shrewd politician, who understands the motives and opinions of others. . . . Ranging through all society, he can talk of love, law, literature, and war; can describe the rulers and thinkers of his time, can gossip of courts and cabinets, of the *boudoir* and the *salon*, of commerce and the Church, of the peer and the pauper, of Dickens and Thackery, of Victor Hugo and Louis Blanc, of Lamartine and Laboulae, of Garibaldi and the Pope, of Lincoln and Stanton, of Buchanan and Pierce, of the North and the South, of the opera and the theater, of General Sickles and Tammany Hall, and of the inner life of almost any capital in the world. With such gifts, aided by an air *distingue*, a fine address and a manner after the English model, Wikoff has the *entree* in many circles which higher intellect and deservings can never penetrate.[72]

Wikoff's relations with Mary Lincoln offended polite society. In December 1861, David Davis told his wife, "Rumors are plenty—that Mrs. Lincoln is acting badly. . . . It is said that she has installed as Master of Ceremonies at the White House, the Chevalier Wikoff. 'My courtship & its consequences' you read. He is a terrible libertine, & no woman ought to tolerate his presence." Washington matrons were "in distress" at this news.[73] A journalist reported in November 1861 that "Mrs. Lincoln is making herself both a fool and a nuisance. Chevalier Wikoff is her gallant, and I have within the week seen two notes signed by him in her name sending compliments and invitation. . . . He is a beautiful specimen to occupy such a position."[74] In disbelief, Joseph R. Hawley asked, "What does Mrs. Lincoln mean by . . . having anything to do with that world-renowned whoremonger and swindler Chevalier Wikoff? Is [Mrs.] Lincoln an old saphead or is she a headstrong fool who thinks she can have a kitchen cabinet? It's a national disgrace."[75] Echoing this sentiment, John Hay deemed Wikoff an "unclean bird," a "vile creature," a "marked and branded social Pariah, a monstrosity abhorred by men and women," and declared it "an enduring disgrace to American society that it suffers such a thing to be at large."[76]

The president intervened when warned of scandal by Matthew Hale Smith, New York correspondent for the *Boston Journal.* Shortly after the Civil War, Smith revealed that full story: Wikoff, "with whom no reputable woman would willingly be seen on Broadway," had been "very officious in his attention to . . . Mrs. Lincoln. His frequent visits to Washington, and his receptions at the White House, were noticed by the friends of the President. At all of the receptions of Mrs. Lincoln he was an early and constant visitor. At the informal receptions he was found. No one went so early but this person could be seen cozily seated in a chair as if at home, talking to the ladies of the White House. None called so late but they found him still there." Wikoff was often "seen riding in the President's coach, with the ladies, through Pennsylvania Avenue. Frequently he was found lounging in the conservatory, or smoking in the grounds, very much at home, and not at all anxious to hide his presence." Wikoff's frequent visits embarrassed the White House staff, and the press began to comment unfavorably.

Friends of the president, suspicious of Wikoff, investigated his background and discovered that he had been hired "by some parties in New York, who were using him as their tool." These men had "furnished him with money and instructions. He was to go to Washington, make himself agreeable to the ladies, insinuate himself into the White House, attend levees, show that he had the power to come and go, and, if possible, open a correspondence with the ladies of the mansion." Once known as an insider, he would be able to wield influence that his backers might find useful in time.

Wikoff carried out his assignment well. Lincoln's friends "considered that the President should be made acquainted with this plot against his honor" and dispatched Smith to do so. Accompanied by a U.S. senator, Smith visited the White House one evening. As he later recalled, Lincoln "took me by the hand, led me into the office of his private secretary, whom he drove out, and locked the door." When Smith showed him documents illuminating the purposes of Wikoff, who at that moment was downstairs in the White House, the president said, "Give me those papers and sit here till I return." Lincoln "started out of the room with strides that showed an energy of purpose." He soon came back, shook Smith's hand, and had Wikoff "driven from the mansion that night."[77]

According to another source, Lincoln "became jealous" of Wikoff and "taxed" his wife. The Chevalier then "volunteered an explanation," telling "the wounded & incensed" president that "he was only teaching the madame a little European Court Etiquette."[78]

When Mary Todd Lincoln left the White House, she took with her "fifty or sixty boxes" and a "score of trunks."[79] Some journalists believed that she "stole a great deal of Government silver, spoons[,] forks[,] etc[.,] and a large quantity of linen and stuffs."[80] Early in 1866, the *New York Daily News* commented that "No one would have said a word against a *few souvenirs* having been taken away. But to despoil the whole house of the best of everything; to send off by railroad more than seventy large packing-cases filled with the newest carpets, curtains, and works of art which have been provided for the adornment of the house, and not for the use of any one family; this was felt to be not exactly in good taste. It is not longer any wonder that the [*White*] house looks empty, dingy, and shabby."[81] The *New York World* reported that "For the $100,00 appropriated in the last four years for alleged repairs and furniture for the White House, there is now actually *nothing* to show on the premises; the Republican officer can be named who says that he furnished ninety boxes to pack up the removed traps. Another prominent Republican says that it required fifteen carts to remove the luggage from the White House; and in addition to this expenditure and these removals, it is a notorious fact that the thirty thousand dollars lately appropriated to furnish the Executive Mansion will nearly all be absorbed by the creditors for the persons who occupied the house ten months ago."[82] Republican Senator Benjamin F. Wade of Ohio stated that Mary Lincoln "took a hundred boxes . . . away with her, and the Commissioner of Public Buildings swore there were fifteen other boxes that she wanted to carry off and he had to interfere to prevent her. At any rate she cleaned out the White House. I didn't know but she was going to run a big hotel with all she carried off."[83] Mary Lincoln heatedly denied the charge,[84] and her biographers have followed suit.[85] But the testimony of David Davis, a close friend of Lincoln and the administrator of his estate, as recorded in Browning's diary, lends credence to the allegation.

The accuracy of David Davis's assertions to Browning about Mrs. Lincoln's purchase of a $2,000 dress, many furs, and 300 pairs of kid gloves can hardly be doubted, for as administrator of Lincoln's estate, he received the bills he described. Others have testified to Mary Lincoln's extravagant shopping propensities. Her closest friend in the White House, Elizabeth Keckley, alleged that the first lady had run up "store bills" totaling $70,000.[86] Mrs. Keckley recalled how Mary Lincoln told her in 1864,

> I have contracted large debts of which he [*Lincoln*] knows nothing. . . . They consist chiefly of store bills. I owe altogether about twenty-seven thousand dollars. . . . Mr. Lincoln has but little idea of the expense of a woman's wardrobe. He glances at my rich dresses, and is happy in the belief that the few hundred dollars that I obtain from him supply all my wants. I must dress in costly materials. The people scrutinize every article that I wear with critical curiosity. The very fact of having grown up in the West subjects me to more searching observation. To keep up appearances, I must have money—more than Mr. Lincoln can spare for me. He is too honest to make a penny outside of his salary; consequently I had, and still have, no alternative but to run in debt.[87]

In addition to going into debt, Mary Lincoln tricked lobbyists to gain money. According to John B. Ellis, she "was much sought after by the lobbyists, who, knowing that they would not dare to hint at a bribe to the President, loaded her with flattery and presents." But, Ellis maintained, the first lady "was not deceived by them" and "made good use of them to secure the reelection of her husband." To a friend, she confided: "I have an object in view. In a political canvass it is policy to cultivate every element of strength. These men have influence, and we require influence to reelect Mr. Lincoln. I will be clever to them until after the election, and then, if we remain at the White House, I will drop every one of them, and let them know very plainly that I only made tools of them. They are an unprincipled set, and I don't mind a little double-dealing with them." When asked if her husband were aware of such schemes, she replied: "No! He would never sanction such a proceeding, so I keep him in the dark, and will tell him of it when all is over. He is too honest to take proper care of his own interests, so I feel it to be my duty to electioneer for him."[88]

In early 1865, Mary Lincoln arranged to have Edward McManus, a White House doorkeeper, fired and replaced with one Cornelius O'Leary, who corruptly charged $50 to expedite the issuance of pardons for Confederate prisoners of war. The proceeds from this racket he allegedly split with the first lady. O'Leary was "instantly dismissed from service when the President ascertained what had been done."[89]

Mary Lincoln's indebtedness may not have totaled $70,000. In 1866, she maintained that her debts amounted to only $6189.[90] She had by that time returned many of the items she had purchased. For example, Galt and Brothers, a jewelry emporium in the capital, billed her $3,200 for diamond and pearl bracelets and rings, as well as four clocks, all purchased early in 1865. She also owed approximately $600 to Joseph J. May and Company of Washington for eighty-four pairs of kid gloves that she had purchased in five separate transactions within one month. Another Washington store, Harper and Mitchell, claimed that she owed them more than $800. She evidently returned all this merchandise.[91] Davis was not the only lawyer who had to deal with Mary Lincoln's creditors after the assassination. Jesse K. Dubois told an interviewer that he "went to N.Y. [and] arranged [a] $64,000 cl[ai]m ag[ain]st [Lincoln's] estate for Jewelry bought by Mrs[.] L[incoln] of Ball[,] Black & Co of N.Y. without L[incoln]'s knowledge."[92]

Davis's story about his refusal to pay the large bill for furs is alluded to in the diary of John Hay. In 1867, Isaac Newton of the Interior Department told Hay that the first lady "has set here on this here sofy & shed tears by the pint a begging me to pay her debt which was unbeknown to the President. There was one big bill for furs which give her a sight of trouble —

she got it paid at last by some of her friends—I don't know for certain—
not Sim Draper for he promised to pay it . . . but after Lincoln's death he
wouldn't do it."[93]

Mary Lincoln told Abram Wakeman that her husband was "almost a
monomaniac on the subject of honesty."[94] In another letter to Wakeman,
she referred to "our opposite natures" when discussing her marriage.[95]
Others have noted that, as Albert J. Beveridge put it, "few couples have
been more unsuited in temperament, manners, taste, and everything else."[96]
Beveridge might well have added that Mary Lincoln's ethical sense was the
opposite of her husband's.

What is to be made of that impaired ethical sense as revealed in Hay's
letters, as well as in the testimony of Thomas Stackpole and David Davis
in the Browning diary, not to mention the evidence supplied by John Watt,
James H. Upperman, Elizabeth Keckley, William P. Wood, Isaac Newton,
Thurlow Weed, Herman Kreismann, Manton Marble, William Wilkins
Glenn, and other members of the press, and by government records? Perhaps the most charitable—and accurate—judgment was the one Lincoln
himself expressed in a conversation with William P. Wood when that gentleman informed the president that the first lady was involved in a corrupt
traffic in "trading permits, favors and Government secrets." Wood recalled
that as he described these shady practices, the president "exhibited more
feeling than I had believed he possessed" and said, "The caprices of Mrs.
Lincoln, I am satisfied, are the result of partial insanity."[97]

And what is to be made of Lincoln's willingness to appoint men such
as Isaac Henderson, William S. Wood, and John Watt to office? The evidence of the Browning diary and other sources confirms the judgment of
William H. Herndon: "Miserable man! Lincoln had to do things which
he knew were out of place in order to keep his wife's fingers out of his
hair."[98]

Notes

Introduction

1. Joseph Bucklin Bishop, "A Friendship with John Hay," *Century Magazine*, 71, no. 5 (March 1906): 777. Later Bishop recalled the words somewhat differently: "Real history is not to be found in books, but in the personal anecdotes and private letters of those who make history. These reveal the men themselves and the motives that actuate them, and give us also their estimate of those who are associated with them. No one should ever destroy a private letter that contains light on public men, or willingly let die an illuminating anecdote disclosing their individuality." Joseph Bucklin Bishop, *Notes and Anecdotes of Many Years* (New York: Charles Scribner's Sons, 1925), 5.

2. John Hay diary, Brown University; Michael Burlingame and John R. Turner Ettlinger, eds., *Inside Lincoln's White House: The Complete Civil War Diary of John Hay* (Carbondale: Southern Illinois University Press, 1997).

3. Hay to John G. Nicolay, Washington, 7 August 1863, infra.

4. Hay to Nicolay, Washington, 20 June 1864, infra. Schuyler Colfax, speaker of the U.S. House in the latter part of the Civil War, recalled that he and Lincoln "often went to Ford's opera house to regale ourselves of an evening, for we felt the strain on mind and body was often intolerable." They found "real relaxation" in watching "those southern girls with their well rounded forms, lustrous hair and sparkling voices. We thought it a veritable treat to see them dance and hear their song." Colfax told this story to Franz Mueller. "Lincoln and Colfax," reminiscences by Mueller, enclosed in Mueller to Ida Tarbell, Spokane, 13 February 1896, Ida M. Tarbell Papers, Allegheny College.

5. Hay to Charles G. Halpine, Washington, 22 November 1863, infra.

6. *Letters of John Hay and Extracts from Diary* (3 vols.; printed privately but not published, 1908).

7. Mrs. Hay, not Adams, decided to print only the initials of people and places. Adams explained to Whitelaw Reid, "I was in no way responsible for the omissions or insertions in the Hay volumes, beyond the material which I placed in Mrs Hay's hands. With that material she has done what she pleased. . . . I am not myself delicate as to the use of names. My view is that we, who set up to be educated society, should stand up in our harness, and should play our parts without the awkward

stage-fright of amateurs." Adams to Reid, Washington, 15 February 1909, J. C. Levenson et al., eds., *The Letters of Henry Adams* (6 vols.; Cambridge: Harvard University Press, 1982–1988), 6:222.

8. Tyler Dennett, ed., *Lincoln and the Civil War in the Diaries and Letters of John Hay* (New York: Dodd, Mead, 1939).

9. *New York Herald Tribune*, 12 February 1939, book review section, front page. After pointing out that Dennett misspelled several names and misidentified some people, Nevins concluded gently, "With all gratitude to Dr. Dennett for what he has presented us, we must hope that when he carries the diary and letters forward . . . he will give closer attention to the niceties of editing." Dennett did not produce another volume of Hay diaries and letters.

10. Horace White to Frank J. Garrison, New York, 8 November 1914, enclosed in Garrison to William R. Thayer, Boston, 10 November 1914, Hay Papers, Brown University.

11. Roosevelt to Henry Cabot Lodge, Washington, 28 January 1909, Elting E. Morison et al., eds., *The Letters of Theodore Roosevelt* (Cambridge: Harvard University Press, 1952), 6:1490.

12. Bishop, "Friendship with Hay," 777.

13. Adams to Mary Cadwalader Jones, Washington, 25 [January 1909], Levenson et al., eds., *Letters of Adams*, 6:215.

14. Adams to Reid, Washington, 15 February 1909, ibid., 6:223.

15. Roosevelt to Henry Cabot Lodge, Washington, 28 January 1909, Morison, ed., *Letters of Theodore Roosevelt*, 6:1489–90.

16. Clara S. Hay to Richard Watson Gilder, Washington, 20 November 1908, Century Collection, New York Public Library.

17. Roy P. Basler et al., eds., *Collected Works of Abraham Lincoln* (8 vols. plus index; New Brunswick, N.J.: Rutgers University Press, 1953–1955).

18. Hay to William H. Herndon, Paris, 5 September 1866, infra.

19. Nicholas Murray Butler to Roy P. Basler, n.p., 23 April 1942, Basler Papers, Library of Congress.

20. Burlingame and Ettlinger, eds., *Hay Diary*, 101 (entry for 26 October 1863).

21. Ibid., 96 (entry for 20 October 1863).

22. Hay to Charles S. Spencer, Washington, 25 November 1864, draft, infra.

23. Justin B. Turner and Linda Levitt Turner, eds., *Mary Todd Lincoln: Her Life and Letters* (New York: Alfred A. Knopf, 1972), 91.

24. Robert Todd Lincoln to Isaac Markens, Manchester, Vermont, 24 November 1916, Robert Todd Lincoln Papers, Chicago Historical Society.

25. Vol. 55, p. 33, Hay Papers, Library of Congress.

26. Hay to Miss H. Louise Hickox, Washington, 10 May 1861, infra.

27. A copy of this document in the Nicolay-Hay Papers at the Illinois State Historical Library in Springfield contains a marginal notation indicating that Hay wrote it.

28. Memo dated 30 September 1863, infra.

29. Hay to Richard Watson Gilder, Washington, 1 March 1902, Hay Papers, Brown University.

30. Hay to Nicolay, Colorado Springs, 14 July 1888, Hay Papers, Brown University.

31. Robert Todd Lincoln to Noah Brooks, Washington, 5 April 1882, Robert Todd Lincoln Papers, Chicago Historical Society.

32. Gilder to Hay, New York, 9 September 1880, Hay Papers, Brown University.

33. William O. Stoddard, *Inside the White House in War Times* (New York: Charles L. Webster, 1890), 179.

34. "One could wish that this remarkable quotation came from a more reliable source." Don. E. Fehrenbacher and Virginia Fehrenbacher, eds., *Recollected Words of Abraham Lincoln* (Stanford: Stanford University Press, 1996), 426.

35. Bishop, *Notes and Anecdotes*, 65–66. See a similar account by an unidentified source, Francis Fisher Browne, *The Every-Day Life of Abraham Lincoln*, 2d ed. (New York: G. P. Putnam's 1913), 477–78.

36. Richard Watson Gilder to Hay, Marion, Massachusetts, 3 July 1890, Hay Papers, Brown University. On another occasion Gilder said "Hay's little paper is excellent, but very general." Helen Nicolay, *Lincoln's Secretary: A Biography of John G. Nicolay* (New York: Longmans, Green, 1949), 308.

37. Charles G. Halpine's headnote to Hay's poem, "God's Vengeance," undated clipping from the *New York Citizen*, scrapbook, Hay Papers, Brown University.

38. Galusha Grow, quoted in James T. DuBois and Gertrude S. Mathews, *Galusha A. Grow: Father of the Homestead Law* (Boston: Houghton Mifflin, 1917), 266–67.

39. *Sedalia* (Missouri) *Times*, 11 May 1871.

40. Nicolay and Hay, *Abraham Lincoln: A History* (10 vols.; New York: Century, 1890), 1:xii.

41. Draft of an introduction to Nicolay and Hay, *Abraham Lincoln: A History*, in the hand of Nicolay, Nicolay-Hay Papers, Illinois State Historical Library, Springfield. According to Hay's biographer Tyler Dennett, "The personal relations of Lincoln and Hay came closely to resemble those of father and son." *John Hay: From Poetry to Politics* (New York: Dodd, Mead, 1934), 39. A pair of more recent scholars has maintained that "John Hay's relationship with Abraham Lincoln was a paramount influence over his life. For Hay, Lincoln proved to be a father figure who combined the values and personalities of both John's father and uncle [*Milton Hay*]." Howard I. Kushner and Anne Hummel Sherrill, *John Milton Hay: The Union of Poetry and Politics* (Boston: Twayne, 1977), 27. On Lincoln's tendency to act as a surrogate father to young men, see Michael Burlingame, *The Inner World of Abraham Lincoln* (Urbana: University of Illinois Press, 1994), 73–91.

42. Hay to Nora Perry, Springfield, 20 May 1859, Hay Papers, Brown University.

43. Draft of an introduction to Nicolay and Hay, *Abraham Lincoln: A History*, in the hand of Nicolay, Nicolay-Hay Papers, Illinois State Historical Library, Springfield.

44. Hay to Hannah Angell, Springfield, 5 May 1860, Amy Angell Montague, ed., *A*

College Friendship: A Series of Letters from John Hay to Hannah Angell (Boston: privately printed, 1938), 55.

45. John W. Bunn to Jesse W. Weik, Springfield, 20 July 1916, in Jesse W. Weik, *The Real Lincoln: A Portrait* (Boston: Houghton Mifflin, 1922), 282–88. During the Civil War, other White House secretaries and clerks, including Gustave Matile and Nathaniel S. Howe, were similarly employed in the Interior Department. Hay was commissioned a major on 12 January 1864 and was promoted on 31 May 1865 to brevet colonel of volunteers for faithful and meritorious service in the war. On 8 April 1867, he was honorably mustered out of the service.

46. John W. Starr, "Lincoln and the Office Seekers," typescript dated 1936, addenda, p. 6, Lincoln files, "Patronage" folder, Lincoln Memorial University, Harrogate, Tennessee.

47. John Russell Young, "John Hay, Secretary of State," *Munsey's Magazine*, 20 (1898): 247; *Philadelphia Evening Star*, 22 August 1891; Young, writing in 1898, quoted in T. C. Evans, "Personal Reminiscences of John Hay," *Chattanooga* (Tennessee) *Sunday Times*, 30 July 1905. Commenting on the 1891 article, Hay told Young: "I read what you say of me, with the tender interest with which we hear a dead friend praised. The boy you describe in such charming language was once very dear to me — and although I cannot rate him so highly as you do, I am pleased and flattered more than I can tell you to know he made any such impression on a mind like yours." Hay to Young, Newbury, N.H., 27 August 1891, Young Papers, Library of Congress.

48. J. B. Angell, *The Reminiscences of James Burrill Angell* (New York: Longmans, Green, 1912), 109.

49. William Evans Norris, quoted in A. S. Chapman, "The Boyhood of John Hay," *Century Magazine*, n.s., vol. 46 (July 1909): 450. Norris (d. 1906) graduated from Brown in 1857.

50. William Leete Stone, "John Hay, 1858," *Memories of Brown: Traditions and Recollections Gathered from Many Sources*, ed. Robert Perkins Brown et al. (Providence, R.I.: Brown Alumni Magazine, 1909), 153–54. William Leete Stone (1835–1908) of New York, author of many books about the American Revolutionary era, had been Hay's roommate at Brown. Stone called Hay "a dear friend and . . . chum." *New York Times*, 12 June 1908, p. 7, c. 6; Stone, "John Hay, 1858."

51. Bishop, "Friendship with Hay," 778.

52. Clark E. Carr, *The Illini: A Story of the Prairies* (Chicago: A. C. McClurg, 1905), 139.

53. Logan Hay, "Notes on the History of the Logan and Hay Families," 30 May 1939, Stuart-Hay Papers, Illinois State Historical Library, Springfield.

54. *St. Louis Dispatch*, 30 May [no year given], clipping in a scrapbook, Hay Papers, Brown University.

55. Mitchel to Hay, East Orange, N.J., 12 February 1905, Hay Papers, Library of Congress.

56. Stone, "John Hay, 1858," 152.

57. Caroline Owsley Brown, "Springfield Society Before the Civil War," *Journal of the Illinois State Historical Society*, 15 (1922): 498.

58. Manuscript diary of Anna Ridgely Hudson, entry for 22 January 1860, Illinois State Historical Library, Springfield.

59. Anna Ridgely Hudson, "Springfield, Illinois, in 1860, by a Native Springfielder," typescript dated December 1912, Hay Papers, Brown University.

60. Amy Duer to Elizabeth Meads Duer, Washington, 6 May 1862, Hay Papers, Brown University.

61. Helen Nicolay, interview with William R. Thayer, Washington, D.C., 18 January 1914, Hay Papers, Brown University.

62. Hannah Angell, interview with William R. Thayer, Providence, 6 December 1913, Hay Papers, Brown University.

63. Octavia Roberts Corneau, "A Girl in the Sixties: Excerpts from the Journal of Anna Ridgely (Mrs. James L. Hudson)," *Journal of the Illinois State Historical Society*, 22 (1929): 437 (entry for 26 June 1864).

64. T. C. Evans, "Personal Reminiscences of John Hay," *Chattanooga* (Tennessee) *Sunday Times*, 30 July 1905. Evans, who represented the *New York World*, befriended Hay on the presidential train trip to Washington in February 1861.

65. *Sedalia* (Missouri) *Times*, 11 May 1871. William E. Doster, provost marshal of the District of Columbia, recalled that Hay in his days as assistant presidential secretary was "genial, bright, and witty." Doster, *Lincoln and Episodes of the Civil War* (New York: G. P. Putnam's Sons, 1915), 31.

66. Stoddard, "White House Sketches," *New York Citizen*, 25 August 1866.

67. Doster, *Lincoln and Episodes of the Civil War*, 17.

68. Stoddard, *Inside the White House in War Times*, 165–66.

69. Stoddard, typescript of memoirs, 2:429, William O. Stoddard Papers, Detroit Public Library.

70. Ibid., 2:364.

71. Hay to Nicolay, Washington, 25 September 1863, infra.

72. Hay to Nicolay, Washington, 7 August 1863, infra.

73. Hay to Nicolay, Warsaw, Illinois, 26 August 1864, infra.

74. Hay to Nicolay, Washington, 11 September 1863, infra.

75. Charles H. Philbrick to Ozias M. Hatch, Washington, 30 December 1864, Hatch Papers, Illinois State Historical Library, Springfield.

76. Hay to Herndon, Paris, 5 September 1866, infra.

77. Hay to Edward D. Neill, Washington, 14 July 1864, infra.

78. Mrs. Milton Hay to her husband, Washington, 13 April 1862, Stuart-Hay Papers, Illinois State Historical Library, Springfield.

79. William O. Stoddard, Jr., ed., *Lincoln's Third Secretary: The Memoirs of William O. Stoddard* (New York: Exhibition Press, 1955), 153.

80. Higginson to his mother, 25 May 1863, Mary Thatcher Higginson, ed., *Letters*

and Journals of Thomas Wentworth Higginson, 1846–1906 (Boston: Houghton Mifflin, 1921), 201–2.

81. King, editor of the *Topeka Record* and later chief editorial writer for the *St. Louis Globe-Democrat*, quoted in "Col. John Hay—A Sketch of His Life," unidentified clipping, scrapbook, Hay Papers, Brown University.

82. Russell to J. C. Bancroft Davis, Washington, 5 October 1861, Martin Crawford, ed., *William Howard Russell's Civil War: Private Diaries and Letters, 1861–1862* (Athens: University of Georgia Press, 1992), 144; Russell, *My Diary North and South*, ed. Eugene H. Berwanger (New York: Alfred A. Knopf, 1988), 51 (entry for 28 March 1861).

83. Seward to John Bigelow, n.p., n.d., quoted in Joseph Bucklin Bishop, "John Hay: Scholar, Statesman" (pamphlet; Providence, R.I.: Brown University, 1906), 8.

84. Weed to John Bigelow, New York, 26 April 1865, John Bigelow, *Retrospections of an Active Life* (5 vols.; Garden City, N.Y.: Doubleday-Page, 1909–1913), 2:521.

85. Henry Smith to Charles Henry Ray and Joseph Medill, [Washington], 4 November 1861, Charles H. Ray Papers, Henry E. Huntington Library, San Marino, California.

86. Washington correspondence, 7 November 1863, *Sacramento Daily Union*, Michael Burlingame, ed., *Lincoln Observed: Civil War Dispatches of Noah Brooks* (Baltimore: Johns Hopkins University Press, 1998), 83.

87. "Hay's Florida Expedition," unidentified clipping, John Hay scrapbook, vol. 57, Hay Papers, Library of Congress.

88. *New York Herald-Tribune Book Review*, 12 February 1939, p. 1.

89. David Rankin Barbee to Stephen I. Gilchrist, Washington, 2 April 1932, copy, William H. Townsend Papers, University of Kentucky, Lexington.

90. Hay to John G. Nicolay, Warsaw, Illinois, 22 November 1872, Hay Papers, Brown University.

91. Hay to Charles Hay, Paris, 9 September 1866, letterpress copy, Hay Papers, Brown University.

92. Hay to Garfield, Washington, 16 February 1881, Hay Papers, Brown University.

93. Hay to John G. Nicolay, Washington, 4 April 1862, infra.

94. Hay to John G. Nicolay, Washington, 5 April 1862, infra.

95. Stoddard, ed., *Lincoln's Third Secretary*, 216.

96. Hay to John G. Nicolay, Washington, ca. 10 November 1861, infra.

97. Dr. and Mrs. Stone paraphrased in the manuscript diary of John Meredith Read, Jr., U.S. minister to Greece, quoted in Old Hickory Book Shop (New York) catalogue, n.d., clipping, Lincoln files, "Wife" folder, Lincoln Memorial University, Harrogate, Tennessee.

98. Hay to John G. Nicolay, Washington, 7 August 1863, infra.

99. Hay to Charles G. Halpine, Washington, 14 August 1863, infra.

100. Hay to Herndon, Paris, 5 September 1866, infra.

101. Nicolay and Hay, *Abraham Lincoln*, 10:355.

1. 1860–1862

1. A. S. Chapman, "Boyhood of Hay," 453. The identity of the addressee is established in Mrs. A. E. Edwards to A. S. Chapman, Warsaw, Illinois, 12 July 1909, enclosed in A. S. Chapman to R. U. Johnson, Gilman, Illinois, 19 July 1909, Century Collection, New York Public Library. In Chapman's article, the letter is dated "Executive Mansion," but the date given, along with the context, makes it clear that Hay was in Springfield, not Washington, at the time. Hay refers to "the annoyances of the chancery court." In 1860, he was unhappily studying law in the office of his uncle, Milton Hay.

2. Hay spent the winter of 1858–1859 in Warsaw.

3. "A Modern Cinderella: or, The Little Old Shoe," *Atlantic Monthly*, 6, no. 36 (October 1860): 425–41.

4. Gilbert Holland Montague Collection of Historical Manuscripts, New York Public Library. Hannah Angell (1839–1921) was the younger sister of one of Hay's professors at Brown, James B. Angell. According to Amy Angell Montague, she "was attractive personally and of a ready wit and was the center of gaiety in her little circle." Montague, ed., *A College Friendship*, vi.

5. Hay was covering the Illinois legislature for the *Missouri Democrat* (St. Louis).

6. In 1860, U.S. Senator Joseph Lane (1801–1881) of Oregon had been the vice presidential running mate of Democrat John C. Breckinridge.

7. The champion prizefighter John C. Heenan, a native of Troy, New York, was called "the Benicia boy" because he first came to prominence in Benicia, California.

8. "Walter" was perhaps Walter B. Noyes (1837–1885), a classmate of Hay at Brown who became an ordained Episcopal minister. Francis B. Peckham (1836–1903), also an alumnus of Brown, was a lawyer in Newport.

9. Thurlow Weed (1797–1882), a New York journalist and powerful political figure, was William Henry Seward's alter ego. Simon Cameron (1799–1889), a prominent Republican leader in Pennsylvania, became Lincoln's secretary of war (1861–1862). Edward Bates (1793–1869), a leading Republican in Missouri, became Lincoln's attorney general (1861–1864).

10. A. Conger Goodyear Collection, Yale University.

11. Copy in the hand of Henry Adams, Hay Papers, Illinois State Historical Library, Springfield. Jane Maria Huntington Ridgely, born in Boston, was the wife of Nicholas H. Ridgely, a prominent banker in Springfield whose autocratic manner earned him the sobriquet *Czar Nicholas*. Hay had spent much time at the Ridgely home, which was known as "the center of musical culture in town" and "the centre of Springfield social life for the younger set — a center where music and jollity reigned, tempered by the Czar's rather rigorous ruling, where there were earnest if rather youthful efforts at improving the mind, and where foreign languages were the fashion." Helen Nicolay, manuscript biography of her father, John G. Nicolay, pp.

29–30, Nicolay Papers, Lincoln Museum, Fort Wayne, Indiana; Caroline Owsley Brown, "Springfield Society Before the Civil War," 492.

12. The dear wife (cara sposa) of Edward Lewis Baker (1829–1897), editor of the Springfield *Illinois State Journal*, was Julia Cook Edwards Baker (b. 1837), the daughter of Lincoln's sister-in-law Elizabeth Todd Edwards and her husband, Ninian W. Edwards.

13. Montague, ed., *A College Friendship*, 59–60.

14. Hay Papers, Brown University. This letter to Miss Hickox is addressed to Genesee, Wisconsin.

15. Barney Papers, Henry E. Huntington Library, San Marino, California. Hiram Barney (1811–1895), a lawyer who belonged to the Bryant-Greeley faction in New York politics, served as collector of the port of New York (1861–1864).

16. George Barrell, born in Maine in 1809, was educated in Massachusetts. After thirty years as a seaman, he came to Springfield in 1855. His wife, Anna Douglas of Connecticut, was a niece of Mrs. Simeon Francis, Lincoln's close friend. John G. Nicolay had written Barney on May 9 reminding the collector of Lincoln's desire to have George Barrell of Springfield appointed deputy collector in the New York Custom House. Barney had been too busy to see Barrell and asked for his address so that he could write to him. George Barrell to Lincoln, Springfield, 11 August 1861, and Barney to Lincoln, New York, 11 May 1861, Lincoln Papers, Library of Congress.

17. Miscellaneous Hay Papers, Illinois State Historical Library, Springfield. Charles L. Huntington, a good friend of Hay in Springfield, had enrolled in the Naval Academy in 1858 and became a naval officer. See Paul M. Angle, "John Hay's Springfield," *Journal of the Illinois State Historical Society*, 38 (1945): 108–9.

18. "Charlie" was perhaps Hay's brother Charles Edward Hay (1841–1916), who served in the Third Illinois Cavalry during the war and became a wholesale grocer in Springfield afterward. He was mayor of Springfield in the 1870s.

19. George Monteiro and Brenda Murphy, eds., *John Hay–Howells Letters: The Correspondence of John Milton Hay and William Dean Howells, 1861–1905* (Boston: Twayne, 1980), 5. In 1860, the young William Dean Howells (1837–1920), who became an eminent novelist, wrote a campaign biography of Lincoln. The following year, Lincoln appointed him U.S. consul in Venice.

20. The bacon state was Ohio. On June 10, Howells had asked Hay about his application for the Munich consulate, which he had filed two months earlier. Ibid., 3.

21. Howells's poem "The Dead" was originally published in a magazine in 1859; the following year it appeared in *Poems of Two Friends* (Columbus, Ohio: Follett, Foster, 1860).

22. King Ludwig I of Bavaria (1786–1868) had abdicated his throne in 1848 after becoming romantically involved with a beautiful dancer, Lola Montez (1818–1861).

23. Jane Parsons Dennison was the daughter of William Dennison (1815–1882), who served as governor of Ohio (1859–1861) and U.S. postmaster general (1864–1866).

24. James Wadsworth Papers, Library of Congress. A slightly different version of this document appeared in the *Louisville Journal*, 9 July 1861, which is reprinted in Turner and Turner, eds., *Mary Todd Lincoln*, 91. John Fry was from Boyle County, Kentucky.

25. Manuscripts department, Butler Library, Columbia University. Charles King was the president of Columbia.

26. William Henry Seward Papers, University of Rochester.

27. A native of Holland, van Reuth had secured the endorsement of Montgomery Blair on his application for a consular appointment. Van Reuth to Hay, Rossville, Maryland, 27 June 1861, Lincoln Papers, Library of Congress.

28. Autograph Catalog, Gary Hendershott, October 1994, sale 84, p. 16.

29. Gilbert Holland Montague Collection of Historical Manuscripts, New York Public Library.

30. Alfred Lord Tennyson wrote the poem "Locksley Hall."

31. On 3 July 1861, Hannah Angell married James Haydon Coggeshall (1820–1890), a Brown University alumnus (class of 1840) and a widower with four children. I am grateful to Martha Mitchell of the Brown University Archives for providing this information. Scituate, Rhode Island, is a small town near Providence.

32. The Ponaganset is a small stream in central Rhode Island.

33. Colonel Elmer E. Ellsworth (1837–1861), a close friend of Hay, was killed in Alexandria, Virginia, on 24 May 1861. See chapter 5, infra.

34. On Noyes, see note 8, supra.

35. Thomas T. Caswell, who graduated from Brown in 1861, became a career naval officer.

36. Hay Papers, Brown University. James Alexander Hamilton (1788–1878), son of George Washington's Treasury Secretary, Alexander Hamilton, was a lawyer and author who served as U.S. attorney for the Southern District of New York (1829–1834). In 1861, he was eager to obtain once again some position in government service.

37. Long Branch was a fashionable beach resort in New Jersey. Hay had accompanied Mrs. Lincoln's party from Washington to New York on August 14 and continued on to Long Branch, where Mrs. Lincoln vacationed briefly. *New York Tribune*, 16 August 1861.

38. The invitation is contained in Hamilton to Hay, Dobbs Ferry, New York, 16 August 1861, Hay Papers, Brown University.

39. A few months later, the merchant-philanthropist Theodore Roosevelt Sr. (1831–1878) called on Hay, who introduced him to the president and did everything he could to expedite Roosevelt's business. "Hay has devoted his whole morning to me and really been of great service," Roosevelt reported to his wife on November 8. Hay Papers, Brown University. Cf. David McCullough, *Mornings on Horseback* (New York: Simon and Schuster, 1981), 59–60.

40. Nevis, James Hamilton's estate in Dobbs Ferry, was named after the Caribbean island where Alexander Hamilton was born.

41. Hay Papers, Brown University. Meigs (1816–1892) was Quartermaster General of the Union Army.

42. Stetson informed Hay that 619 men of his regiment answered roll call on August 19.

43. Hay Papers, Brown University.

44. Hay Papers, Library of Congress. Fanny Campbell Eames was one of the foremost hostesses in Washington. After her death in 1890, a newspaper ran the following description of her accomplishments:

> During the twenty-eight years of her married life in Washington Mrs. Eames's house was one of the favorite resorts of the most conspicuous and interesting men of the nation; it was a species of neutral ground where men of all parties and shades of political opinion found it agreeable to foregather. Though at first in moderate circumstances and living in a house which rented for less than $300 a year, there was no house in Washington except for the President's, where one was sure of meeting any evening throughout the year so many people of distinction.
>
> Mr. and Mrs. [*William L.*] Marcy were devoted to Mrs. Eames; her *salon* was almost the daily resort of Edward Everett, Rufus Choate, Charles Sumner, Secretary [*James*] Gutherie, Governor [*John A.*] Andrew of Massachusetts, [*Henry*] Winter Davis, Caleb Cushing, Senator Preston King, N. P. Banks, and representative men of that ilk. Mr. [*Samuel J.*] Tilden when in Washington was often their guest. The gentlemen, who were all on the most familiar terms with the family, were in the habit of bringing their less conspicuous friends from time to time, thus making it quite the most attractive *salon* that has been seen in Washington since the death of Mrs. [*James*] Madison, and made such without any of the attractions of wealth or luxury. . . . [*D*]uring her residence there she was intellectually quite the most accomplished woman in Washington.

Marian Gouverneur, *As I Remember: Recollections of American Society During the Nineteenth Century* (New York: D. Appleton, 1911), 178–79, quoting an unidentified newspaper.

45. *Jenkins* was a slang term for a journalist. The *Herald* covered Mrs. Lincoln's doings at Long Branch in elaborate detail.

46. George Denison was appointed naval officer for the port of New York in 1861.

47. "Bing" was perhaps Julius Bing (d. 1867), "an obscure free-lance journalist and literary dilettante of New York and Washington" who wrote a biography of Adam Gurowski. LeRoy H. Fischer, *Lincoln's Gadfly, Adam Gurowski* (Norman: University of Oklahoma Press, 1964), 272.

48. Charles Eames (1812?–1867), a Harvard graduate who achieved renown as an admiralty lawyer, was chief counsel for the Navy Department. In the 1840s, he had served as chief correspondence clerk of that department and as associate editor of the *Washington Union*. President Polk assigned him to negotiate a treaty with the

Hawaiian Islands, and President Pierce named him minister to Venezuela. Marian Gouverneur, *As I Remember*, 171–73.

49. Hay described Robert Bourke as "a briefless young barrister of Irish parentage who . . . has a natural inclination for rebellions." Washington correspondence, 14 October 1861, *Missouri Republican* (St. Louis), 19 October 1861, in Michael Burlingame, ed., *Lincoln's Journalist: John Hay's Anonymous Writings for the Press, 1860–1864* (Carbondale: Southern Illinois University Press, 1998), 110.

50. Nathaniel Parker Willis (1806–1867), a poet and journalist, edited the *Home Journal,* which on 17 August 1861 ran an account of Lincoln preparing for a state dinner on August 6:

> The official dinner for the Prince [*Napoleon*] was to come off at 7 P.M.; but that was not to interfere, fortunately, with the playing of the Marine Band, in the grounds of the White House. . . . I chanced to be one of three who occupied, for the last half hour of the performance, a long settee, which stood opposite the Presidential mansion — not the least interesting operation, of the beautiful picture before us, being a chance view of *the President himself,* who sat at the window of his private room, on the second story, reading his letters and listening to the music, but evidently wholly unconscious of being visible to the public.
>
> Of course, neither our own party nor the rest of the gay crowd had the least expectation of seeing any portion of the royal entertainment that was to take place in the great White Mansion before us; but, as it approached within thirty minutes of the dinner hour, (which Mrs. Lincoln had chanced to mention to me, the night before) I could not help wondering, to the friend sitting at my side, whether "Abe," lounging there in his gray coat, with his knees up to his chin, would have time enough for his toilet. But the words were scarce out of my mouth, when up jumped the lively successor to George Washington, and took a seat in another chair — the body-servant, who had entered the room, proceeding immediately to put the cloth around the respected throat and shave that portion of the honored face which had not "taken the veil." In three minutes more, said holder of the Executive by the nose shook his official napkin out of the window, giving to the summer wind, thus carelessly, whatever had fallen from the Inaugurated beard; and the remainder of the toilet was prompt enough! The long arms were busy about the tall head for a moment, probably with brush or comb — there was a stoop, probably for bi-forked disencumberment, and, immediately after, a sudden gleam of white linen lifted aloft — a momentary extension of elbows with the tying of the cravat, and a putting on of the black coat — and, then, the retiring figure of the dressed President was lost to our sight. The toilet of the sovereign of the great realm of the West — (which we had been thus privileged to see, through the open window of his dressing-room) — had occupied precisely twenty-two minutes, by my anxiously consulted watch.

"The Tonsorial Ablutions of Honest Abe," unidentified clipping, Lincoln Museum, Fort Wayne, Indiana.

51. Hay Papers, Brown University.

52. No dispatch by Nicolay could be found for August 22, but the day before he wrote to Hay thus: "Governor Andrew very earnestly desires that Capt Thomas J. C. Armory of the seventh Regiment Infantry now on recruiting service in Boston which could be Just as well discharged by one of less experience be permitted to become Colonel of the 19th Mass Volunteers. I have just seen the Govr & think it important that he be gratified. See the president & get if possible a favorable answer to me at once." Nicolay to Hay, Newport, Rhode Island, 21 August 1861, telegram, Lincoln Papers, Library of Congress.

53. "Dr. Pope" was perhaps Gustavus W. Pope, listed in *Boyd's Washington and Georgetown Directory* for 1862 as a "homeopathic physician."

54. Nicolay spent most of August vacationing in Newport, Rhode Island.

55. William O. Stoddard (1835–1925) assisted Nicolay and Hay in the White House (1861–1864). At first, he served as the "Secretary to the President to Sign Land Patents." After the war began, as Nicolay recalled, "business became very slack so that he had scarcely any official work to do. He was therefore assigned to duty as one of my clerks at the White House, being able just as well to sign there the few Land Patents which were issued from time to time. Also on one or two occasions when Hay and I were both absent, he carried a message to Congress. So that you see he . . . was not in any proper sense either a real or acting President's Private Secretary." Nicolay to Paul Selby, Washington, 11 March 1895, draft, Nicolay Papers, Library of Congress.

56. *Shab* was a slang term meaning to sneak or run away.

57. Joe Gargery was a character in Charles Dickens's novel *Great Expectations*.

58. Hay Papers, Brown University. The recipient was perhaps James B. Swain (d. 1895) of New York City, who was appointed second lieutenant in the First Cavalry on 1 November 1861. On August 28, Lincoln had indicated his willingness to gratify Senator Ira Harris of New York, who urged that Swain be named a quartermaster. Lincoln to Simon Cameron, Washington, 28 August 1861, Basler et al., eds., *Collected Works of Lincoln*, 4:501.

59. Seward Papers, University of Rochester.

60. "Bleeker" was perhaps Anthony J. Bleeker (1790–1884) of New York, a prominent New York real estate broker and auctioneer, as well as an active Republican. In 1862, Lincoln appointed him an assessor of internal revenue. *New York Times*, 18 January 1884, p. 8, c. 1.

61. A. S. Chapman, "Boyhood of Hay," 453.

62. Hiram Barney Papers, Henry E. Huntington Library, San Marino, California. Albert Marshman Palmer (1838–1905), confidential secretary to the collector of the port of New York, Hiram Barney, was thought to be "the Collector *de facto*."

63. Hay Papers, Brown University. This dating of this letter is calculated thus: Nicolay left Washington on October 10 and returned on November 13; Mrs. Lincoln left Washington on November 4 for Boston and Cambridge, and she doubtless stopped in New York *en route*. Watt may have accompanied her, for he told Simon Cameron, "You know very well what difficulties I had to contend with in regard to Mrs. Lincoln. . . . I paid about $700.00 for Mrs. Lincoln on one trip to Cambridge, Mass." Watt to Cameron, n.p., n.d., Turner and Turner, eds., *Mary Todd Lincoln*, 103n.

64. White House gardener John Watt (1824–1892) helped Mrs. Lincoln obtain money for herself by padding White House expense accounts and payrolls. See infra, appendix 2.

65. During the Lincoln administration, the stationery fund was $1000 per year.

66. Hay Papers, Brown University. The recipient was perhaps the L. B. Wyman who was in Hilton Head, South Carolina, in February 1864 and was described by a journalist as someone whose name "we have seen in connection with New York politics." Unidentified newspaper clipping, "Hay's Florida Expedition," scrapbook, vol. 57, Hay Papers, Library of Congress.

67. Caton Papers, Library of Congress. John D. Caton (1812–1895), chief justice of the Illinois state supreme court (1855–1864), was the principal shareholder in the Illinois and Mississippi Telegraph Company.

68. Anson Stager (1825–1885) of Cleveland was general superintendent of the Western Union Company.

69. Copy provided by Frederick William Seward, Lincoln Papers, Library of Congress.

70. Undated note on the back of an envelope postmarked St. Louis, November 2, addressed to Nicolay, Hay Papers, Brown University.

71. Hay Papers, Brown University. One of the foremost American landscape painters of the nineteenth century, Bierstadt (1830–1902) was also a photographer.

72. Hay explained that this photo "was made of me in 1861" while "sitting on the window ledge of the White House with the blind behind me." Hay to the *Century*, 3 March 1904, in A. S. Chapman, "Boyhood of Hay," 448. It is reproduced in Burlingame, ed., *Lincoln's Journalist*.

73. The German-born Emanuel Leutze (1816–1868) was an artist known for his historical paintings, among them *Washington Crossing the Delaware* (or as one wag called it, poking fun at Leutze's Teutonic style, "Washington Crossing the Rhine.") The painting he was executing for the capitol was *Westward the Course of Empire Takes Its Way*.

74. [Adams, ed.], *Letters of Hay*, 1:7–8. Mary Ridgely, daughter of Nicholas and Jane Huntington Ridgely, was a good friend of Hay; in May 1865, she married Hay's brother Charles. See Hay to Charles Edward Hay, 8 May 1864, infra.

75. George Bancroft-Alexander Bliss Papers, Library of Congress.

76. Mrs. Bliss was presumably Mrs. Alexander Bliss.

77. Leroy P. Graf et al., eds., *The Papers of Andrew Johnson* (Knoxville: University of Tennessee Press, 1967–), 5:109.

78. Confederate General Felix K. Zollicoffer (b. 1812) was killed at the battle of Mill Springs, Kentucky, on January 19. Union General Albin F. Schoepf (1822–1886), born in Polish Austria, was a protege of Joseph Holt, who obtained for him a command in Kentucky.

79. Hay Papers, Brown University. On January 18, Josiah D. Canning, who styled himself "the Peasant Bard," sent to the president from Gill, Massachusetts, a song entitled "Columbia's Bright Banner."

80. Hay Papers, Brown University.

81. Hay Papers, Brown University. Anson G. Henry (1804–1865), surveyor general of the Washington Territory, was a close friend and political ally of Lincoln in Illinois. Henry moved to Oregon in 1852.

82. Hay Papers, Brown University. Bedell lived in Warsaw, Illinois.

83. William A. Richardson (1811–1875) represented an Illinois district in the U.S. House (1861–1863) and later served in the U.S. Senate (1863–1865).

84. Hay Papers, Brown University.

85. Miguel Maria Lisboa was Brazil's minister. F. L. Asta Buraga was Chile's *chargé d'affaires* (1860–1867).

86. At the Eames home, society often gathered at parties like the one described by John G. Nicolay:

> Both he [*Eames*] and his wife are very intelligent, amiable, and hospitable, and by reason of their position and long residence here as well as abroad, know almost everybody, and constantly draw around them the most interesting people who visit Washington. Although they have but a small house, and live in a very moderate style, their parlor is really a sort of focal point in Washington society, where one meets the best people who come here. By the "best" I do not mean mere fashionable "society people," but rather the brains of society — politicians, diplomats, authors and artists, and occasionally too, persons whose social and political positions merely, and not their brains, entitle them to consideration, such as titled foreigners, pretty women &c. Politically it is a sort of neutral ground, where men of all shades of opinion — Republicans, Democrats, Fossil Whigs, with even an occasional spice of Secessionist, come together quietly and socially. Usually we go there on Sunday evenings — say from 8 to 11 — without any formality whatever; merely "drop in," coming and going entirely at pleasure, and talking to whom and about whatever one pleases. A variety of people, of course, bring with them a variety of languages; and so, while the key note is almost always English, the conversation runs into variations of French, German, and Spanish.

Nicolay to Therena Bates, Washington, 30 June 1861, Nicolay Papers, Library of Congress. See note 44, supra.

87. In February and March, Mary Todd Lincoln's sister, Elizabeth Todd Edwards, stayed at the White House to help console the first lady as she mourned the death of her son Willie.

88. Austin Coleman Woolfolk (d. 1880) wed Hay's sister Mary (1836–1914). After the war, he became an attorney in Denver, Colorado.

89. In March, Mrs. Milton Hay of Springfield, daughter of Lincoln's second law partner, Stephen T. Logan, visited Washington to see her sister, Sally (Mrs. Ward Hill Lamon). With her came another sister, Jennie. Mrs. Hay to her husband, Washington, 13 April 1862, Stuart-Hay Papers, Illinois State Historical Library, Springfield.

90. This was written on the verso of the letter of March 31.

91. "Beckwith" was perhaps Major Amos Beckwith (d. 1894) of Vermont, a member of the Commissary Department.

92. William Howard Russell (1820–1907), a special correspondent for the *London Times* whose dispatches describing the Union rout at Bull Run angered many Northerners, wanted to accompany McClellan to the Peninsula, but Secretary of War Stanton refused the necessary permission. When the exasperated journalist appealed to Lincoln, the president declined, hinting that the pro-Confederate stance of the *Times* was the main obstacle in Russell's way. In despair, Russell returned to England. Russell to Hay, Washington, 2 April 1862, Hay Papers, Brown University; Russell to Stanton, Washington, 2 April 1862, Russell to Randolph Marcy, Washington, 2 April 1862, and Russell to Mowbray Morris, Washington, 4 April 1862, Crawford, ed., *Russell's Civil War*, 235–38. See infra, Hay to Russell, 4 April 1862.

93. A small Confederate force under General John B. Magruder fooled McClellan into thinking it was much larger than it really was. Hence the Union commander hesitated to attack and resorted to a siege operation.

94. Hay Papers, Brown University. This note is written on the back of an envelope.

95. McClellan advanced on Yorktown on April 4 and laid siege to the town the following day.

96. W. Douglas Wallach was proprietor of the *Washington Evening Star*, which during the war had the largest circulation of any newspaper in the capital. Originally a Democrat, Wallach strongly supported the Lincoln administration.

97. According to Thomas Stackpole, a White House watchman, Mrs. Lincoln was collecting the $100 monthly salary supposedly being paid to Jane Watt for her work as White House stewardess. See appendix 2, infra.

98. Draft, Hay Papers, Brown University.

99. Hay Papers, Brown University.

100. Thomas Stackpole, a native of New Hampshire, was a White House watchman; in 1863 he became a steward. See appendix 2, infra.

101. Mrs. John Watt (nee Jane Masterson) had served as White House stewardess from June 1861 to March 1862. See appendix 2, infra.

102. Hay Papers, Brown University.

103. General John Pope (1822–1892) captured Island No. 10 in the Mississippi River

on April 7. Confederate General Pierre Gustave Toutant Beauregard (1818–1893) attacked Grant at the battle of Shiloh (or Pittsburg Landing), Tennessee, April 6–7.

104. On April 7, visitors, including Mrs. Milton Hay, called on Mary Lincoln, who "did not make her appearance." A White House servant explained that "she was in one of her moods and would not see any one." Mrs. Milton Hay to her husband, Washington, 8 April 1862, Stuart-Hay Papers, Illinois State Historical Library, Springfield.

105. Lincoln intervened to quash Lamon's threat. Greeley to Lincoln, New York, 6 January 1863 [misdated 1862], Lincoln Papers, Library of Congress.

106. James H. Van Alen (1819–1889) of New York was promoted to Brigadier General on 15 April 1862. He had raised a cavalry regiment at his own expense.

107. Baron Friedrich Karl Joseph von Gerolt (1798?–1879) was the Prussian minister to the United States. He was "an intellectual man and, prior to his career in the United States, his name was much associated with Alexander von Humboldt." Gouverneur, *As I Remember*, 232.

108. Miss Hooper was the daughter of Samuel Hooper (1808–1875), a Boston merchant and ironmaster who served in Congress from 1861 to 1874. Count Adam Gurowski (1805–1866), who had been a Polish revolutionary, worked in the State Department as a translator.

109. *Minutes of the Twenty-Second Session of the Providence Annual Conference of the Methodist Episcopal Church, Held at Provincetown, Mass., April 2–7, 1862* (Boston: James P. Magee, 1862), 22. Brown was secretary of the conference.

110. The resolutions commended the administration and Lincoln's emancipation message of the previous month.

111. Hay Papers, Brown University.

112. Edward Haight (1817–1885) and Moses Fowler Odell (1818–1866) were Democratic Congressmen from New York. On this day, Congress abolished slavery in Washington, D.C.

113. Former mayor of Washington James Berret declined appointment to the commission established by the bill emancipating slaves in the District of Columbia, a statute that Berret opposed and could not in good conscience execute. See Lincoln to Berret, Washington, 22 April 1862, Basler et al., eds., *Collected Works of Lincoln*, 5:195–96; Washington correspondence, 19 April 1862, *Chicago Tribune*, 20 April 1862, p. 1, c. 4. The previous August, Berret had been arrested and jailed for refusing to take the oath of allegiance as a member of the Board of Police Commissioners. He was released the following month.

114. Democrat James Alexander McDougall (1817–1867) represented California in the U.S. Senate (1861–1867). Republican Benjamin F. Wade (1800–1878) represented Ohio in the U.S. Senate (1851–1869).

115. Edwin Forrest (1806–1872) was a leading actor.

116. Carl Schurz Papers, Library of Congress. Schurz (1829–1906) commanded a division in the Eleventh Corps of the Army of the Potomac.

117. Copied in Hiram Ketchum to John J. Crittenden, New York, 19 May 1862, Crittenden Papers, Library of Congress.

118. Letitia Howe Collection, Miscellaneous Manuscripts, Library of Congress. Caleb Lyon (1822–1875) represented a New York district in the U.S. House (1853–1855) and served as governor of the Idaho Territory (1864–1865).

119. Hay Papers, Library of Congress.

120. The undated reply written on the back of this letter reads: "It is our *especial* desire that the Band, does not play in these grounds, this Summer. We expect our wishes to be complied with—Mrs Lincoln."

121. Hay Papers, Library of Congress.

122. The undated reply written on the back of this letter reads: "It is hard that in this time of our sorrow, we should be thus harassed! The music in LaFayette square, would sound quite as plainly as here. For this Summer, at least, our feelings should be respected. Mrs Lincoln." The following year, she continued to refuse permission, much to the irritation of Secretary of the Navy Gideon Welles, who recorded in his diary on 8 June 1863:

> Spoke to the President regarding weekly performances of the Marine Band. It has been customary for them to play in the public grounds south of the Mansion once a week in the summer, for many years. Last year it was intermitted, because Mrs. Lincoln objected in consequence of the death of her son. There was grumbling and discontent, and there will be more this year if the public are denied the privilege for private reasons. The public will not sympathize in sorrows, which are obtrusive and assigned as a reason for depriving them of enjoyments to which they have been accustomed and it is a mistake to persist in it. When I introduced the subject to-day, the President said Mrs. L. would not consent, certainly not until after the 4th of July. I stated the case pretty frankly, although the subject is delicate, and suggested that the band could play in Lafayette Square. Seward and Usher who were present advised that course. The President told me to do what I thought best.

Howard K. Beale, ed., *Diary of Gideon Welles, Secretary of the Navy under Lincoln and Johnson* (3 vols.; New York: Norton, 1960), 1:325.

123. Gilder-Lehrman Collection, Pierpont Morgan Library, New York. Mary Jay was the daughter of John Jay (1817–1894), a leading antislavery spokesman in New York.

124. In early July, McClellan's peninsular campaign ended in failure as Lee drove the Union army from the outskirts of Richmond. Hay's poor opinion of McClellan's generalship during that campaign was most vividly expressed in a book review he wrote in 1881: "McClellan was really never interfered with, . . . he was treated by Lincoln with a long-suffering forbearance without any parallel in history, . . . [H]e had at all times more troops than he knew how to use, and . . . he failed from sheer moral incapacity ever to assume the initiative when an enemy stood in the way." Hay denounced McClellan's "utterly unfounded expectation that the Navy would take Yorktown for him; his complete ignorance of the topography of the Peninsula . . .; his failure to divine the presence of the enemy at the Yorktown line; his clamor for

Franklin's and McCall's divisions to be sent to him, and his utter inability to do anything with them when they came; his ignominious delay before Yorktown till the rebels, at their leisure, withdrew; the terrible mismanagement at the battle of Gaine's Mill." Scathingly, he wrote of "the worthlessness of McClellan as the commander of a great army." The general, Hay concluded, was "weak, vacillating, insubordinate, [*and*] more alive to his own interests and those of his political party than to those of the country." Review of Alexander S. Webb, *The Peninsula: McClellan's Campaign of 1862*, *New York Tribune*, 23 December 1881, reproduced in George Monteiro, ed., "John Hay and the Union Generals," *Journal of the Illinois State Historical Society*, 69 (1976): 49, 51.

125. On May 9, Hunter unilaterally freed the slaves in his department, which included Georgia, Florida, and South Carolina. Ten days later, Lincoln revoked that order. On July 12, Lincoln praised Hunter. Basler et al., eds., *Collected Works of Lincoln*, 5:222–23, 318.

126. Edward McPherson Papers, Library of Congress. McPherson (1830–1895), clerk of the U.S. House (1863–1875), compiled *The Political History of the United States of America During the Great Rebellion* (1864) and *The Political History of the United States of America During the Period of Reconstruction* (1871).

127. George S. Boutwell (1818–1905), the former governor of Massachusetts, was commissioner of internal revenue (1862–1863). From 1863 to 1869, he served in the U.S. House, where he championed the Radical cause. On July 29, 1862, Boutwell told McPherson that the Pennsylvania appointments would not be made before August 10 or 12.

128. Hay Papers, Brown University. William Almon Wheeler (1819–1887) represented a New York district in the U.S. House (1861–1863, 1869–1877) and served as vice-president of the United States (1877–1881).

129. Endorsed by Lincoln on 8 December 1862: "Sec. of War please let this appointment be made at once. It is due that it be done under the circumstances."

130. Hay Papers, Brown University.

131. On 1 July 1862, Congress passed a statute levying taxes on property and on income. To implement the law, many federal assessors and collectors were appointed.

132. Hay Papers, Brown University.

133. John Blair Smith Todd (1814–1872) served a delegate to Congress from the Dakota Territory (1861–1863). The Pembina River flows from North Dakota to Canada.

134. Dr. William Jayne (1841–1916), a Springfield physician, was a good friend of Lincoln, who appointed him governor of the Dakota Territory.

135. Hay Papers, Brown University.

136. At Cedar Mountain on August 9, General Nathaniel P. Banks fought a bloody battle with Stonewall Jackson's corps.

137. Robert King Stone, a professor of medicine and ophthalmology at Columbia

Medical College (later renamed George Washington University), was the White House physician.

138. [Adams, ed.], *Letters of Hay*, 1:68–70.

139. Miss Kennedy was the daughter of Joseph Camp Griffith Kennedy (1813–1887), superintendent of the seventh and eighth censuses.

140. Leonard Grover (1835–1926) was an actor-turned-director who ran the National Theater (sometimes called "Grover's Theater") in Washington, which had been closed for renovation and expansion. Dahlgren was probably either Captain John A. Dahlgren (1809–1870), USN, or his son Ulric.

141. "The new clubhouse" was perhaps the Metropolitan Club.

142. Cartter Family Papers, Library of Congress. David Kellogg Cartter (1812–1887) represented an Ohio district in the U.S. House (1849–1853), served as the U.S. minister to Bolivia (1861–1862), and presided over the Supreme Court of the District of Columbia as its chief justice (1863–1887).

143. Hay Papers, Brown University.

144. "Heslop" was perhaps Lt. Frederick William Heslop of the provost marshal's office of the Second Cavalry Division of the Army of the Potomac.

145. Records of the Treasury Department, Settled Miscellaneous Accounts, Record Group 217, entry 347, account no. 148092, box 352, National Archives.

146. Gawler billed the president $40.75 for repairing furniture, for 180 yards of cambrick, and for "Draping the Presidents House in black." The bill was dated 16 September 1862. On 16 July 1863, Gawler acknowledged payment in full.

147. Lincoln Papers, Library of Congress.

148. The enclosed papers were Robert B. Nay to Jackson Grimshaw, New Orleans, 1 September 1862, in which Nay accused Col. Jonas H. French, provost marshal in New Orleans, of misconduct; a testimonial from members of the Adams County bar lauding Nay as an estimable gentleman, dated Quincy, 15 September 1862; and a letter to the president, dated Quincy, 17 September 1862, from Jackson Grimshaw, defending Nay and urging an investigation into the circumstances that led to Nay's court-marital.

149. Copy, Willard Family Papers, Library of Congress. Williams was aide-de-camp to General Irvin McDowell.

150. George W. Carlin, a Union soldier imprisoned in Richmond, wrote on September 17 to Williams asking his help in winning his freedom through an exchange. His brother was William P. Carlin.

151. Hay Papers, Brown University. The letter was sent to Bradley at 81 Madison Avenue, New York City.

152. The enclosure was Thomas M. [Nucent ?] to Hay, War Department [Washington], 7 October 1862.

153. Hay Papers, Brown University.

154. Alice Huntington, known as a "fine pianist," married Thomas L. Knapp. Hay, who frequently visited the Huntington home in Springfield, "always addressed [*her*]

as 'La Princesse.'" Emily Huntington Stuart, "Some Recollections of the Early Days in Springfield and Reminiscences of Abraham Lincoln and Other Celebrities who Lived in that Little Town in My Youth," unpublished typescript, bound in Daughters of the American Revolution, State of Illinois, Genealogical Records, 3:124, 127, Illinois State Historical Library, Springfield. The Huntingtons were a musical family. Alice's father George Lathrop Huntington "played on the flute and was the leader of Springfield's first orchestra." Caroline Owsley Brown, "Springfield Society Before the Civil War," 492.

155. Charles Henry Philbrick (1837–1885), a resident of Griggsville, Illinois, and a graduate of Illinois College, became Nicolay and Hay's assistant in 1864. Clark E. Carr called him "a man of singularly sweet and gentle nature." Carr, *The Illini*, 140. In 1860, a young woman in Springfield described him as "a sweet little fellow," "short and rather stout," with "light [h]air and bright blue eyes with a small nose and the sweetest mouth I almost ever saw," "quite bashful, but intelligent," and, in sum, "a real true honest young man." Diary of Anna Ridgely Hudson, entry for 26 February 1860, Illinois State Historical Library, Springfield. In that year, Philbrick replaced Nicolay as assistant to Illinois Secretary of State Ozias M. Hatch. Wayne C. Temple, "Charles Henry Philbrick: Private Secretary to President Lincoln," *Lincoln Herald*, 99 (1997): 6–11.

156. Clement L. Vallandigham (1820–1871), leader of the northern Peace Democrats, represented an Ohio district in the U.S. House of Representatives (1858–1863).

157. General Don Carlos Buell (1818–1898) commanded the Army of the Ohio; he was relieved of that command on October 24, after failing to follow up on his quasi victory at Perryville, Kentucky, on October 8.

158. George Clayton Latham (1842–1921) was a close friend of Robert Lincoln. "Irwin" was perhaps Robert T. Irwin, son of Robert Irwin, cashier of the Springfield Marine and Fire Insurance Company and Lincoln's financial agent during his presidency.

159. Lincoln Papers, Library of Congress.

160. Edward Salomon (1828–1909), governor of Wisconsin (1862–1864), urged the president to order a trial for over one hundred men who resisted the draft in Wisconsin. An endorsement, dated December 16, by Joseph Holt indicates that the matter was taken care of by General John Pope. Salomon to Lincoln, Madison, Wisconsin, 1 December 1862, Lincoln Papers, Library of Congress.

161. Hay Papers, Brown University. Jean Margaret Davenport Lander (1829–1903), a celebrated English-born actress, took over the direction of Union hospitals in Port Royal, South Carolina, following the death of her husband, General Frederick West Lander, on 2 March 1862. After the war, she returned to the stage, where she again won acclaim. Hay described her in 1861 as "the Medea, the Julia the Mona Lisa of my stage-struck salad days." Burlingame and Ettlinger, eds., *Hay Diary*, 1 (entry for 18 April 1861).

2. 1863

1. Hay Papers, Brown University.

2. Hay perhaps refers to Stone, *Life and Times of Sir William Johnson, Bart.* (2 vols.; Albany: J. Munsell, 1865), the first seven chapters of which had been written by Stone's father, William L. Stone (1792–1844), author of *The Life of Joseph Brant, The Poetry and History of Wyoming, Tales and Sketches*, and *Ups and Downs in the Life of a Distressed Gentleman.*

3. Manuscript Collection, "Abraham Lincoln and His Cabinet," Beinecke Library, Yale University. Badeau (1831–1895), a staff officer for General Thomas W. Sherman, was stationed in New Orleans. He later became U.S. Grant's military secretary.

4. Lincoln Papers, Library of Congress. George Plumer Smith of Franklin, Pennsylvania, was a genealogist and local historian who wrote *Descendents of Francis Plumer of Newbury, Massachusetts* (Philadelphia, 1875). He moved to Philadelphia in 1879 and corresponded with Hay throughout the 1870s.

5. Smith's statement described Lincoln's conduct during the secession crisis:

A few days after the Convention at Richmond passed the ordinance of secession, I accompanied a delegation from Western Virginia to Washington, to procure Arms for their defense at home.

The President received us with much interest and kindness.

During the interview, on my mentioning to him the fact that one of the Committee, Mr. [*Campbell*] Tarr, of Wellsburg—had been a member of the convention, Mr Lincoln spoke very freely of the attempts he had made to hold Virginia firm for the Union—and then, greatly to Mr Tarr's surprise mentioned, that amongst other influences, he had sent for Mr [*John B.*] Baldwin, of Augusta Co. a member of the Convention, and had him in the White House with him alone—and told him, if they would pass resolutions of adherence to the Union, then adjourn and go home—he, the President, would take the responsibility, at the earliest proper time—to withdraw the troops from Fort Sumpter—and do all within the line of his duty to ward off collision.

He then imposed strict silence upon us in regard to what he then had told us.

Will you please now ask him whether what I state is correct, and whether he now cares about its becoming known.

Smith to Hay, Philadelphia, 9 January 1863, Lincoln Papers, Library of Congress. Cf. Joseph Applegate to John Hay, Wellsburg, West Virginia, 11 March 1878; Tarr to George P. Smith, near Wellsburg, 28 February 1878; Tarr to Nicolay, near Wellsburg, 11 April 1878, Nicolay Papers, Library of Congress; Tarr to John Minor Botts, *Baltimore American*, 16 July 1866.

6. [Adams, ed.], *Letters of Hay*, 1:70–72.

7. Franklin Philp with his partner Adolpheus S. Solomon (1826–1910) ran the Metropolitan Book Store at 332 Pennsylvania Avenue.

8. Monteiro and Murphy, eds., *Hay–Howells Letters*, 6.

9. John Julius Thomasson (b. 1841) was Hay's cousin. His father, William Poindexter Thomasson (1797–1882), when a congressman (1843–1847), was the only Southerner to vote for the 1846 Wilmot Proviso.

10. Hitchcock Papers, Library of Congress. General Ethan Allen Hitchcock (1798–1870) was commissioner for the exchange of prisoners.

11. An endorsement states that "The letter was sent by the President to Genl. McClellan in October 1863[2]." This was evidently Lincoln's letter to McClellan, dated 13 October 1862.

12. Butler Papers, Library of Congress.

13. The letter referred to was from the Foreign Affairs Committee of Sheffield, England.

14. Hay Papers, Brown University. The recipient was Hay's mother.

15. According to press reports, Hay left Washington on March 12 to join General Hunter's staff and took sick in New York shortly thereafter. Washington correspondence, 11 and 17 March 1863, *Chicago Tribune*, 12 and 18 March 1863.

16. On March 15, Nicolay told his fiancée that "John Hay went to New York last Thursday [*March 12*] and goes from there sometime this week to Hilton Head S.C. for a two or three weeks' visit to Gen. Hunter. I see the newspapers report that he goes to accept a place on Gen. Hunter's staff, which is not correct. He does hope to help the General take Charleston, but in an amateur and not a professional capacity." Nicolay to Therena Bates, Washington, 15 March 1863, Nicolay Papers, Library of Congress.

17. Hay was devoted to his older brother, Augustus Leonard Hay (1834–1904), who entered the Union army as a private during the war and retired as a captain in 1891.

18. George Hay Stuart Papers, Library of Congress. Stuart was a leading member of the U.S. Christian Commission.

19. Hay Papers, Brown University. Hay indicates no day of the month on which this letter was written.

20. Hay Papers, Brown University.

21. Charles G. Halpine (1829–1868), an Irish-born New York journalist, served as assistant adjutant to General Hunter, as well as liaison with the press. Writing under the pen name *Miles O'Reilly*, he contributed humorous pieces to the *New York Herald*.

22. George Henry Gordon (1823–1886) commanded a division besieging Charleston. Israel Vogdes (1816–1889) helped plan the artillery strategy in the Charleston campaign.

23. General Truman Seymour (1824–1891) was a veteran artillery officer who served with the Tenth Corps. In 1864, his troops were routed at the battle of Olustee, Florida.

24. In the battle of Charleston Harbor (7 April 1863), the Union fleet of nine iron-clads was decisively repulsed by Confederate batteries in Forts Sumter and Moultrie.

25. The *Keokuk* and *Patapsco* were ironclad steamers of the monitor class.

26. Colonel Milton Smith Littlefield (1830–1899) of the Twenty-first U.S. Colored Troops was in charge of recruiting at Hilton Head. During Reconstruction, he achieved prominence as a railroad lobbyist in North Carolina and Florida.

27. The *Ben De Ford* was a U.S. transport steamer.

28. Admiral Samuel Francis Du Pont (1803–1865) commanded the South Atlantic Blockading Squadron.

29. Christopher Raymond Perry Rodgers (1819–1892), fleet commander of the South Atlantic Blockading Squadron, served as superintendent of the Naval Academy (1874–1878). Preston was Lt. Samuel W. Preston (1841–1865), flag lieutenant for Admiral Dahlgren, who praised him as a man with "a fine capacity for business" who "knew all about the squadron." Dahlgren's diary entry for 30 July 1863, in Madeleine Vinton Dahlgren, ed., *Memoir of John A. Dahlgren* (Boston: James R. Osgood, 1882), 406.

30. Hay Papers, Brown University.

31. Hay Papers, Brown University.

32. The USS *New Ironsides*, an ironclad steamer, had served as the Union flagship during the battle of Charleston Harbor.

33. Gideon Welles to S. F. Du Pont, Washington, 2 April 1863, Clarence Clough Buel and Richard Underwood Johnson, eds., *Battles and Leaders of the Civil War* (4 vols.; New York: Century, 1887–1888), 4:41; Gustavus V. Fox to S. F. Du Pont, Washington, 2 April 1863, Robert Means Thompson and Richard Wainwright, eds., *Confidential Correspondence of Gustavus Vasa Fox, Assistant Secretary of the Navy, 1861–1865* (2 vols.; New York: Naval History Society, 1918), 1:197.

34. [Adams, ed.], *Hay Letters*, 1:79.

35. In late March, when Mary Brooks visited Hilton Head with Mrs. Henry J. Raymond, wife of the editor of the *New York Times*, and publisher Fletcher Harper (1806–1877), General Hunter ordered Charles G. Halpine to make Miss Brooks an acting aide-de-camp. On March 25, Halpine dashed off a lighthearted poem, "Special Orders A, Number 1, Headquarters, Army of the South," which appeared in *Harper's Monthly*. William Hanchett, *Irish: Charles G. Halpine in Civil War America* (Syracuse: Syracuse University Press, 1970), 64. The text is given in [Adams, ed.], *Hay Letters*, 1:79–81.

36. The Ks were probably Captain Arthur Magill Kinzie, from Chicago, and his wife. He was an aide-de-camp to General Hunter and the nephew of Mrs. Hunter.

37. Hay Papers, Brown University.

38. Hay Papers, Brown University.

39. Hay Papers, Brown University.

40. Surgeon John Joseph Craven (1822–1893) was the chief medical officer of the Department of the South.

41. Connecticut's Republican governor, William A. Buckingham (1807–1868), had defeated his Democratic challenger, Thomas H. Seymour (1804–1875), earlier in April. At the same time the Republicans won three of the state's four seats in the U.S. House of Representatives.

42. Hay Papers, Brown University.

43. Major Edward W. Smith was assistant adjutant general to General Quincy A. Gillmore.

44. The *New South* was an army camp newspaper.

45. Halpine vigorously defended Du Pont in a letter to Nicolay, Folly Island, South Carolina, 25 April 1863:

> Our friend, Major Wright, showed me one paragraph of your letter to him, in which you referred, apparently with surprise, to the fact that the attack on Charleston by the iron-clads should have been discontinued "when so few casualties had occurred." This is so obvious a reflection, on the first hasty view of the affair, and one so radically unjust when we look calmly at the facts, that, in Major Wright's absence (he has gone down the posts along the Florida coast on a tour of inspection) I will venture to occupy your time a few moments on the subject.
>
> In ordinary warfare the amount of casualties will give a fair idea of the strength of the resistance and the power and persistency of the attack. With wooden vessels, your remark, as previously quoted — and I know it to be an all but universal one — would apply with truth; and it is because we have all become so accustomed to measure battles on land or sea by the amount of slaughter and maiming inflicted, that we are apt to err in judging an utterly uncommon and unprecedented battle by the ordinary or common standard. Let me also add that this standard is both a vulgar and false one. McClellan's victory at Yorktown was a bloodless one, but, nevertheless, a triumph of the highest importance in its results. Of Halleck's siege and capture of Corinth, the same may be said — that victory, although a bloodless one, having thrown open the doors of the entire South-West to the conquering advance of our armies.
>
> And now, let me submit to you, more in detail, some few hasty reflections on the subject of the recent operations for the capture of Charleston: —
>
> 1. It is to be borne in mind that this (so far as the navy was concerned) was purely an experiment as to the possibility of taking a city by machinery. The Monitors might be called blood-saving instruments, with this penalty attached to them: that whenever the loss of life should begin, it would involve the almost certain destruction of every man on board. The number of men in the whole iron-clad squadron was less than a regiment; and these few hundred men, rushing against thirty or forty thousand behind powerful fortifications, were to have no other part in the fight than to supply the necessary power for working the machines. If Charleston were to fall, it was by machinery; and the

moment the experiment was tested to the point of proving that the machines were inadequate to their work, it was wisdom to withdraw them, and would have been dangerous foolhardiness to have held them longer exposed.

2. The experiment was fully prosecuted up to this point, with a magnificence of gallantry before which every generous and just spectator, not directly involved in the attack, must have bowed in reverence. The machines were untried, and the conflict was the first practical test we have ever had of the power of the new kinds of ordnance and ordnance material employed against them. I refer to the Blakely and Whitworth English guns, firing bolts and steel-pointed shot. The warfare was almost as new to Admiral Du Pont and his Captains as it would have been to you or myself—new kinds of projectiles raining on them from above; vast torpedoes [*mines*] known to be underneath their keels, and every channel of entrance blocked up with triple rows of torpedo-armed obstructions.

3. After less than an hour's conflict, five out of the eight Monitors were disabled—the Keokuk sinking. Behind the forts, calmly waiting their opportunity, lay three of the enemy's iron-clads in plain view: vessels not able in fair fight to live an hour before one of our Monitors; but held in readiness to cruise out and capture any Monitor disabled by the artillery practice of the forts and batteries. This should not be let out of sight.

4. With two or three of our vessels of this kind disabled, captured, repaired, and in the enemy's service, what force would it require to maintain the blockade of Charleston? Wooden vessels—our gunboats and steam-sloops—would be useless; and our iron vessels could not live outside of Charleston bar in rough weather. Nor, even if they could, unless we had enough of them to cross-fire over every inch of the mouth of the harbor permanently, could a blockade be maintained against the fast clipper steamers built as blockade-runners in English shipyards. In a word, the enemy, with a single Monitor of ours, could drive every wooden boat from the blockade: and the blockade would thus practically be raised.

5. Could we afford to have Charleston, a free port—the greatest free port in the world, when viewed as the only outlet and inlet for the commerce of eight millions of people; with arms and all other requisites pouring into it unmolested, and cotton, tobacco, naval stores, and so forth, pouring out? Would not such an event of necessity—a moral and political necessity—compel France, and perhaps other wavering foreign Powers, to acknowledge the Confederacy? Are we in a position lightly to hazard these consequences?

6. Bear in mind that the weakness of the Monitor-turrets was increasing in geometrical ratio under the force of each concussion. Each bolt started, each plate cracked, each stancheon bent by the first ball, left weaker protection against the second; and the second transmitted this deterioration, increased by its own impact, to the third. Thus onward—the element of the calculation

being that three hundred guns, worked with every advantage of space and fixity, were arrayed against thirty-two guns cramped up in delicate machines, and requiring to be fired just at the exact right moment of turretal rotation.

7. Fort Sumter itself, we should not forget, was but the fire-focus of two long, converging lines of forts and batteries; and while, for aggressive purposes, and from its position, its armament was more to be dreaded than that of any other work,—the fort itself, being built of masonry, fully exposed to fire, was the most pregnable point in the harbor. Nor would its fall have terminated the contest, nor given any further ease to the iron-clads, than the withdrawal of so many guns from against them. Their work would still lie before them, in silencing the other forts and removing the triple line of powerful and cunningly devised obstructions.

The foregoing, my dear Nicolay, are only a few of the most prominent suggestions to be used in forming a right estimate of the struggle. Busy and overworked as I am, this explanation has appeared necessary to my conscience as a point of duty: insomuch that I could not rest until my very utmost was done to let you see this affair from the standpoint of a deeply interested spectator, who had given some thought and observation to the problem, and who certainly has no other interest in this matter than to see that no injustice is done to brave, true patriots whom he honors—honors with his whole heart and soul.

How I should have felt if in the Weehawken, commanded by John Rodgers, who had the post of honor in the van, I do not know; but suppose that pride and the busy sense of duty and responsibility would have held me firm to my work. Only a spectator, however, with no immediate cares to distract my attention, I am not ashamed to say that I trembled like a leaf for the gallant souls on board the Weehawken, when she first steamed into the hell-made-visible fronting and around Fort Sumter.

The chief officers, as you know, who took part in this fight were Admiral Du Pont, Commodore [*John W.*] Turner, Fleet Captain Raymon Rodgers, Dupont's chief of staff; and Commanders John Rodgers, [*Percival*] Drayton of South Carolina, brother to General [*Thomas F.*] Drayton of the Confederate army; George W. Rodgers, Daniel Ammen, [*John A.*] Downs, [*Donald M.*] Fairfax, [*John L.*] Worden, who commanded the original Monitor in her fight with the Merrimac in Hampton Roads; and [*Alexander C.*] Rhind who, with rash gallantry, ran his vessel, the Keokuk, right under the walls of Fort Sumter, in which position she was so badly riddled and ripped up with bolts and percussion shells, that she sank next morning, despite all efforts to keep her afloat and send her down for repairs to Port Royal. I record these names because it gives me pleasure to write them. It is with names such as these that the future crown of the Republic will be most brightly jewelled. . . .

Before concluding this letter—hastily written, but containing points, it seems to me, which you might do the country a service by bringing to the notice of Mr. Lincoln—let me call attention to the manifest impolicy of further increasing our fleet of Monitor built iron-clads. These vessels, admirable perhaps for attacking fortified places along our coasts—although they have been badly repulsed at Forts McAlister and Sumter—are manifestly unfit to cross the ocean, except when a guaranty-deed of "dead calm" shall have been obtained from the Clerk of the Weather; and are just as manifestly unfit for human beings to live in for any length of time. Besides, it is clear, that, with the reduction of Charleston and Mobile, all the work for which this class of vessels is peculiarly fitted will have been accomplished.

I know it is said that they could be used as floating batteries with which to defend our harbors; but ask the men best competent to judge of their capacities as against vessels like the Warrior, Guerriere, La Gloire, etc., and this illusion will be dissipated. In the judgment of men who have commanded these little, low-lying, two-gun, slow sailing, floating batteries, one of the vast iron-clad frigates of France or England could receive the fire of any two of them—eight or ten guns at most—and then run right over them, the vast ploughs which such frigates carry in front, beneath the water, ripping the whole lower skin of the Monitor-hulls to pieces, and their tall prows moving on undisturbed over the little circular towers and pilot-houses, which would go down in eddying whirlpools beneath their irresistible weight and impetus.

Believe me, my dear Nicolay, that we need iron-clad frigates; and fast vessels to fight fast vessels. There is not one of our grass-grown Monitors to-day that can make, to save her life, even in tideless water, over five miles an hour, if so much; while the mailed frigates of France and England make from seven to eleven and a half. In this respect also, the Roanoke is a failure, only making six knots per hour; and our only safeguard against invasion, and our only means of aggression in case of a foreign war, must be looked for in such vessels as Mr. Webb, of New York, is now constructing.

Could the Navy Department be made to realize these obvious facts? Cannot Mr. Assistant Secretary Fox—whose abilities and zeal are highly spoken of by many who are in the best position to judge—cannot he be brought to comprehend that all vessels-of-war must be in their nature a compromise between the best shape and construction for the immediate purposes of battle—occurring, mayhap, once in several years; and the necessity for having such accommodations, ventilation, comforts, etc., as will preserve the health of the men and officers forming the respective crews? These questions are asked by every unprejudiced naval officer at this station; and it is important that the matter should receive the prompt attention of all who are interested in city property along the Atlantic and Pacific sea-boards.

Halpine, *The Life and Adventures, Songs, Services, and Speeches of Private Miles O'Reilly* (New York: Carleton, 1864), 11–24.

46. Hay had William C. Morrill purchase several lots for him at the St. Augustine tax sale of 21–28 December 1863. He apparently bought an orange grove for $500 that produced a crop worth $2500 in 1864. Hay told Whitelaw Reid that "incidental expenses" had consumed the profits and that "he had never seen an orange or received a penny from it!" He also bought property in Fernandina in a joint venture with Morrill, Lyman Stickney, William Alsop, and gentlemen named Ayer and Hoyt. Hay sank all his capital ($4,000) into Florida real estate, thinking he would reap profits of "several hundred percent." Hay to William Alsop, Paris, 9 October and 12 December 1865; to an unknown correspondent, Paris, 26 September 1866; and to Lyman Stickney, Paris, 4 June 1866, all in a letterpress copybook, Hay Papers, Brown University; Alsop to Hay, New York, 29 August 1866, ibid.; Whitelaw Reid, *After the War: A Tour of the Southern States, 1865–66* (Cincinnati: Moore Wilstach & Baldwin, 1866; Harper Torchbook paperback reprint, 1965), 171–72. Hay objected to Reid's mention of his orange groves, saying "it would have been more merciful for him to have passed that orange grove in St. Augustine without the *infandum muovare dolorem* of my enterprise." Hay to Salmon P. Chase, Paris, 19 October 1866, letterpress copybook, Hay Papers, Brown University.

47. Hay Papers, Brown University. Hay's grandfather was also John Hay (1775–1865).

48. Hay Papers, Brown University.

49. The *Arago* was a U.S. transport steamer.

50. General Joseph Hooker (1814–1879) commanded the Army of the Potomac (1863). General William S. Rosecrans (1819–1898) commanded the Army of the Cumberland (1862–1863).

51. Congressman Charles A. Wickliffe (1788–1869), postmaster general under President Tyler and a leading Kentucky Unionist, protested against Hunter's recruitment of black troops. Hunter issued a defiant rejoinder. On May 9, Hunter, disappointed by the failure of blacks to volunteer for the army, ordered that all black males between eighteen and forty-five living in or near Port Royal be drafted. Edward L. Pierce, a Treasury Department agent stationed in Port Royal to supervise the affairs of the freed slaves, protested that Hunter's order would have an unfavorable effect on the "ignorant, suspicious, and sensitive" blacks, for they "have not so far recovered the manhood which two centuries of bondage have rooted out." Pierce quoted in Edward A. Miller, Jr., *Lincoln's Abolitionist General: The Biography of David Hunter* (Columbia: University of South Carolina Press, 1997), 100. See also Pierce to Salmon P. Chase, Port Royal, 13 May 1862, and Beaufort, 2 April 1863, John Niven et al., eds., *The Salmon P. Chase Papers* (Kent, Oh.: Kent State University Press, 1993–1875), 3:198–99, 4:2–3. A firsthand account of Hunter's recruiting efforts in the spring of 1862 can be found in [Charles G. Halpine], *Baked Meats of the Funeral* (New York: Carlton, 1866), 171–207.

52. General Lorenzo B. Thomas (1804–1875) had been recruiting black troops in the South since April.

53. In 1857, George Alfred Lawrence (1827–1876) published the controversial novel *Guy Livingston, or Thorough*, which scandalized polite society. He tried to join the Confederate army, but was arrested by Union forces. Eventually he was released on the condition that he return forthwith to England.

54. Hay Papers, Brown University.

55. When Hay left South Carolina at the end of May, he took with him his brother, who had obtained a twenty-day medical leave. *New South* (Port Royal, S.C.), 30 May 1863.

56. Draft, Hay Papers, Brown University.

57. General Quincy A. Gillmore (1825–1888), who commanded the Tenth Corps, Department of the South, had led a successful campaign against Fort Pulaski in Georgia.

58. Andrew Hull Foote (1806–1863) was sent to command the fleet at Charleston but died en route to his new assignment.

59. In a three-hour conversation at the White House, Lincoln explained his decision to Hunter in much the same terms that Hay spelled out. Hunter to Halpine, 21 July 1863, Hanchett, *Halpine*, 73–74.

60. Draft, Lincoln Papers, Library of Congress.

61. Julian Campbell's letter of June 10 is not in the Lincoln Papers, though one from him dated Providence, R.I., 10 March 1864, is. In that document, Campbell forwards pro-Lincoln resolutions adopted by the "R.I. State League, A.L. of A."

62. Seward Papers, University of Rochester.

63. William Marsh was a writer; he continued to serve in Altona, a major German fishing port near Hamburg, through the late 1860s.

64. Cf. William Marsh to Hay, Altona, 30 October 1863, Seward Papers, University of Rochester.

65. Hay Papers, Brown University.

66. Janet (Nettie) Ralston Chase (1847–1925) was the daughter of Secretary of the Treasury Salmon P. Chase.

67. Carlota Wilhelmina Mariana von Gerolt and John Ward of the Bengal Civil Service were married on July 21.

68. Hay Papers, Brown University.

69. Hay Papers, Brown University.

70. "Bosco" was perhaps Ferdinando Beneventano Bosco, who led Bourbonists against Garibaldi's forces at Milazzo, Sicily, on 20 July 1859, in a losing battle.

71. Hay Papers, Brown University.

72. Draft of a telegram, Hay Papers, Brown University.

73. Hay had asked that his brother Charles be assigned to temporary duty in the provost marshal general's office. Later in 1863, he was stationed in Springfield. Charles E. Hay to the War Department, Washington, 22 July 1863, and Hay's reports dated Springfield, 1 and 15 August, 1 September, 1 October, and 1 November 1863, Record Group 725, National Archives.

74. Hay Papers, Brown University.

75. James B. Fry (1827–1894) was provost marshal general.

76. Hay Papers, Brown University. Edward Geer Bush (1838–1892) was the son of Daniel Brown Bush, editor of the *Pike County Journal* and brother-in-law of Ozias M. Hatch. A schoolmate of Hay in Pittsfield, Bush graduated from West Point in 1859; he was wounded at Gettysburg.

77. General George Gordon Meade (1815–1872) of Pennsylvania commanded of the Army of the Potomac (1863–1865). Colonel Edmund Brooke Alexander of the Tenth U.S. Infantry was provost marshal for Missouri. See Alexander to Colonel J. B. Fry, St. Louis, 4 June 1863, Lincoln Papers, Library of Congress.

78. Gilder-Lehrman Collection, Pierpont Morgan Library, New York.

79. Hay Papers, Brown University.

80. The letter referred to was Bush to Nicolay, Camp, Second Brigade, Second Division, Fifth Army Corps, 11 June 1863, Lincoln Papers, Library of Congress.

81. Nicolay had left Washington on July 14 to help negotiate a treaty with Indian tribes in Colorado.

82. Edward Davis Townsend (1817–1893) was adjutant general of the army.

83. George Washington Cullum (1809–1892) was chief of staff to the commander of the Union armies.

84. Theodore was Bush's brother, whose death was imminent.

85. Hay Papers, Brown University.

86. Nicolay was among those drafted. Washington correspondence, 4 August 1863, *Chicago Tribune*, 5 August 1863, p. 1, c. 4.

87. A black servant whom Lincoln had brought with him from Springfield, Johnson (d. 1864) worked in the White House attending to Lincoln's wardrobe, shaving him, and performing similar services. To earn extra money, Johnson also worked as a messenger for the Treasury Department. See Roy P. Basler, "Did President Lincoln Give the Smallpox to William H. Johnson?" *Henry E. Huntington Library Quarterly*, 34 (1972):279–84, and John E. Washington, *They Knew Lincoln* (New York: E. P. Dutton, 1942), 127–34.

88. Henry Stoddard worked as a clerk in the Treasury Department. He was an accountant whose job had been obtained through some clever maneuvering by his brother William O. Stoddard. Henry Stoddard and Hay "were good friends. He was always a welcome visitor in the northeast room [*of the White House*], whenever his really severe and responsible duties at the Treasury gave him an hour off to come for a chat with the private secretaries." William O. Stoddard, typescript of memoirs, 2:331, Stoddard Papers, Detroit Public Library.

89. "Ramsey" was perhaps Samuel Ramsey, a clerk in the Surgeon General's Office.

90. Henry A. Blood was a clerk in the Interior Department.

91. It is difficult to identify specific items in the *Washington Chronicle* by Hay (save for a squib about Schuyler Colfax on August 20 and editorials that he pasted into his scrapbooks), but several editorials are written in Hay's baroque style, e.g., "The

Returned Soldiers" (3 August 1863) and "General Gillmore and Admiral Dahlgren" (20 August 1863). From 1860 through 1862, Hay had written anonymous and pseudonymous dispatches for several newspapers, including the *Missouri Republican* (St. Louis), the *Springfield Illinois State Journal*, the *New York World*, and the *Providence Journal*. Burlingame, ed., *Lincoln's Journalist*.

92. John P. Hale (1806–1873) represented New Hampshire in the U.S. Senate (1855–1865).

93. In 1863 and 1864, Nathaniel S. Howe of Haverhill, Massachusetts, was technically a clerk in the Interior Department; he and Gustavus E. Matile, both of whom actually worked in the White House assisting Nicolay and Hay, were two of ten clerks listed as serving in the office of the Secretary of the Interior. *Register of Officers and Agents, Civil, Military, and Naval, in the Service of the United States on the Thirtieth of September, 1863* (Washington: Government Printing Office, 1864), 97. In the *Register* for 1865 he is listed as a pension clerk. Howe, a lawyer and a probate judge in Haverhill, had served in the Massachusetts state senate (1853) but sought a U.S. government post because he could not make enough money practicing his profession. After the war, he served as collector of internal revenue in the Sixth District of Massachusetts and was a political operative for Nathaniel P. Banks. See Howe to Charles Sumner, Haverhill, Massachusetts, 1 January 1863, and Washington, 3 November 1864, Sumner Papers, Harvard University; *Boyd's Washington and Georgetown Directory* (1864); D. W. Gooch to William Henry Seward, Boston, 14 November 1861, Letters of Application and Recommendation during the Administration of A. Lincoln and A. Johnson, Record Group 650, reel 23, National Archives; letters of Howe to Banks, Haverhill, Massachusetts, 17 and 21 September, and 29 November 1867; 8 January, 21 February, 12 and 13 March, 18 June, 3 July, 28 September, 12 and 28 October, and 9 December 1868; and 14 and 29 January and 16 March 1869, Banks Papers, Library of Congress.

94. "Miss Carroll" was perhaps Anna Ella Carroll (1815–1893), a Maryland writer whose patriotic pamphlets Lincoln commended.

95. Hay Papers, Brown University.

96. "John A. Nicolay" was probably John H. Nicolay (?–1870), John G. Nicolay's nephew. His father, Frederick Lewis Nicolay (?–1872), was John G. Nicolay's older brother. He served in the U.S. Treasury during the war in a job that John G. Nicolay helped him obtain. *Pike County Republican* (Pittsfield, Illinois), 20 October 1937.

97. Nicolay was enrolled for the draft in Springfield and thus ineligible to be drafted by the District of Columbia authorities. When drafted on 20 September 1864, he hired a substitute. Helen Nicolay memo, n.d., and "Certificate of Exemption," Washington, 27 September 1864, scrapbook, box 1, Nicolay Papers, Library of Congress.

98. Halpine Papers, Henry E. Huntington Library, San Marino, California. By this time, Halpine had resigned from the army and was serving as the civilian commissary-general of subsistence on the staff of Horatio Seymour, governor of New York.

99. Nelson J. Waterbury (b. 1819) was Judge Advocate General of the State of New

York and grand sachem of the Tammany Society. Waterbury to Horatio Seymour, New York, 7 August 1863, Lincoln Papers, Library of Congress.

100. Robert H. Nugen (1809–1872) was a Democratic Congressman from Ohio.

101. "The Question of Reconstruction," *New York Times*, 3 August 1863, p. 4, cc. 2–3.

102. Draft, Hay Papers, Brown University.

103. Many of Charles C. Fulton's letters are preserved in the Lincoln Papers, Library of Congress.

104. Hay Papers, Brown University.

105. HON. SCHUYLER COLFAX. This distinguished Western orator and statesman was in the city yesterday. He seems to have lost much of his old vivacity of manner, which may be attributed to his recent severe domestic affliction. He remained but a few hours, and went to his home in Indiana. Mr. Colfax is very generally spoken of as the Union candidate for the Speakership of the next House of Representatives. Of course we do not wish to announce any special preference in this matter, choosing rather to leave it to the decision of the Union members of Congress, as a nomination by them, it now appears, will be equivalent to an election. But no one can be insensible to the fact that the long and brilliant parliamentary career of Mr. Colfax, his unstained political record, his spotless personal character, over which a suspicion of wrong has never hovered, his industry and sagacity, and his intimate connection with the struggles and triumphs of the West in the war, form a combination of rare qualifications for the important position for which his friends are preparing to present him.

Washington Chronicle, 20 August 1863, p. 2, c. 3.

106. *Official Records of the War of the Rebellion*, (129 vols.; Washington: Government Printing Office, 1880–1900), series III, 3:712.

107. Nelson J. Waterbury to Lincoln, New York, 19 August 1863, *Official Records of the War of the Rebellion*, series III, 3:712–14.

108. Hay visited Long Branch, New Jersey, for a brief while. Washington correspondence, 25 August 1863, in an unidentified journal, paraphrased in *Illinois State Journal* (Springfield), 28 August 1863, p. 3, c. 2.

109. Sumner Papers, Harvard University. Charles Sumner (1811–1874) of Massachusetts was chairman of the Senate Foreign Relations Committee.

110. Richard Cobden (1804–1865) and John Bright (1811–1889) were celebrated English reform leaders.

111. James Wadsworth Papers, Library of Congress.

112. Hay Papers, Brown University.

113. Attorney G. Rush Smith had supported Simon Cameron's appointment to the cabinet in 1861.

114. Hay Papers, Brown University.

115. At commencement exercises on September 1, Hay spoke in response to the invitation of Professor John Larkin Lincoln. He delivered "verses of great beauty and

grace, which showed that the lyre, which in former days charmed the hearers, had not lost its charms, even in the prosaic atmosphere of Washington." *Providence Journal*, 3 September 1863. Hay had been the class poet at Brown in 1858.

116. William Tod Otto (1816–1905) of Indiana was assistant secretary of the interior.

117. After maneuvering Braxton Bragg's Confederate forces out of Chattanooga, Rosecrans entered the city on September 10.

118. Lincoln to James C. Conkling, Washington, 26 August 1863, Basler et al., eds., *Collected Works of Lincoln*, 6:406–10.

119. Sarah Forbes Hughes, ed., *Letters and Recollections of John Murray Forbes* (2 vols.; Boston: Houghton Mifflin, 1900), 2:76. John Murray Forbes (1813–1898) was a prominent Boston businessman who helped raise black troops for the Union army. On September 8, Forbes had praised Lincoln's public letter to James C. Conkling and urged the president to inform the world "that our quarrel is that of the people against an aristocracy." Benjamin P. Thomas speculated that Forbes's letter may have inspired the Gettysburg address. In an unpublished autobiographical sketch, Thomas explained his reasoning: "I don't mean that Forbes's letter influenced Lincoln's thinking; he had entertained that very opinion about the true issue of the war from the beginning. But I do believe it was his letter that induced him to accept the invitation to speak at Gettysburg, and that it is due to Forbes' suggestion that the world gained the immortal words 'That government of the people, by the people, for the people shall not perish from the earth.'" Autobiographical sketch, ca. 1953, Benjamin P. Thomas Papers, Illinois State Historical Library, Springfield.

120. James Wadsworth Papers, Library of Congress.

121. Frederick Lander Papers, Library of Congress.

122. George Henry Boker (1823–1890), a playwright and poet, was secretary of the Union League of Philadelphia (1862–1871).

123. Barney Papers, Henry E. Huntington Library, San Marino, California.

124. Barney had asked when it would be convenient for the president "to sit to our great portrait painter Elliott." Barney to Lincoln, New York, 21 September 1863, Lincoln Papers, Library of Congress. Charles Loring Elliott (1812–1868) of New York was a popular portrait painter.

125. Photocopy, Letitia Howe Collection, Miscellaneous Manuscripts, Library of Congress. Brainerd (1831–1910) was a New York attorney and champion of school reform.

126. James Wadsworth Papers, Library of Congress.

127. Hay Papers, Brown University.

128. Margaret Julia Mitchell (1837–1918) was a popular actress famous for her performance in the title role of *Fanchon the Cricket*. In 1862, John T. Ford, manager of Baltimore's Halliday Street Theater, organized a resident stock company in Washington to perform with visiting stars at the Athanaeum, a remodeled Baptist church on Tenth Street. The following year, after the Athenaeum had burned down, Ford opened a new twenty-four-hundred-seat theater on the same site.

129. The Canterbury was a music hall with a dubious reputation. A journalist

called it "a sink of corruption . . . whose matinees are attended by the shameless sort of Treasury girls." *New York Citizen*, 27 October 1866. Another correspondent described both the Canterbury and the Oxford music halls as "very low theaters — something between a 'model artist' establishment and a Bowery — where the principal attraction is the 'development' of the female performers, and where double entendre always brings down the house." *Cincinnati Commercial*, 4 December 1865.

130. Nicolay-Hay Papers, Illinois State Historical Library, Springfield.

131. Seventy delegates from Missouri arrived in Washington on September 27 "and spent two days in preparing a formal address and arranging the necessary preliminaries to make their interview as impressive as possible. A number of delegates from the State of Kansas also appeared in Washington at the same time with similar views and objects, and joined in the interview and address." Nicolay and Hay, *Abraham Lincoln*, 7:214.

132. Charles D. Drake (1811–1892), a leading Missouri Radical, represented his state in the U.S. Senate (1867–1870).

133. *Pike* was a slang term, originally applied to Missourians from Pike County, then to Missourians in general; it came to mean a vagrant or an incompetent person.

134. On September 1, Radical Republicans held a convention in Jefferson City.

135. John M. Schofield (1831–1906) commanded the Department of Missouri. Lincoln spoke of the "pestilent factional quarrel" in his letter to Schofield of 27 May 1863, Basler et al., eds., *Collected Works of Lincoln*, 6:234.

136. Hamilton R. Gamble (1798–1864) was the Unionist governor of Missouri.

137. Gamble to Lincoln, 13 July 1863, and Lincoln to Gamble, Washington, 23 July 1863, Basler et al., eds., *Collected Works of Lincoln*, 6:344–45.

138. Democrat Claiborne F. Jackson, who favored secession, was elected governor in 1860. In June 1861, he fled the capital, Jefferson City, creating a power vacuum that was filled in July when a Unionist convention established a provisional government, headed by Hamilton R. Gamble.

139. By the fall of 1861, it was clear that the understaffed, poorly equipped Missouri militia needed reorganization. Since some Missourians would serve in the militia but not the Union army, and since the state government was strapped for cash, the federal government agreed to finance the militia, which would be under the control of the state government.

140. Schofield angered the Radicals by arresting a proprietor of the *Missouri Democrat* and threatening to arrest others, including newspaper editors, stirring up dissatisfaction within the armed forces or inciting civilians to violence against the government. Lincoln supported these measures.

141. Hay adds this footnote here: "An hour afterward the Governor of Kansas and some prominent citizens of Kansas called on the President to state that Gen. Schofield was entirely satisfactory to the people of Kansas and that they did not wish him removed at all."

142. On August 21, Confederates under William C. Quantrill slaughtered 150 men and boys in Lawrence, Kansas.

143. On October 28, Lincoln told Hay: "I believe, after all, those Radicals will carry the State & I do not object to it. They are nearer to me than the other side, in thought and in sentiment, though bitterly hostile personally. They are utterly lawless — the unhandiest devils in the world to deal with — but after all their faces are set Zion-wards." Burlingame and Ettlinger, eds., *Hay Diary*, 101.

144. Later in the document, a note was inserted indicating that at this point Lincoln referred to the following letter written by Joseph A. Hay from St. Louis on September 11:

> Excuse me for thus intruding upon your time and attention but I felt as though you ought to be posted as to who are your friends & who are the opposers of your Administration in this State.
>
> Mr C D Drake in a speech in my town (La Grange) on the 19th of August denounced you as a Tyrant and a Dictator and to prove it called the attention of the meeting to what he said was an attempt on your part to dictate to the Loyal Masses of Missouri by some report which Gen Schofield brought to Jefferson City to deliver to the Members of the State Convention from effecting their decision on the Emancipation question.
>
> He said he did not learn the nature of it (the Message) until after the Convention adjourned[.] [I]f he had he should have blown the President & the Convention sky high. He would show him how he attempted to dictate to a free people and much more of like talk not necessary to mention.

Lincoln Papers, Library of Congress.

145. A Republican leader from Keokuk, Iowa, Taylor had been appointed mail agent in Kansas at the behest of Jim Lane. He had known Lincoln in New Salem in the 1830s.

146. *Drabs* was a slang term for slatternly women.

147. A few days later, Drake called on Lincoln, without success. Whitelaw Reid reported on October 5, "The streets are laughing this morning over a rebuff given by Mr. Lincoln to the Chairman of the Missouri Delegation. Calling at the White House, at an early hour, he sought an interview with the President. In a moment the servant came out with the message 'The President is sorry, but he really can't see you. He has a hundred pages of the manuscript you left him to read yet!'" Washington correspondence by "Agate," 5 October 1863, *Cincinnati Gazette*, 8 October 1863, p. 1, c. 2. On October 3, Drake had left four supplementary addresses at the White House. Two days later, Lincoln wrote a long response to Drake and his colleagues. Basler et al., eds., *Collected Works of Lincoln*, 6:499–504.

148. Hitchcock Papers, Library of Congress.

149. Hay Papers, Brown University.

150. John Brough (1811–1865) was governor of Ohio (1863–1865).

151. William Dennison (1815–1882) had been governor of Ohio (1860–1861) and was to serve as U.S. postmaster general (1864–1866).

152. Andrew G. Curtin (1817–1894) was governor of Pennsylvania.

153. Montague, ed., *A College Friendship*, 63–64. Caroline Angell (d. 1909) was a younger sister of Hay's friend Hannah Angell Coggeshall.

154. Francis Preston Blair Family Papers, Library of Congress.

155. The enclosed was a letter from C. W. Hibbard of the *Rochester Evening Express*, Rochester, New York, 16 October 1863, asking for copies of a letter by J. Stubbs to Blair and Blair's reply, concerning the draft.

156. Basler et al., eds., *Collected Works of Lincoln*, 6:533–34. For unknown reasons, Hay backdated the letter from October 26 to October 24. On October 26, Hay recorded in his diary that he "wrote Boker letter (dated 24) accepting the gold medal and honorary membership of the Philadel[phi]a Union League." Burlingame and Ettlinger, eds., *Hay Diary*, 101. The original is in Hay's handwriting, signed by Lincoln.

157. Hay Papers, Library of Congress.

158. The piece on the banquet appeared in the *New York Herald*, 23 October 1863, reprinted in Halpine, *Life and Adventures of Miles O'Reilly*, 73–113.

159. Halpine had criticized Fox and Wise in his letter to Nicolay, Folly Island, South Carolina, 25 April 1863, in Halpine, *Life and Adventures of Miles O'Reilly*, 11–24.

160. Gurowski's letter and Edward W. Smith's speech are part of the banquet account in Halpine, *Life and Adventures of Miles O'Reilly*, 82, 101–3.

161. General Rosecrans had been removed from command of the Army of the Cumberland on October 17.

162. Kate Chase (1840–1899), daughter of Salmon P. Chase, was a Washington belle who married Rhode Island senator William Sprague.

163. Sumner Papers, Harvard University.

164. Sumner's letter read thus: "I am obliged by your kind attention. Will you be good enough to call the attention of the Presdt. to *two* letters which I forwarded for his perusal from (1) Joshua Bates of London (2) John Bright. As I presume, he does not desire to keep them, I should be glad to have them returned so that they need not be lost in the Presidential pile." Hay Papers, Brown University. This document is addressed to "Dear Sir" and is identified in pencil as a letter to Hay. But Hay's letter to Sumner of October 26 indicates that it was written to Hay's assistant, Nathaniel S. Howe.

165. Joshua Bates was a resident of London.

166. On 17 January 1864, Hay sent Bates's letter to Sumner with this covering note: "I find this letter in the files of the President, and return it as you requested." A pencilled annotation indicates that the letter returned was by Joshua Bates, 3 September 1863. Sumner Papers, Harvard University.

167. James Wadsworth Papers, Library of Congress.

168. Hay Papers, Brown University. Lossing (1813–1891) wrote popular works about American history.

169. Halpine Papers, Henry E. Huntington Library, San Marino, California.

170. On November 18, Halpine wrote to Hay:

Private Miles is about to visit Washn. And be introduced to the Prest., of whom for reelection (*vide* Herald passim) he is a warm and devoted supporter. Have you any annecdote you could give me of what *anybody* said about Miles? Also, this is very important, give me the name of James, your doorkeeper, who was so under Pierce & Buckn. He comes from the same part of "the ould [*dart?*]" with OReilly. *Any* annecdote from the Presdt. if new would be worth its weight in gold. . . . I promise if you help me in this my hour of need that OReilly will be discreet and give you no cause to blush for him. He will do the handsome by Fox and take Wise to his bosom. *He* never had any quarrel with either — never saw either: but it was necessary to hit them as part of the fight for Du Pont. Can you give me any *fresh saying* or *annecdote* of the Prest. No matter what it may be, it can be worked in. Anything like his "plowing round the stumps that couldn't be either grubbed or burnt out," with which I commenced my article on Jim Lane and the Kansas Missouri troubles some five or six weeks ago. Mr [*James Gordon*] Bennet wishes the next OReilly paper on the Presidency and to be a strong political & Irish document for Mr. Lincoln. Your note shall be destroyed five minutes after its receipt: and no living soul shall know of its receipt.

Halpine to Hay, New York, 18 November 1863, Hay Papers, Brown University.

171. George B. Lincoln had visited Abraham Lincoln (no relation) in 1860 at Springfield. He published reminiscences of his encounters with the president. *St. Johnsbury* (Vermont) *Caledonian*, 23 October 1890. He also shared his recollections of Lincoln with Gideon Welles. See G. B. Lincoln to Welles, Rivervale, New Jersey, 25 April 1874, *Lincoln Lore* (April 1981), 2–3.

172. Jesse K. Dubois (1811–1876), a political ally of Lincoln, had been elected Illinois state auditor in 1856.

173. Edward McManus was described by William O. Stoddard as a "short, thin, smiling, humorous-looking elderly Irishman . . . who has been so great a favorite through so many administrations. He is as well liked by his seventh President [*Lincoln*] as he was by even General Taylor. There is no end of quiet fun in him as well as intelligence, and his other name is Fidelity. He is said to have been the first man met in the White House by Mr. Lincoln who succeeded in making him laugh." Stoddard, *Inside the White House in War Times*, 10. For unclear reasons, he was dismissed in January 1865, evidently at the behest of Mary Lincoln, who called him a "serpent." Turner and Turner, eds., *Mary Todd Lincoln*, 200–2. In March 1865, his replacement, Cornelius O'Leary, was fired after being caught peddling influence to obtain pardons. It was alleged that he shared with Mary Lincoln the illegal fees he received. Noah Brooks, Washington dispatch, 12 March 1865, Burlingame, ed., *Lincoln Observed*, 171–74. See appendix 2, infra.

174. Thomas Burns, a native of Ireland, was an assistant doorkeeper.

175. Prussian-born Louis Burgdorf was a doorkeeper.

176. In September 1863, General Richard Busteed (1822–1898) of New York was appointed a judge of the U.S. District Court for Alabama. In that post, he was accused of corruption and resigned to avoid impeachment.

177. Hay's poem is based on a poem by Halpine that appeared in the *New York Herald* in October. Halpine, *Life and Adventures of Miles O'Reilly*, 61.

178. Hay Papers, Brown University. No note is filed with this letter.

179. Hay Papers, Brown University.

180. General Orlando Bolivar Wilcox (1823–1907) commanded the First Division of the Ninth Corps.

181. George H. Thomas of Virginia (1816–1870) commanded the Fourteenth Corps of the Army of the Cumberland. In September 1863, he earned the sobriquet *The Rock of Chickamauga* when he prevented a complete Union rout at the battle of Chickamauga. General William T. Sherman (1820–1891) commanded the Army of the Tennessee.

182. Hay Papers, Brown University.

183. Lincoln Collection, Brown University.

184. Dix had asked the president for a statement regarding the ground-breaking ceremony in Nebraska for a section of the Union Pacific Railroad. Lincoln suffered from varioloid fever, a mild form of smallpox.

185. Halpine Papers, Henry E. Huntington Library, San Marino, California.

186. Walter S. Collins was the son of James H. Collins, a prominent Chicago lawyer. On November 24, Halpine wrote Hay about Collins:

> I send herewith a letter to which I beg you will ask Mr. Lincoln's attention. If the subject matter of the "Miles OReilly" which will appear tomorrow, if there be room in the *Herald* pleases him,—pray say that Mr. Collins' request is Private OReillys *only* request of him,—and I think that's cheap when he makes Busteed a judge! Mr. Collins was a friend of Mr. L's, whom he admired greatly as a lawyer, and on seeing Mrs. Collins some weeks ago, or on being spoken to by one of her friends, I forget which, he was most kind and flattering in his reminiscences of Mr. C., who was a wealthy and prominent lawyer of high character in Chicago. Her son Walter is a really fine high spirited, handsome young fellow of 17, now a student at the Military Academy Poughkeepsie, having come from Clinton College. He has a good income and is crazy to be a West Pointer.

Hay Papers, Brown University.

187. "Miles O'Reilly at the White House," Washington, 26 November 1863, was published in the *New York Herald* and reprinted in Halpine, *Life and Adventure of Miles O'Reilly*, 154–197.

188. Conservative Unionist Emerson Etheridge (1819–1902), a slaveholder from west Tennessee, was clerk of the U.S. House of Representatives. He hoped to disqualify many Republican Representatives on a technicality.

189. Wilkes (1817–1885) edited a New York newspaper, the *Spirit of the Times*.

190. Hay alludes to passages in "Miles O'Reilly at the White House," Halpine, *Life and Adventures of Miles O'Reilly*, 170–72, 178–79.

191. Hay Papers, Brown University. Kansas senator Samuel C. Pomeroy (1816–1891), a spokesman for the Radical Republicans in Congress, achieved wide notice in 1864 when he issued a circular denigrating Lincoln and promoting the candidacy of Salmon P. Chase.

192. Hay Papers, Brown University. The addressee was the daughter of Edward Everett and wife of Hay's friend Henry A. Wise.

3. 1864–1865

1. Hay Papers, Brown University. Hay misdated this letter 1863. Samuel Phillips Lee (1812–1897) commanded the North Atlantic Blockading Squadron.

2. The Union army maintained a prisoner of war camp at Point Lookout, Maryland.

3. In his diary entry for 2–4 January 1864, Hay described his misadventures aboard the *Clyde*. Burlingame and Ettlinger, eds., *Hay Diary*, 137–40.

4. Holt Papers, Library of Congress. Joseph Holt of Kentucky (1807–1894) was judge advocate general of the army (1862–1875).

5. Draft of telegram, Hay Papers, Brown University.

6. Hay Papers, Brown University.

7. Lincoln to Gillmore, Washington, 13 January 1864, Basler et al., eds., *Collected Works*, 7:126.

8. Ephraim Brewer (b. 1827), a well digger originally from Tennessee, lived on Gemini Street in Springfield.

9. General John Wesley Turner (1833–1899) of Chicago later commanded a division in the Eighteenth Corps of the Army of the James.

10. Albert Gallatin Brown Sr. was the supervising special agent at Beaufort, South Carolina. Lyman D. Stickney told Chase, "Your treasury agent, A. G. Browne, is a good man, his impulses are good, if he gave his thoughts less tongue, no one could find serious objection to him." Stickney to Chase, Jacksonville, 24 February 1864, Niven, ed., *Chase Papers*, 4:306.

11. Judge Lyman D. Stickney was a northern-born Florida Unionist who served as superintendent of freedmen in his adopted state. A friend of Salmon Chase, the judge speculated financially and politically, leading to charges of corruption and misfeasance in office. Herbert Reed to Salmon P. Chase, New York, 3 November 1863, Chase Papers, Library of Congress; House of Representatives, Executive Document 18, 38th Congress, 2nd Session. Stickney's activities on behalf of Chase alienated at least one Radical, Joseph R. Hawley, who told a friend early in 1864:

> I am growing more and more confident that we will do better to re-elect President Lincoln than to attempt to make any change. I used to be a Chase man

and I admire his ability and statesmanship, but I don't like the eagerness with which he schemes for the Presidency or rather many of the tools he works with. Some of his agents and appointees down here have been infernal scoundrels and he sticks to them though they have been exposed. The leading Tax Commissioner for Florida and the getter-up of the humbug Union meetings they have had down here is old Stoops on a larger scale, and a *more* unblushing rascal, a thorough going scoundrel. Had I continued in the management of Fernandina or St. Augustine affairs, ten to one I should soon or late have had him jugged. I routed out one or two as it were, and I exposed Stickney's character in a letter to Mr. Sumner, which he read to the President and Messrs. Blair and Chase. But the latter gives Stickney full control. If Mr. Lincoln is to be reelected through Seward's aid, that will put a great load on us for four years more, — that is if a condition of that support shall be the retention of Seward and his counsels.

Joseph R. Hawley to Charles Dudley Warner, St. Helena Island, South Carolina, 22 January 1864, in Arthur L. Shipman, "Letters of Joseph R. Hawley," 187, typescript dated 1929, Connecticut Historical Society, Hartford. Elsewhere, Hawley called Stickney a "lying adventurer" and added that the citizens who were to form the basis of a loyal, reconstructed Florida government "are poor, white-livered, clay-eating, timid, useless or else treacherous" people led by "scoundrelly intriguers." Hawley to his father, Jacksonville, Florida, 28 February 1864, ibid., 195. Cf. Hawley to Warner, n.p., 30 January 1864, ibid., 189:

aside from a little undue influence exercised by that monstrous mixture of blind selfishness and philosophic statesmanship, Seward, "Old Abe" makes the best approach to George Washington that we can get. . . . Of course, there has been what we may fairly term imbecility in some things, a mixture of discordant counsels in the management of the war — sometimes Halleck and sometimes Lincoln and sometimes nobody telling a General and a grand army what to do. But the whole nation has much stumbling to do and an infinite deal to learn. Old Abe has sat down with us and we have all "spelled out" the sore lesson together.

12. In the *Address of E. W. Gantt, of Arkansas (Brigadier General in the Confederate Army) in Favor of Re-union in 1863* (Little Rock: n.p., 1863), Edward Walton Gantt (1812–1883) urged Arkansans to quit the war, reorganize the state, and bring it back into the Union. Cf. *New York Times*, 6 February 1864.

13. In his annual message to Congress on 8 December 1863, Lincoln put forth a plan of amnesty and pardon stipulating that amnesty would be granted to those Confederates who took an oath of future loyalty to the Constitution and pledged to support the presidential proclamations concerning slavery. When enough residents of a Confederate state took such an oath, the state could be restored politically. Hay went to Florida to help implement that policy.

14. Hay Papers, Brown University.

15. Lincoln to Gillmore, Washington, 13 January 1864, Basler et al., eds., *Collected Works of Lincoln*, 7:126.

16. Hay Papers, Brown University.

17. Thomas B. Brooks was an aide-de-camp to General Gillmore.

18. According to John Russell Young, "Hay's yearning for the field became an active force. He had the military instinct. . . . Hay used to talk of active duty, counting the days until the day would come." Young, "John Hay, Secretary of State," 248.

19. Lincoln Papers, Library of Congress.

20. Copy, Nicolay-Hay Papers, Illinois State Historical Library, Springfield.

21. Confederate General William Joseph Hardee (1815–1873) commanded the Department of Georgia, South Carolina, and Florida.

22. Colonel James Montgomery (1814–1871) commanded the Second South Carolina (Colored) Infantry. The surgeon of the Eighth U.S. Regiment later wrote of his unit's participation in the battle of Olustee:

> The Eighth colored marched on the railroad, came up first, and filed to the right, when they were soon met with a most terrific shower of musketry and shell. General T. Seymour now came up, and pointing in front toward the railroad, said to Colonel Fribley, commander of the Eighth, "Take your regiment in there"—a place which was sufficiently hot to make veterans tremble, and yet they were to enter it with men who had never heard the sound of a cannon. Colonel Fribley ordered the regiment, by company, into line, double-quick march; but, before it was fairly in line, the men commenced dropping like leaves in autumn. Still, on they went, without faltering or murmuring, until they came within two hundred yards of the enemy, when the struggle for life and death commenced. Here they stood for two hours and a half, under one of the most terrible fires I ever witnessed; and here, on the field of Olustee, was decided whether the colored man had the courage to stand without shelter, and risk the dangers of the battle-field; and when I tell you that they stood with a fire in front, on their flank, and in their rear, for two hours and a half, without flinching, and when I tell you the number of dead and wounded, I have no doubt as to the verdict of every man who has gratitude for the defenders of his country, white or black.

A. P. Aeichhold to E. M. Davis, near Jacksonville, Florida, 23 February 1864, Frank Moore, ed., *The Rebellion Record: A Diary of American Events* (12 vols.; New York: G. P. Putnam, 1861–1868), 8, documents section, 416.

23. Joseph R. Hawley was skeptical about Hay's mission: "The reorganization of Florida is a gigantic humbug," he told Charles Dudley Warner. "Besides the Floridians who were already with the Union forces at St. Augustine, Fernandina, Key West, etc., we have scarcely met a man who would be allowed to vote in Connecticut,—that is with sufficient intelligence and education. Not enough white men have we picked up to make one good country school district at the north. We have some pris-

oners, a good many deserters and a lot of stragglers, poor white-livered, fever-stricken, scrawny, ignorant creatures, with hardly intelligence enough to be made even the tool of a political intriguer." Hawley to Warner, Jacksonville, Florida, 4 March 1864, Shipman, ed., "Letters of Hawley," 199.

24. N. P. Banks Papers, Library of Congress.

25. Daniel P. Woodbury (1812–1864) commanded the District of Key West and the Tortugas.

26. On February 22, Louisiana voters chose delegates to a constitutional convention.

27. Hay Papers, Brown University. Greene was chief quartermaster in the Department of Washington.

28. Edward Lyulph Stanley was the Baron Sheffield of Roscommon (1840–1925).

29. Telegrams Collected by the Office of the Secretary of War, 1861–1882, RG 473, reel 1, National Archives.

30. Telegrams Collected by the Office of the Secretary of War, 1861–1882, RG 473, reel 1, National Archives.

31. Copy, Edwin M. Stanton Papers, Library of Congress.

32. On April 6, Butler replied: "Telegram received. Points will be submitted. I beg leave to assure the President that I have no desire to visit Washington, but wish he should visit Fortress Monroe." *Private and Official Correspondence of Benjamin F. Butler During the Period of the Civil War* (5 vols.; Norwood, Mass.: Plimpton, 1917), 4:29. The next day, Lincoln told him that he and the first lady planned to visit Fort Monroe the following week. Ibid.

33. Halpine Papers, Henry E. Huntington Library, San Marino, California.

34. On 23 February 1864, the *New York Herald* denounced Hay:

It is stated that a curious development of Executive intermeddling with military movements has been developed by inquiries about the recent Florida expedition. It is said that upon hearing of it General Halleck was quite taken by surprise, and wrote to General Gillmore to know what he was doing at Jacksonville, a place that had been two or three times in our possession and was not considered worth holding, and asking how he came to go there, not only without orders but without the knowledge and contrary to the positive instructions of the Secretary of War and General Halleck. In reply General Gillmore is said to have enclosed a letter of instructions from the President, transmitted to him by Mr. Hay, late private secretary of Mr. Lincoln, directing the movement to be made. Since this statement has been in circulation it is rumored that the expedition was intended simply for the occupation of Florida for the purpose of securing the election of three Lincoln delegates to the National Nominating Convention, and that of John Hay to Congress. The cost of the operation to the government is estimated at about one million of dollars.

This touched off a press controversy about the Olustee disaster. In late February, one journalist reported that "the very highest authority" claimed "that the President never issued any order or made any suggestion to Gen. Gillmore relative to military operations in Florida," "that the contrary statement . . . is untrue," and "that the expedition was made by Gen. Gillmore on his own responsibility." Washington correspondence, 28 February 1864, *Chicago Tribune*, 29 February 1864, p. 1, c. 5. Press criticism continued into March. On the first of that month, the *New York Herald* condemned "the President and his private secretary, who are the recognized originators and managers of this whole movement" and endorsed "the popular conviction that the President and his secretary are the only ones to blame in the business." Lyman Stickney observed that "Maj Hay was greatly excited at the notice taken of his Florida mission by the *Herald*." Stickney to Chase, 2 March 1864, Chase Papers, Library of Congress.

35. Lincoln Papers, Library of Congress. Lorenzo Thomas (1804–1875), adjutant general of the army, was in charge of recruiting black troops in the Mississippi Valley.

36. Thomas complained that Alpheus Lewis had proposed an unwise plan for taxing crops grown on plantations worked by freed slaves. The Kentuckians who commended Lewis to Lincoln's attention were Green Clay Smith and Brutus J. Clay. See Basler et al., eds., *Collected Works of Lincoln*, 6: 145–46, 212, 217–18.

37. Lincoln Papers, Library of Congress. Amos Myers (1824–1893) represented a Pennsylvania district in the U.S. House (1863–1865).

38. Myers had asked Lincoln to name Joseph C. Hays of Meadville, Pennsylvania, to be an assistant quartermaster. Myers to Lincoln, Washington, 18 April 1864, Lincoln Papers, Library of Congress.

39. Draft, Hay Papers, Brown University.

40. Hay Papers, Brown University. Manning Leonard was a cousin of Hay. Hay enclosed the following note, from Washington, 30 April 1864: "I take pleasure in introducing to the acquaintance and confidence of any diplomatic or consular representatives of the United States whom he may meet, my friend Manning Leonard Esq. of Massachusetts, a gentleman of high character and earnest loyalty, who will spend some time in Europe for the benefit of his health. I take especial pleasure in presenting Mr. Leonard to any friends of mine whom he may meet in his journey."

41. Telegrams Collected by the Office of the Secretary of War, 1861–1882, RG 473, reel 1, National Archives.

42. Copy in the hand of Henry Adams, Hay Papers, Illinois State Historical Library, Springfield.

43. Charles Hay wed Mary Ridgely in May 1865.

44. The letter, written in an unidentified hand, is reproduced in Bonnie B. Collier, "A New Lincoln Letter," *Yale University Library Gazette*, 48 (January 1974): 192. A newspaper clipping of this item is pasted into Hay's scrapbook, vol. 54, Hay Papers Library of Congress. It appeared in the *New York Times*, 29 May 1864. Colonel Francis B. Loomis of New London, Connecticut, had made a fortune in the textile busi-

ness. His letter, from New London, 29 April 1864, is in the Lincoln Papers, Library of Congress.

45. Fort Trumbull is in New London, Connecticut.

46. Hay Papers, Brown University. The document was addressed to Chase in Boston. On 28 December 1864, Lincoln wrote to John G. Foster: "Mr. Charles D. Chase, visits your Department on business. He is a gentleman with whom I am personally acquainted and whom I can commend to your courteous consideration." Basler et al., eds., *Collected Works of Lincoln*, 8:186.

47. Miscellaneous Hay Papers, Illinois State Historical Library, Springfield. Richard C. McCormick (1832–1901) of New York was secretary of the Arizona Territory (1863–1866).

48. John N. Goodwin of Maine was chief justice and later governor of the Arizona Territory.

49. In May 1864, Grant's army fought Lee's at Spotsylvania Court House, Virginia; the Union casualties amounted to 17,500 out of 110,000. Earlier that month, Grant's casualties at the battle of the Wilderness were 15,500.

50. The Republican national convention was to be held in Baltimore in early June.

51. Draft, Hay Papers, Brown University.

52. Hay Papers, Brown University, inserted in a copy of [Henry S. Burrage], *Brown University in the Civil War: A Memorial* (Providence: Providence Press, 1885).

53. Hay Papers, Brown University.

54. Nicolay wrote Hay from Baltimore on June 5, saying:

Arrived here safely—find quite a number of delegates already in, but have not yet talked much with them.

One of the first men I met was B. C. Cook, who stands at the head of our Illinois delegation, and had quite a long and confidential chat with him. He told me he had thought of going to Washington to-morrow, but seeing me he concluded he could sufficiently post himself.

He premised by telling me that the milk-and-water Lincoln resolution which was first reported to the Illinois State Convention, was cooked up by a few plotters, to the utter surprise and astonishment of nine-tenths of the Convention, and by only a part of the Committee, and was with the others reported to the Convention when there was but a small attendance, it being late at night, but that the Convention very handsomely repudiated them, referred them to a new Committee, which introduced and passed others of the right stripe. Cook does not seem to know thoroughly who were at the bottom of the matter. He thinks Turner was the chief manager. [*Joseph*] Medill is understood to have declared himself opposed to the resolution in Committee but seems to have contented himself with the mere expression of his dissent, after which he went away without further active opposition. Strangely enough one or two men have told me that W[*illia*]m A. Grimshaw, either of his own volition or under the influence of others, was in the scheme. Jack[*son Grimshaw*] on the contrary, Cook told me, was open and hearty for Lincoln.

Cook says there will be three or four disaffected members in the delegation from Illinois, but that nevertheless the delegation will vote and act as a unit, under the instructions of the Convention and also the will of the large majority of the delegation. He says the delegation will in good faith do everything they can for Lincoln that is in arranging the Vice P[*resident*], the Committees, Platform &c. taking his own nomination of course as beyond question.

What transpired at home, and what he has heard from several sources, have made Cook suspicious that [*Leonard*] Swett may be untrue to Lincoln. One of the straws which lead him to this belief is that Swett has telegraphed here urging the Illinois delegation to go for Holt for Vice President.

I told Cook that I thought Lincoln would not wish even to indicate a preference for V.P. as the rival candidates were all friendly to him.

There will be some little trouble in arranging the matter of the contested seats from Missouri. The Radicals seem to have the technical right to be admitted. They threaten to withdraw from the Convention if the Conservatives are also admitted; but promise to abide by the action of the Convention if they (the Radicals) obtain the seats. Cook says they intimated to him that they would even promise to vote for Lincoln in the Convention, for the promise of an admission to seats.

Whitelaw Reid is here and told me this evening that the Radicals conceded Lincoln's re-nomination, but their present game was to make a very radical platform.

Cook wants to know confidentially whether Swett is all right — whether in urging Holt for V.P. he reflects the President's wishes — whether the President has any preference, either personally or on the score of policy — or whether he wishes not even to interfere by a confidential indication. Also whether he thinks it would be good policy to give the Radical delegates from Missouri the seats, on their promising to vote for him.

Please get the information for me, if possible. Write and send your letter by express so that it will reach me by the earliest practicable hour on tomorrow (morning).

Hay Papers, Brown University. Burton C. Cook (1819–1894), who was to represent an Illinois district in the U.S. House of Representatives (1865–1871), nominated Lincoln at the 1864 Republican national convention in Baltimore. He was chairman of the Illinois Republican State Central Committee.

55. Leonard Swett (1825–1889) of Illinois, an old friend and political ally of Lincoln, was a delegate to the Baltimore convention.

56. Telegram, Hay Papers, Brown University.

57. Hay Papers, Brown University.

58. Hay Papers, Brown University.

59. Hay Papers, Library of Congress.

60. Swiss-born Gustave E. Matile (1841–1908) was an assistant to Hay, though officially listed as a clerk in the Interior Department. He had studied law with Abram

Wakeman, whom Lincoln named postmaster of New York. In the 1864 Washington city directory, he is listed as a White House clerk. He received a second-class clerkship on 1 September 1863, which he resigned on 31 March 1865. William A. Steiger to Marion E. Brown, Springfield, Illinois, 10 May 1955, Hay Papers, Brown University. On 26 March 1864, Matile wrote, "I may not remain in public office very long, for I find that my experience in law matters is getting rusty." Matile to S. N. Holmes, Washington, 26 March 1864, photocopy, Illinois State Historical Library, Springfield. See Homer Croy, "Discovered—An Authentic Lincoln Fingerprint," *Journal of the Illinois State Historical Society,* 49 (1956): 263–70.

61. Unlike Lincoln, General Rosecrans believed that the Knights of the Golden Circle posed a serious threat to the war effort in the West.

62. In May 1863, Clement L. Vallandigham was arrested by General Burnside for uttering sedition; Burnside's act embarrassed the president, who banished Vallandigham to the Confederacy. He returned to Ohio in mid-June 1864.

63. Democrat William Ralls Morrison (1824–1909) represented an Illinois district in the U.S. House (1863–1865, 1873–1887). Fernando Wood (1812–1881) was mayor of New York (1855–1858, 1861–1862) and member of the U.S. House (1863–1865, 1867–1881).

64. The Lorings were perhaps the family of Dr. Francis Bott Loring of Washington.

65. Mrs. C. Young Kretchmar was a teacher of vocal music.

66. Photocopy, Letitia Howe Collection, Miscellaneous Manuscripts, Library of Congress.

67. Curtis (1824–1892), editor of *Harper's Weekly,* was a member of the committee appointed to notify Lincoln of his renomination for president at the Baltimore convention. The letter referred to, by Curtis informing Lincoln of his nomination, dated June 14, is in Basler et al., eds., *Collected Works of Lincoln,* 7:411–12n.

68. Telegrams Collected by the Office of the Secretary of War, 1861–1882, RG 473, reel 1, National Archives.

69. Draft, Lincoln Papers, Library of Congress.

70. Kappes, who had deserted the Army of the Potomac after the battle of Antietam, wished to rejoin. Kappes to Lincoln, Philadelphia, 21 June 1864, Lincoln Papers, Library of Congress.

71. Draft of a telegram, Hay Papers, Brown University.

72. The letter referred to was Lincoln to William Dennison et al., Springfield, Washington, 27 June 1864, Basler et al., eds., *Collected Works of Lincoln,* 7:411.

73. Draft, John G. Nicolay Papers, Library of Congress.

74. Hay Papers, Brown University. General Stephen A. Hurlbut (1815–1882), a friend of Lincoln from Illinois, commanded the Department of the Gulf (1864–1865).

75. Draft of a telegram, Hay Papers, Brown University.

76. Greeley had written to Lincoln on July 7. That document and Lincoln's response are in Basler et al., eds., *Collected Works of Lincoln,* 7:435–36.

77. Draft of a telegram, sent to 302 Second Avenue, New York, Hay Papers, Brown University.

78. Draft of a telegram, Hay Papers, Brown University.

79. Hay Papers, Library of Congress. In 1864, Edward Duffield Neill (1823–1893) of Minnesota joined the White House staff as Nicolay and Hay's principal assistant.

80. Telegram, Lincoln Papers, Library of Congress. Filed with this telegram is an undated note by Hay:

> The President of the United States directs that the four persons whose names follow, to wit:
> Hon. Clement C. Clay
> "   Jacob Thompson
> Prof. James B. Holcombe
> "   George N. Sanders
> shall have safe conduct to the City of Washington in company with the Hon. Horace Greeley, and shall be exempt from arrest or annoyance of any kind from any officer of the United States during their journey to the said City of Washington.

81. Lincoln to Greeley, Washington, 15 July 1864 (two letters), Basler et al., eds., *Collected Works of Lincoln*, 7:440–42.

82. See Greeley to Lincoln, New York, 13 July 1864, Basler et al., eds., *Collected Works of Lincoln*, 7:441n.

83. Lincoln answered on July 16, suggesting that Hay write the safe conduct. Basler et al., eds., *Collected Works of Lincoln*, 7:443.

84. Telegram, Lincoln Papers, Library of Congress.

85. A newspaper clipping of this item is pasted into Hay's scrapbook of his own writings, vol. 54, Hay Papers, Library of Congress. Another copy of this letter, dated 18 July, is pasted into the same scrapbook. Jewett, a descendant of an old Maine family, had settled in Colorado, where he was involved in gold mining interests. He had begun his career as a peacemaker as early as 1861, when he tried to win appointment as a delegate to the Peace Convention from Colorado. With former president Millard Fillmore, he then attempted to arrange a compromise peace between North and South. Failing in that, he sought to enlist the aid of European powers to mediate the dispute between the sections. One historian called him an "imbecile optimist." Edward Chase Kirkland, *The Peacemakers of 1864* (New York: Macmillan, 1927), 70.

86. Draft, Hay Papers, Brown University. Hay flirted with Alice Skinner of Buffalo, New York. Alice Skinner to Hay, Buffalo, 4 November and 1 December 1864, Lincoln Papers, Library of Congress.

87. Draft, Lincoln Papers, Library of Congress. Samuel Cony (1811–1870) served as governor of Maine (1864–1867).

88. Cony had invited the president to accompany the House Committee on the Defenses of the North Eastern Frontier when they inspected fortifications in Maine

in mid-August. Cony to Lincoln, Augusta, 22 July 1864, Lincoln Papers, Library of Congress.

89. Montague, ed., *A College Friendship*, 62.

90. Hay Papers, Brown University.

91. William H. Marston's address was 35 Wall Street, New York. His wife was "an early friend and old schoolmate of Mrs. Lincoln." The first lady visited her in the summer of 1862. *New York Herald*, 16 July 1862.

92. Telegrams Collected by the Office of the Secretary of War, 1861–1882, RG 473, reel 1, National Archives.

93. Schurz Papers, Library of Congress.

94. General Schurz, who had been sidelined because of his spotty record in the field, complained that his appeals for permission to visit Washington in search of a new command were ignored. "I wrote a private letter to Maj. Hay, requesting him to . . . let me know what my chances as to obtaining employment might be. To this letter, as well as to others previously addressed to Mr. Nicolay I never received a reply, a circumstance which could not but appear strange to me." Schurz to Lincoln, Bethlehem, Pennsylvania, 8 August 1864, Lincoln Papers, Library of Congress.

95. In the spring, Schurz had complained to Nicolay that General Hooker had abolished his command and General Sherman could find no place for him. He practically demanded a field command. Schurz to Nicolay, Nashville, 29 and 30 April 1864, Lincoln Papers, Library of Congress.

96. Hay Papers, Brown University. Captain Young, an assistant quartermaster in Colonel E. D. Baker's brigade (the Seventy-first Pennsylvania), had been court martialed early in the war on a technicality. In June 1864, he asked for an appointment to the staff of General W. F. Smith. Young to Lincoln, New York, 14 June 1864, Lincoln Papers, Library of Congress.

97. Montague, ed., *A College Friendship*, 63.

98. Telegram, Schurz Papers, Library of Congress.

99. Hay Papers, Brown University.

100. Hay was searching for a school for his sister.

101. "Peace snakes" refers to the Democratic National Convention in Chicago at the end of August.

102. Joseph Medill (1823–1899) was editor of the *Chicago Tribune*. His letter, dated Chicago, 10 August 1864, is in the Hay Papers, Brown University.

103. Lt. William Archer Dubois, the son of Jesse K. Dubois, was helped by Nicolay when the young man faced a court martial. W. Archer Dubois to Nicolay, Springfield, 4 January 1864, Nicolay Papers, Library of Congress. Jesse K. Dubois felt cheated by Lincoln, whom he later described as "a singular man" whom he really "never knew." In 1865, he complained that Lincoln

has for 30 years past just used me as a plaything to accomplish his own ends — but the moment he was elevated to his proud position he seemed all at once to have entirely changed his whole nature and became altogether a new being—knows no one and the road to favor is always open to his enemies whilst the door is systematically sealed to his old friends. I was not as much disappointed as my friends were at my late defeat as I never did believe Lincoln would appoint me though he time and again urged I had more talent than any of them. But I was his old friend and I could afford to be disappointed.

Dubois to Henry C. Whitney, Springfield, 6 April 1865, Douglas L. Wilson and Rodney O. Davis, eds., *Herndon's Informants: Letters, Interviews, and Statements about Abraham Lincoln* (Urbana: University of Illinois Press, 1998), 620. On 8 November 1864, Republican Richard J. Oglesby (1824–1899) defeated his Democratic opponent for the governorship of Illinois by the vote of 190,376 to 158,711.

104. Hay Papers, Brown University.

105. James C. Derby was a proprietor of the New York firm of Derby and Miller, which published Henry J. Raymond's *History of President Lincoln's Administration, including His Speeches, Addresses, Letters, Messages and Proclamations, with a Preliminary Sketch of His Life.* See the circular announcing this and other books enclosed in Derby & Miller to Lincoln, New York, 21 July 1864, Lincoln Papers, Library of Congress.

106. Henry J. Raymond (1820–1869) had established the *New York Times* in 1851 and was its editor. He sat in Congress from 1865 to 1867. In 1864, he chaired the National Union Executive Committee and took charge of campaign fund-raising. In August he had complained, "We are not in funds at present," but contributions did increase after the fall of Atlanta on September 2. On August 25 Raymond and the Executive Committee called on Lincoln, urging him to settle for a compromise peace and to back down on the commitment to abolish slavery. On August 18 a group of twenty-five disenchanted Republicans met at the home of New York mayor George Opdyke to plan a convention that would dump Lincoln and choose an alternative presidential candidate.

107. In May, some Radical Republicans, dissatisfied with Lincoln, nominated John C. Frémont for the presidency. His candidacy was disproportionately popular among German American Republicans.

108. John Todd Stuart (1807–1885), Lincoln's first law partner (1837–1841), represented the Springfield district of Illinois in the U.S. House (1863–1865). He vainly implored Millard Fillmore, who had been president from 1850 to 1853, to seek that office once again.

109. William O. Stoddard had held the post of land patent secretary but had resigned for reasons of health. He was, in effect, a clerk for Nicolay and Hay.

110. Philbrick had a drinking problem. In 1873, Hay reported a conversation with a man "who told me that he had passed an evening with Charlie Philbrick in Pittsfield. He gives a discouraging account of him. Horrible power of drink." Because he drank heavily, Philbrick led a "checkered life, with more shadows than sunshine,—shadows that enveloped all who held him dear." John Hay recruited

Philbrick, who left Springfield in early September and was appointed to the land patent secretaryship on September 14. Wayne C. Temple, "Charles Henry Philbrick: Private Secretary to President Lincoln," *Lincoln Herald*, 99 (1997): 6–11. Presumably, the "subject" was the possibility of Philbrick taking a job in the White House.

111. Hay Papers, Brown University.

112. Philbrick was in Chicago on September 10 and was appointed to the land patent secretaryship four days later. Philbrick to Ozias M. Hatch, Chicago, 10 September 1864, Hatch Papers, Illinois State Historical Library, Springfield; Temple, "Philbrick," 9.

113. In 1839, many Mormons settled in Nauvoo, Illinois, on the Mississippi River. Five years later, they fled, soon after their leader, Joseph Smith, was murdered in nearby Carthage.

114. At the end of August, the Democrats nominated George B. McClellan for president.

115. Draft, Hay Papers, Brown University.

116. Hay Papers, Brown University.

117. General Philip H. Sheridan (1831–1888) defeated Confederate forces under Jubal Early on September 19 at Winchester and three days later at Fisher's Hill.

118. Hay Papers, Brown University.

119. Hay Papers, Brown University.

120. "I found Mr Weed absent when I arrived here, and although he was expected this morning, he has not yet returned. A friend of his telegraphed him today that I was here, and wished to see him, and he thinks he will be here tomorrow." Nicolay to Lincoln, New York, 22 September 1864, Lincoln Papers, Library of Congress.

121. Philbrick obtained lodging at a home at 284 G Street, about three blocks from the White House. Temple, "Philbrick," 11. On September 28, the stenographic reporter R. R. Hitt called at the White House and saw Philbrick. After meeting with the president, Hitt chatted with Nicolay and Hay: "Going outside I met Leonard Sweet [*Swett*] and went in and filed the papers with the secretaries who were with Charlie Philbrick. I had seen them the day before, when they treated me with apparent good feeling as usual and Charlie this day appeared very sociable." R. R. Hitt journal, Hitt Papers, Library of Congress, 364–69 (Washington, 28 September 1864).

122. George F. Schafer was a tailor on Pennsylvania Avenue.

123. Hay Papers, Brown University, misfiled as a Nicolay letter. German-born Francis Lieber (1800–1872) of Columbia University was a leading political scientist who in February 1864 became head of the New York Loyal Publication Society. His campaign pamphlet, *Lincoln or McClellan*, was widely distributed in 1864.

124. Earlier in September, Lieber had favored Lincoln's withdrawal from the presidential race: "We must have a new man against a new man, and we cannot have him without Mr. Lincoln's withdrawal. Oh, that an angel could descend and show him what a beautiful stamp on his name in history such a withdrawal would be! He could say in his letter that it is a universal law that names wear out in revolutions and civil

wars, and that he withdraws, &c. If he does not speedily withdraw we are beaten. . . . Sometimes I feel as if I should write to the President; but then, how would he listen to a private individual in a matter of such moment?" Lieber to Henry W. Halleck, New York, 1 September 1864, Thomas Sergeant Perry, ed., *Life and Letters of Francis Lieber* (Boston: Houghton Mifflin, 1882), 146.

125. Draft, Lincoln Papers, Library of Congress. Holyoake was the editor of a London newspaper, the *English Leader.*

126. Holyoake had sent Lincoln a clipping from the *English Leader* of Prof. F. W. Newman's letter to William Lloyd Garrison, dated 1 September 1864, in which he disputed Garrison's interpretation of his earlier remarks on Lincoln.

127. Hay Papers, Brown University.

128. William N. Grover of St. Louis was U.S. district attorney for the eastern district of Missouri.

129. Lt. John R. Meigs was killed by Confederate guerrillas on 3 October 1864. Believing he had been murdered after surrendering, General Philip Sheridan ordered all houses within five miles of the site where he had been killed to be burned.

130. Photocopy, "Lincoln's Secretaries" file, Lincoln Museum, Fort Wayne, Indiana. This document is in the handwriting of Edward D. Neill. Mrs. Westerman lived in Pekin, Illinois.

131. Hay Papers, Brown University.

132. U.S. Representative William D. ("Pig Iron") Kelley (1814–1890), a leading Radical from Philadelphia, served in Congress from 1861 to 1890.

133. Telegrams Collected by the Office of the Secretary of War, 1861–1882, RG 473, reel 1, National Archives.

134. Telegrams Collected by the Office of the Secretary of War, 1861–1882, RG 473, reel 1, National Archives.

135. Telegrams Collected by the Office of the Secretary of War, 1861–1882, RG 473, reel 1, National Archives.

136. Hay Papers, Brown University.

137. On October 13, voters in Indiana reelected Republican governor Oliver P. Morton by a 20,000 majority. The Republicans gained control of the legislature and won eight of the state's eleven seats in the U.S. House.

138. In Pennsylvania, the Republican state ticket, headed by Governor Andrew G. Curtin, won by a 13,000 vote margin. Republicans in the Keystone State captured sixteen of twenty-four U.S. House seats. The soldier vote was decisive.

139. John W. Forney (1817–1881) was editor of the *Washington Chronicle* and *Philadelphia Press.*

140. Roger Brooke Taney (1777–1864) was chief justice of the U.S. Supreme Court.

141. The Radical Republican Henry Winter Davis (1817–1865) represented a Maryland district in the U.S. House (1855–1861, 1863–1865).

142. John Lee Chapman was the incumbent mayor of Baltimore; he received 11,237 votes while his Radical opponent, Archibald Stirling Jr. received 3,290.

143. George E. Jones Papers, New York Public Library.

144. James H. Lane (1814–1866) represented Kansas in the U.S. Senate.

145. James Harlan (1820–1899) represented Iowa in the U.S. Senate (1857–1865).

146. Photocopy, Letitia Howe Collection, Miscellaneous Manuscripts, Library of Congress.

147. Draft of a telegram, Hay Papers, Brown University. Gustav P. Koerner (1809–1896), a German-born Republican leader from Belleville, had served as lieutenant governor of Illinois (1852–1856).

148. Lincoln Papers, Library of Congress. Isaacs was a journalist who worked for the *New York Jewish Messenger* and served as secretary of the New York Jewish Board of Delegates.

149. Isaacs, believing reports that the Jewish delegation which had visited Lincoln on October 23 had received money in return for a promise to deliver the Jewish vote, protested, "There is no 'Jewish vote' — if there were, it could not be bought." Isaacs to Lincoln, New York, 26 October 1864, Lincoln Papers, Library of Congress.

150. Hay Papers, Brown University. Allen was president of the Quincy, Illinois, Western Illinois Sanitary Fair. His letter is in the Lincoln Papers, Library of Congress.

151. Hay Papers, Brown University.

152. Sergeant H. Warren Stimson of the 142nd Pennsylvania Volunteers was nineteen years old and wished an appointment at West Point. He had dropped out of Columbia College in his sophomore year to join the army, in which he had been serving for over two years. Stimson to Hay, near Petersburg, 25 October 1864, Lincoln Papers, Library of Congress.

153. Hay Papers, Brown University. The artist Francis Bicknell Carpenter (1830–1900) painted *First Reading of the Emancipation Proclamation of President Lincoln*.

154. On October 27, Carpenter had appealed to Hay on behalf of Franklin F. Pratt, who wished to be discharged from the navy. Lincoln ordered his release on November 19, provided that Pratt refund his bounty money.

155. Hay Papers, Brown University.

156. Hay Papers, Brown University.

157. See appendix 1, "The Authorship of the Bixby Letter," infra.

158. A copy of this letter, clipped from a newspaper, is pasted into Hay's scrapbook of his own writings, Hay Papers, vol. 54, Library of Congress. The Lincoln Papers in the Library of Congress, contain a copy in the hand of Edward D. Neill. A copy in Hay's hand with Lincoln's signature allegedly was obtained by Ralph Newman. Newman to David C. Mearns, Chicago, 2 August 1965, Mearns Papers, Library of Congress.

159. Draft of a telegram, Hay Papers, Brown University. Thomas was the mayor of St. Louis.

160. In March 1864, Alfred Pleasonton (1824–1897) had been removed from the command of the cavalry of the Army of the Potomac and sent to Missouri. On November 16, Thomas, on behalf of "all classes of loyal men," had sent a telegram urging Lincoln to nominate Pleasonton for a brigadier generalship in the regular army.

161. Draft, Hay Papers, Brown University.

162. Edmond About (1828–1885) was a French journalist, novelist, and playwright.

163. Lieutenant Thomas Poynton Ives (1834–1865), USN, graduated from Brown University in 1854. He later married the daughter of John Lothrop Motley, the historian and diplomat. Hay to his father, Paris, 15 September 1865, letterpress copy, Hay Papers, Brown University.

164. Draft, Lincoln Papers, Library of Congress.

165. Smith sent the beef as a token of his esteem for Lincoln, who, he hoped, would be able to eat it for Thanksgiving. Smith to Lincoln, Troy, N.Y., 21 November 1864, Lincoln Papers, Library of Congress.

166. Draft, Hay Papers, Brown University. President of the Lincoln and Johnson Central Campaign Club in New York City, Spencer had passed an evening the previous October visiting with Lincoln at the Soldiers Home in Washington, in the company of Rufus Andrews, surveyor of the customs house in New York. Spencer to Lincoln, New York, 21 March 1864, Lincoln Papers, Library of Congress. Spencer had requested a toast from the president to be given at the New York banquet. Spencer to Lincoln, New York, 23 November 1864, telegram, Lincoln Papers, Library of Congress.

167. Butler Papers, Library of Congress.

168. Jeremiah Clemens (1815–1865) of Alabama was a lawyer and novelist who had served in the U.S. Senate (1849–1853). In his letter to Butler, he urged that Lincoln offer generous peace terms to the Confederates. Clemens to B. F. Butler, 16 November 1864, copy, Lincoln Papers, Library of Congress.

169. Hay Papers, Brown University.

170. Simeon Draper (d. 1866), a prominent New York Republican leader, became collector of the port of New York in September 1864. See appendix 2, infra.

171. Hay Papers, Brown University.

172. Congressman Shelby M. Cullom (1829–1914) of Springfield had been the speaker of the Illinois house of representatives.

173. Photocopy, Letitia Howe Collection, Miscellaneous Manuscripts, Library of Congress.

174. Undated draft of a telegram, Hay Papers, Brown University. Worthen lived in Warsaw, Illinois.

175. "Franklin in France," a talk prepared for delivery in December 1904, in *Addresses of John Hay* (New York: Century, 1906), 40.

176. Hay Papers, Brown University.

177. McPherson Papers, Library of Congress.

178. Lincoln's letter to Eliza P. Gurney is in Basler et al., eds., *Collected Works of Lincoln*, 7:535. Mrs. Gurney met with the president in late September 1862.

179. [Adams, ed.], *Hay Letters*, 1:253–54.

180. John Bigelow (1817–1911) became U.S. Minister to France in April 1865.

181. Hay Papers, Brown University.

182. On the verso, Philbrick wrote the following note to Edward D. Neill: "As per

within I 'report' to you 'by letter' this morning. I really need and desire to be excused from the office until Monday morning. By that time I will have arranged some matters important to me; as important as the business which has kept others in the office away for several days at a time. This is honestly important to me and I therefore ask it. Meanwhile if I am imperatively needed I can be found at 136 'Willards,' 34 'National' Lewis Johnson's Bank (upstairs) or 222 F street in Davis & Swinton's room. On Monday I will be ready to work with a will and fix up things as you may direct."

183. Butler Papers, Library of Congress.

184. Hay Papers, Brown University.

185. Raymond Papers, New York Public Library.

186. For the letter, see note 77 supra. Hay endorsed the document thus: "This safe conduct was written and handed to Mr. Greeley on the 16th July 1864 in pursuance of the President's instructions by telegram of that date." Greeley returned it to Hay on April 10. Greeley to Hay, New York, 10 April 1865, Hay Papers, Brown University.

187. Lincoln to "whom it may concern," Washington, 16 July 1864, Basler et al., eds., *Collected Works of Lincoln*, 7:451. In this brief note, Lincoln announced that he was willing to negotiate peace if the South agreed to return to the Union and accept the abolition of slavery.

188. Andrew Johnson Papers, Library of Congress.

189. A black man born in Petersburg, Virginia, Solomon James Johnson (1842–1885) not only shaved Lincoln but, at his recommendation, was appointed in 1864 a laborer in the Treasury Department.

190. Stanton Papers, Library of Congress.

191. Colonel William G. Moore was President Johnson's private secretary.

4. Hay's Reminiscences of the Civil War

1. Herndon-Weik Papers, Library of Congress.

2. On 29 September 1863, Hay recorded in his diary: "Today came to the Executive Mansion an assembly of cold-water men & cold water women to make a temperance speech at the Tycoon . . . in which they called Intemperance the cause of our defeats. He could not see it, as the rebels drink more & worse whiskey than we do." Burlingame and Ettlinger, eds., *Hay Diary*, 89. Cf. Basler et al., eds., *Collected Works of Lincoln*, 6:487.

3. George Bancroft, *Memorial Address on the Life and Character of Abraham Lincoln, Delivered, at the Request of Both Houses of the Congress of America, Before Them, in the House of Representatives at Washington, on the 12th of February, 1866* (Washington: Government Printing Office, 1866). In September 1861, Bancroft (1800–1891), a leading historian, diplomat, and Democratic Party intellectual, deplored Lincoln's "monstrous political imbecility" and "criminal dilitoriness." He told his wife, "We suffer for want of an organizing mind at the head of government." Lillian Handlin, *George Bancroft: The Intellectual as Democrat* (New York: Harper & Row, 1984), 274;

M. A. De Wolfe Howe, *Life and Letters of George Bancroft* (2 vols.; New York: Charles Scribner's Sons, 1908), 2:132.

4. *New York Tribune*, 17 July 1871, p. 4, c. 6.

5. Lecture delivered in Buffalo, New York, and other cities in 1871 and 1872, galley copy, with many handwritten emendations by Hay, Hay Papers, Brown University. Evidently it was never published. See George Monteiro, "John Hay's Lyceum Lectures," *Western Illinois Regional Studies*, 9 (1986): 48–58.

6. "The Dividing Line Between Federal and Local Authority: Popular Sovereignty in the Territories," *Harper's Monthly*, 19 (September 1859), reprinted in Harry V. Jaffa and Robert W. Johannsen, eds., *In the Name of the People: Speeches and Writings of Lincoln and Douglas in the Ohio Campaign of 1859* (Columbus: Ohio Historical Society, 1959), 58–125.

7. The Virginia state legislature summoned delegates from around the country for a "peace conference," which assembled on 4 February 1861 in Washington. Its recommendations to avert civil war—primarily by extending to California the 1820 Missouri Compromise line of thirty-six degrees, thirty minutes, separating slave from free territory—were ignored by Congress.

8. Basler et al., eds., *Collected Works of Lincoln*, 4:190–91.

9. New York politician and attorney William Henry Seward (1801–1872) had been chosen by Lincoln to become secretary of state, a post he held from 1861 to 1869. Winfield Scott (1786–1866) was General in Chief of the U.S. Army (1841–1861). Fearing that reports of assassination plots might be accurate, both men urged Lincoln not to proceed through Baltimore, as originally planned, on his train journey to Washington. The president-elect took their advice and was ridiculed by some for his timidity.

10. Louis T. Wigfall (1816–1874) represented Texas in the U.S. Senate (1860–1861).

11. Thomas Hart Benton (1782–1858) was a U.S. senator from Missouri (1821–1850).

12. "Harry Wise" was probably Hay's recently deceased friend, Henry Augustus Wise. See note 35 infra.

13. James Buchanan (1791–1868) of Pennsylvania was president of the United States (1857–1861).

14. This sentence appears in the penultimate paragraph of Lincoln's first inaugural address.

15. Massachusetts Governor John A. Andrew (1818–1867) was a staunch Republican. Massachusetts politician Benjamin F. Butler (1818–1893) was a Democrat who had supported Jefferson Davis for the presidency in 1860.

16. Millard Fillmore (1800–1874), a conservative Whig, had been president of the United States (1850–1853). Wendell Phillips (1811–1884) of Massachusetts was a leading abolitionist.

17. The First Rhode Island Regiment. Cf. Hay's diary entry for 26 April 1861: "I called on Sprague the Governor of R. I. . . . A small, insignificant youth, who bought his place. . . . He is very proud of his Company of its wealth and social standing." Burlingame and Ettlinger, eds., *Hay Diary*, 12.

18. Colonel Edward D. Baker (1811–1861), a close friend of Lincoln, was killed at the battle of Ball's Bluff on 21 October 1861. Colonel Elmer E. Ellsworth (1837–1861), another close friend of Lincoln, was killed in Alexandria, Virginia, on 24 May 1861. See Hay's obituaries of the two infra.

19. David C. Broderick (1820–1859), a U.S. senator from California (1857–1859), was killed in a duel.

20. Senator John C. Breckinridge (1821–1875) of Kentucky had been vice-president of the United States (1857–1861).

21. Hay described this unit, known as "Ellsworth's Avengers," thus:

> It is the People's Ellsworth Regiment of New York, selected from every town in the State with the exception of the cities of New York and Troy. Magnificent in physique and morale, well dressed, well equipped, well armed, officered by the perfectly trained Chicago boys and commanded by Ellsworth's friend and companion, Col. Stryker, lacking the effeminacy of the Seventh and the brutality of the Fire Boys, it unites the refinement of the one with the muscle of the other, and goes into the field animated by the loftiest motives of patriotism and the highest incentives to daring.

Washington correspondence, 26 October 1861, *Missouri Republican* (St. Louis), 31 October 1861, in Burlingame, ed., *Lincoln's Journalist*, 127.

22. One day, after "closing a protracted local squabble with a brilliant compromise," Lincoln told Hay that "all there is of honest statesmanship consists in combining individual meanness for the public good." *Springfield Republican*, n.d., copied in an unidentified clipping, ca. early 1870s, Hay scrapbook, Hay Papers, Brown University. Cf. Nicolay and Hay, *Abraham Lincoln*, 10:355.

23. "Artemus Ward" was the pen name of the humorist Charles Farrar Browne (1834–1867).

24. See Roy P. Basler, *President Lincoln Helps His Old Friends* (Springfield: Abraham Lincoln Association, 1977).

25. "Meditation on the Divine Will," ca. early September 1862, Basler et al., eds., *Collected Works of Lincoln*, 5:403–4.

26. "Reply to Emancipation Memorial Presented by Chicago Christians of All Denominations," 13 September 1862, and "Preliminary Emancipation Proclamation," 22 September 1862, Basler et al., eds., *Collected Works of Lincoln*, 5:419–25, 433–36.

27. Confederate troops under General Jubal A. Early (1816–1894) menaced Washington in July 1864.

28. In the fall of 1863, Union General Ambrose E. Burnside (1824–1881) led forces that were threatened by Confederates under General James Longstreet (1821–1904). Hay's diary for 24 November 1863 records a different version of Lincoln's remarks: "Like Sally Carter when she heard one of her children squall would say 'There goes one of my young uns, not dead yet, bless the Lord.'" Burlingame and Ettlinger, eds., *Hay Diary*, 118. During the war, a newspaper reported yet another version: "It reminds me of Mistress Sallie Ward, a neighbor of mine, who had a very large fam-

ily. Occasionally some of her numerous progeny would be heard crying in some out-of-the-way place, upon which Mrs. Sallie would exclaim, 'There's one of my children that isn't dead yet.'" Quoted in *Old Abe's Jokes* (1864), in Paul M. Zall, ed., *Abe Lincoln Laughing* (Berkeley: University of California Press, 1982), 30.

29. A slightly different version of these remarks is given in Nicolay and Hay's biography of Lincoln: "An Austrian deputy said to the writer, 'Among my people his memory has already assumed superhuman proportions; he has become a myth, a type of ideal democracy." *Abraham Lincoln*, 10:346.

30. Cf. Hay's diary for 19 April 1863: "Good things by [*Captain Edward W.*] Hooper. Talk about Linkum! No man see Linkum. Linkum walk as Jes[us] walk! no man see L." Burlingame and Ettlinger, eds., *Hay Diary*, 47.

31. Friedrich August von Kaulbach (1850–1920) of Munich was a noted painter of historical subjects.

32. Manuscript in Hay's hand, Hay Papers, reel 22, Library of Congress. This essay was published, with slight variations, in *Century Magazine*, 41 (November 1890): 33–37.

33. Wilson to William H. Herndon, Natick, Massachusetts, 30 May 1867, Wilson and Davis, eds., *Herndon's Informants*, 561–62.

34. In the margin, Hay noted, "Gen. J. B. Fry, who was present." Hay refers to James B. Fry's contribution to Alexander Thorndike Rice, ed., *Reminiscences of Abraham Lincoln by Distinguished Men of His Time* (New York: North American Publishing Company, 1886), 393.

35. General James A. Garfield (1831–1881) of Ohio had been General William S. Rosecrans's chief of staff. In 1880, he was elected president. John Adolph Dahlgren (1809–1870) commanded the Washington Navy Yard and invented the Dahlgren gun, a rifled cannon. Gustavus Vasa Fox (1821–1883) was the assistant secretary of the navy. Lieutenant Henry Augustus Wise, USN (1819–1869), author of *Los Gringos* (1849) and *Tales from the Marines* (1855), became chief of the Bureau of Ordnance and Hydrography. He published under the pen name *Harry Gringo*. Hay, who called Wise "the best man in this wicked world," enjoyed what he called Wise's "fantastic fun." Hay to Charles G. Halpine, 24 October 1863, supra; Hay to Harriet Loring, Madrid, 30 June 1870, Hay Papers, Brown University. William Howard Russell considered Wise, with whom he occasionally dined, "really smart clever quick." Crawford, ed., *Russell's Civil War*, 114 (entry for 31 August 1861).

36. In the margin, Hay noted, "Ms. Letter from Col. Wm. H. Harris." William Hamilton Harris, who graduated from West Point in 1861 and served in the Ordnance Department, was the son of Ira Harris (1802–1875), U.S. senator from New York (1861–1869). Romeyn Beck Ayers (1825–1875) served in the Army of the Potomac.

37. In 1862, 1863, and 1864, the president and his family spent the summers in a stone cottage on this site, which was established for disabled troops. Located on a hilltop three miles outside the District of Columbia, it was much cooler than the White House.

38. Cf. Hay's diary for 19 August 1863:

This evening and yesterday evening an hour was spent by the President in shooting with Spencers new repeating rifle. A wonderful gun loading with absolutely contemptible simplicity and ease with seven balls & firing the whole readily & deliberately in less than half a minute. The President made some pretty good shots. Spencer the inventor a quiet little Yankee who sold himself in relentless slavery to his idea for six weary years before it was perfect did some splendid shooting. . . . An irrepressible patriot came up and talked about his son John who when lying on his belly on a hilltop at Gettysburg, feeling the shot fly over him like to [*have*] lost his breath — felt himself puffing up like a toad — thought he would bust. Another seeing the gun recoil slightly said it wouldnt do; too much powder: a good piece of audience [*ordnance*] should not rekyle: if it did at all, it should rekyle a little forrid.

Burlingame and Ettlinger, eds., *Hay Diary*, 75.

39. A renowned marksman, Hiram Berdan of New York (1823?–1893) formed two regiments of sharpshooters that served with the Army of the Potomac. C. A. Stevens, *Berdan's United States Sharpshooters in the Army of the Potomac, 1861–1865* (St. Paul, Minn.: Price-McGill, 1892), 9–11.

40. A temperance movement led by former alcoholics.

41. See Hay's obituary of Tad Lincoln, supra.

42. Basler et al., eds., *Collected Works of Lincoln*, 6:392–93, 558–59. James Henry Hackett (1800–1871) was a noted Shakespearian actor with whom Lincoln corresponded until finally Hackett asked for an appointment as U.S. consul to London. David Rankin Barbee, "Mr. Lincoln Goes to the Theater," 24–40, typescript, Barbee Papers, Georgetown University. David Homer Bates said that Lincoln "was very fond of Hackett personally and of the character of Falstaff, and frequently repeated some of the latter's quaint sallies. I recall in his recitation for my benefit he criticized some of Hackett's readings." Bates, *Lincoln in the Telegraph Office: Recollections of the United States Military Telegraph Corps During the Civil War* (New York: Century, 1907), 223.

43. Cf. Hay's diary for 23 August 1863: "Last night we went to the Observatory with Mrs Young. They were very kind and attentive. The Prest. took a look at the moon & Arcturus. I went with him to the Soldiers' Home & he read Shakespeare to me, the end of Henry VI and the beginning of Richard III till my heavy eye-lids caught his considerate notice & he sent me to bed." Burlingame and Ettlinger, eds., *Hay Diary*, 75–76.

44. Journalist T. C. Evans recalled how Lincoln recited this speech at Cincinnati in February 1861. Evans, "Personal Reminiscences of John Hay," *Chattanooga* (Tennessee) *Sunday Times*, 30 July 1905.

45. The English poet Thomas Hood (1799–1845) wrote humorous verse, full of word play, that appealed to Lincoln. On 30 April 1864, Hay noted in his diary:

A little after midnight . . . the President came into the office laughing, with a volume of Hood's works in his hand to show Nicolay & me the little Caricature "An unfortunate Bee-ing," seemingly utterly unconscious that he with his short shirt hanging about his long legs & setting out behind like the tail feathers of an enormous ostrich was infinitely funnier than anything in the book he was laughing at. What a man it is! Occupied all day with matters of vast moment, deeply anxious about the fate of the greatest army of the world, with his own fame & future hanging on the events of the passing hour, he yet has such a wealth of simple bonhommie & good fellow ship that he gets out of bed & perambulates the house in his shirt to find us that we may share with him the fun of one of poor Hoods queer little conceits.

Burlingame and Ettlinger, eds., *Hay Diary*, 194.

46. William Knox of Scotland (1789–1825) wrote "Mortality." Lincoln evidently became acquainted with this poem in his midthirties, not in his youth. Douglas L. Wilson, *Lincoln Before Washington: New Perspectives on the Illinois Years* (Urbana: University of Illinois Press, 1997), 123–48.

47. In 1862, Nathaniel Hawthorne, a close friend of ex-president Franklin Pierce, wrote an irreverent sketch of Lincoln. "Chiefly About War Matters," *Atlantic Monthly*, 10 (July 1862): 43–61.

48. Richard Bickerton Pemell Lyons (1817–1887) was the British minister to the United States during the Civil War.

49. Assistant Secretary of War Charles A. Dana (1819–1897) was a journalist whom Lincoln used as a troubleshooter. The quote comes from Dana's contribution in Rice, ed., *Reminiscences of Lincoln*, 369.

50. Frederick Douglass (1817?–1895) was the leading black abolitionist. The quote comes from his contribution ibid., 195.

51. Leonard Wells Volk (1818–1895) made a life mask of Lincoln on 31 March 1860 and a cast of his hands in May 1860. Clark Mills (1810–1883) made a life mask of Lincoln on 11 February 1865.

5. Biographical Sketches

1. "Ellsworth," *Atlantic Monthly*, 8 (July 1861): 119–25. Hay wrote two other articles about Ellsworth, the first appearing in the Washington *Chronicle*, 26 May 1861, and the other in *McClure's Magazine* in March 1896.

2. Arthur Forrester Devereux of Salem, Massachusetts, had moved to Chicago where he first worked with the Galena and Chicago Union Railroad before entering the patent-soliciting business. His father, George H. Devereux, was adjutant general of Massachusetts and captain of the Salem Light Infantry. Charles A. Ingraham, *Elmer E. Ellsworth and the Zouaves of '61* (Chicago: Chicago Historical Society, 1925), 87–90. Hay described him thus in a footnote: "Arthur F. Devereux, Esq., now in com-

mand of the Salem Zouave Corps, Eighth Massachusetts Regiment, distinguished for the gallant part borne by it in opening the route to Washington through Annapolis, and in the rescue of the frigate Constitution, 'Old Ironsides,' from the hands of the rebels."

3. William Walker (1824–1860) was a soldier of fortune who led informal militia units into Nicaragua and elsewhere in Central America on filibustering expeditions.

4. Icarius was a mythological figure in Attica who extended hospitality to Dionysus, who rewarded him with the gift of wine.

5. William J. Hardee (1815–1873) wrote the standard textbook, *Rifle and Light Infantry Tactics* (New Orleans: H. P. Lathrop, 1861).

6. Charles A. DeVilliers was "a surgeon in the French Army in Algiers, and an accomplished swordsman, having served with a French Zouave regiment in the Crimean War." Ingraham, *Ellsworth and the Zouaves of '61,* 7.

7. Pierre Terrail, seigneur de Bayard (1473?–1524), was a French soldier known as "the knight without fear and without reproach."

8. In Rockford, Ellsworth met and fell in love with Caroline Spafford.

9. James W. Jackson, proprietor of a hotel in Alexandria that flaunted the Confederate flag, killed Ellsworth and was in turn killed immediately thereafter by Francis E. Brownell, corporal of the guard in the Ellsworth Zouaves.

10. The standard biography of Ellsworth is Ruth Painter Randall, *Colonel Elmer Ellsworth* (Boston: Little, Brown, 1960).

11. "Colonel Baker," *Harper's Monthly,* 24 (December 1861): 103–10.

12. The Italian War of 1859 began on April 30, when Austrian General Gyulai led his forces across the Ticino River to attack the Sardinian army.

13. Karl Theodor Koerner (1791–1813) was a leading German patriot in the war against Napoleon. By the time of his death at the age of twenty-two, he had seen three of his plays produced at the Burgtheater in Vienna.

14. Baker's father was a schoolteacher.

15. Baker's mother was Lucy Dickinson. Her brother fought under the leadership of Vice Admiral Cuthbert Collingwood (1750–1810).

16. The Bakers lived in the Utopian community founded by Robert Dale Owen in New Harmony, Indiana.

17. Pierre Laclede (1724?–1778) was a French trader who founded St. Louis in 1764.

18. Joseph Lancaster (1778–1838) established a monitorial form of instruction for schools, designed to help facilitate the education of poor children.

19. Ninian Edwards (1775–1833) was governor of the Illinois Territory (1809–1818) and a U.S. senator from Illinois (1818–1831).

20. Alfred W. Caverly (1793–1876) was a Democratic lawyer and state legislator.

21. In 1831, Baker wed Mary Ann Lee, the widow of his employer, Samuel Lee, clerk of Greene County.

22. Daniel Stone of Springfield was a lawyer and Whig politician.

23. "Protest in Illinois Legislature on Slavery," Basler et al., eds., *Collected Works of*

Lincoln, 1:74–77. In this document, Lincoln and Stone denounced slavery as "founded on both injustice and bad policy."

24. John Calhoun (1808–1859) was a surveyor and Democratic politician who served as mayor of Springfield (1849–1851) and surveyor general of the Kansas Territory. While in Kansas, he presided over the fateful Lecompton Constitutional Convention. When the territorial legislature investigated the suspicious vote on the constitution, it discovered returns buried inside a candle box. Calhoun fled to Missouri during the subsequent investigation.

25. William Taylor Barry (1785–1835) of Kentucky served as U.S. postmaster general (1829–1835).

26. Felix Grundy (1777–1840) represented Kentucky in the U.S. Senate (1829–1838, 1839–1840) and served as U.S. attorney general (1838–1839).

27. Stephen T. Logan (1800–1880) was Lincoln's second law partner (1841–1844).

28. Milton Hay (1817–1893), uncle of John Hay, was a Springfield lawyer and friend of Lincoln.

29. Albert Taylor Bledsoe (1809–1877) had been a Whig lawyer and politician in Springfield in the 1840s.

30. James A. McDougall (1817–1867) represented California in the U.S. Senate (1861–1867).

31. William H. Bissell (1811–1860) fought in the Mexican War as colonel of the Second Illinois Volunteers. He served as governor of Illinois (1856–1860).

32. James Shields (1810–1879) of Illinois had been a U.S. senator (1849–1855) and became a general during the Civil War.

33. Lyman Trumbull (1813–1896) was a U.S. senator from Illinois (1855–1873).

34. Stephen A. Douglas (1813–1861) represented Illinois in the U.S. Senate (1847–1861).

35. Robert Anderson (1805–1871) commanded Union forces at Fort Sumter when the Confederates attacked it in April 1861.

36. Cerro Gordo was a Mexican village where a battle took place on 17–18 April 1847, which helped determine the outcome of the Mexican War.

37. At the battle of Churubusco, Colonel W. B. Burnett was wounded at the head of his regiment of New Yorkers.

38. William Henry Harrison (1773–1841) briefly served as president of the United States (1841).

39. Zachary Taylor (1784–1850) served as president of the United States (1849–1850).

40. Isaac G. Strain (1821–1857) wrote *A Paper on the History and Prospects of Interoceanic Communication by the American Isthmus* (1856).

41. Stephen T. Logan, who was Baker's law partner, said that "Baker was a brilliant man but very negligent." Logan told an interviewer: "I could not trust him in money matters. He got me into some scrapes by collecting and using money though he made it all right afterwards. You know Baker was a perfectly reckless man in matters

of money." Logan, interview with John G. Nicolay, Springfield, 6 July 1875, in Burlingame, ed., *Oral History of Lincoln*, 38, 37. When Baker was killed early in the Civil War, he left unaccounted for ten thousand dollars he had been granted to raise a regiment. Benjamin P. Thomas, "Edwin M. Stanton Takes Over the War Department," typescript, Benjamin P. Thomas Papers, Illinois State Historical Library, Springfield. See also Benjamin P. Thomas and Harold M. Hyman, *Stanton: The Life and Times of Lincoln's Secretary of War* (New York: Alfred A. Knopf, 1962), 160. John G. Nicolay noted that Baker "acquired a habit of negligence in study and preparation and business, which largely thwarted his high promise of usefulness and fame." Nicolay, undated memorandum dictated to Maud Williams, "Military" folder, box 11, Nicolay Papers, Library of Congress. When Baker lobbied hard for a cabinet post in 1849, Kentuckians, including Governor John J. Crittenden, opposed him, for they thought "Bakers moral weight is not as great as it should be. His career is regarded as erratic, and he is not thought to possess those patient, plod[d]ing, business qualifications so necessary to make a first rate Cabinet officer." Joshua F. Speed to Lincoln, House of Representatives [*of Kentucky*], 13 February 1849, Lincoln Papers, Library of Congress.

42. Leland Stanford (1824–1893), who had run unsuccessfully for governor in 1859, won that post in 1861. He later achieved fame and wealth as a railroad builder.

43. Joseph A. Nunes, president of the California Republican conventions in 1856 and 1860, served during the Civil War as a paymaster.

44. Frederick P. Tracy was a leading Republican renowned for his oratorical prowess.

45. John C. Frémont (1813–1890), the Republican candidate for president in 1856, lived in California.

46. Democrat Joseph C. McKibbin (1824–1896) represented a California district in the U.S. House (1857–1859).

47. David Logan was the son of Lincoln's second law partner, Stephen T. Logan.

48. Nathaniel Lyon (1818–1861) commanded loyal troops in Missouri; he was killed at the battle of Wilson's Creek in August 1861.

49. Alexander Stewart Webb (1835–1911) was chief assistant to W. F. Barry, the commander of the artillery of the Army of the Potomac.

50. George Archibald McCall (1802–1868) was commander of the Pennsylvania Reserves Division.

51. Charles P. Stone (1824–1887) was confined for 189 days without charges for his role in the debacle at Ball's Bluff.

52. At the battle of Ball's Bluff, Charles Devens Jr. (1820–1891) was saved by a uniform button that deflected a bullet.

53. Major John Mix of the Third New York Cavalry.

54. *Charles Stewart* was the pseudonym of Lord Ernest Vane-Tempest of England, who served as assistant adjutant general in Baker's division. His father was Lord Adolphus Frederick William Vane-Tempest (d. 1864), who sat in Parliament (1854–1864).

55. William Raymond Lee (1804?–1891) of the Twentieth Massachusetts was captured by the Confederates at Ball's Bluff.

56. Isaac Jones Wistar (1827–1905) commanded the Seventy-first Pennsylvania Regiment, which Baker had raised in Philadelphia.

57. Walter M. Bramhall served in the New York State Militia artillery.

58. Frank S. French served in the First Artillery.

59. John J. Hardin (1810–1847), Lincoln's political ally and sometime rival in Illinois, was killed at the battle of Buena Vista during the Mexican War.

Appendix 1. The Authorship of the Bixby Letter

1. J. G. Randall and Richard N. Current, _Last Full Measure_ (vol. IV of _Lincoln the President_; New York: Dodd, Mead, 1955), 48–52. Randall wrote the chapter in which the Bixby letter is discussed.

2. Carl Sandburg, _Abraham Lincoln: The War Years_ (4 vols.; New York: Harcourt, Brace & World, 1939), 3:669.

3. Carl Sandburg, _Abraham Lincoln: The Prairie Years and the War Years_ (New York: Harcourt, Brace, 1954), 640.

4. David A. Anderson, ed., _The Literary Works of Abraham Lincoln_ (Columbus, Ohio: Charles E. Merrill Publishing Company, 1970), vi. I am grateful to Professor Gabor S. Boritt of Gettysburg College for calling this work to my attention.

5. Herbert Joseph Edwards and John Erskine Hankins, _Lincoln the Writer: The Development of His Literary Style_ (University of Maine Studies, Second Series, no. 76; Orono: University of Maine, 1962), 90, 92.

6. "The Emotional and Intellectual Side of Lincoln," typescript enclosed in Dodge to David Kinley, Urbana, Illinois, 17 February 1924, Dodge Papers, Lincoln Shrine, A. K. Smiley Public Library, Redlands, California.

7. Dr. J. Herbert Claiborne to Isaac Markens, New York, 13 February [19]14, Markens Papers, Jewish American Historical Society, Brandeis University, Waltham, Massachusetts.

8. Quoted in Sherman Day Wakefield, "Abraham Lincoln and the Bixby Letter," _The Amateur Book Collector_, 6 (1955):1.

9. Basler et al., eds., _Collected Works of Lincoln_, 8:116–17.

10. Helen R. Towers of Athol, Massachusetts, quoted in the _Providence Evening Bulletin_, 12 August 1925.

11. Arthur March Bixby to David C. Mearns, New York, 31 August 1948, Mearns Paper, Library of Congress; Arthur March Bixby to the editor of the _New York Sun_, East Haven, Connecticut, 28 October 1949, clipping collection, Lincoln Museum, Fort Wayne, Indiana.

12. George C. Shattuck, ed., "Sarah Cabot Wheelwright's Account of the Widow Bixby," _Proceedings of the Massachusetts Historical Society_, 75 (1963):107–8. Shattuck reproduces this excerpt from "The Reminiscences of Sarah Cabot Wheelwright," 20

April 1904, a typed copy of which he found in the papers of Mrs. Wheelwright's only child, Mary Cabot Wheelwright (1878–1958). Sarah Cabot Wheelwright (1835–1917) was the wife of Andrew Cunningham Wheelwright and the daughter of Samuel Cabot (1784–1863).

13. William E. Barton, *A Beautiful Blunder: The True Story of Lincoln's Letter to Mrs. Lydia A. Bixby* (Indianapolis: Bobbs-Merrill, 1926) and F. Lauriston Bullard, *Abraham Lincoln and the Widow Bixby* (New Brunswick, N.J.: Rutgers University Press, 1946).

14. David Rankin Barbee, "The Bixby Letter—Did Lincoln Write It?" typescript, Barbee Papers, box 1, folder 8, Georgetown University.

15. Barton, *A Beautiful Blunder*, 62–63.

16. "Authorship of Happy Sayings," *New York Times*, 14 May 1933, section 4, p. 4E, c. 4.

17. Rollo Ogden to F. Lauriston Bullard, n.d., in Bullard, *Lincoln and the Widow Bixby*, 108. Brownell was an editor at Scribner's. Rollo Ogden, *W. C. Brownell: Tributes and Appreciations* (New York: Charles Scribner's Sons, 1929).

18. E. V. Lucas, *Post-Bag Diversions* (London: Methuen & Co., 1934), 132–33.

19. Butler, *Across the Busy Years: Recollections and Reflections* (2 vols.; New York: Charles Scribner's Sons, 1939–1940), 2:391–92.

20. Spender to E. C. Stone, 15 June 1941, quoted in Stone to William H. Townsend, Boston, 17 November 1941, William H. Townsend Papers, University of Kentucky, Lexington.

21. Bullard, *Lincoln and the Widow Bixby*, 109–10.

22. Memo by Catherine Eddy Beveridge (widow of Albert J. Beveridge), 22 July 1949, Albert J. Beveridge Papers, Library of Congress.

23. Hay to Herndon, Paris, 5 September 1866, supra.

24. Hay to Francis B. Carpenter, Washington, 19 November 1864, supra.

25. Hay to Spencer, Washington, 25 November 1864, supra.

26. Basler, "Who Wrote the 'Letter to Mrs. Bixby'?" *Lincoln Herald*, 45 (February 1943): 3–8.

27. Basler to F. Lauriston Bullard, Fayetteville, Arkansas, n.d., Bullard Papers, Boston University.

28. Basler, "Who Wrote the 'Letter to Mrs. Bixby'?" 3–8. Cf. Joe Nickell, "Lincoln's Bixby Letter: A Study in Authenticity," *Lincoln Herald*, 91 (1989): 135–40.

29. Fehrenbacher, *Lincoln in Text and Context: Collected Essays* (Stanford: Stanford University Press, 1987), 275.

30. Bullard, *Lincoln and the Widow Bixby*, 106–37.

31. Tyler Dennett to Roy P. Basler, Hague, N.Y., 8 September 1942, Basler Papers, Library of Congress.

32. Tyler Dennett to Edward C. Stone, n.d., quoted in Stone to William H. Townsend, 17 November 1941, copy, Bullard Papers, Boston University. Basler told Stone, "If John Hay wrote the letter, then he becomes as an editor of Lincoln's *Com-*

plete Works, a complete and bald-faced liar. It is one thing to say nothing—that is not to admit anything, but quite another to foster a lie." Ibid. Basler fails to understand that if Lincoln approved what Hay had written and affixed his signature to it, it was a legitimate Lincoln document.

33. Townsend, "Bullard's Bixby Book," *Lincoln Herald*, 48:2–10 (October 1946).

34. Warren to Edward C. Stone, Ft. Wayne, Indiana, 20 July 1945, Bullard Papers, Boston University.

35. William H. Townsend to F. Lauriston Bullard, Lexington, Kentucky, 5 March 1945, Bullard Papers, Boston University.

36. Paul M. Angle to Roy P. Basler, Springfield, 3 December 1940, Basler Papers, Library of Congress.

37. Angle to Basler, Springfield, 6 May 1942, Basler Papers, Library of Congress.

38. Pratt to Basler, Springfield, 22 March 1942, Basler Papers, Library of Congress.

39. Wakefield, "Abraham Lincoln and the Bixby Letter"; "Who Wrote Lincoln's Letter to Mrs. Bixby?" *Hobbies Magazine* (February 1941): 12–14; *Abraham Lincoln and the Bixby Letter* (pamphlet; New York: n.p., 1948), and *Abraham Lincoln and the Widow Bixby* (pamphlet; New York: n.p., 1947); Barbee, "The Plain Truth about the Bixby Letter," *Tyler's Quarterly Historical and Genealogical Magazine*, 26 (January 1945): 149–70, and "The Bixby Letter—Did Lincoln Write It?" typescript, Barbee Papers, Georgetown University.

40. Barbee, "The Bixby Letter Not There," dated Washington, 31 July 1947, typescript, Bullard Papers, Boston University. In this essay Barbee comments on the opening of the Lincoln Papers to the public in 1947.

41. Townsend to George A. Dondero, n.p., 25 July 1946, copy, and Townsend to Lawrence S. Thompson, n.p., 9 December 1948, copy, Townsend Papers, University of Kentucky, Lexington; memo enclosed in Bullard to Townsend, n.p., 15 November 1947, ibid.

42. Basler et al., eds., *Collected Works of Lincoln*, 8:117n.

43. Randall and Current, *Lincoln the President: Last Full Measure*, 50–52. Cf. Randall to Edward C. Stone, 12 July 1943, copy, Randall Papers, Library of Congress.

44. Neely, *The Abraham Lincoln Encyclopedia* (New York: McGraw-Hill, 1982), 28–29.

45. *New York Times*, 16 August 1925.

46. I am grateful to Jennifer Lee of the New York Public Library (and formerly of the John Hay Library) for calling that scrapbook to my attention.

47. Vol. 54, Hay Papers, Library of Congress.

48. Lincoln to John Phillips, Washington, 21 November 1864, Basler, ed., *Collected Works of Lincoln*, 8:118.

49. *Lincoln Lore*, no. 601 (14 October 1940).

50. W. L. Werner, "Who Wrote the Bixby Letter," article from an unidentified, undated magazine, folder 396, Carl Sandburg Papers, Illinois Historical Survey, University of Illinois, Urbana-Champaign. I am grateful to the late Don E. Fehrenbacher

for calling this item to my attention. The article was published after the Lincoln Papers at the Library of Congress were opened to the public in 1947.

51. Werner, "Who Wrote the Bixby Letter," 16–17.

52. Ibid.

53. The word *republic* appears in what is probably a spurious letter to James W. Wadsworth, in Basler et al., eds., *Collected Works of Lincoln*, 7:101.

54. Hay to Mrs. Manning Leonard, Cleveland, 12 August 1885, Hay Papers, Brown University.

55. Hay to William Henry Seward, Paris, 15 November 1866, letterpress copy, Hay Papers, Brown University.

56. Hay to Mrs. [H. H.] Richardson, Washington, 29 April 1886, draft, Hay Papers, Brown University.

57. Hay to Mr. Marshall, Paris, 20 October 1865, letterpress copy, Hay Papers, Brown University.

58. Hay to Gillmore, Washington, 2 July 1864, supra.

59. Lincoln to Salmon P. Chase, Springfield, 21 September 1859, Basler et al., eds., *Collected Works of Lincoln*, 3:471.

60. Hay to Sarah Helen Whitman, Warsaw [Illinois], 15 December 1858, Hay Papers, Brown University.

61. Hay to Seward, Paris, 2 March 1866, letterpress copy, Hay Papers, Brown University.

62. Hay to Emilio Castelar, Madrid, [21?] June 1870, letterpress copy, Hay Papers, Brown University.

63. Hay to Mr. [McEntee?], Cleveland, 27 September 1874, Hay Papers, Brown University.

64. Hay to James, Cannes, 24 December 1882, in George Monteiro, ed., *Henry James and John Hay: The Record of a Friendship* (Providence: Brown University Press, 1965), 90.

65. Hay to Mrs. [H. H.] Richardson, Washington, 29 April 1886, draft, Hay Papers, Brown University.

66. Supra, Hay to Manning Leonard, Washington, 9 June 1864.

67. Hay to Seward, Paris, 26 July 1865, letterpress copy, Hay Papers, Brown University.

68. Hay to Mr. Marshall, Paris, 20 October 1865, letterpress copy, Hay Papers, Brown University.

69. Hay to "My Dear Curtis," Paris, 10 January 1867, letterpress copy, Hay Papers, Brown University.

70. Hay to Nicolay, Cleveland, 27 November [1885], Lincoln's Secretaries File, Lincoln Museum, Fort Wayne, Indiana.

71. Lincoln to Fanny McCullough, Washington, 23 December 1862, in Basler et al., eds., *Collected Works of Lincoln*, 6:16–17.

72. Lincoln to Ephraim D. and Phoebe Ellsworth, Washington, 25 May 1861, Basler et al., eds., *Collected Works of Lincoln*, 4:385–86.

73. David Rankin Barbee, "The Bixby Letter—Did Lincoln Write It?" typescript, Barbee Papers, box 1, folder 8, Georgetown University.

74. I am grateful to David Herbert Donald, who had the collected works of Lincoln scanned onto discs so that they could be searched by computer; Professor Donald kindly performed several searches for me. For similar aid I am indebted to Dr. C. A. Tripp of Nyack, New York.

75. To tarnish Lincoln's image, some of his detractors, like Barbee, maintain that Hay wrote the Bixby letter. See Ira D. Cardiff, *The Deification of Lincoln* (Boston: Christopher, 1943), 62–65.

76. *New York Sun*, 6 August 1925.

Appendix 2. Mary Todd Lincoln's Unethical Conduct as First Lady

1. Ruth Painter Randall, *Mary Lincoln: Biography of a Marriage* (Boston: Little Brown, 1953), 258.

2. See Browning's interview with John G. Nicolay, Springfield, Illinois, 17 June 1875, in Burlingame, ed., *Oral History of Lincoln*, 3–4.

3. Browning to Issac N. Arnold, Quincy, Illinois, 25 November 1872, Isaac N. Arnold Papers, Chicago Historical Society.

4. Harlan Hoyt Horner, "Lincoln Rebukes a Senator," *Journal of the Illinois State Historical Society*, 44 (1951): 116.

5. Maurice Baxter, *Orville Hickman Browning: Lincoln's Friend and Critic* (Bloomington: Indiana University Press, 1957); Theodore Calvin Pease, "Introduction," *The Diary of Orville Hickman Browning*, ed. Theodore Calvin Pease and James G. Randall (2 vols.; Springfield: Illinois State Historical Library, 1925, 1933), 1:xii–xxxii.

6. Ten years after the war, Browning told an interviewer that Lincoln "many times . . . used to talk to me about his domestic troubles. He has several times told me there that he was constantly under great apprehension lest his wife should do something which would bring him into disgrace." Browning interviewed by John G. Nicolay, Springfield, 17 June 1875, in Burlingame, ed., *Oral History of Lincoln*, 3.

7. Henry Villard, *Memoirs of Henry Villard, Journalist and Financier: 1835–1900* (2 vols.; Boston and New York: Houghton Mifflin, 1904), 1:58.

8. William Allen Butler, *A Retrospect of Forty Years, 1825–1865* (New York: Charles Scribner's Sons, 1911), 350.

9. Villard, *Memoirs*, 1:58–59.

10. Harry J. Carman and Reinhard H. Luthin, *Lincoln and the Patronage* (New York: Columbia University Press, 1943), 278–80, 59–60.

11. Ibid., 62–63.

12. Turner and Turner, eds., *Mary Todd Lincoln*, 431; Jean H. Baker, *Mary Todd Lincoln: A Biography* (New York: W. W. Norton, 1987), 274.

13. "Deplorable—Exceedingly," editorial, *New York Citizen*, 5 October 1867. Cf. *New York Herald*, 4 October 1867, p. 7, cc. 4–5; *New York World*, 3 October 1867, p. 4, c. 6, p. 5, c. 1.

14. Mary Lincoln to W. H. Brady, Chicago [actually New York], 14 September [1867], in Turner and Turner, eds., *Mary Todd Lincoln*, 435.

15. *Albany Express*, 7 October 1867, reprinted in the *New York World*, 16 October 1867, p. 1, c. 5.

16. *Cincinnati Commercial*, n.d., reprinted ibid.

17. Carman and Luthin, *Lincoln and the Patronage*, 62–63.

18. Horace White to William H. Herndon, New York, 26 January 1891, Wilson and Davis, eds., *Herndon's Informants*, 700–1; Herndon to Jesse Weik, Springfield, 5 February 1891, Herndon-Weik Papers, Library of Congress; Carl Schurz, interview with Ida M. Tarbell, 6 November 1897, Ida Tarbell Papers, Allegheny College; Henry Villard, *Lincoln on the Eve of '61: A Journalist's Story*, ed. Harold G. and Oswald Garrison Villard (New York: Alfred A. Knopf, 1941), 70–71. Cf. Villard, *Memoirs*, 1:147–48. Ruth Painter Randall doubts this story (*Mary Lincoln*, 195–97). Mrs. Randall suggests that Mary Lincoln would not have fought with her husband in front of others. But she clearly did in 1865, as a letter she wrote to Abram Wakeman on January 30 indicates. Turner and Turner, eds., *Mary Todd Lincoln*, 200. She also belittled Lincoln before Richard Oglesby. Carl Sandburg and Paul M. Angle, *Mary Lincoln: Wife and Widow* (New York: Harcourt, Brace, 1932), 111. Jean Baker accepts the story as true (*Mary Lincoln*, 200–1), though she wrongly indicates that Henderson wished a post in Boston and also misidentifies the source of this information as "Henry Kreisman."

19. Godwin to William Cullen Bryant, Roslyn, 31 July 1865, Bryant-Godwin Papers, New York Public Library; Byant to Gideon Welles, New York, 25 June 1864, draft, ibid.; William E. Chandler to Gideon Welles, Washington, 2 June 1865, plus enclosure, Gideon Welles Papers, New York Public Library; Basler et al., eds., *Collected Works of Lincoln*, 4:334, 7:409–10; Beale, ed. *Welles Diary*, 2:54 (entry for 20 June 1864); Charles H. Brown, *William Cullen Bryant* (New York: Charles Scribner's Sons, 1971), 459–63. On Henderson, see Allan Nevins, *The Evening Post: A Century of Journalism* (New York: Boni and Liveright, 1922), 426–30.

20. *Washington Sunday Gazette*, 16 January 1887.

21. Receipt on Executive Mansion stationery, 10 May 1865: "Received of John D. Hammack Eighty four dollars for Sundry &c in full payment[.] Mrs. Lincoln." Ward Hill Lamon Papers, Henry E. Huntington Library, San Marino, California.

22. Turner and Turner, eds., *Mary Todd Lincoln*, 251, 332–34.

23. Mary Todd Lincoln to Alexander Williamson, Chicago, 2 February [1866], ibid., 332–33.

24. Villard, *Memoirs*, 1:148.

25. Barbee to Mrs. James G. Randall, Washington, 27 April 1951, J. G. Randall Papers, Library of Congress. On 18 January 1861, Henry Villard talked with the president-elect about the route he would take to Washington. Lincoln's preferences, it seemed to Villard, were "for a southerly route, via Cincinnati, Wheeling and Baltimore, doubtless to demonstrate how little fear he entertains for his personal safety." But, Villard noted, "there is a great pressure brought to bear on him in favor of a

more northerly one, via Pittsburgh and Harrisburg." Villard, *Lincoln on the Eve of '61*, 49 (dispatch to the *New York Herald*, 19 January 1861).

26. "Reminiscences of William P. Wood," *Washington Sunday Gazette*, 23 January 1887.

27. The *New York Times* reported that "Mr. W. S. Wood, of New York, called upon Mrs. Lincoln, and in the most delicate manner, tendered her, on behalf of certain New Yorkers, whose names were not given, a pair of magnificent black horses, with the request that if she preferred any other color, she would specify it. Mrs. Lincoln accepted them, and was highly gratified at the esteem and delicacy of feeling manifested by the donors." *New York Times*, 7 March 1861.

28. *Boston Daily Evening Transcript*, 1 March 1861; Baker, *Mary Lincoln*, 200–2.

29. *New York World*, 16 October 1867, p. 1, c. 5.

30. This story allegedly appeared in a book written by Mary Lincoln in 1868 and submitted to an Illinois publisher, who related it to a journalist. "Mrs. Lincoln's Book," *Albany Argus*, 15 April 1868, in John A. Williams, *They Knew Lincoln* (New York: E. P. Dutton, 1942), 228–29. Such evidence casts doubt on Ruth Painter Randall's conclusion that Mary Lincoln's "participation in politics, however injudicious, stemmed from her intense desire to watch out for and assist the mild and unselfseeking man she loved." Randall, *Mary Lincoln*, 251. That judgment is true only in part; she sought material rewards for her meddling. Moreover, as Professor Baker maintains, "she expected to gain recognition, and thus her interest in public affairs displayed a quirky feminism located not in principle but in the psychological necessity to be somebody." Baker, *Mary Lincoln*, 134.

31. Mary Lincoln to Ward Hill Lamon, Washington, [11] April [1861], Turner and Turner, eds., *Mary Todd Lincoln*, 83; Lamon to Mrs. Lincoln, Washington, 11 April 1861, Lamon Papers, Henry E. Huntington Library, San Marino, California.

32. Davis to Ward Hill Lamon, Bloomington, Illinois, 6 May 1861, and Clinton, Illinois, 31 May 1861, Lamon Papers, Henry E. Huntington Library, San Marino, California.

33. "Union" to Lincoln, Washington, 26 June 1861, typed copy, Illinois State Historical Library, Springfield.

34. Colfax to John G. Nicolay, South Bend, Indiana, 17 July 1875, Nicolay Papers, Library of Congress. Jean Baker mistakenly identifies this as a letter from Nicolay to Colfax. Baker, *Mary Lincoln*, 184. Cf. Randall, *Mary Lincoln*, 308–9.

35. The source of this story was Lincoln King, who claimed that he knew Mrs. Lincoln's paramour "intimately" in New York in the late nineteenth century. The *Primghar Sky Rocket* (Iowa), 15 March 1929, p. 4, c. 1; King to William E. Barton, Primghar, Iowa, 9 August 1930, Barton Papers, University of Chicago.

36. Baker, *Mary Lincoln*, 301.

37. George W. Adams to [David Goodman] Croly, Washington, 7 October 1867, Manton Marble Papers, Library of Congress.

38. Government Contracts, House Report No. 2, 37th Congress, 2d session, vol. 1

(serial no. 1142), 72–73, 501–505. The exact chronology of this story is confused. On August 8, it was reported that the President would remove Wood and name Benjamin Brown French in his stead. Lincoln told French that he would appoint him commissioner of public buildings on September 1. In fact, the appointment was made on September 6. Benjamin Brown French, *Witness to the Young Republic: A Yankee's Journal, 1828–1870*, ed. Donald B. Cole and John J. McDonough (Hanover, N.H.: University Press of New England, 1989), 370–74. Mary Todd Lincoln claimed that her husband, "to save his [*Wood's*] family from disgrace—When the Senate would not confirm him, [*re*]nominated him until the 1st of Sep. with a promise from him, he would resign." Mary Todd Lincoln to John F. Potter, Washington, 13 September 1861, Turner and Turner, eds., *Mary Todd Lincoln*, 104.

39. Mary Todd Lincoln to John F. Potter, Washington, 13 September 1861, Turner and Turner, eds., *Mary Todd Lincoln*, 104.

40. U.S. Senate, 59th Congress, 2nd Session, Report 69 (1903); Watt "Declaration for Invalid Pension," 25 August 1890, and Jane M. Watt, "Dependent Widow's Declaration for Pension," 29 January 1892, Pension Records, National Archives; Watt to General [name indecipherable], Washington, 16 January 1861; Watt to Lorenzo Thomas, 10 September and 3 December 1861, Records of the Adjutant General's Office, Letters Received, Main Series, Record Group 94, ibid.; Watt's service record, ibid.

41. John B. Blake, commissioner, to John Watt, Washington, 10 June 1858, copy, enclosing "a copy of the decision of the Secretary of the Interior upon the charges preferred against you by Mr. John Saunders," and Blake to Watt, Washington, 5 July 1859, copy, Records of the Commissioner of Public Buildings, letters sent, vols. 13 and 14, Record Group 42, Microcopy 371, reel 7, National Archives.

42. *New York Tribune*, 28 January 1862, p. 3,c. 4.

43. Mary Todd Lincoln to John F. Potter, Washington, 13 September 1861, Turner and Turner, eds., *Mary Todd Lincoln*, 104.

44. Browning diary, 3 March 1862, Illinois State Historical Library, Springfield.

45. Bill from John Watt to Abraham Lincoln, [1 February] 1863, Ward Hill Lamon Papers, Henry E. Huntington Library, San Marino, California; *New York Commercial Advertiser*, 4 October 1867, p. 2, cc. 1–2; Bayly Ellen Marks and Mark Norton Schatz, eds., *Between North and South; A Maryland Journalist Views the Civil War: The Narrative of William Wilkins Glenn, 1861–1869* (Rutherford, N.J.: Fairleigh Dickinson University Press, 1976), 175–76, 296 (entries for 16 March 1865 and 4 October 1867); Randall, *Mary Lincoln*, 254–58. Cf. Harry Pratt and Ernest E. East, "Mrs. Lincoln Refurbishes the White House," *Lincoln Herald*, 47:13–22 (February 1945). The gardener, John Watt, denied the story, but according to a New York wine merchant, Secretary of the Interior Smith verified it. George W. Adams to [David Goodman] Croly, Washington, 7 October 1867, and Frederic S. Cozzens to Manton Marble, New York, 12 October 1867, Manton Marble Papers, Library of Congress. Cozzens named Caleb B. Smith as his source. Some believed Mary Lincoln was "close" with money because she wanted to preserve her husband's salary "as much as possible to build

them a house after [*his*] term at Washington expires." Comments of Mrs. Owen Lovejoy, paraphrased in the Reverend David Todd to the Reverend John Todd, Providence, Illinois, 11 June 1862, copy, James G. Randall Papers, Library of Congress.

46. Upperman to Caleb B. Smith, Washington, 21 October 1861, copy, Records of the U.S. Senate, Committee on Public Buildings, 37th Congress, Record Group 46, National Archives. William H. Johnson was paid $50.00 for services as furnace-keeper at the White House for April, June, and August 1861, $43.75 for carting manure in June, $37.75 for whitewashing the Executive Mansion in July 1861. Alexander McKerichar received $50.00 as a laborer on public grounds for June 1861, $54.00 for hire of horse and covered wagon and driver in July 1861, $47.25 for cartage in August. Augustus Jullien and Charles F. Cone were paid for working in June as laborers under Watt on Lafayette Square. Burke received $31.25 for working as a laborer on the square south of the White House for June 1861. Upperman sent Smith copies of eight receipts. Financial Records of the Office of Public Buildings and Grounds, Record Group 42, entry 19, box 13, National Archives. The originals are located in the First Auditor's Records, Miscellaneous Records, Treasury Department, Record Group 217, ibid. Sutter approved Watt's bills for monthly pay as superintendent of President's Square and for hire of his horse and cart in hauling manure in June and July 1861. He also approved Watt's payroll for twenty-two laborers working under him. Records of the Commissioner of Public Buildings, letters sent, vols. 13 and 14, Record Group 42, Microcopy 371, reel 7, ibid.

47. Caleb B. Smith to W. H. Seward, Washington, 27 October 1861, Seward Papers, University of Rochester Library.

48. Memo by Smith, Washington, 11 December 1861, Records of the Commissioner of Public Buildings, Letters Received, Record Group 42, microcopy 371, reel 7, National Archives. Three days later, French disallowed the payments to Jullien, Burke, and Vermeren. French to Joseph Ingle, Washington, 14 December 1861, Records of the First Auditor, Miscellaneous Records, Treasury Department, no. 143610, Record Group 217, National Archives. Cf. penciled annotations on "Account No. 1," Annual Repair of the President's House, 30 September 1861, enclosed in First Auditor's Certificate on the account of B. B. French, no. 142505, ibid. This "return" was evidently made on January 7, 1862. See annotation on the First Auditor's Certificate on the account of B. B. French, no. 142506, and no. 142416, ibid.

49. Upperman to Foot, Washington, 6 December 1861, Records of the U.S. Senate, Committee on Public Buildings, 37th Congress, Record Group 46, National Archives. Cf. Washington correspondence by "Iowa," 4 February 1862, *Burlington* (Iowa) *Hawk-Eye*, 8 February 1862, p. 2, c. 3.

50. *New York Commercial Advertiser*, 4 October 1867, p. 2, cc. 1–2.

51. Democrat Benjamin M. Boyer (1823–1887), who represented a Pennsylvania district in the U.S. House (1865–1869) and served on the Ways and Means Committee, told this story to Maryland journalist William Wilkins Glenn. Marks and Schatz, eds., *Narrative of Glenn*, 175–76, 296 (entries for 16 March 1865 and 4 October 1867).

52. Donn Piatt in the *Cincinnati Commercial*, 22 February 1869.

53. Cole and McDonough, eds., *French Journal,* 479 (entry for 24 May 1865).

54. Lincoln to Whittlesey, Washington, 11 March 1862, *Lincoln Memorial Association Bulletin,* 21 (1992), 1–2.

55. John Hay heard this in 1867 from Isaac Newton, who "launched off in his buzzing way about Mrs. Lincoln how imprudent she was—how he protected & watched over her & prevented dreadful disclosures." John Hay diary, 13 February 1867, Brown University.

56. Washington correspondence, 16 October 1867, *New York Tribune,* 17 October 1867, p. 4, c. 6.

57. George W. Adams to [David Goodman] Croly, Washington, 7 October 1867, Manton Marble Papers, Library of Congress.

58. John Hay diary, 13 February 1867, Hay Papers, Brown University.

59. D. P. Holloway to John Watt, Washington, 14 March 1862, copy, Lincoln Papers, Library of Congress. When Watt asked for instructions, he was put off by the secretary of the interior. Caleb B. Smith to Watt, Washington, 29 March 1862, copy, ibid.

60. In the Ward Hill Lamon Papers at the Henry E. Huntington Library is the following document, dated on its folder [Feb. 1] 1863:

His Excellency
Abraham Lincoln
Due to John Watt
1863
To Commissary stores for the use of the Presidents House $361.00
the items and vouchers for this sum of money are in the hand [*of*] Genl Simm Draper
To Cash sent to Mrs Lincoln from this city [*Washington?*] to Mrs L by a draft at her request $350.00
the authority to send the same to Mrs Lincoln to New York is also in the hand of Mr Draper
To Cash paid Mrs Lincoln Hotel bill in Boston, receipt in Mr Lincoln['s] hand 15.00
To Cash handed Mrs Lincoln NY 10[.*oo*]
$736.00
Mr. Watts presents this account with reluctance & never intended to present it for payment and departs from his purpose originally intended as the wishes of the Hon Secretary Smith has not been carried out by Mr Newton the head of the Agriculture bureau in not compensation [*compensating*] me him for ~~my~~ time and services in his ~~my~~ visit to Europe for that Bureau, as that has not been done Mr Watts feels bound to present the above bill for payment as he cannot afford now to lose it. Mr Watts parted with the vouchers refer[*re*]d to with the understanding that the account would be promptly paid.

61. Watt to Cameron, n.p., n.d., Turner and Turner, eds., *Mary Todd Lincoln,* 103n.

62. Davis to his wife, St. Louis, 23 February 1862, David Davis Papers, Chicago Historical Society. See same to same, St. Louis, 19 February 1862, ibid.

63. Washington correspondence by "Iowa," 4 February 1862, *Burlington* (Iowa) *Hawk-Eye*, 8 February 1862, p. 2, c. 3; Marks and Schatz, eds., *Narrative of Glenn*, 176 (entry for 4 October 1867).

64. *New York World*, 26 September 1864, p. 4, c. 3; E. V. Haughwout & Co. to Marble, New York, 26, 27, and 28 September 1864; [Marble] to Col. Frank E. Howe, New York, 26 September 1864; and Marble to [E. V. Haughwout & Co.], "Wednesday 2 AM", filed at the end of September 1864, and [3 October 1864], draft, Marble Papers, Library of Congress. According to a Maryland journalist, Mrs. Lincoln "once bought a lot of China for $1500 in New York & made the seller give her $1500 in cash & sent a bill for $3000. When Lincoln refused to put his signature to the Bill prior to sending it to the Department to be paid, on the ground that it was exorbitant, [*the merchant said,*] 'You forget, sir, . . . that I gave Mrs Lincoln $1500.[']'" Marks and Schatz, eds., *Narrative of Glenn*, 296 (entry for 4 October 1867). Cf. entry for 16 March 1865, ibid., 175.

65. George W. Adams to [David Goodman] Croly, Washington, 7 October 1867, Manton Marble Papers, Library of Congress. In 1862, Congress passed a supplemental appropriation of $2,613 to cover expenses involved in plating gas fittings at the White House. Elisha Whittlesey to George Harrington, Washington, 6 March 1862, Letters Received, vol. 27, Records of the Commissioner of Public Buildings, microfilm edition, Record Group 42, microcopy 371, National Archives. On 30 July 1862, Haughwout received $2,343 from the Commissioner of Public Buildings for plating White House cutlery. Financial Records of the Commissioner of Public Buildings, entry 19, box 13, ibid.

66. New York correspondence by "Metropolitan," 9 October 1867, *Boston Post*, 11 October 1867, p. 1, c. 8.

67. Marks and Schatz, eds., *Narrative of Glenn*, 167 (entry for 16 March 1865).

68. A H[omer] B[yington] to [Sidney Howard] Gay, Washington, 23 March [1864], Gay Papers, Columbia University.

69. Ben: Perley Poore, *Reminiscences of Sixty Years in the National Metropolis* (2 vols.; Philadelphia: Hubbard Brothers, 1886, 2:142–43; Washington correspondence, 13 February 1862, *New York Tribune*, 14 February 1862, p. 5, c. 3, *Chicago Tribune*, 14 February 1862, p. 1, c. 4, and *New York Herald*, 14 February 1862, p. 1, c. 2; Randall, *Mary Lincoln*, 303–6. Cf. Douglas Fermer, *James Gordon Bennett and the New York Herald: A Study of Editorial Opinion in the Civil War Era, 1854–1867* (New York: St. Martin's, 1986), 214–16.

70. McClure to an unidentified correspondent, n.p., 9 May 1907, in Emanuel Hertz, ed., *Abraham Lincoln: A New Portrait* (2 vols.; New York: Horace Liveright, 1931), 2:248.

71. Frank Malloy Anderson, *The Mystery of "A Public Man": A Historical Detective Story* (Minneapolis: University of Minnesota Press, 1948), 126–28.

72. John W. Forney, *Anecdotes of Public Men* (2 vols.; New York: Harper and Brothers, 1873, 1881), 1:366–67.

73. Davis to his wife, St. Louis, 15 December 1861, David Davis Papers, Chicago Historical Society.

74. Henry Smith to Charles Henry Ray and Joseph Medill, [Washington], 4 November 1861, Ray Papers, Henry E. Huntington Library, San Marino, California. Cf. Adam Gurowski to Horace Greeley, Washington, 1 October 1861, Greeley Papers, New York Public Library.

75. Hawley to Charles Dudley Warner, n.p., n.d., in Arthur L. Shipman, ed., "Letters of Joseph R. Hawley," typescript dated 1929, 387, Connecticut Historical Society, Hartford.

76. Washington correspondence, 21 October 1861, *Missouri Republican* (St. Louis), 25 October 1861, in Burlingame, ed., *Lincoln's Journalist*, 120.

77. Matthew Hale Smith, *Sunshine and Shadow in New York* (Hartford: J. B. Burr, 1868), 284–89. Another journalist confirmed that Lincoln had unceremoniously ejected Wikoff from the White House, evidently in early February. Washington correspondence, 11 February 1862, *New York World*, 12 February 1862, p. 1, c. 2.

78. T. J. Barnett to S. L. M. Barlow, Washington, 27 October 1862, Barlow Papers, Henry E. Huntington Library, San Marino, California.

79. Elizabeth Keckley, *Behind the Scenes, or Thirty Years a Slave, and Four Years in the White House* (New York: G. W. Carlton, 1868), 203.

80. Marks and Schatz, eds., *Narrative of Glenn*, 296 (entry for 4 October 1867).

81. Washington correspondence, 7 January 1866, *New York Daily News*, 9 January 1866.

82. Washington correspondence, 7 January 1866, *New York World*, 9 January 1866.

83. Jefferson, Ohio, correspondence, *Cincinnati Commercial*, 2 November 1867.

84. Mary Todd Lincoln to Sally Orne, Chicago, 13 January [1866], to Alexander Williamson, Chicago, 17 and 26 January [1866], and to Oliver S. Halsted Jr., Chicago, 17 January [1866], Turner and Turner, eds., *Mary Todd Lincoln*, 326–30.

85. Randall, *Mary Lincoln*, 388–89; Baker, *Mary Todd Lincoln*, 249–50.

86. Keckley, *Behind the Scenes*, 204.

87. Ibid., 149–50.

88. Dr. John B. Ellis, *The Sights and Secrets of the National Capital* (New York: United States Publishing Company, 1869), 186–87.

89. Noah Brooks, Washington dispatch of 12 March 1865, Burlingame, ed., *Lincoln Observed*, 171–74; *New York World*, 15 March 1865.

90. Turner and Turner, eds., *Mary Todd Lincoln*, 331.

91. Willard L. King, *Lincoln's Manager: David Davis* (Cambridge: Harvard University Press, 1960), 235–37.

92. Dubois, undated interview with Jesse W. Weik, Weik Papers, Illinois State Historical Library.

93. Hay diary, 13 February 1867, Brown University.

94. Mary Lincoln to Abram Wakeman, Washington, 23 September [1864], in Turner and Turner, eds., *Mary Todd Lincoln*, 180.

95. Mary Lincoln to Abram Wakeman, Washington, 30 January [1865], ibid., 200.

96. Beveridge, *Abraham Lincoln, 1809–1858* (2 vols.; Boston: Houghton, Mifflin, 1928), 1:312.

97. *Washington Sunday Gazette*, 16 January 1887.

98. Herndon to Horace White, Springfield, 13 February 1891, White Papers, Illinois State Historical Library, Springfield.

Index

The following abbreviations are used throughout the index:

AL   Abraham Lincoln

JH   John Hay

Abolition Act, 21, 220n. 113

About, Edmund, 101, 257n. 162

Abraham Lincoln and the Widow Bixby (Bullard), 174, 176

Adams, Henry, xi, xii, 173, 205–6n. 7

Address of E. W. Gantt (Gantt), 73, 244n. 12

Aeichhold, A. P., 245n. 22

African Americans. *See* blacks

Alexander, Edmund Brooke, 234n. 77

Allen, Charles E., 99, 256n. 150

Alsop, William, 232n. 46

American Bank Note Company, 192

Ames, Mrs., 47

Ammen, Daniel, 230n. 45

Anderson, Robert, 154, 265n. 35

Andrew, John A., 120, 124, 171, 214n. 44, 259n. 15

Andrews, Rufus, 257n. 166

Angell, Caroline, 65, 240n. 153

Angell, Hannah (Coggeshall), xxi, 4–5, 6, 9–10, 90–91, 211n. 4, 213n. 31, 240n. 153

Angell, James B., 211n. 4

Angle, Paul, 176–77

Arago, USS, 40, 43

Arkansas, 76

Armory, Thomas J. C., 216n. 52

Armstrong, 49

Army of the Cumberland, 232n. 50, 240n. 161, 242n. 181

Army of the James, 243n. 9

Army of the Ohio, 224n. 157

Army of the Potomac, xvi, 28, 234n. 77, 256n. 160, 262n. 39

Army of the Tennessee, 242n. 181

assassination plots, 190

Asta Buraga, F. L., 18, 218n. 85

Athanaeum theater, 237n. 128

Atlantic Monthly, 4

Ayers, Romeyn Beck, 133, 261n. 36

Badeau, Adam, 29–30, 225n. 3

Baker, Alfred, 156

Baker, Edward D., xvii, 121–22, 180, 252n. 96, 260n. 18; in California, 156–58, 160; death of, 165; financial matters and, 265–66n. 41; JH on, 151–66; military prowess of, 154–55; as orator, 155–62,

Baker, Edward Lewis, 6, 212n. 12

Baker, Jean, 272n. 18, 273n. 30

Baker, Julia Cook Edwards, 6, 212n. 12

Ball, Black & Co., 202

Ball's Bluff, battle of, 122, 151, 266nn. 51, 52

Baltimore: assassination plots, 259n. 9; elections, 83, 97, 255n. 142

Baltimore & Ohio Railroad, 190

Baltimore convention, 248–49nn. 54, 55, 250n. 67

Bancroft, George, 110–11, 258n. 3

Bancroft, Nancy, 110–11

Banks, Nathaniel P., 24, 78–79, 214n. 44, 222n. 136, 235n. 93

Barbee, David Rankin, xxiv, 177, 190, 262n. 42, 271n. 75

Barney, Hiram, 7, 13–14, 55, 188, 212n. 15, 216n. 62, 237n. 124

Barrell, George, 7, 14, 212n. 16

Barry, William Taylor, 154, 265n. 25

Barton, William E., 171–72, 175, 178

Basler, Roy P., xiii, 174, 175, 177, 185, 268–69n. 32

Bates, David Homer, 262n. 42

Bates, Edward, 5, 67, 211n. 9

Bates, Joshua, 67, 240n. 164

Bayard (Pierre Terrail), 145, 264n. 7

Bayard, James A., 195

Beauregard, Pierre Gustave Toutant, 20, 220n. 103

Beautiful Blunder, A (Barton), 171–72

Beckwith, Amos, 18, 219n. 91

Bedell, Edward A., 17–18, 218n. 82

Ben De Ford, USS, 32

Bennett, James Gordon, 198

Benton, Thomas Hart, 118, 259n. 11

Berdan, Hiram, 133, 262n. 39

Berrett, James, 220n. 113

Beveridge, Albert J., 203

Bierstadt, Albert, 14, 217n. 71

Bigelow, John, 103, 257n. 180

Bing, Julius, 12, 214n. 47

Bishop, Joseph Bucklin, xii, xx, 205n. 1

Bissell, William H., 154, 165, 265n. 31

Bixby, Arthur March, 170, 267n. 11

Bixby, Lydia, xiii, 100; appearance of, 170–71

Bixby letter, 169–86; terms used in, 179–86

Black Hawk War, 154

blacks: Eighth U.S. Regiment, 77, 245n. 22; Second (South Carolina) Colored Infantry, 245n. 22; troops, 31–32, 41, 43, 77, 227n. 26, 232n. 51, 237n. 119, 245n. 22, 247n. 35; Twenty-first U.S. Colored Troops, 227n. 26

Blair, Francis P., Jr., 9

Blair, Montgomery, 49, 65, 243–44n. 11

Blake, John B., 193

Bledsoe, Albert T., 154, 265n. 29

Bleeker, Anthony J., 13, 216n. 60

Bliss, Mrs. Alexander, 16

Blood, Henry A., 48, 234n. 90

Blucher, Gebhart Leberecht von, 53

Boker, George H., xiii, 55, 66, 237n. 122, 240n. 156

Bosco, Ferdinando Beneventano, 46, 233n. 70

Boston Herald, 175

Boston Journal, 199

Bourke, Robert, 12, 215n. 49

Boutwell, George S., 25, 89, 222n. 127

Boyer, Benjamin M., 195, 275n. 51

Brady, William, 188

Bragg, Braxton, 77, 237n. 117

Brainerd, Cephas, 55, 237n. 125

Bramhall, Walter M., 164, 267n. 57

Breckinridge, John C., 122, 166, 211n. 6, 260n. 20

Brewer, Ephraim, 73, 243n. 8

Bright, John, 53, 67, 236n. 110

Broadway, Jesse, 97

Broderick, David C., 122, 158–59, 260n. 19

Brooks, Mary, 36, 227n. 35

Brooks, Noah, xiv, xxiv

Brooks, Thomas B., 73, 245n. 17

Brough, John, 65, 79, 239n. 150

Brown, Albert Gallatin, 73, 243n. 10

Brown, Caroline Owsley, xxi

Brown, Charles Farrar (Artemus Ward), 125, 260n. 23

Brown, Samuel C., 21, 220n. 109

Brownell, Francis E., 264n. 9

Brownell, William Crary, 172, 174, 177, 186, 268n. 17

Browning, Orville Hickman, 185–88, 193, 196, 201, 203, 271n. 6

Brown University, xi, xviii, 53, 178–79, 236–37n. 115

Bryant, William Cullen, 138, 188, 189

Buchanan, James, xv, 118–19, 198, 259n. 13

Buckingham, William A., 49, 228n. 41

Buell, Don Carlos, 28, 224n. 157

Buena Vista, battle of, 165, 267n. 59

Bullard, F. Lauriston, 175, 176, 177

Bull Run: first battle of, xv, 126, 193; second battle of, xxiv

Bunker's Hill, 141
Bureau of Militia, 147–49
Burgdorf, Louis, 68
Burke, Francis P., 194, 275n. 46
Burnett, W. B., 155, 265n. 37
Burns, Robert, 137–38
Burns, Thomas, 68
Burnside, Ambrose E., xv, 69, 70, 128, 250n. 62, 260n. 28
Bush, Daniel Brown, 234n. 76
Bush, Edward Geer, 47–48, 94, 97, 234n. 76
Bush, Theodore, 47, 234n. 84
Busteed, Richard, 68–69, 242n. 176
Butler, Benjamin F., 31, 64, 72, 104
Butler, Nicholas Murray, xiii, 172–73, 174, 175, 176–78

Cabinet, 50, 58, 133; AL's rule of, xi, 49
Cabot, Samuel, 268n. 12
Calhoun, John, 154, 265n. 24
California, 156–58, 160, 259n. 7
Cameron, Simon, 5, 97, 196, 211n. 9, 236n. 113
Campbell, Julian R., 44, 233n. 61
Canning, Josiah D., 16, 218n. 79
Canterbury (music hall), 56, 237–38n. 129
Carlin, George W., 26, 223n. 150
Carlin, William P., 26, 223n. 150
Carpenter, Francis Bicknell, 99, 100, 174, 256n. 153
Carr, Clark E., xx, 224n. 155
Carroll, Anna Ella, 49, 235n. 94
Cartter, David Kellogg, 64, 223n. 142
Cartter, Mrs. David Kellogg, 25
Caswell, Thomas T., 10, 213n. 35
Caton, John Dean, 15, 217n. 67
Caverly, Alfred W., 15, 264n. 20
Cedar Mountain, battle of, 222n. 136
Century Magazine, xvii
Cerro Gordo, battle of, 155, 265n. 36
Chandler, William E., 175, 177
Chapman, A. S., 1
Chapman, John Lee, 97, 255n. 142
Charleston (S.C.), 51
Charleston Harbor (S.C.), 32–38, 41, 44, 51, 120, 141, 228–31n. 45

Chase, Charles D., 83, 85, 248n. 46
Chase, Janet (Nettie) Ralston, 45, 233n. 66
Chase, Kate, 67, 240n. 162
Chase, Salmon P., 7–8, 24, 66, 71, 110, 233n. 66, 243n. 191
Chattanooga, battle of, 54, 237n. 117
Chicago, 114, 126
Chicago Tribune, xxiv, 252n. 102
Chickamauga, battle of, 133, 242n. 181
Choate, Rufus, 214n. 44
Churubusco, battle of, 265n. 37
Clay, Brutus J., 247n. 36
Clay, Clement C., 251n. 80
Clemens, Jeremiah, 102, 257n. 168
Clyde, USS, 72, 243n. 3
Cobden, Richard, 53, 236n. 110
Coggeshall, James Haydon, 213n. 31
Colfax, Schuyler, 52, 191, 205n. 4, 234n. 91, 236n. 105
Collected Works of Abraham Lincoln, The (Basler), 174, 177
Collingwood, Cuthbert, 152, 264n. 15
Collins, James H., 242n. 186
Collins, Walter S., 70, 242n. 186
Colorado, 251n. 85
Columbia College, 8–9
Comanches, 117
Commager, Henry Steele, xxiv
Cone, Charles F., 194, 275n. 46
Confederate prisoners of war, 202
Congress, 63, 83, 89, 110, 118, 133, 155, 156, 236n. 105; Radicals in, 62; slavery and, 21, 220n. 112
Conkling, James C., 237nn. 118, 119
Connecticut, 38, 228n. 41
Conrad's Ferry, 163
Conservatives, 62–63, 75–76, 249n. 54
Cony, Samuel, 89, 251–52nn. 87, 88
Cook, Burton C., 248–49n. 54
Coolidge, Louis A., 173, 174, 177, 185
Copperheads (peace Democrats), 85, 92, 93, 252n. 101
Craven, John Joseph, 37, 227n. 40
Crittenden, John J., 266n. 41
Cronan, John, 85
Cullom, Shelby M., 47, 102, 257n. 173

Cullum, George Washington, 46, 234n. 83
Cumming's Point battery (S.C.), 41
Current, Richard N., 177
Curtin, Andrew G., 65, 97, 239n. 152, 255n. 138
Curtis, George William, 85–86, 250n. 67
Cushing, Caleb, 214n. 44
Cuthbert, Mrs., 187

Dahlgren, John A., 25, 44, 51–52, 133, 223n. 140
Dahlgren, Ulrich, 25, 223n. 140
Dakota Territory, 24, 222n. 133
Dana, Charles A., 141, 263n. 49
Dant, George W., 195
Davis, David, 187, 191, 196, 199, 201, 202, 203
Davis, Henry Winter, 39, 97, 214n. 44, 255n. 141
Davis, Jefferson, 154–55, 259n. 15
Defrees, John D., 187
Democratic National Convention (Chicago), 91, 252n. 101
Democrats, 27, 91, 92, 158, 228n. 41. *See also* Copperheads
Denison, George, 11, 65, 192, 214n. 46
Dennett, Tyler, xi-xii, 175–76, 206n. 9, 207n. 41
Dennison, George. *See* Denison, George
Dennison, Jane Parsons, 8, 212n. 23
Dennison, William, 64, 239n. 151
Department of the Gulf, 250n. 74
Derby, James C., 92, 253n. 105
Devens, Charles, Jr., 163–64, 266n. 52
Devereux, Arthur Forrester, 142, 263–64n. 2
Devereux, George H., 263n. 2
DeVilliers, Charles A., 144, 264n. 6
Dickinson, Lucy, 264n. 15
Dickinson, Thomas, 152
Dix, John A., 70, 242n. 184
Dobb's Ferry, 10, 11
Dodge, Daniel Kilham, 169
Donald, David Herbert, 271n. 74
Doster, William E., 209n. 65
Douglas, Anna, 154, 212n. 16, 265n. 34

Douglas, Stephen A., xvi, 115–16, 120, 148, 158, 165, 259n. 6
Douglass, Frederick, 141, 263n. 50
Downes, John A., 230n. 45
Drake, Charles D., 57, 64, 238n. 132, 239nn. 144, 147
Draper, Simeon, 102, 187, 188, 189, 196, 203, 257n. 170
Drayton, Percival, 230n. 45
Drayton, Thomas F., 230n. 45
Dubois, Jesse K., 68, 91, 202, 241n. 172, 252–53n. 103
Dubois, William Archer, 252n. 103
Du Pont, Samuel Francis, 33, 34–37, 41, 43, 227n. 28, 228–31n. 45, 241n. 170

Eames, Charles, 12, 214–15n. 48
Eames, Fanny Campbell, 11–12, 18, 19, 214n. 44, 218n. 86
Early, Jubal E., 128, 260n. 27
Eddy, Spencer, 173, 186
Edwards, Elizabeth Todd, 218n. 87
Edwards, Mrs. A. E., 3–4, 13
Edwards, Ninian, 153, 264n. 19
Edwards's Ferry, 163, 164
Eighteenth Corps, Army of the James, 243n. 9
Eighth Massachusetts Regiment, 263–64n. 2
Eliot, George, 15–16
Elliott, Charles Loring, 55, 237n. 124
Ellis, John B., 201–2
Ellsworth, Elmer E., xvii, 9–10, 121, 122–24, 141–51, 260n. 18; appearance of, 144–45; and Bureau of Militia proposal, 147–48; character of, 142–43; early years of, 141–42; JH on, 141–51; and Lincoln's letter of condolence, 182–85; Mexico and, 143; military reform and, 143–44; murder of, 150–51, 264n. 9
Ellsworth's Avengers, 260n. 21
Emancipationists, 63–64
Emancipation Proclamation, 27, 60, 66, 78, 127
England, 121

Etheridge, Emerson, 71, 242n. 188
Evans, T. C., xxii, 262n. 44
Everett, Edward, 214n. 44

Fairfax, Donald M., 230n. 45
Fanchon the Cricket (play), 237n. 128
Fehrenbacher, Don E., 174–75,
    269–70n. 50
Fernandina (Fla.), 74
Fillmore, Millard, 93, 120, 251n. 85,
    253n. 108, 259n. 16
Fire Zouaves, 10–11, 123, 260n. 21
First Cavalry, 216n. 58
First Rhode Island Regiment, 259n. 17
Fisher's Hill, battle of, 254n. 117
Fitch, Henry S., 98
Florida, 40; and Olustee incident, 245n.
    22, 246–47n. 34; voters, 77, 245–46n. 23
Folly Island (S.C.), 37
Foote, Andrew Hull, 44, 233n. 58
Forbes, John Murray, 55, 237n. 119
Ford, John T., 237n. 128
Ford's Theater, 56, 85, 205n. 4
Forney, John W., 97, 198, 255n. 139
Forrest, Edward, 21, 220n. 115
Fort Monroe, 19, 246n. 32
Fort Pulaski, 233n. 57
Fort Sumter, 35, 36, 37, 41, 43, 44, 51,
    119–20, 141, 230n. 45
Fort Trumbull, 81, 248n. 45
Forty-fourth New York Regiment,
    260n. 21
Foster, John Gray, 128, 248n. 46
Fox, Gustavus Vasa, 43, 66, 67, 133, 231n.
    45, 240n. 159, 261n. 35
Francis, Mrs. Simeon, 212n. 16
Franklin, William B., 221–22n. 124
Fredericksburg, battle of, xvi
Frémont, John C., 92, 158, 253n. 107,
    266n. 45
French, Benjamin Brown, 195,
    273–74n. 38, 275n. 48
French, Frank S., 164, 267n. 58
French, Jonas H., 223n. 148
Fribley, Col., 245n. 22
Fry, James B., 52–53, 85, 261n. 34

Fry, John, 8, 46, 47, 50, 213n. 24
Fulton, Charles C., 51–52, 236n. 103

Gaine's Mill, battle of, 222n. 124
Galt and Brothers, 202
Gamble, Hamilton R., 58–59, 238nn. 136,
    138
Gantt, Edward Walton, 73, 244n. 12
Garfield, James A., xxv, 133, 261n. 35
Gawler, Joseph, 26, 223n. 146
German American Republicans, 253n. 107
Gerolt, Carlota Wilhelmina Mariana von,
    25, 45, 46, 48, 233n. 67
Gerolt, Friedrich Karl Joseph von, 20,
    220n. 107
Gettysburg address, 169–70, 174, 237n. 119
Gilder, Richard Watson, xv, 175, 207n. 36
Gillmore, Quincy A., 43, 73, 74–75, 76, 77,
    83, 86, 181, 228n. 43, 233n. 57,
    246–47n. 34
Glenn, William Wilkins, 203
Godwin, Parke, 189
Goodwin, John N., 83, 248n. 48
Gordon, George Henry, 32, 226n. 22
Grant, Ulysses S., 20, 43, 56, 59, 69, 70, 85,
    130, 220n. 103, 225n. 3; Spotsylvania
    Court House and, 83, 248n. 49
Greeley, Horace, 20, 71, 87, 89, 91, 105, 180,
    188, 220n. 105, 251n. 80, 258n. 186
Greene, Elias M., 79
Grimshaw, Jackson, 223n. 148
Grimshaw, William A., 248n. 54
Grover, Leonard, 223n. 140
Grover, William N., 98, 255n. 128
Grover's Theater, 25, 223n. 140
Grow, Galusha, xvii
Grundy, Felix, 154, 265n. 26
Gurney, Eliza P., 103, 257n. 178
Gurowski, Adam, 66, 220n. 108, 240n. 160
Gutherie, James, 214n. 44
Guy Livingston, or Thorough (Lawrence),
    41, 233n. 53

habeas corpus, suspension of, 59
Hackett, James Henry, 262n. 42
Haight, Edward, 21, 220n. 112

Hale, John P., 49, 235n. 92

Halleck, Henry W., 44, 230n. 45, 233n. 59, 243n. 11, 246–47n. 34

Halliday Street Theater, 237n. 128

Halpine, Charles G., xiii, xvii, 32, 35, 38, 42, 228–31n. 45; Fox and, 66, 240n. 159; JH's letters to, 50–51, 66–67, 68–69, 70–71, 72, 80; *Life and Adventures of Miles O'Reilly,* 66, 67, 68, 69, 70, 240nn. 158–60, 242n. 177, 242n. 186, 243n. 191

Hamilton, Alexander, xix

Hamilton, James Alexander, 10, 11, 213n. 36

Hamilton, Mary, 18

Hamlin, Hannibal, 81

Hammack, John, 190, 272n. 21

Hardee, William Joseph, 77, 144, 245n. 21, 264n. 5

Hardin, John J., 165, 267n. 59

Harlan, James, 98, 256n. 145

Harper, Fletcher, 227n. 35

Harper and Mitchell (store), 202

Harper's Magazine, xvi, 115–16

Harris, Ira, 133, 216n. 58, 261n. 36

Harris, William Hamilton, 261n. 36

Harrison, William Henry, 156, 265n. 38

Harrison's Island, 163, 164

Hatch, Ozias M., xviii, 224n. 155, 234n. 76

Haughwout & Co., 197

Hawley, Joseph R., 199, 243–44n. 11, 245–46n. 23

Hawthorne, Nathaniel, 138, 263n. 47

Hay, Augustus Leonard, 32, 226n. 17

Hay, Charles Edward, 7, 18, 32, 33, 36, 94, 212n. 18, 217n. 74; illness of, 36, 37–38, 39, 40, 43, 233n. 55; JH's letters to, 81–82, 103–4

Hay, Clara Stone, xi, 205–6n. 7

Hay, Helen, 88, 93

Hay, John, 40; as aid to AL, xviii-xix, xxiii-xxiv; on AL's greatness, xxv-xxvi; appearance of, xix-xxv; in army, xix, 208n. 45; Bixby letter and, 169–86; character of, xix-xxv; Civil War diary of, xi; early years of, xviii; on G. B.

McClellan, 27, 221–22n. 124; and Hay Papers, 178–79; on history, xi, 225n. 1; imitative capacity of, 175–76; as journalist, 234–35n. 91; on journalists, 78; letters of, xi-xii; on Mary Todd Lincoln's debt, 202–3; military instinct of, 245n. 18; on modesty, xxiv-xxv; and nomination to Congress, 80, 246n. 34; and Paris appointment, 103, 104; photo of, 14, 217n. 72; real estate ventures of, 92, 232n. 46; and relationship with AL, xix, 207n. 41; reminiscences of, xiv-xv; scrapbooks of, 178; vanity of, xxiv; verse by, 53, 55, 56, 65, 69; on W. O. Stoddard, xxiii; in Warsaw (Ill.), 3, 211n. 2; on Washington, D.C., 25, 26, 48–49, 54, 67, 89; on Wikoff, 199

Hay, Joseph A., 239n. 144

Hay, Leonard, 87

Hay, Logan, xx, 176

Hay, Mary, 82, 89, 90, 91, 219n. 88

Hay, Milton, xviii, 154, 265n. 28

Hay, Mrs. Charles, 31–32

Hay, Mrs. Milton, 18, 219n. 88, 220n. 104

Hays, Joseph C., 247n. 38

Heenan, John C., 5, 211n. 7

Henderson, Isaac, 189, 203, 272n. 18

Henry, Anson G., 17, 218n. 81

Herndon, William H., xiv, xv, xxvi, 109, 148, 173, 177, 185, 203

"Heroic Age in Washington, The" (Hay), xv, xvi, 113–31, 259n. 5

Hertz, Emanuel, 177

Heslop, Frederick William, 26, 223n. 144

Hickox, H. Louise, 7

Higginson, Thomas Wentworth, xxiv

Hilton Head (S.C.), 33

Hitchcock, Ethan Allen, 31, 65, 103, 226n. 10

Hitt, R. R., 254n. 121

Holcombe, James B., 251n. 80

Holt, Joseph, 72, 84, 218n. 78, 224n. 160, 243n. 4, 249n. 54

Holyoake, George Jacob, 96

Home Journal, 215n. 50

Hood, Thomas, 138, 262–63n. 45

Hooker, Joseph, 41, 51, 53, 69, 232n. 50, 252n. 95
Hooper, Samuel, 220n. 108
Hopkins, Samuel A., 192
House of Representatives, 156, 251–52n. 88
House Select Committee on the Loyalty of Government Employees, 193
Howe, Nathaniel S., xxiii, 49, 54, 66, 208n. 45, 235n. 93
Howells, William Dean, 7–8, 31, 212nn. 19–21
How Lincoln Became President (Wakefield), 177
Hugo, Victor: *Les Miserables,* 30–31
Hunter, David, 22, 32, 33, 36–37, 38, 41, 42, 43–44, 66, 74, 222n. 125, 226n. 16, 232n. 51
Hunter, Mrs., 66
Huntington, Alice, 27, 223–24n. 154
Huntington, Charles H., 7, 212n. 17
Huntington, George Lathrop, 224n. 154
Hurlbut, Stephen A., 86, 250n. 74

Idaho Territory, 221n. 118
Illinois State Convention, 83, 248–49n. 54
Illinois State Historical Society, 185–86
Illinois State Journal, 212n. 12
Indiana, 97, 255n. 137
Interior Department, 193, 195, 196
inventors, 134, 262n. 38
Irvington, 10, 11
Irwin, Robert, 224n. 158
Irwin, Robert T., 28, 224n. 158
Isaacs, Meyer S., 98, 256nn. 148, 149
Island No. 10 (Miss.), 219–20n. 103
Italian War (1859), 151, 264n. 12
Ives, Thomas Poynton, 99, 257n. 163

Jackson, Claiborne F., 238n. 138
Jackson, G. A., 172
Jackson, James W., 264n. 9
Jackson, Stonewall, 222n. 136
James, Henry, 181
James Wadsworth Papers, xiv
Jay, John, 221n. 122
Jay, Mary, 22–23, 221n. 122

Jayne, William (Bill), 24, 222n. 134
Jewett, William Cornell, 88, 251n. 85
Jewish delegation, 98, 256nn. 148, 149
Johnson, Andrew, 16, 105
Johnson, Solomon James, 103, 258n. 189
Johnson, William, 48, 194, 195, 234n. 87, 275n. 46
Joseph J. May & Co., 202
journalists, 77, 120, 246–47n. 34
Jullien, Augustus, 194, 195, 275nn. 46, 48

Kansas, 93, 154, 265n. 24; delegates, 57, 238n. 131; and Lawrence massacre, 61, 238n. 142; Radicals, xiv
Kappes, Charles, 86, 250n. 70
Kaulbach, Frederick August, 130–31, 261n. 31
Keckley, Elizabeth, 190, 201, 203
Kelley, William D. ("Pig Iron"), 97, 255n. 132
Kennedy, Joseph Camp Griffith, 25, 223n. 139
Kentucky, 8
Keokuk, USS, 32, 35, 227n. 25, 228n. 45
Keyes, S. C., 188
King, Charles, 8–9
King, Henry, xxiv
King, Lincoln, 273n. 35
King, Preston, 214n. 44
Kinzie, Arthur Magill, 35, 42, 43, 227n. 36
Knapp, Thomas L., 223n. 154
Knights of the Golden Circle, 250n. 61
Knox, James, 263n. 46
Koerner, Gustav P., 98, 256n. 147
Koerner, Karl Theodor, 152, 264n. 13
Kreismann, Herman, 189, 203, 272n. 18
Kretchmar, C. Young, 85, 250n. 65

Laclede, Pierre, 152, 264n. 17
Lamon, Mrs. Ward Hill (Sally), 219n. 89
Lamon, Ward Hill, 20, 48, 191, 220n. 105
Lancaster, Joseph, 264n. 18
Lancasterian plan, 153, 264n. 18
Lander, Frederick West, 224n. 161
Lander, Jean Margaret Davenport, 28, 49, 54, 224n. 161

Land Patent Secretary, 93
Lane, James H. (Jim), 57, 61, 98, 239n. 144, 241n. 170, 256n. 144
Lane, Joseph, 4, 160, 211n. 6
Latham, George Clayton, 27, 224n. 158
Lawrence, Albert G., 97
Lawrence, George Alfred, 41, 233n. 53
Lawrence massacre, 61, 238n. 142
Lecompton Constitutional Convention, 265n. 24
Lee, Mary Ann, 153, 264n. 21
Lee, Robert E., xvi; peninsular campaign and, 221–22n. 124; and Spotsylvania Court House, 82, 248n. 49
Lee, Samuel Phillips, 72, 243n. 1
Lee, William Raymond, 164, 267n. 55
Leonard, Manning, 81, 84, 104–5, 181, 185, 247n. 40
Leutze, Emanuel, 15, 25, 217n. 73
Library of Congress, xiv, 178
Lieber, Francis, 95–96, 254nn. 123, 124
Life and Letters of John Hay (Thayer), 174
"Life in the White House in the Time of Lincoln" (Hay), xvii, 131–42
Lincoln, Abraham, 48, 77, 118–19, 155, 260n. 22; accessibility of, 109, 132–33; on Civil War, xv-xvi; Confederate amnesty and, 244n. 13; courts-martial and, 45, 46, 97; death of, 105, 129–30; and Gettysburg address, 169–70, 174, 237n. 119; habeas corpus and, 238n. 140; habits of, 109, 110, 133; Hawley on, 243–44n. 11; humor of, xi, xv, xxii-xxiii, 49, 67, 128, 138–41, 260–61n. 28; illness of, 70, 242n. 184; and inaugural address, 116, 119, 259n. 14; introspection of, 126–28; JH as correspondence ghostwriter for, 8, 66, 82, 100, 110, 256n. 158; JH's letters to, 34–36, 65, 74, 75–76, 87, 88; J. K. Dubois on, 252–53n. 103; and journey to Washington, 190; leisure of, 85, 110, 136–38, 205n. 4, 262n. 43; letters of, xiii, 54; and letters of introduction, 80; letters to, 110, 173–74; and life-masks, 142, 263n. 51; magnanimity of, 128–29; Mary Todd Lincoln

and, 186–87, 189, 192, 194–96, 199–203, 271n. 6, 272n. 18; Message of the President (1863), 73, 83, 244n. 13; message to Congress, 186–87, 197–98; military strategy of, 32, 50–51, 54, 246–47n. 34; on Missouri, 59–63; Missouri delegates and, 59–64; as myth, 130, 261n. 29; on negotiation of peace, 258n. 187; on office-seekers, 260n. 22; office-seekers and, xvi-xvii, 5, 125, 131–32; patience of, xvii; patriotism of, 116–17; and the press, 246–47n. 34; on Radicals, 239n. 143; reading and, 137–38, 262n. 43; and relationship with JH, xix, 207n. 41; on rights, 103; second inaugural address of, 127, 169, 174; on slavery, xvi, 22–23, 264–65n. 23; somberness of, 141–42, 165; state events and, 134–35, 215n. 50; statesmanship of, xi, xxvi, 125–26; temperance and, 110, 258n. 2; as tyrant, xiv, 63; workday of, 133
Lincoln, George B., 68, 241n. 170
Lincoln, John Larkin, 236–37n. 115
Lincoln, Mary Todd, 7, 18, 22, 45, 85, 219n. 87, 221n. 120; AL and, 186–87, 189, 192, 194–96, 199–203, 271n. 6, 272n. 18; AL's message to Congress and, 186–87, 197–98; character of, 220n. 104; and debt, 201, 202–3, 277nn. 64, 65; JH as ghostwriter for, xiv, 8; and leaks to press, 197–98; lobbyists and, 201–2; office-seekers and, 190–91; and relationships with men, 190–91, 198–99; temper of, 187, 189; and trips, 8, 217n. 63; unethical conduct of, xxv, 14, 19–20, 185–203, 219n. 97, 241n. 173; White House furnishings and, 200–201
Lincoln, Robert Todd, xiii, xiv, xv, 12, 14, 17, 45, 48, 112, 113, 135, 186
Lincoln, Thomas Todd (Tad), xv, 109, 111–13, 135–36
Lincoln, William (Willie), 111, 135, 219n. 87, 221n. 120
Lincoln and Johnson Central Campaign Club, 257n. 166

Lincoln Group of Boston, 175
Lincoln Group of New York, 177
Lincoln or McClellan (Lieber), 94, 254n. 123
Lincoln the President: Last Full Measure (Randall and Current), 177
Lincoln the Writer (Edwards and Hankins), 169
Lisboa, Miguel Maria, 218n. 84
Littlefield, Milton Smith, 227n. 26
Logan, David, 92, 160, 266n. 47
Logan, John A., 191
Logan, Stephen T., 18, 92, 154, 219n. 89, 265n. 27, 265–66n. 41
Londen, Robert, 81
London Times, xxiv, 50, 219n. 92
Long Branch (N.J.), 10, 12, 213n. 37
Longstreet, James, 70, 128, 260n. 28
Lookout Mountain, 69
Loomis, Francis B., xiii, 82, 247–48n. 44
Loring, Francis Bott, 85, 250n. 64
Lossing, Benson J., 67, 240n. 168
Louisiana, 76, 79, 246n. 26
Louisville Journal, 213n. 24
Ludwig I (king of Bavaria), 8, 212n. 22
Lyon, Caleb, 22, 221n. 118
Lyon, Nathaniel, 162, 266n. 48
Lyons, Richard Bickerton Pemell, 138–41, 263n. 48

Madison, Mrs. James, 214n. 44
Magruder, John B., 219n. 93
Marble, Manton, 197, 203
Marcy, Mrs., 7
Marine Band, 22, 221n. 120
Marsh, William, 44–45, 233n. 63
Marston, William H., 89, 252n. 101
Mary Todd Lincoln: Her Life and Letters (Turner and Turner), xiv
Massachusetts regiments: Eighth, 263–64n. 2; Fifteenth, 163; Nineteenth Volunteers, 216n. 52; Sixteenth, 97; Twentieth, 164, 266n. 55
Matile, Gustavus E., 85, 96, 208n. 45, 235n. 93, 249–50n. 60
McCall, George Archibald, 163, 222n. 124, 266n. 50

McClellan, George B., 18, 19, 22, 219nn. 92, 93, 95; JH on, 27, 92, 94, 95, 221–22n. 124; and peninsular campaign, 22, 221–22n. 124; presidential campaign of, 93, 94, 254n. 123, 254–55n. 124; at Yorktown, 228n. 45
McClure, Alexander K., 198
McCormick, Richard, 83
McCullough, Fanny, 182
McDougall, James Alexander, 21, 154, 220n. 114, 265n. 30
McHenry, Capt., 102
McKerichar, Alexander, 194, 195, 275n. 46
McKibbin, Joseph C., 158, 266n. 46
McManus, Edward, 68, 202, 241n. 173
McMichael, Morton, 90
McPherson, Edward, 23, 103, 222n. 127
Meade, George Gordon, 47, 97, 234n. 77
Medill, Joseph, 91, 248n. 54, 252n. 102
Meigs, John R., 96, 255n. 129
Meigs, Montgomery C., 10–11, 26, 98
Methodist Church conference, 120
Methodist Episcopal Church, 21, 220n. 109
Metropolitan Club, 25, 223n. 141
Mexican War, 155, 165, 265n. 36, 267n. 59
Miller, Eliza, 185–86
Mills, Clark, 142, 263n. 51
Mill Springs (Ky.), 218n. 78
Miserables, Les (Hugo), 30–31
Mississippi River, 35, 43, 151
Missouri: delegation, 57–64, 238n. 131; militia, 238n. 139; Radicals, xiv; state politics, 59–60
Missouri Compromise, 259n. 7
Missouri Democrat, 238n. 140
Mitchell, Frederick Augustus, xxi
Mitchell, Margaret Julia, 55, 237n. 128
Mix, John, 163, 266n. 53
Monk Girls, xi, 85
Montague, Amy Angell, 211n. 4
Montgomery, James, 77, 245n. 22
Moore, William G., 105, 258n. 191
Morley, John, 172–73, 174, 175, 177, 178, 185
Mormons, 94, 254n. 113
Mormon War, 148

Morrill, William C., 232n. 46

Morris Island (S.C.), 36, 37, 40, 44, 75

Morrison, William Ralls (Billy), 85, 250n. 63

Morton, Oliver P., 255n. 137

My Courtship and Its Consequences (Wikoff), 198

Myers, Amos, 80, 247nn. 37, 38

Napoleon, 193

National Bank Note Company, 192

National Nominating Convention, 246n. 34

National Rifle Corps, xiii

National Theater (Grover's Theater), 25, 223n. 140

National Union Executive Committee, 91, 253n. 106

Navy Department, 34, 41–42, 43, 51, 66, 100

Nay, Robert B., 26, 223n. 148

Neely, Mark E., Jr., 178

Neill, Edward Duffield, 87, 104, 251n. 79, 257–58n. 182

Nevins, Allan, xii, 206n. 9

Nevis (Hamilton estate), 10, 213n. 40

"New Cinderella, The," 4, 211n. 3

New Harmony (Ind.), 264n. 16

New Ironsides, USS, 34, 227n. 32

New South, 38, 228n. 44

New Theater, 21

Newton, Isaac, 196, 203, 276nn. 55, 60

New York, 51, 52; People's Ellsworth Regiment of New York, 260n. 21

New York Daily News, 200

New York Evening Post, 189

New York Herald, 11, 51, 80, 197, 246–47n. 34

New York Loyal Publication Society, 254n. 123

New York Times, 172, 253n. 106

New York World, xxii, 197

Nicolay, Frederick Lewis, 235n. 96

Nicolay, Helen, xxi

Nicolay, John G., xiii, xvii, xxiii–xxiv, 68, 182; C. Schurz and, 88, 252nn. 94, 95; draft and, 46, 49, 235n. 97; on E. Baker,

266n. 41; illness of, 104; JH's letters to, 12–13, 14, 18, 19–20, 21, 23–25, 27–28, 32–34, 36–38, 40–43, 45, 46, 48–50, 52–53, 56, 69–70, 72, 73–74, 75–77, 79, 84, 85, 88, 89, 91–94, 95, 96, 97, 99, 248–49n. 54; job description of, 110; on society parties, 218n. 86

Nicolay, John H., 48, 235n. 96

Ninth Corps, First Division, 242n. 180

Norris, William Evans, 208n. 49

North Atlantic Blocking Squadron, 243n. 1

Noyes, Walter, 5, 10, 211n. 8

Nugent, Robert H., 50, 236n. 100

Nunes, Joseph A., 158, 266n. 43

Odell, Moses Fowler, 21, 220n. 112

office-seekers, xvi–xvii, 5, 111, 112–13, 125, 131–34, 149, 190–91

Ogden, Rollo, 172

Oglesby, Richard J., 91, 253n. 103, 272n. 18

Ohio, 7, 65, 212n. 20

O'Leary, Cornelius, 202, 241n. 173

Olustee (Fla.), 246–47n. 34

Opdyke, George, 253n. 106

Oregon, 17, 159–60

Otto, William Tod, 54

Owen, Robert Dale, 264n. 16

Page, Walter Hines, 172, 174, 175, 177, 185

Paine, Mrs. Charles, 170, 171

Palmer, Albert Marshman, 216n. 62

Panama Railroad Company, 156

Patapsco, USS, 32, 227n. 25

Peace Convention, 116, 251n. 85

Peace Democrats. *See* Copperheads

Peckham, Francis B., 5, 211n. 8

Pembina River (N.Dak.), 24, 222n. 133

Pennsylvania, 97, 255n. 138

People's Ellsworth Regiment of New York, 260n. 21

Philadelphia Press, 255n. 139

Philadelphia Union League, 66, 240n. 156

Philbrick, Charles Henry, xxiii, 27, 92, 95, 104, 224n. 155, 253–54nn. 110, 112, 121, 257–58n. 182

Phillips, John, xiii, 100, 178
Phillips, Wendell, 120, 259n. 16
Philp, Franklin, 30, 226n. 7
Pierce, Edward L., 233n. 51
Pierce, Franklin, 68, 263n. 47
"Pike" (Missourian), 57, 238n. 133
Pittsfield (Ill.), xviii
Pleasonton, Alfred, 100, 256–57n. 160
Point Lookout (Md.), 72, 243n. 2
Pomeroy, Samuel C., 71, 243n. 191
Pope, Gustavus W., 12, 216n. 53
Pope, John, 20, 24, 219–20n. 103, 224n. 160
Porter, Dr., 96
Potomac River, 151
Potter, John F., 193
Pratt, Franklin F., 99, 100, 256n. 154
Pratt, Harry E., 177
Preston, Samuel W., 33, 227n. 29
prisoners of war, 202

Quakers, 68, 162, 164
Quantrill, William C., 238n. 142

Radicals, xiv, 63, 96, 222n. 127, 238nn. 134, 140, 243n. 11, 249n. 54, 253n. 107, 255n. 142; AL on, 239n. 143
Raleston, 83
Ramsey, Samuel, 48, 234n. 89
Randall, James G., 169, 177–78, 267n. 1
Randall, Ruth Painter, 272n. 18, 273n. 30
Raymond, Henry J., 92, 98, 105, 253nn. 105, 106
Raymond, Mrs. Henry J., 36, 227n. 35
Read, John Meredith, Jr., 210n. 97
Reconstruction, 50
Reid, Whitelaw, xii, 205n. 7, 232n. 46, 239n. 147, 249n. 54
Reinmüller (deserter), 19
Republican National Committee, 173
Republicans (see also Radicals), 27, 92–93, 111, 157–58, 228n. 41; German American, 253n. 107
Rhind, Alexander C., 230n. 45
Rhode Island, 4, 9, 121; First Rhode Island Regiment, 259n. 17
Richardson, Mrs. H. H., 180

Richardson, William A., 17, 218n. 83
Ridgely, Anna, xxi
Ridgely, Jane Huntington, 5–6, 211n. 11
Ridgely, Mary, 15–16, 30–31, 81–82, 217n. 74
Ridgely, Nicholas H., 211n. 11
Rodgers, Christopher Raymond Perry, 33, 34–35, 227n. 29, 230n. 45
Rodgers, George W., 230n. 45
Rodgers, John, 230n. 45
Roosevelt, Theodore, xii, 172–73
Roosevelt, Theodore, Sr., 10, 213n. 39
Rosecrans, William S., 41, 54, 67, 81, 85, 232n. 50, 240n. 161, 250n. 61, 261n. 35
Rowland, Col., xiii
Russell, William Howard, xxiv, 19, 219n. 92, 261n. 35

Sabin, John A., 23
Sacramento Union, xxiv
Salem Zouave Corps, 263–64n. 2
Salomon, Edward, 28, 224n. 160
Sandburg, Carl, 169
Sander, George N., 251n. 80
Sanderson (Fla.), 76
Schafer, George F., 95, 254n. 123
Schoepf, Albin F., 16, 218n. 78
Schofield, John M., 58–59, 61–63, 238nn. 135, 140, 141, 144
Schouler, William, 171
Schurz, Carl, 19, 90, 91, 220n. 116, 252nn. 94, 95
Schurz, Mrs. Carl, 21
Scott, Winfield, 259n. 9
Scribner's Magazine, xv
Sedalia (Missouri) Times, xvii
Seventh Regiment Infantry, 216n. 52
Seventy-first Pennsylvania Brigade, 252n. 96
Seward, Frederick William, 9, 44–45, 181
Seward, William Henry, xxiv, 13, 71, 128–29, 179–81, 188, 193–95, 259n. 9
Seymour, Horatio, 50, 235–36n. 99
Seymour, Thomas H., 228n. 41
Seymour, Truman, 32, 36–37, 76–78, 226n. 23, 245n. 22
Shakespeare, William, 137, 262nn. 42, 43

Sheridan, Philip H., 94, 95, 254n. 117, 255n. 129
Sherman, Thomas W., 225n. 3
Sherman, William T., 69, 126, 130, 188, 196, 242n. 181, 252n. 95
Shields, James, 154, 265n. 32
Shiloh (Pittsburg Landing), battle of, 20, 219–20n. 103
ships: iron-clad frigates, 41, 230–31n. 45; monitors, 32–33, 37, 228–31n. 45
Silas Marner (Eliot), 15–16
Skinner, Alice W., 88–89, 101, 251n. 86
slavery, xvi, 21, 22–23, 220n. 112, 264–65n. 23
Smith, Caleb B., 24, 193–94, 197, 274n. 45, 276n. 59
Smith, Edward W., 39, 66, 74, 228n. 43, 240n. 160
Smith, G. Rush, 53, 236n. 113
Smith, George Plumer, 30, 225nn. 4, 5
Smith, Green Clay, 247n. 36
Smith, Henry Martin, xxiv
Smith, Joseph, 254n. 113
Smith, Matthew Hale, 199
Soldiers' Home, 109, 133, 137
"Soldier Song," 71
South Atlantic Blockading Squadron, 227nn. 28, 29
Spafford, Caroline, 146, 264n. 8
Speed, James, 102
Spencer, Charles S., xiii, 101–2, 174, 257n. 166
Spender, J. A., 173
Spirit of the Times (newspaper), 243n. 189
Spotsylvania (Va.), 83, 248n. 49
Sprague, William, 240n. 162, 259n. 17
Springfield (Ill.), xviii, 6
Stackpole, Thomas, 19, 28, 186–87, 190, 193, 197–98, 203, 219n. 97
Stager, Anson, 14, 217n. 68
Stanford, Leland, 158, 266n. 42
Stanley, Edward Lyulph, 79, 80–81, 246n. 28
Stanton, Edwin M., 19, 20, 26, 28, 44, 50, 53, 66–67, 69, 79, 105–6, 130, 219n. 92
St. Augustine (Fla.), 39
Stetson, Alexander M. C., 11

Stewart, Becky, 56
Stewart, Charles. *See* Vane-Tempest, Ernest
St.-Gaudens, Augustus, 140
Stickney, Lyman D., 73, 232n. 46, 243–44n. 11, 246–47n. 34
Stimson, H. Warren, 99, 256n. 152
Stirling, Archibald, Jr., 255n. 142
St. John's River (Fla.), 75
St. Louis (Mo.), 152
Stoddard, Henry, 48, 234n. 88
Stoddard, William O., xvi, xxii–xxv, 12, 25, 53, 54, 62, 234n. 88, 253n. 109; on E. McManus, 241n. 173; JH's view of, 48, 56, 93, 216n. 55
Stone, Charles P., 163, 164, 266n. 51
Stone, Daniel, 153, 264nn. 22, 23
Stone, Edward C., 176
Stone, Robert King, xxv, 24, 222–23n. 137
Stone, William Leete, xx, xxi, 208n. 50, 225n. 2; letters to, 5, 29, 84, 102
Strafford, Lady, 172
Strain, Isaac G., 156, 265n. 40
Stuart, George Hay, 32
Stuart, John Todd, 93, 253n. 108
Sumner, Charles, 53, 54, 66, 110, 122, 214n. 44, 240n. 164, 166, 244n. 11
Sutter, Thomas J., 195, 275n. 46
Swain, James B., 13, 216n. 58
Swett, Leonard, 84, 249nn. 54, 55, 254n. 121

Taggart, Sally, story of, xv, 128, 260–61n. 28
Taney, Roger Brooke, 97, 255n. 140
Tarr, Campbell, 225n. 5
taxes, 24, 222n. 131, 247n. 36
Taylor, Hawkins, 63, 239n. 145
Taylor, Zachary, 156, 265n. 39
Tenth Corps, Department of the South, 233n. 57
Tenth U.S. Infantry, 234n. 77
Terrail, Pierre. *See* Bayard
Thayer, William Roscoe, 174
Thirty-eighth Illinois Volunteers, 26
Thomas, Benjamin P., 237n. 119
Thomas, George H., 69, 242n. 181
Thomas, James S., 100, 256nn. 159, 160

Thomas, Lorenzo B., 41, 80, 232n. 52,
    247n. 35, 36
Thomasson, John Julius, 31, 226n. 9
Thomasson, William Poindexter, 31,
    226n. 9
Thompson, C. G., 32
Thompson, Jacob, 251n. 80
Tilden, Samuel J., 214n. 44
Todd, Charles H., 13
Todd, John Blair Smith, 24, 222n. 133
Towers, Helen R., 170, 267n. 10
Townsend, Edward David, 47, 234n. 82
Townsend, William H., 176, 177
Tracy, Frederick P., 158, 266n. 44
Treasury Department, 23, 222n. 127
Trumbull, Lyman, 154, 265n. 33
Turner, John Wesley, 73, 230n. 45, 243n. 9,
    248n. 54
Turner, Justin B., xiv
Turner, Levi C., 42
Turner, Linda Levitt, xiv

Union League, 66, 71, 92
Upperman, James H., 194, 195, 203,
    275n. 46
U.S. Christian Commission, 226n. 18
Usher, John P., 186, 193

Vallandigham, Clement L., 27, 39, 63, 65,
    85, 224n. 156, 250n. 62
Van Alen, James H., 20, 163, 220n. 106
Vanderhoff, E. W., 86
Vane-Tempest, Ernest (Charles Stewart),
    163, 266n. 54
van Reuth, Felix, 9, 213n. 27
Vermeren, Peter, 194, 195
Villard, Henry, 188, 190, 272–73n. 25
Virginia, 116, 259n. 7
Vogdes, Israel, 32, 77, 226n. 22
Volk, Leonard Wells, 142, 263n. 51
Voris, A. C., 15

Wade, Benjamin F., 21, 201, 220n. 114
Wakefield, Sherman Day, 177
Wakeman, Abram, 188–89, 203,
    249–50n. 60, 272n. 18

Walker, William, 143, 264n. 3
Wallach, W. Douglas, 19, 219n. 96
Ward, Artemus (Charles Farrar Browne),
    125, 260n. 23
Ward, John, 233n. 67
War Department, 83, 100, 147, 149
Warner, Charles Dudley, 245–46n. 23
Warren, Joseph, 141
Warren, Louis A., 176, 178
Washington, G., 48
Washington, George, xix
Washington, Miss "C. H.", 94
Washington Chronicle, 48–49, 52, 234n. 91,
    255n. 139
Washington Evening Star, 219n. 96
Washingtonian reform, 134, 262n. 40
Washington Union, 214n. 48
Waterbury, Nelson J., 50, 52, 235–36n. 99
Watt, Jane (nee Masterson), xxv, 20, 186,
    193, 219nn. 97, 101
Watt, John, xxv, 14, 19–20, 186–88, 191–98,
    203, 217n. 64, 274n. 45, 276n. 59
Watterson, Henry, 170
Webb, Alexander Stewart, 163, 266n. 49
Weed, Thurlow, xxiv, 5, 188, 190, 193–94,
    195, 203, 211n. 9, 254n. 120
Weehawken, USS, 230n. 45
Welles, Gideon, 221n. 122
Werner, William L., 179, 185
Westerman, Mrs. Henry P., 96, 255n. 130
Western Committee, 64, 98
Wheeler, William Almon, 23, 222n. 128
Wheelwright, Andrew Cunningham,
    268n. 12
Wheelwright, Mary Cabot, 267n. 12
Wheelwright, Sarah Cabot, 170, 174,
    267–68n. 12
White, Horace, xii
Whittlesey, Elisha, 195–96
Wickliffe, Charles A., 41, 232n. 51
Wigfall, Louis T., 117–18, 259n. 10
Wikoff, Henry, 197, 198–200, 278n. 77
Wilcox, Orlando Bolivar, 69, 242n. 180
Wilkes, George, 71, 95, 243n. 189
Willard's Hotel, xxi, 5, 12, 48, 149
Williams, J. C., 47

Williamson, Alexander, 190
Willis, Nathaniel Parker, 12, 215n. 50
Wilmot Proviso (1846), 226n. 9
Wilson, Henry, 132
Wilson's Creek, battle of, 162, 266n. 48
Winchester, battle of, 254n. 117
Wisconsin, 224n. 160
Wise, Charlotte Brooks Everett, 71,
   243n. 191, 261n. 35
Wise, Henry Augustus, 49, 66, 118, 133,
   259n. 12
Wistar, Isaac Jones, 164, 267n. 56
women, Civil War and, 124–25
Wood, Fernando, 85, 250n. 63
Wood, William P., 190, 203, 273–74n. 38
Wood, William S., 186, 190, 191–92, 203,
   273n. 27
Woodbury, Daniel P., 77, 246n. 25

Woolfolk, Austin Coleman, 18, 37, 82,
   219n. 88
Worden, John L., 230n. 45
Worthen, Fay, 102, 257n. 174
Wright, Maj., 228n. 45
Wycoff, Henry, 186–87
Wyman, L. B., 14, 217n. 66
Wyoming Conference of the Methodist
   Church, 120

Yates, Richard, 147, 191
Young, Francis G., 90, 252n. 96
Young, John Russell, xix-xx, 208n. 47,
   245n. 18
Younger, Miss, 56

Zollicoffer, Felix K., 16, 218n. 78
Zouaves, 10–11, 123, 145–47, 260n. 21, 264n. 9

Michael Burlingame is a professor of history at Connecticut College in New London. His previous books include *The Inner World of Abraham Lincoln*; *Lincoln's Journalist: John Hay's Anonymous Writings for the Press, 1860–1864*; *Inside Lincoln's White House: The Complete Civil War Diary of John Hay* (coedited with John R. Turner Ettlinger); *Lincoln Observed: Civil War Dispatches of Noah Brooks*; and *An Oral History of Abraham Lincoln: John G. Nicolay's Interviews and Essays*, which won the 1995 Abraham Lincoln Association Prize.